The Politics of
Immigrant Workers

The Politics of
Immigrant Workers
Labor Activism and Migration
in the World Economy since 1830

edited by
Camille Guerin-Gonzales
and Carl Strikwerda

Foreword by David Brody

Holmes & Meier
New York / London

Published in the United States of America 1993 by
Holmes & Meier Publishers, Inc.
30 Irving Place
New York, NY 10003

This book has been printed on acid-free paper.

Library of Congress Cataloging-in-Publication Data

The politics of immigrant workers: labor activism and migration in the world
    economy since 1830 / edited by Camille Guerin-Gonzales and Carl
    Strikwerda: foreword by David Brody.
        p.   cm.
        Includes bibliographical references and index.
        ISBN 0-8419-1297-1 (cloth: acid-free paper)
    1. Alien labor—Political activity—History. 2. Immigrants—
Political activity—History. 3. Labor movement—History. I. Guerin-Gonzales,
Camille. II. Strikwerda, Carl.
HD8081.A5P65   1993
322'.2'-0—dc20   91-36174
                                                                          CIP

Manufactured in the Unted States of America

To

Kerrie, Ronald, and Michael
&
Laurna and Timothy

The Descendants of Immigrants

Contents

AN INTERNATIONAL PERSPECTIVE

Foreword

David Brody

Immigration has been a central theme in American historiography for at least fifty years. The pioneering work was done by Marcus Lee Hansen before World War II and afterward on a grander scale by Oscar Handlin. The book that seized the profession's imagination, and probably more than any other sparked its enthusiasm for social history, was Handlin's *The Uprooted* (1951), a poetic evocation of the mass migration to the United States as experienced by the immigrants. That novel approach, Handlin explained, was a kind of strategic retreat from his larger ambition: he had intended to write a history of immigrants in America, only to discover "that the immigrants *were* American history" and "that adequately to describe the course and effects of immigration involved no less a task than to set down the whole history of the United States." Others might put that proposition less boldly or perhaps qualify it, but few, and assuredly no one in the growing ranks of American social historians, would deny its implications. For a great range of subjects, there seems to be no way of proceeding without taking account of ethnicity. It is true that, with an increasingly specialized scholarship, this fact has become unremarkable. The political historian thinks about ethnicity in relation to party affiliation, the urban historian in relation to neighborhoods and spatial patterns, the labor historian in relation to class formation. One need only consider the task of integrating our fragmented scholarship to gain a proper perspective on ethnicity. Linking so many historical strands as it does, immigration stands at, or somewhere close to, the center of American history, and is for Americanists, perforce, a quintessentially *national* subject.

This collection of essays proceeds from an entirely different premise, namely, that of immigration as *international* history. Such a notion is sure to find an eager reception among American historians, painfully aware as they are that theirs is a parochial scholarship. (Parochialism is, of course, not an American monopoly; it has been just much a part of the immigration scholarship of, say, the Germans and Scandinavians, only from the rather different perspective of societies that experienced mass emigration from the homeland.) It is exhilarating, certainly, to find, side by side with essays on German bakers in New York City and Mexican agricultural migrants in California, treatments of indentured servitude in Natal, Polish miners in Germany, and Chinese labor militancy in colonial Malaya. Or to discover, reading almost at random in these essays, parallels from distant places and other times strikingly close to what we know to have happened in North America. But what meaning is to be extracted from this stimulating encounter? One might put the problem this way: To what extent are we dealing with actual international history, that is, history in which the parts--however disparate they may seem--are in fact related in some functional or organic way? To what extent is the unity we are seeing only apparent, that is, consisting of like, but not connected, events? In the comparative analysis of that latter class of events, finally, how much utility are we likely to find, that is, how much explanatory power of major historical questions?

By focusing their collection on labor, Camille Guerin-Gonzales and Carl Strikwerda have narrowed down these issues and made them more tractable. And in their subtitle, they themselves call attention to the fault line between international and comparative immigration history.

Insofar as labor migration is linked to a "world economy," there surely we have the makings of an actual international history. In their incisive and wide-ranging introduction, Guerin-Gonzales and Strikwerda rightly reject as overly simplistic any rigid core/periphery explanation for the international movement of workers. But, however variegated we find that migration to have been, clearly it was set in motion and sustained by world economic forces, and clearly, too, those forces applied to host no less than to sender countries. If they have not yet studied the problem systematically, Americanists have increasingly incorporated into their scholarship the notion that immigration to (and remigration from) the United States has to be understood in an international context. How much, beyond the process of migration itself, can be subsumed under international history? Regulation by the state, insofar as governments control the flow of immigration, certainly is to be characterized as a subset of international migration history, a fact that underscores the importance of the systematic analysis of state regulation by James Foreman-Peck in this collection. Major patterns of entry and settlement—chain migration, segmented labor markets, and community building—extend the international linkages deep into the host society.

At some indeterminate point, however, the balance shifts, the particularities of the host country overshadow the international linkages, and immigration history is absorbed into national history. Labor activism—another theme identified by the subtitle—seems to me to fall over the line into national history. That line is permeable, to be sure, and more than that, important transnational linkages cut through it, as, for example, in the circulation of seasoned leaders (as with the entry of the Belgian socialists Eduard Anseele and Edmond VanBeveren into the Nord), in the transfer of labor institutions (thus the American Federation of Labor modeled itself after the British Trades Union Congress), and most obviously in the active proselytizing across national boundaries by radical movements. Even so, it is not so much those linkages as the interaction among ethnically diverse workers that makes immigration a significant determinant of class formation. And that interaction, since it is part of discrete working-class histories, is of utility in a transnational context only to the degree that, when subjected to comparative analysis, it yields significant consistent patterns.

The essays in this collection are richly suggestive of parallel experiences in highly diverse contexts. Under what circumstances does economic competition between foreign and native workers or between rival ethnic groups give way to solidarity? Does the presence of foreign workers strengthen or weaken labor movements? Under what circumstances do ethnic characteristics make for greater or lesser militancy among immigrant workers? Or cross-class ties within immigrant communities? Or labor exploitation specific to the vulnerabilities of immigrant groups? In John Laslett's essay, we have a telling example of how comparative analysis might be brought to bear on this range of questions. Why Lanarkshire miners opted for the Labour party, while their brothers in Illinois opted for labor lobbying, can only be explained, Laslett tells us, by differences in national political systems. And America's system, as it happens, had its origins very considerably in the nation's ethnic development.

Handlin had said that immigration was American history. The application of his dictum to American working-class history can perhaps best be observed in Herbert Gutman's famous essay "Work, Culture and Society in Industrializing America" (1973). Much of the specifics about ethnicity in that essay could well be replicated in the essays in this collection on France, Germany, colonial Malaya, and the Natal, but not the conclusion Gutman meant to draw from those specifics: namely, that labor migration—the constant replenishment of the work force from outside the industrial order over an entire century—was the central fact of American working-class experience.

This stimulating collection forces us to be attentive to immigration as international history. It also challenges us to think harder about immigration in the context of national histories.

ACKNOWLEDGMENTS

The editors would like to thank the following people: for their assistance in finding contributors to the volume, John Jentz, Bruce Levine, David Montgomery, Donald Reid, William Rowe, and G. William Skinner; for her patience and professionalism in preparing the manuscript, Pam LeRow of the Wescoe Word-Processing Center of the University of Kansas; for their hard work on the index, Kerrie Chappell and Thelma Kime; and for their skill in editing and overseeing the publication, our editors, Sheila Friedling, Anne Hebenstreit, Katharine Turok, and designer Adrienne Weiss of Holmes & Meier.

INTRODUCTION

1

Labor, Migration, and Politics

Carl Strikwerda and Camille Guerin-Gonzales

From Mexican "undocumented workers" in California agriculture to Turkish "guest workers" in German auto factories, immigrant workers in countries all over the world are as economically crucial as they are politically controversial. Historically, the fears provoked by immigrant workers have been many. Native workers have been anxious about protecting their own jobs. Others have feared that the cultural and linguistic differences of immigrants meant that immigrants would disrupt the social order, make unusual demands on welfare programs, or undermine political parties or labor movements because they were unable or unwilling to participate. At the same time, immigrant leaders and other observers have argued that the discrimination and even repression that immigrant workers often face is an indictment against the societies that need their labor but refuse to grant them equal rights.

The debate surrounding immigrants thus stimulates larger questions about modern society—questions about the strength of class consciousness, the power of culture, and the role of the state. Many Marxists have argued that class and the demands of the economy are the most powerful forces influencing workers, while others have contended just as strongly that culture and politics, independent of economic forces, are paramount. The case of immigrant workers brings this debate to the fore. When does the pressure of being in a common economic class unite immigrant and native workers, and when do cultural or political differences keep them apart? Which is more powerful—the demands of the economy to allow immigrant workers to come in or the political pressure to exclude them?

The essays in this volume focus on immigrants who are workers—as opposed to settlers, refugees, and professionals—both because workers have typically been the largest group among those who cross national borders and because they capture more precisely the tensions between economic factors and ethnic and cultural ones. Settlers, business and technical personnel, and professionals, in contrast to workers, have usually had much greater freedom to choose where they want to go or whether or not they wish to return to their homelands. Thus, they have not felt the same pressures to find work and to depend on their own ethnic group for support. Refugees are also a special case since political or military threats are usually a more overriding influence on their migration than the economy of the country to which they flee.[1]

The essays in this volume reflect on the general question of how economic, cultural, and political forces interact in modern society by examining the more specific case of how immigrant workers organize themselves collectively—in strikes, unions, and political activities. In a broad sense, we are interested in immigrant workers' "politics" and "collective action," that is, by what means they defend or advance their interests, with whom they ally, and by whom they are opposed. Specifically, some of the questions we are seeking to answer are: Are immigrants more conservative or more radical than native workers? When and why do immigrants and natives sometimes act together and at other times fail to cooperate? How does the special status of immigrants as a distinct cultural or racial group or as noncitizens influence their collective action?

To answer these questions, we believe, it is important to examine immigrant workers in a wide variety of settings—in different types of work, at different times over the last centuries, and in interaction with workers of different nationalities and cultures. Too often, a stereotype of the immigrant worker as passive and exploited or as alienated and radical has been taken from one historical situation and imposed on another. Only a truly comparative approach can aid us in testing and reevaluating this stereotype. Because most historical scholarship on immigrant labor focuses on Europeans going to the United States in the nineteenth century or on Third World workers in Western Europe since World War II, we have included essays on other important streams of migration: migration internal to Europe; Asian migration to Africa, the Pacific islands, and Southeast Asia; and Mexican migration to the United States before World War II. Together, the essays look at agricultural as well as industrial workers, and at skilled craftsmen, miners, and factory workers. By looking at this variety of settings, students of labor and immigration history will be able to see more clearly the features common to immigrant workers' experiences everywhere.

One of the crucial obstacles to such a comparative approach is the difficulty in finding any basis of comparison between immigrant workers who have lived in radically different settings. Can scholars, for example, make any meaningful comparisons between German bakers in nineteenth-century New York and Algerians in twentieth-century France? We believe that, in fact, we can make some fruitful comparisons between how these different groups of workers acted and organized themselves. Before turning to the essays in this volume, then, it is important to lay out, in very broad terms, the major factors that impinge on almost all immigrant workers. We can synthesize these diverse factors by grouping them into five important categories: (1) the world economy; (2) the state; (3) the structure of work; (4) labor organizations and political institutions involving workers; and (5) workers' community, or, in Ira Katznelson and Aristide Zolberg's phrase, "workers' way of life"—customs, family structure, religion, and leisure.[2] By examining how these forces have affected immigrant workers, we can acquire a framework for comparison before turning to the specific essays in the volume. These categories of factors can be seen as a set of concentric circles, moving from the level of large-scale formations—the international economy and the state—to the midrange level of immigrants' work and their place in the economy, and, finally, to the small-scale and specific level of political organizations and communities, most of which are peculiar to each group of immigrant workers.

The World Economy

The expansion and contraction of economic growth in the world economy has largely determined the size of immigration streams over the last 150 years. During the change to full-scale industrialization, it was often critical for countries such as Britain, Germany, Italy, and Belgium to export their unemployment. For the United States and France, labor shortages were more often typical: the United States industrialized with labor imported from countries such as Britain and Germany, while France utilized Belgians and Italians. When the world economy as a whole fell into recession, as it did in the 1880s, 1930s, and 1970s, migration in many places all over the world contracted dramatically.

One way in which the world economy has controlled migration, according to David Montgomery, is that workers have moved from agricultural to industrialized areas, both within and across national borders. Using a variant of Immanuel Wallerstein's definition of a world economy, Montgomery argues that by the late nineteenth century there was an industrial "core" stretching from the American Midwest to northwestern Europe. Migrants to industry came from the unindustrialized "periphery" into the industrialized core or from the less industrialized areas within the core, such as the countryside, to the industrial cities.[3] This industrial world economy cuts through the conventional nation-state units and helps us see that the economic forces that encourage immigration across national borders are often similar to those stimulating migration within a country. The essays in Dirk Hoerder's edited collection *Labor Migration in the Atlantic Economies* show that German and Polish peasants and workers, for example, could choose between migrating to Berlin and to Milwaukee.[4] For the contemporary world, Michael Piore has argued that immigrants from less industrialized countries in Latin America, North Africa, and the Mideast act as a kind of reserve labor force for the more developed economies of North America and Western Europe. These "birds of passage," as he calls them, come into the industrialized economies when needed, are generally not assimilated into the new societies, and frequently return to their countries of origin when work is difficult to find.[5]

The flow of immigrants from nonindustrialized areas to the industrialized core, however, is only one way the world economy has determined migration. The model that scholars such as Montgomery, Hoerder, and Piore have developed, while it certainly accounts for a large amount of migration, puts too much emphasis on the gap between the levels of industrialization in the countries that immigrants leave and the countries that they enter. As early as the nineteenth century, large numbers of migrants moved from nonindustrialized areas near the core to other, nonindustrialized areas. Many of these regions produced raw materials for the industrial core. Argentina, which supplied Europe with grain and meat, experienced immigration, much of it from Italy and Spain, at an even higher rate than the United States. Carl Solberg has shown how Argentina drew immigrants in direct proportion to the demand for its products in the industrial core.[6] Similarly, large movements of immigration occurred in the nineteenth and twentieth centuries within the periphery, that is, between nonindustrialized areas, to supply labor to economies producing raw materials for the core. At least a million Mexican immigrants entered the southwestern United States between 1880 and 1930, many of them to work in agriculture and mining.[7] Meanwhile, workers from India went to work in construction, transport, and plantations in South Africa, the West Indies, and the South Pacific, and Chinese immigrated to do similar work in Southeast Asia.[8] Labor migration to South Africa provides a particularly striking example. As Surendra Bhana points out in his essay in this volume, the movement of workers from India and China to Africa was a product of the activities of British businessmen trying to develop the resources of South Africa. In this case, then, workers moved between two nonindustrialized areas as a result of the capital and markets created in an industrialized economy thousands of miles away.[9]

In some cases, therefore, economic factors other than the level of industrialization in migrants' home countries or in their countries of destination help to set the pattern of migration. Workers do not move within the world economy only from nonindustrialized regions to industrialized ones. Instead, a complex set of economic factors affects migration: movements from low-wage to high-wage areas, from areas with expanding populations or high unemployment to those with low employment, and from declining economies to expanding ones. The emphasis on wages, labor security, and economic prosperity helps to explain otherwise incongruous movements of immigration, movements that do not fit into the simple model of migration from nonindustrialized regions to an industrial core. Britain was the most industrialized country in the world in the nineteenth century, yet it was also one of the greatest sources of out-migration. Industrialization in Britain did not grow fast enough to create jobs for a quickly growing population, nor did workers want to accept jobs where the wages or the level of skill, status, or security was not as high as they desired. By the late nineteenth century, the large majority of migrants from Britain went, not to the United States, but to less industrialized countries such as Australia, New Zealand, and Canada where labor scarcity made for high wages.[10] Another seemingly incongruous movement occurred in the mid-nineteenth century, when many skilled German craft workers migrated to the United States and took jobs demanding less skill than those they had had in Germany. These jobs, nonetheless, were more attractive to the Germans because they had higher wages and were in urban areas with more opportunity for advancement and security.[11]

Although population pressure has often been pointed to as a cause for out-migration, this factor has to be treated very cautiously. The causes of a "surplus" population that wishes to emigrate are usually underemployment, poverty, and lack of economic growth, rather than simple population growth. Countries that experienced huge out-migration in the nineteenth century today have populations twice as large—and import rather than export workers. It seems natural that population pressure creates migration from Puerto Rico to the United States as the island has a population density more than twelve times that of the mainland. Natural, that is, until one realizes that most Puerto Ricans migrate to New York City, which has a population density more than one hundred times that of their homeland.[12]

Migrants have frequently—both before World War I and again after World War II—moved between industrialized countries as well. For almost the whole of the nineteenth century, the United States had been a labor-scarce economy, and Britain, despite its level of industrialization, a labor-exporting economy. Yet, abruptly with the start of World War I, the movement of workers into the British military and the temporary economic slump in the United States caused by the outbreak of the war created opportunities for American skilled workers to try to find jobs of higher status or pay in Britain. The employment of American workers helped set off the first major strike in Britain during World War I when the British workers still on the job feared that the newly hired Americans would undercut the position of the established unions. In the 1960s German companies sometimes hired British skilled workers, for even though Britain was still more industrialized than Germany, its economy was not growing fast enough to provide new jobs with high wages, while the booming German economy was.[13]

This more complex picture of the world economy helps to explain why groups of migrants replace each other and helps to illuminate the choices potential migrants face. One of the best examples of these changing flows of migration is Germany. German migration to the United States reached enormous heights in the 1880s but dropped dramatically ten years later when German industrialization finally absorbed the country's underemployment. Instead of Germans, a wave of Polish immigrants then flowed to the United States and eventually even to Germany itself, where industrialization outran the labor supply.[14] The contrast between the Dutch in the Netherlands and the Flemish in Belgium in the late nineteenth century illustrates the ways in which migrants weigh the advantages and disadvantages created by their cultural background and economic position. The Dutch and Flemish were both Dutch-speaking, agricultural populations living within two hundred miles of each other, who faced heavy unemployment. The poorer Flemish had two choices: permanent migration to a Belgian or French city and seasonal migration to France with the hope of accumulating enough savings to purchase or rent a farm. The Dutch too faced two possibilities: Those who lacked a significant amount of capital could move to a Dutch or North American city, while whose with slightly greater capital could choose to migrate to North America in hopes of obtaining a farm. In both cases, cultural and economic links intermixed to explain the choices open to potential migrants: the Netherlands, through trade and international shipping with nearby Britain, possessed long-established ties to English-speaking America, while the Flemish shared a common history of textile production and Francophone culture with nearby France.[15]

The concept of a world economy also helps us understand "circular" migration, in which seasonal change determines when workers move back and forth between two countries. Workers migrate when there is a demand for work in another country and then return home when demand slackens. Before World War I, Italian harvest workers and

English housepainters were just two of many immigrant groups that migrated back and forth between Europe and North or South America each year. By the early 1900s, approximately one-tenth of the Italians entering the United States had been there before.[16] And in Argentina, the decision to allow Italian "swallows" to harvest crops, rather than to encourage a settled farming population, may have harmed the country's long-term prospects for a stable society.[17]

The complex workings of the world economy are also important because they set the stage for migration long before workers actually move and often at tremendous distances from where migrants eventually end up settling. Far from the areas that were industrializing in the late nineteenth century, farmers and rural laborers in central India, Sicily, the Philippines, Mexico, and Romania saw their traditional livelihood upset as the effects of international markets in grain and commercial goods began to be felt in their regions. The expansion of large, more capitalistic landholdings and freer markets for land and small consumer items began undermining the economic status of tenants, rural workers, and small farmers. The results, often combined with surging population growth, pushed the more destitute and the more ambitious to leave in search of work. Although cultural ties and political controls shaped where these people could go, some of the underlying patterns were the same in widely different societies around the globe. The indentured Indians in South Africa, the Romanian laborers in Cleveland, the Filipino plantation hands in Hawaii, and the Mexican and Italian miners in southern Colorado and the Appalachian region of the United States were all part of the "ripple effects" of a new, more international, and more capitalistic economy.[18]

The changing position of an economy within the larger world economy can help explain one of the paradoxes of migration. Scholars have sometimes puzzled over why migrants should leave less-developed economies that are experiencing considerable growth. Saskia Sassen points out that some of the countries that have sent large numbers of migrants to the United States in the 1970s and 1980s—South Korea, Mexico, and several Caribbean states, for example—have been undergoing industrialization themselves.[19] This migration has troubled policymakers, who argue, correctly, that in the long run the only solution to problems caused by migration to industrialized countries is for emigrant-sending countries to develop their own economies. One must remember, however, that, although these economies as a whole have growing employment or output, many workers are losing their traditional occupations through the very process of economic change. In many cases, these workers might prefer to take their chances on a better life in a more developed society than to settle for taking an unfamiliar and perhaps more difficult job in their own country. The experience of these Asian and Latin American societies is similar in some ways to that of nineteenth-century Germany and early-twentieth-century Italy. There, too, rapid industrialization went along with large-scale emigration. Many were migrating because the traditional economy they had known was declining. There have also been, however, important streams of migrants from countries undergoing economic growth who move even though they have already begun participating in the modern sector of their economies. In part, these migrants move as a result of "rising expectations," but their movement also indicates that traditional economic sectors can decline more quickly than modern economic sectors can provide numerous, well-paying jobs. Workers in less-developed countries who have already moved out of small towns or rural areas to take jobs in modern, urban occupations may choose to take the further step of migrating to a more developed industrial economy. Many of the Latin Americans and North Africans who migrate to the United States or Western Europe are not the most unskilled or impoverished of their countries' populations. Thus, the process of economic growth in poorer countries may actually increase migration.

As crucial as the perspective of the world economy is, it never gives a complete picture of migration, or even of the major determinants affecting flows of migration. Immigrants lack perfect information about the demand for employment elsewhere; indeed, at times out of sheer destitution they migrate to almost any place they are allowed to enter. Immigrants, furthermore, make choices on the basis of cultural and family ties as well as of employment or economic opportunities. Italian migration overseas began to South America rather than North America, in part because of linguistic and religious affinities with Catholic, Portuguese-speaking Brazil and Spanish-speaking Argentina. Almost all migration tends to move in "streams," as later migrants depend on earlier ones for housing, information, and companionship in a strange country. As Charles Tilly has put it, migrants to America formed networks: "By and large the effective units of migration were (and are) neither individuals nor households but sets of people linked by acquaintance, kinship, and work experience."[20]

Once in their new country of residence, migrants form new networks, as individuals and families spread to new cities without completely breaking their ties to parts of old networks. Money and information sent back to the country of origin maintain, for a time at least, the networks at the other end of the migration stream. And, as will be pointed out below, the composition of the networks helps determine which jobs immigrants take and what kinds of communities they form.

The Role of the State

As crucial as the world economy is, migration also has to be placed within the framework of the state. The huge, circulating labor system of the late nineteenth and early twentieth centuries was itself a product of political as well as economic forces. Free trade policies, the gold standard, and relatively lax regulations on the movement of labor made possible the flourishing world economy before 1914. Large-scale immigration existed only as long as governments permitted it. For example, in the United States, once Americans of European descent became alarmed at the importance of Asian immigrants in the labor force in the western United States, the government simply prohibited the immigration of Asians. The U.S. Immigration Act of 1924, the so-called Quotas Act, drastically curtailed immigration from Italy and eastern Europe, and greatly weakened the ability of these societies to deal with their unemployment.[21] Also, the United States, Belgium, and France all expelled foreign workers during the Great Depression of the 1930s—France to such an extent that many charged the government with exporting its unemployment.[22] Nigeria, faced with the economic depression caused by the collapse of the oil market in the early 1980s, tried to expel up to two million immigrant workers from other West African countries. Even while allowing immigration to occur, governments can profoundly affect what kind of person can immigrate, whether immigrants can settle and become permanent residents, and what rights immigrant communities can enjoy. By trying to grant work permits only to single males for limited periods, Germany before World War I created a far different immigrant work force than did France, which allowed families to settle and extended citizenship.[23] Further, the Arab states near the Persian Gulf, as discussed below, during less than ten years' time recruited their foreign laborers from three different areas, in part to ensure a more pliable work force.

This emphasis on the power of the state to control migration modifies the picture painted by theorists such as Piore, who argue that migration, at least in the contemporary world economy, is largely determined by the need of capitalist economies for labor. In contrast, W. R. Böhning insists that, although the receiving country's economy has to exercise a "pull" for migration to be possible, governments have enormous power to decide whether and how migrants will come. As Böhning puts it, "Demand, then, is caused economically, screened politically, and given effect to administratively."[24] The state, in other words, often can control migration, albeit at high costs, and thereby counteract or offset economic pressure. Labor scarcity and a booming economy, for example, have only recently begun to weaken the Japanese government's controls on immigration. Instead, by using subsidies and tax advantages, the government, for a long period, encouraged some labor-intensive enterprises to continue to use "high-cost" Japanese workers rather than import foreign labor at lower wages. At the same time, other employers have been encouraged to become less labor-intensive, in part again, to avoid the temptation to import labor. The result presents a striking counterexample to those who argue that industrialization and economic growth always bring about immigration. Despite being one of the fastest-growing and most industrialized economies in the world, Japan until very recently had remarkably little immigration.[25]

The same power of the state to shape immigration can also be seen in the case of countries that choose the opposite route, and become overwhelmingly dependent on foreign labor. The Arab states around the Persian Gulf, while recruiting workers during the oil boom of the 1970s and early 1980s, deliberately shifted their recruitment, first from the non-oil Arab states—Egypt, Yemen, and Syria—to South Asia—India, Pakistan, and Bangladesh—and finally to East Asia—South Korea and Taiwan. The Arabs from the non-oil states, despite their being closer geographically and culturally, proved more dangerous because of the threat that they would stay permanently and bring into the Gulf states conflicts between Sunnis and Shi'ites and between conservatives and radicals. The South Asians could be controlled more easily and had less opportunity to stay, but eventually posed the threat of labor militancy. The East Asians, finally, were brought in on a strictly contract basis, to finish a project and then be shipped out by their employers. These changes also coincided with the changing employment needs of the Gulf states for more skilled, "targeted" labor. Nonetheless, the changing economic needs for labor were combined with careful attempts by the governments to balance political threats and security interests.[26]

The state is critical on a deeper level, because it defines immigration as we perceive it today. The "immigrant," the person who moves from one nation-state to another, is an artifact of modern history. Far back in the recorded past large groups have moved from place to place in search of work. But only the rise of state bureaucracies that confer citizenship and police borders has made it possible to demarcate immigrants as a group. Even when immigration was controlled in Europe before the nineteenth century, it was usually towns or guilds, not national governments, that determined whether "foreigners" could work.[27] Nor is it even true that proportionately more immigration has occurred in the industrial or modern nation-state than in earlier forms of society. Huge numbers of people moved over large distances in preindustrial Europe and China.[28] In the nineteenth century, however, modern governments acquired the ability to keep track of each resident within their territory. Immigrants, therefore, could be clearly identified as different from citizens. At the same time, this differentiation of immigrants from citizens was reinforced by modern nationalism, which divided some groups and merged others. Saxons and Bavarians, who for centuries had immigrated to France, the Netherlands, and eastern Europe with their own provincial identities, suddenly became "German" no matter where they went. The area of Flanders, meanwhile, where peasants and artisans had for centuries moved back and forth between various districts, suddenly became split between France and Belgium. What had been interregional migration became migration between two nations, France and Belgium.[29] The annexation of Polish areas by Prussia in the eighteenth century meant that, in the early twentieth century, most "Poles" in Ruhr mining towns were German citizens and could not be controlled as easily as the Poles from Austrian- and Russian-annexed areas who entered Germany to work.[30]

The crucial importance of state boundaries can also be seen in the way in which European colonialism could reshape migration long after colonial empires had disappeared. Much of the "international" migration in Africa today flows between areas that have long been connected by trade and cultural ties but are now divided as a result of independent nations being formed by arbitrarily drawn colonial boundaries. European colonialism could also strengthen links between areas, links that made migration more possible between the two areas long after colonialism's end. British rule over India and Pakistan, on the one hand, and over the Mideast, on the other, resulted in steamship lines and in the common use of English as a lingua franca linking the two areas together. These ties made it easier for the Arab states in and around the Gulf to turn to India and Pakistan for immigrant laborers in the 1970s.

Further, the state impinges on migration in both sending and receiving countries. During the late nineteenth century, immigrants to the United States began to come from eastern Europe and Italy, rather than northwestern Europe, in part because governments abolished old controls on land in eastern Europe and Italy and, as a result, a new mobile, "propertyless" class was created.[31] In the 1920s, the Italian government negotiated with employers and the government in France to obtain better working conditions and wages for many Italian workers in France.[32] Countries as diverse as Pakistan and El Salvador today have active policies encouraging emigration.[33] Sending countries can also decisively affect who migrates within their populations through passports and work permits. The Mexican government, during the *bracero* program of regulated, seasonal workers in American agriculture, regularly gave over one-half of the program's work permits to one region that had only 25 percent of the country's population.[34]

The receiving country is nonetheless far more decisive, as a rule, in controlling migration. As mentioned above, in the 1930s, France, Belgium, and the United States expelled and repatriated thousands of immigrant workers in what many saw as attempts to lessen unemployment. Even when immigrants mobilize politically or seek legal redress of grievances, the state sets the terms under which they can act. That most West Indians, South Americans, Asians, or Africans in the Netherlands and Britain have Dutch or British citizenship confers upon them some important legal rights that North African and Turkish guest workers lack in other Western European countries. Even when some governments expel immigrants only rarely, the possibility of expulsion or the fear of losing legal status has a powerful inhibiting influence on immigrants. Switzerland is probably the most dramatic example among contemporary industrial countries. With over half of its industrial labor force being non-Swiss, the country gives very few rights to its immigrant workers. As a result, immigrant workers are extremely vulnerable to pressure by the government and by employers, pressure that can keep them from organizing strikes or demanding better working conditions.[35] Leaving aside the tragic cases of forced labor in dictatorships such as Nazi Germany and Soviet Russia, immigrant workers have often been denied rights that native workers enjoy. Indentured and contract labor is perhaps the largest category today of immigrant workers placed in a legally disadvantaged position that divides them from native labor. At its most extreme, of course, indentured and contract laborers could be treated almost as badly as forced laborers or slaves. One of the major prejudices of native workers—in the United States, Australia, and western Europe, at various times—has often been the perception that immigrant workers were contract labor and thus were a threat to "free" labor. At one extreme, the fear of contract or indentured labor was a desire to protect the hard-won rights of native labor; at the other extreme, it could be outright prejudice—blaming the victims, the laborers, rather than the employers or governments who exploited them.[36]

Because national governments have such enormous power to control immigrant workers, it is essential to emphasize the difference between citizenship and national or ethnic identity. States impose legal status as alien or citizen, while individuals and groups evolve national or ethnic identity, partly in relation to other groups around them. Naturally, the two categories overlap and intersect, but this makes it all the more necessary to keep them analytically separate. States increase and decrease the requirements for citizenship, the openness of borders, and the rights of aliens. Meanwhile, the dominant ethnic or national group within a state may be defining its own identity in reaction to immigration, as well as to other contacts with foreigners, and putting pressure on the state to change its policies regarding immigrants.[37] Thus, white, Protestant, Northern European "native" Americans in the nineteenth century tried to define and redefine their identity as Americans to exclude, at various times, blacks, Irish, Catholics, Slavs, Jews, Asians, and Mexicans.[38] Indeed, as James Foreman-Peck points out in his essay in this volume, anti-immigrant feeling may be more easily translated into action by the state in democratic countries than in authoritarian ones.

At the same time, the national identity of immigrants is not necessarily equivalent to that of the state from which they come. Immigrants in the United States often defined themselves as "Italian" or "Polish" only once they were in the United States. Their national identity remained loosely defined because village, regional, and religious identities were often stronger than national ones. Ethnic or regional divisions within immigrant-sending countries can even affect which countries workers choose to migrate to. As Joel Michael Halpern has pointed out, among Yugoslav workers migrating to the rest of Europe, Serbs have been more likely to go to France and Austria, Croats to West Germany.[39] The ethnic identity of immigrants has also often been decisively shaped by the environment of their new country. Thus, immigrants from the same home country can soon differ a good deal depending on which host country they live in. In the late nineteenth century, for example, the identity of "Italian-Americans"—faced with a large, often hostile Protestant majority in the United States, as well as with rival Catholic immigrant communities—soon had a much different content from that of Italians in Argentina. Italians in Argentina, as the largest immigrant group in an overwhelmingly Catholic and heavily immigrant country, tended to be much more upwardly mobile and more involved in the Catholic church than did "Italian-Americans" who were often near the bottom of the labor market and who faced a Catholic church dominated by Irish and German Catholics.[40]

Because ethnic identity is often so fundamental to immigrants, scholars have had to insist that ethnic or national identity is not exclusively a problem for immigrants but also one for natives of the host country. Because immigrant workers usually form a smaller group than native workers and are distinguished, in the eyes of native workers, by their separate racial or ethnic background, it is tempting to see immigrant workers as defined by their separate identity. Native workers, by contrast, are supposed to have ethnic or national identity as only one of their distinguishing characteristics—along with class, political allegiance, level of skill, and so on. Instead, immigrant workers, too, can feel a similar mix of class, religious, and ideological loyalties. Ironically, both groups may be groping for a sense of ethnic or national identity in opposition to each other. As John J. Kulczycki points out,

earlier historians saw the union of Polish miners in pre–World War I
Germany as a "nationalist" union, whereas, in fact, the German Catholic
and socialist unions, which excluded these workers and virtually forced
them to form their own union, were often more nationalistic.[41] As Ruth
Mandel shows in her essay, the community of guest workers in western
Germany today that is labeled "Turkish" includes a complex mix of
Kurdish and Alawi Moslem groups who do not feel Turkish, except in
the sense of their legal citizenship, and whom many Turks do not accept
as truly Turkish.[42]   Similarly, the immigrant workers in the United
States who were just beginning to see themselves as "Italian" or "Slovak"
were probably less nationalist than the "native" Americans or the
earlier, northwestern European immigrants who sought to exclude them
from their workplaces and unions. How the dominant group changes its
identity may be more critical than what immigrants do: one of the
fundamental transformations in British working-class history has been
the decline of prejudice against the Irish and its replacement with
prejudice against "coloreds"—West Indians, Pakistanis, Indians, and
Africans.[43] The complexities of ethnic and national identity run very
deep; one cannot infer identity even from something as fundamental as
language. The Polish workers in Germany, who were largely Catholic,
tried to bring into their unions Masurian workers who spoke a dialect of
Polish. The Masurians refused, however, because they were Protestant
and identified themselves politically and culturally with German rather
than Polish nationalism.[44] At the same time, English, Scottish, and
English Canadian immigrants were almost always assimilated into
American working-class communities, whereas Irish, Mexican, and
other Catholic workers often were seen as different even when they
spoke English and were third-generation U.S. citizens. Thus, one has to
see the lines demarcating ethnic groups and the lines demarcating
citizenship and alien status as distinct but intersecting boundaries.

The Structure of Work

The international migration of workers is also one element in a
struggle for control over labor power and the conditions of work between
industrial capitalists and workers. A vital and an often overlooked
characteristic of labor migration is that in-migration of workers is
actively encouraged and even initiated by employers in advanced
industrial countries despite the presence of unemployed native-born
workers who could be recruited for these jobs.[45] The vast majority of
immigrant workers enter the labor force in advanced industrial
countries at the bottom. They fill low-wage jobs and form the most
vulnerable sector of the labor force. This is not necessarily because they
lack skills but rather is a result of their immigrant status: their
inexperience with the ways of the receiving country, the differences in

culture and traditions, their legal status, and attitudes held by the native-born of the receiving country. As a result of both their vulnerability as immigrants and the presence of unemployed native-born workers, immigrant workers play a pivotal role in the ongoing struggle between employers and workers for control of the workplace. Employers can often use immigrant workers to depress wages and to undermine labor organizing. Sometimes employers are successful in this strategy, and at other times immigrant and native-born workers join forces in their fight for higher wages, better working conditions, and greater control over production.

To help understand how employers' strategies affect the labor market, some economists have developed theories that describe the labor market in capitalist countries as divided, or "segmented," into two or more sectors. Whereas most neoclassical economists treat the labor market as a unified whole with different occupations and individuals bidding for each other, dual and segmented labor market theorists see employment opportunities divided into primary and secondary labor markets. Job seekers in the primary market are favored over those in the secondary.[46] Mobility between the two labor markets is nearly nonexistent for many first-generation immigrants and, depending on the resources of the immigrant group and the amount of discrimination it faces, can be extremely difficult for later generations as well. The distinction between workers in the primary and secondary labor markets is not always one of skill, since workers confined to the secondary labor market could be trained for jobs in the primary market at a cost no higher than that for training workers already in the primary labor market. Instead, it is a distinction between "good" and "bad" jobs.[47]

Segmented labor market theory has been applied historically by economists David Gordon, Michael Reich, and Richard Edwards in a number of works, but especially in their book *Segmented Work, Divided Workers*. The three authors argue that the American working class was essentially transformed in the late nineteenth and early twentieth centuries when industrial employers substituted controls by managers for the quasi monopoly previously held by skilled, industrial workers. The result, by the mid-twentieth century, was a labor market split between unionized workers, to whom employers made concessions, and nonunionized, unskilled laborers who suffered the worst effects of unemployment and discrimination. Segmentation of the labor market, according to these theorists, provided employers with a way to divide the work force. Employers made the development of a working-class consciousness more difficult by confining blacks, women, and immigrants to the secondary labor market and by restricting access to jobs with higher pay, more security, and better working conditions to white, male, native-born workers—the very workers employers had the most reason to fear. This is not to say that a sudden shift took place. Native-born white males had enjoyed an advantage over nonwhites, women, children, and new immigrants since the early stages of industrial development, due to their privileged position in industrializing countries. Rather, the advantage became more rigid and more structured, and two separate job sectors developed to be filled by two separate labor markets, each with different criteria.[48]

It appears that this theory could be applied to much of industrialized North America and Western Europe during the nineteenth and twentieth centuries. Labor market segmentation grew out of conflict between workers and employers for control of the workplace. In a sense, it was a compromise between industrial capitalists and white, native-born male workers. Employers agreed to higher wages, job security, and other benefits in exchange for industrial peace. White, native-born male workers agreed to overlook the low wages, high turnover, and poor working conditions of a larger part of the labor force in exchange for good jobs.

Immigrant workers fill jobs primarily in the secondary labor market, the "bad" jobs. They are initially recruited for jobs that offer low wages, high turnover, and poor working conditions. The level of skill of immigrants does not correlate with the jobs they are recruited for or have access to once in the receiving country. They are, with few exceptions, locked into the secondary labor market at the very bottom of the wage and job structure. It is these jobs and the working conditions that go with them that pose the greatest threat to employer control over workers and over the workplace, since these jobs offer the greatest potential for worker dissatisfaction and protest.

By dividing the work force, the immigrant status of workers lessens the chance that workers can successfully pressure employees. As the essays by Guerin-Gonzales and Kulczycki show, immigrants become the scapegoat for unemployment, for depressed wages, and for other social tensions. The fact that they have been recruited, or at least that their initial entrance into the economy resulted from recruitment by employers, goes largely unrecognized. That the jobs they hold will continue to be low-wage, "bad" jobs without a concerted move on the part of workers, native-born males included, often goes unrecognized as well.[49]

At the same time, it is not clear that immigration necessarily increases unemployment among native workers. To the extent that migrants move in response to job opportunities, they appear to be filling new jobs or, more likely, finding jobs that native workers do not wish to fill. Data from both the United States and the Netherlands suggest that, in fact, in moderate numbers immigrants themselves can provide a stimulus to employment and economic growth. Immigrants demand services and may create further job opportunities. The area of employment, however, may be separate from wages. To the extent that immigrants are confined to unskilled and irregular employment, they may continue to work at relatively low wages and thus help hold down overall wage levels.[50]

The perspective of labor market segmentation helps to explain much of the historical evidence of inequality among job seekers. In his study of a Pennsylvania steel town, John Bodnar found that for a generation and a half, very few Italians, Slavs, or blacks were promoted to certain jobs that were, in effect, reserved for Irish, German, or English Americans.[51] Peter Shergold, investigating wages in the late nineteenth century, argued that the high wages of American skilled workers—which seemed fabulous by European standards of the time—had as their counterpart very low, and very insecure, wages paid to a mass of unskilled laborers.[52]

Another value of labor segmentation theory is that it provides a healthy antidote to the view that work, especially industrial work, unites workers while noneconomic factors—ethnicity, religion, family patterns, and gender—divide them. From both Marxist and neoclassical liberal perspectives, the tendency has been to argue that industrialization acts as a homogenizing or unifying force, overriding the peculiar characteristics that individuals or groups bring to the labor market and substituting a uniform, economic dimension that responds only to wages and unemployment. As both labor market theorists and labor historians have argued, however, modern industry has almost always divided workers as much as it has united them. Even as factory owners broke down small units of production in the late nineteenth century, for example, they organized factory workers into job hierarchies, created ranks, and enforced differing pay scales.[53] That the exact relationship between labor markets and industrialization remains only dimly understood perhaps reflects the problem that labor markets represent for economic analysis. In contrast to the development of capital markets, corporations, and governmental economic policy, labor markets seem much more resistant to the tools of mainstream economics. Why some workers move to seek new jobs while others stay unemployed and why so much employment recruitment remains informal and unbureaucratized are still important questions.[54]

One problem remaining with labor market segmentation theory is that it still emphasizes the structure of work as something that acts upon immigrants and other workers and rarely suggests how ethnicity acts upon work and the division of labor. A somewhat richer theoretical perspective than Gordon, Reich, and Edwards' is that of Charles Sabel in his *Work and Politics*. Sabel argues that workers must be seen as coming to work with values, prior experiences, and expectations. These "worldviews," as he calls them, shape which jobs workers will prefer, whether they see their jobs as permanent, and how they will perceive themselves in relation to other workers. Workers with similar worldviews—craftsmen valuing their jobs in part for status reasons, peasant workers intending to return to agriculture—form groups, Sabel argues, that must create alliances in order for any kind of working-class solidarity to emerge.[55] Although Sabel deals with immigration only briefly, his larger framework allows us to see the specific customs and prior experiences of immigrants not as epiphenomenal but as critical to their behavior in the workplace.

One problem, however, is that, like Gordon, Reich, and Edwards and indeed almost all scholars on labor, Sabel treats industrial or factory labor as the archetypal form of work. In fact, immigrants have as often if not more often been found in agriculture, casual labor, and domestic service. These occupations are especially critical because whole groups of immigrant workers, women being perhaps the most important example, work in nonindustrial occupations or move back and forth between industrial work and domestic service. Nor is a divided labor market only a phenomenon of industry. In Californian agriculture—where in fact labor market segmentation was first documented—employers sometimes organized workers by racial and ethnic group. With the work force split into separate gangs of Japanese, Mexicans, blacks, and Filipinos, union organizers found they had to organize the workers into similarly divided unions.[56]

Just as labor theorists have sometimes focused too narrowly on industrial work, so both labor theorists and labor historians working on ethnic or immigrant groups have sometimes assumed only that work influences ethnic groups, not that ethnic groups can affect work. Ethnicity is something that the unifying effect of a capitalist economy supposedly will break down. David Montgomery, by contrast, shows that Italians maintained a favored position in construction in pre–World War I America because they alone maintained a *padrone* system whereby straw bosses could mobilize large numbers of workers quickly and move them over long distances. Even when employers tried to dispense with Italians because they could force higher wages and better working conditions, they found that no other ethnic group of workers was organized to fit the demands of the industry.[57]

Montgomery's insight could be broadened considerably: other ethnic groups found their place in the economy because they possessed special customs as a social and economic group. Chinese citrus pickers in southern California for years waged a successful battle against the attempts of growers to replace them, as did Flemish seasonal workers in French agriculture whose employers tried to replace them with Poles and native workers. In both cases, the labor contract system, as it had with the Italians in construction, proved indispensable to employers. In both cases, enormous group solidarity, enforced not only by the straw bosses but by the workers themselves and reinforced by racial or ethnic distinctiveness, gave the workers leverage against competing groups. The Chinese were finally driven out only by outright violence and legal exclusion, while machinery and better employment elsewhere drew away the Flemish.[58] Similarly, when scholars such as Piore argue that labor immigration grows out of demands of the capitalist system, there is a danger that workers' own bargaining power is overlooked. Piore argues that in almost every case, immigrant labor is "pulled in" by management. This management initiative demonstrates, for Piore, the control exercised over immigration by employers. Nonetheless, his argument overlooks—in part, because it has been less often studied—the cases where employers tried but failed to pull in labor. In pre-World War I Europe, Poles often refused to take jobs in France, and Flemings and Italians refused to replace the Poles in Germany.[59] How many more cases might there be of immigrant workers' ability to exercise some choice or control, albeit limited, in labor markets against employers' wishes?

Determining the degree of choice that immigrant workers have in labor markets is critical because it can also help us understand why certain groups are concentrated in specific occupations, and why some groups move out of the unskilled labor force. The importance of prior skills among immigrant workers has often been noted: Cornish miners took their experience with them to mining towns all over the English-speaking world. During the nineteenth-century move to the cities, Irish women in Britain and black southern women in the United States, despite prejudice and discrimination, managed to carve out a place for themselves as domestic servants.[60] Some groups succeeded, over time, in turning small, marginal places in the economy into conduits through which they could move into the middle class. In the United States, Poles and Belgians transformed pockets of urban land into truck farms, while Greeks and Italians moved from street hucksters to owners of produce supply houses and candy factories. The prosperous owners of "waste management" companies in Chicago—whom their Italian neighbors labeled "garbios"—owed their success to Dutch immigrant teamsters who began hauling refuse.[61] The niches in the economy filled by immigrants can also be crucial because within some immigrant groups a large proportion of workers are hired by small businessmen of their own nationality. In garment making in West Germany, the anthropologist A. Ersan Yücel found that many new enterprises were begun by Turks who could more easily hire their own compatriots than could German employers.[62] Just as the greater success or failure of small businesses may help explain the degree of social mobility among certain immigrant groups, so the ability or opportunity to create self-help organizations has been a factor determining whether immigrant workers can better themselves. Discrimination, as well as coming into urban areas at the very bottom of the labor markets, made it much more difficult for blacks, Mexicans, and some southern and eastern Europeans to establish the small businesses and self-help organizations that some Asians, Poles, and a variety of Protestant European immigrant groups used with success.[63]

Politics, Institutions, and Organizations

Within the confines set by the world economy, the state, and the structure of work, immigrant workers face the challenge of defending their interests in competition with other groups holding power in society. Workers, both immigrant and native, can exercise bargaining rights by creating informal coalitions or formal associations, by engaging in strikes, and by organizing themselves in political organizations and parties. The typical argument has been that immigrant workers check or undermine the solidarity between workers necessary for such action. From the literature, however, it is often not clear whether immigrant workers themselves weaken solidarity by refusing to ally, or whether the divisions between immigrants and native workers are an obstacle that working-class leaders cannot or choose not to overcome. Furthermore, the evidence for immigrant workers' weakening solidarity comes almost exclusively from the pre–World War I United States or contemporary Western Europe, both of which are situations where scholars have often been intent on explaining an apparent "failure" or "conservatism" of the labor movement as a whole. In a number of other cases, which have been treated much less widely in the general literature, immigrants have been seen as more radical than native workers. In contrast to the United States, much of the militancy of Argentinian and Brazilian workers in the late nineteenth century, for example, has been attributed to the influence of immigrants. Whereas Italians, for example, were often seen as the quintessentially conservative group among the "new immigrants" in the United States, in Brazil and Argentina they supplied a disproportionate amount of leadership for the labor movements.[64]

Labor historians studying immigrants have sometimes been too anxious to acquit their subjects of the charge of being "outside agitators," although systematically examining the role of immigrant workers as radicals is difficult because the definition of *radical* often differed widely between immigrants and natives. Certainly within the ranks of their own nationality, workers who migrated were often leaders in developing new political ideologies and organizations. The Chinese revolutionary leader Sun Yat-sen found his first following among immigrant communities in Hawaii, Canada, and the western United States and was actually in Denver, Colorado, when the Chinese Revolution of 1911 broke out.[65] The Chinese, Vietnamese, and Peruvian Communist parties were all founded by exiles in France, and Bismarck was worried enough about the revolutionary sentiments of German workers in the United States to have his consular agents spy on a large number of immigrants.[66]

Indeed, one of the parallels between German workers in the nineteenth-century United States and Algerians in France in the 1950s is that both groups had a vital interest in debates over nationalism in the home countries. Much of this immigrant radicalism, however, could be cut off from the militancy of native workers in the host countries, both because of differences in language and culture and because the political issues the groups were addressing were so different. Furthermore, the radicalism of immigrant workers has to be seen in its full context: the majority of workers, both native and immigrant, were usually only intermittently militant, and one has to carefully examine the divergent strands of apathy and mobilization before concluding whether an immigrant group was more or less radical than native workers. Political activism could also be harnessed in favor of conservatism. Many Italian immigrants in the United States in the interwar period supported Mussolini and fascism, although many others only responded to subsidies and manipulation by the Fascist government.[67] Turkish guest workers in Western Europe and Arab immigrant workers in the Gulf states are examples of two groups among whom right-wing political activity and religious fundamentalism have been strong. Nonetheless, the ability of even some of the most oppressed immigrant workers to organize strikes and engage in political activity must be emphasized, especially because so much of this activity remained cut off from that of native workers. The Koreans in interwar Japan, for example, were stripped of their ethnic identity and often brutally treated, yet still managed to organize themselves and even to participate in the embryonic Communist party of Japan.[68] Similarly, the indentured Indian workers in South Africa could mobilize occasionally, despite enforced isolation from other workers and severe legal restrictions on them.[69]

Yet immigrant workers, by their very presence, are still often assumed to undermine the possibility of labor militancy. Because they come to the labor market as outsiders, it is assumed that they lack the knowledge and experience to support protest or organizations. The evidence, however, is mixed. Rather than the immigrants refusing to ally with native workers, native workers have often created divisions by excluding immigrants. In both the United States and western Europe, native workers often initiated much of the divisiveness between immigrant and native workers. American historians such as John Higham have pointed out the deep xenophobia and racism that set workers against each other. More recently, Robert Parmet has argued that the anti-Chinese agitation of the 1880s solidified a deep antiforeign feeling among American workers that eventually supported the curtailing of immigration in 1924.[70] One political scientist has even gone so far as to argue that anti-immigrant policy was the leading factor in shaping the conservatism of organized labor in the United States.[71] That labor history has often failed to integrate these divisions into the larger picture of working-class action points up that labor historians as a group have frequently avoided confronting nationalism or ethnicity as a theoretical problem. In one of the rare attempts to do so, one of the most prominent of labor historians, E. J. Hobsbawm, waffles on the issue. The evidence, he says, suggests that "working class consciousness is probably secondary to other kinds of consciousness" such as nationalism, but at the same time, he asserts, "internal conflicts" within the working class "usually remain subordinate."[72]

The exceptional position of immigrant workers can easily be exaggerated: in many cases, their attempts to challenge employers have failed for the same reasons that actions by native workers have failed. Thus, the mere presence of immigrant workers is not a sufficient explanation for a weak labor movement. In the most widely known work on immigrant workers in contemporary Western Europe, Stephen Castles and Godula Kosack argue that "immigration is advantageous to the employers, through its effect in weakening the labour movement and in dividing the working class."[73] Yet there is not always a close correlation between the numbers of immigrant workers in Western European countries and the strength or weakness of labor movements. With large and approximately equal numbers of foreign workers, western Germany and France possess markedly different wage levels and union movements. Why? West German unions have been both politically stronger and more open to organizing immigrants than French unions. Indeed, Castles and Kosack's own evidence presents a much more contradictory picture than their assertions. They describe twelve labor disputes at length and conclude: "The evidence of the disputes indicates that the trade unions have not been successful in representing immigrant workers, nor in defending them from special forms of exploitation and victimization by employers and authorities." Yet among the nine disputes involving unions, there are only five cases where unions fail to help immigrant workers, while in four they do. Similarly, there is only one case of native and immigrant workers not allying, whereas there are four cases where they do. The problems which Castles and Kosack show that immigrants have in getting unions to defend them are, in fact, quite similar to problems native Western

European workers have with the same overly bureaucratized, co-opted unions. In addition, the one other factor that emerges from Castles and Kosack's work is the role of the state: in five of their twelve examples, governments acted against immigrant workers, while in none of the cases did they intervene on the behalf of immigrants.[74] There is little evidence, furthermore, that guest workers in Western Europe have served as a "reserve army of the unemployed." Some of them have reasonably good jobs, and the number of unemployed among them is not exceptionally high.[75]

Increasingly, some labor historians and other social scientists have argued that ethnicity is not simply a divisive factor that undermines working-class solidarity. Working-class organizations and institutions, it appears, possess a crucial ability to create or stifle solidarity by the alliances and tactics they choose when they confront divisions among workers. The western German unions, perhaps in part because of their country's troubled past, have followed a strikingly different policy toward guest workers than did the German unions of the pre–World War I period. The contrast between the high rate of union organization among Turks and Italians in western Germany and their disorganization in Switzerland, Barbara Schmitter argues, can be accounted for only by the decisive role that unions have played in Germany. Here, organizations have been more critical than have any ethnic tendencies.[76] The conventional picture of immigrants in the United States causing the failure of a radical American labor movement has to be altered as well. In contrast to earlier American labor historians, writers such as Victor Greene, David Montgomery, Michael Nash, and Rudolph Vecoli have argued that immigrant workers could be militant and politically active. Much of the immigrants' action had to take place outside of the established labor unions and political parties dominated by unsympathetic native workers or nativist middle-class leaders. When, belatedly, the Socialist party of America created "ethnic federations" in order to mobilize recent immigrants, it was the weakness of native Socialists that left the ethnic Socialists isolated.[77] In one of the richest portrayals of how workers developed a tradition of protest against industrialization, Herbert Gutman showed that the peasant customs and preindustrial rituals which European immigrant workers brought with them to the United States helped them to fashion a new working-class culture to defend their interests.[78]

In both the United States before World War I and contemporary Western Europe, the role of organized labor has been critical—within the limits set by the state—in determining whether or not immigrant workers' militancy had any success. In Fall River, Massachusetts, for example, established unions succeeded at first in allying with French Canadian immigrants but later failed to do so with Poles and

Portuguese workers.[79] In the Chicago packinghouses, which had an extremely diverse work force, historian James Barrett found that "the existence of separate racial and ethnic communities could lead to either unity or fragmentation, depending upon the role played by important community leaders and institutions."[80] The relative success of German unions in recruiting foreign workers, by contrast with the French, has occurred even though the relations between natives and foreigners are probably equally poor in the two countries. The weakness of French unions in this regard is probably due less to any inherently greater antiforeign prejudice than to the historic weakness of French unions—divided into rival federations and lacking direct political pressure on the state.[81]

Not only can unions and their leadership at times bring ethnic groups together in alliance, but ethnic consciousness can itself act as a unifying force. A number of the essays in Dirk Hoerder's edited collection *Struggle a Hard Battle* argue that ethnic consciousness, at times, helped North American workers rise above individualism and apathy and led them toward collective action. Ethnic consciousness could even help workers of different ethnic groups ally. David Montgomery argues that nationalism among Italian and eastern European workers at the end of World War I fed into a kind of class consciousness. The concepts of "oppressed nationalities" and oppressed groups of workers were closely linked.[82] As these writers emphasize, solidarity between ethnic groups was often fragile and frequently broke down. But it is not clear that solidarity based on ethnicity or on alliances between ethnic groups was more fragile than other kinds of solidarity—political, ideological, economic—formed between workers of different jobs and levels of skill. There seem, indeed, to be as many cases of ethnic solidarity as there are of ethnic divisiveness. As Allen Seager concludes about workers in Alberta, "Class consciousness, community-based solidarities, political ideologies, and ethnic identities are not easily sorted out and neatly compartmentalized."[83]

Workers' class consciousness and workers' ethnic or national identity, in other words, can be interwoven. At times, they may be alternatives, but at other times, they may reinforce or complement each other. This points to a larger argument in recent scholarship on labor: collective consciousness and solidarity among workers is almost always built up tactically by working-class leaders out of diverse elements. Groups of workers divided by levels of skill, age, race, nationality, gender, or geography have to be brought together on the basis of a complex set of loyalties and shared or compromised interests. Even a coalition of workers ostensibly based on purely economic similarities almost always has other ties that bind the members together and outweigh the divisiveness created by still other loyalties. In other words, the same factors can create either solidarity or divisiveness. The test for which result they will produce depends on the institutions, leadership, and tactics used to bring workers together. Whereas socialist rhetoric, for example, has often been used to demonstrate that workers were bound together by class consciousness, it could also be part of a distinct ethnic tradition. Richard Oestreicher captures this mixture nicely: in nineteenth-century Detroit, he says, "for German unionists, a certain amount of socialist phraseology was accepted cultural practice."[84] In other words, German workers could be bound together both by a sense of class consciousness and by a distinctive cultural tradition that encouraged class consciousness within ethnic boundaries.

"Workers' Community" or "Way of Life"

Among the most important elements that may divide or unite workers are the habits and loyalties growing out of what might be called workers' "way of life"—family structure, neighborhood ties, religious symbols, customs, leisure activities, and clubs and informal associations. Although often neglected by an earlier generation of labor scholars more interested in purely economic and political action, these habits and loyalties often are the building blocks for more formal or overtly political collective action. Among bronze workers in nineteenth-century Brussels, a singing club kept alive a sense of occupational solidarity during a period when no union existed in their trade, while Fourth of July picnics helped maintain what has been called an "artisans' republic" among American skilled workers.[85] As John Foster and Michael Anderson have shown, marriage and family patterns help explain why some communities and occupations acquire or maintain more solidarity than others.[86] Although much of the best work on "workers' way of life" has focused on early industrialization, scholarship on workers' culture in mature industrial society now makes it more possible to trace over time how changes in leisure, family, and informal associations support or undermine changes in working-class organization. In industrial towns in a number of European countries in the late nineteenth century, consumer cooperatives served as a focus for entertainment, festivals, and socializing and thereby strengthened the sense of community among workers' families that was necessary for political and labor union activity. As these institutions developed, they appear to have gathered around them some of the customs and solidarity that, in earlier phases of industrialization, had been centered on craft and local identities.[87] Even within an occupation, leisure and rituals could change to reflect the alterations in working-class life. Klaus Tenfelde has described how miners' festivals changed from local events to corporate ones identified with all miners and finally to celebrations linked to the mass of workers.[88] These institutions, experiences, and rituals outside of work could be the crucial cement holding together working-class solidarity; their absence, or their limitations, could point to reasons why workers have failed to mobilize successfully. Significantly, Tenfelde notes that Polish miners often had their own festivals apart from those of their German co-workers.

Despite the research done on workers' way of life and working-class culture, the argument has frequently been made that workers are more likely to be militant if they are separated from their communities—in other words, that loyalties to family, customs, and local institutions encumber workers rather than provide them with resources. At times, this argument takes the form of what might be called the "nothing-to-lose" hypothesis, that is, that single, usually male immigrant workers with few long-lasting ties to their host region may be more willing to strike than other workers. Research on strikes and collective action, however, indicates that the resources provided by organizations and families are critical to actually winning strikes and creating enduring solidarity. Young, predominantly male, Belgian textile operatives in France in the 1880s and young, single Filipino workers on Hawaiian plantations in the 1930s are but two examples of workers whose militancy, scholars have claimed, came from their feeling that they had little to lose by boldly challenging their employers. Yet when these workers actually were successful in launching strikes, it was often because they acquired loyalties to their communities or to institutions or because they allied themselves with other groups who were more involved in their communities. These workers, in other words, in contrast to the "nothing-to-lose" hypothesis, appear to have been willing to acquire "something to lose" if this could help create solidarity. The most successful strikes by Belgians in the French Nord came when they were backed by consumer cooperatives that gave the strikers new resources and new allies. The cooperatives lent strikers money and reached both French and Belgian families as consumers, thereby tapping the resources of many workers in different industries. The Filipinos, too, won their strikes when they allied with Japanese coworkers, who were supported, in turn, by Japanese small businessmen. The Japanese small businessmen who opposed Hawaii's Anglo business elite, in other words, were linked by ethnic and cultural ties to Japanese workers in a working-class alliance with Filipinos.[89] The Japanese small businessmen, in this case, acted in a similar fashion to tavernkeepers and shopowners in many working-class communities in North America and western Europe who supported their customers and neighbors on strike against the employers who ran large, more capitalist enterprises.

Religion, at times, has provided both solidarity and material resources. The Polish miners' union in pre–World War I Germany was almost as much a Catholic as an ethnic Polish union, while many of the German miners belonged to their own Catholic union, rather than the socialist one. The striking Japanese workers in Hawaii received support from Buddhist temples, and Sikhs on strike on London in the 1960s received aid from their coreligionists outside their industry.[90] Both Catholicism and Protestantism have sometimes provided the ideological glue to hold together diverse groups of workers in militant labor movements.[91]

Yet religion, family patterns, and community structure have also been divisive factors. Anti-Catholic feeling plagued, and in some cases permanently divided, the working class in America, Ireland, Belgium, Germany, and Austria, while both Catholic and Protestant churches at times denounced socialist or radical workers, created separate labor organizations, and allied with employers and the government against unions or workers' parties.[92] In addition, one of the crucial obstacles to allying ethnic groups together is not simple prejudice or linguistic differences but the contrasting cultures and ways of life they have developed. In the United States, the Irish proclivity toward employment in the church or in politics versus the Italian preference for small business or property ownership, the Slovak commitment to communal ties in contrast to the Romanian emphasis on individual advancement, and the close identification of Catholics with the Democratic party as opposed to the Jews' allegiance to several parties are all examples of the differences that set groups off from each other.[93]

Distinctive gender relationships that allowed more of an independent role for single women and legitimized males' support for women workers could be a unique source of strength for immigrant groups but, at the same time, could make it more difficult for other immigrant groups with different gender relationships to work with them. It could be argued, for example, that among the Irish in the United States and the Flemish in Belgium and northern France there was a high degree of acceptance of single women workers and of mutual support between male workers in one trade and striking women workers in another.[94] Although there is no easy solution to determining why these differences sometimes lead to division and at other times do not or actually aid in solidarity, it is clear that immigrant workers' collective action cannot be understood without investigating workers' culture and way of life.

Conclusion

The picture one is left with is perhaps best described as a series of priorities for research. First, the world economy, understood in its widest sense as the relation between all industrialized and nonindustrialized countries, acts as a kind of control on immigrant workers, shaping which choices they have open to them and raising or lowering the costs of movement to different places. Second, the state, in both sending and receiving countries, can curtail migrants' freedom of movement across borders and close off or open up the potential for collective action. Finally, it appears that where native and immigrant workers meet, the potential for conflict is enormous. While much of labor scholarship has assumed that simply being in a common economic class can draw workers together, the history of immigrant labor may suggest the reverse: ethnic, racial, and cultural differences are extremely deep. Yet the surprising instances of cooperation between divided groups of workers have to be explained as well. Explaining cooperation by economic pressures is not the only option. Scholars could also look at the three areas of work, institutions and politics, and family and community life to see how ethnicity and culture shape groups of workers in adopting or rejecting strategies of cooperation. Why have certain ethnic groups been more disposed, because of their beliefs, customs, or community structure, to support working-class solidarity? Have workers in certain communities been more shaped to seek alliances with other groups—alliances that can either make workers more accepting of paternalism or give them new resources for militancy? When do work, institutions, and family and community life provide or deny resources to immigrant workers who are trying to act together?

These questions are quite broad in part because the potential for immigration in the future may be increasingly complex. Few observers would have predicted that, by the 1970s and 1980s, Pakistanis and South Koreans would be working in the Persian Gulf states, that Nigeria, the Ivory Coast, and Argentina would be magnets for nearby Third World migration, or that the Communist bloc would be bringing Algerians to East Germany and North Koreans and Bulgarians to Russia.[95] Non-Western societies that Western observers have long thought of only as sources of emigrants have themselves become homes for migrants. While Egypt continues to send workers and professionals to other Arab countries such as the oil sheikdoms, West Africans have begun taking jobs in Egypt.[96] Even countries that deliberately try to stop migration from certain other areas find themselves contradicting their policies: the United States has recently imported Japanese, Jamaican, and Filipino workers while Israel has become dependent on Arab workers.[97] After passing what appeared to be landmark legislation in 1986 designed to slow immigration from Mexico, the United States almost immediately began allowing thousands of workers to come into the country on a temporary basis.[98]

Together, the essays in this volume capture a great deal of the diversity in immigration over the last two centuries. The authors utilize concepts such as the world economy, segmented labor, ethnic consciousness, and workers' culture to explain how immigrant workers organized themselves. In the process, they not only offer a sample of the recent scholarship on immigration and labor but suggest some ways in which the study of labor and migration can contribute to social science as a whole.

The first two essays examine the importance of immigrant workers' European heritage for their struggles in the United States during the nineteenth century. Dorothee Schneider demonstrates how the German bakers in New York City could draw on their common ethnic and occupational identity to try to create a powerful labor union. John Laslett looks at Scottish miners who brought over to Illinois their experience with independent labor political action. On the one hand, both scholars find that the structure of work and workers' way of life could, at least for a brief period, forge a strong sense of workers' solidarity. Laslett found that the Scottish miners' political activism in Illinois was much more similar to what they had engaged in in Britain than arguments about American exceptionalism have suggested. Both Schneider and Laslett found that immigrant groups, in different ways, eventually appeared to have lessened their distinctive European identity and to have adapted to the decentralized, less communitarian nature of American politics and labor activism. Yet it is striking that in both cases immigrant workers were not held back by their ethnic identity from engaging in political or labor activism. Instead, for both Scottish miners and German bakers ethnic heritage and distinctive traditions encouraged their activism. Indeed, Laslett raises the possibility that it was the American political system, not the immigrant workers' traditions, that encouraged a more apolitical role for labor.

On the other hand, the two essays also point out the crucial relationship between immigrant workers' way of life and their political organizations. Schneider shows that for the German bakers the very strength that they drew from their ethnic identity and neighborhood ultimately proved a hindrance when their unions could not adjust to the entrance of new groups such as Italians and Jews or to the expansion of baking factories. By contrast, Laslett found that the Scottish immigrant miners in Illinois much more successfully carried their labor activism along with them as they were forced to mobilize other groups of workers.

Europeans not only migrated to the United States, they also migrated within Europe itself. Carl Strikwerda examines the Belgian workers who migrated to France to work in textiles, agriculture, and mining, while John J. Kulczycki looks at the Poles who worked in Imperial Germany's industrial heartland of the Ruhr before World War

I. Scholars have paid a good deal of attention to both of these groups of immigrants, in part because they represented two of the largest streams of labor migration in nineteenth-century Europe. Both Strikwerda and Kulczycki argue, however, that scholars have largely followed the lead of the contemporary observers who saw the Belgians and the Poles as either passive and easily exploited or undisciplined and disease-ridden.

In the case of the Belgians, Strikwerda argues that they were not, for the most part, a passive or easily exploited work force. State regulation of migration and changes in the Belgian and French economies, furthermore, help explain many of the instances where Belgian immigrants appear to have been uninvolved in strikes and labor unions. In the case of the Polish miners, Kulczycki argues, their way of life was not more squalid, undisciplined, or disease-ridden. The Poles suffered some of the same disabilities that German miners did, in roughly the same proportion. Contemporary observers and later historians, however, took the Poles and their problems as a symbol of the difficulties that nineteenth-century industrialization caused for German society as a whole.

The structure of work and the role of the state as an arbitrator of identity are probably the two most important themes that emerge from these two essays. The differences between Belgians who were settled textile workers and those who were seasonal farm workers were almost as great as between Belgians and French, while Kulczycki points out that mining work created its own world, whether those engaged in it were Poles or Germans. At the same time, the distinctions that the German government could make between Poles who lived within the Reich and those who did not, coupled with the intense German nationalism fostered by the state, divided and isolated the Poles from Germans. Similarly, the French state transformed the Belgian immigrant community by extending citizenship and raising tariffs.

Two essays help remind us that Europeans were not alone in their migration to the United States in the nineteenth and early twentieth centuries and that the recent Asian and Latin American migrants to the United States are not a completely new phenomenon. Looking at plantation workers in Hawaii, Ruth Akamine examines an immigrant work force that faced unusual disabilities as a result of the way their work was organized and the diversity of the ethnic groups that managers had recruited. Working in often isolated plantations, Chinese, Filipinos, Japanese, and Pacific islanders labored for large companies that dominated Hawaii's economy. Despite these odds, Japanese workers were able to draw on their larger ethnic community and, once allied with the other large ethnic group, the Filipinos, were able finally to pressure employers and the government to improve their condition. In her essay on Mexican workers in early-twentieth-century

California, Camille Guerin-Gonzales shows that problems faced today by many Latinos have deep roots in past discrimination. California agriculture for decades was the classic example of labor segmentation, where workers of different ethnic and racial backgrounds labored and lived in separate communities. The freedom with which large agricultural employers could segment their Mexican workers, Guerin-Gonzales argues, was strengthened by the state and the antiurban myths that Anglo-Americans held about their own way of life. During the Depression, the U.S. government sent many Mexicans out of the country, while the American myth of the independent family farm allowed agricultural employers to operate with very little interference from the government or other social groups.

Why should immigrant agricultural workers in Hawaii and California have had such differing success in organizing and improving their conditions? As Guerin-Gonzales and Akamine point out, the structure of work on settled sugar and pineapple plantations in Hawaii created radically different conditions from seasonal migratory work in California citrus. The repression exercised by Californian growers, too, forced Mexican workers into a marginal way of life unlike the more integrated way of life that Japanese and Filipino workers managed to build in Hawaii.

The same world economy that drew Japanese and Filipinos to Hawaii and Mexicans into the United States also formed the economic foundation for the movement of products and workers within the British Empire. Two of the most important movements of workers within the empire brought Indians to South Africa and Chinese to Malaya. The migration of the Indians, according to Surendra Bhana, demonstrates the crucial role of the state, as most of the migrants came as indentured laborers. Once in South Africa, the indentured Indians organized themselves into immigrant communities in the face of enormous pressure exercised by employers backed by the colonial state. A slightly less strict form of indenture brought Chinese workers to Malaya in the early twentieth century. By the 1930s, as Donald Nonini argues, changes in the imperial colonial economy and the Chinese workers' own activism created the basis of a new labor movement that eventually succeeded in weakening imperial control itself and laying the foundation for an independent Malaya.

Bhana's and Nonini's essays show perhaps most clearly the way in which migration history begins with the powerful forces of the world economy and the state. The demand of the European and North American markets for colonial products from South Africa and Southeast Asia was supplied through the British Empire's control of trade routes and indentured labor. The distinctively segregated way of life in which Indians and Chinese found themselves in South Africa and

Malaya by the twentieth century emerged from the interaction of one powerful nineteenth-century state over a portion of the world economy.

One of the ironies of world economic history is that Third World countries that had been colonized by Europe in the nineteenth century have now sent thousands of workers to Europe itself. In a wide-ranging essay, Donald Reid examines the immigration into France in the twentieth century from all major sources—Poland, Italy, Portugal, and, of special importance since World War II, Algeria. Reid demonstrates how Algerians in France helped define the Algerian identity in new ways in the midst of the Algerian war of independence against France, 1954–62. Another common characteristic of this post–World War II migration is that the state has played a much more important role than before World War I. Reid points out how state-to-state agreements have regulated the flow of Italians, Poles, and Algerians to France.

The role of the state has been equally decisive in shaping the migration of Turks to West Germany. With the Cold War blocking the possibility of East Germans, Poles, or other Eastern Europeans from working in western Germany, thousands of Turks were brought instead. Yet, as Ruth Mandel demonstrates, the way of life created by the Turks in western Germany is much more complex than the opposition of German and Turk. The Turks themselves come from a society that nurtures a variety of religious and ethnic communities, and the reactions of immigrants to life in Western Europe create further diversity within the Turkish population. Mandel thus reminds us that fully grasping the reality of immigrant workers requires paying close attention to their way of life in all its complexity, even though the opposition of immigrant and native created by the state still influences all aspects of immigrant life.

The last essay in the book looks at the political process in which the state determines whether migration is restricted. In a wide-ranging contribution, economist James Foreman-Peck argues that in modern history the structure of work and the nature of the state have usually combined to restrict immigration. Most workers have tended to see immigrants as competitors and have been able to express that fear through the political process. This tendency to restrict immigration, he argues, has been checked only episodically by employers' desire for labor, by the inability of restrictionist sentiment to impose its views, or by an expanding economy.

If anyone needed further evidence of the immense power of the state to shape immigration, it was provided by the dramatic events of 1990 in Eastern Europe, the Mideast, and West Africa. With the end of the Communist hegemony over Eastern Europe, refugees, smugglers, and, most often, immigrant workers began moving over borders that had been closed for decades.[99] Iraq's seizure of Kuwait set off not only a

major military and economic crisis but an international upheaval of
migration as thousands of Indians, Egyptians, Bangladeshis, and
Koreans and workers of a dozen other nationalities struggled to reach
home. The ripple effects of the crisis were quickly felt in Thailand and
the Philippines as remittances of immigrant workers fell off.[100] Less well
known, but just as revealingly, the civil war in Liberia threatened the
migrant workers from a half-dozen West African countries. Indeed, one
reason that other nearby African states sent in their troops was to
protect their countries' workers in Liberia.

These examples demonstrate the continuing importance of
migration as a political as well as an economic and social issue. Barring
a global depression, the world economy will continue to encourage
migration and states will attempt to regulate, control, and channel
migrants. And immigrant workers will continue to seek to organize and
shape their communities to defend their way of life. Together, these
essays, we hope, will broaden students' and scholars' understanding of
migration, labor, and politics and help provide perspectives both for
further study of the past and for making decisions about an important
phenomenon in the world today.

Notes

1. W. R. Böhning lists four "distinct types of foreign migrants: 1) Refugees
or persons who leave their own country because of a well-founded fear of
persecution by reasons of race, religion, nationality, political association or social
grouping; 2) Economically active persons for the purpose of employment; 3) A
residual category such as pilgrims, ministers of religion, diplomatic and
unassimilated personnel, students, volunteers sponsored publicly or by charity,
retired or other persons living entirely on their own means; and 4) A derivative
category, namely the parents, spouses, siblings and children of some or all of the
preceding three groups." W. R. Böhning, "Elements of a Theory of International
Economic Migration to Industrial Nation States," in *Global Trends in Migration:
Theory and Research on International Population Movements,* ed. Mary M. Kritz,
Charles B. Keely, and Silvano Tomasi (New York, 1983), 28–29. We are focusing
here on workers as the largest subgroup within Böhning's second category of those
who migrate as economically active people seeking employment.
2. Ira Katznelson and Aristide Zolberg, eds., *Working-Class Formation:
Nineteenth Century Patterns in Western Europe and the United States* (Princeton,
1986), 16.
3. David Montgomery, *The Fall of the House of Labor: The Workplace,
the State, and American Labor Activism, 1865-1925* (Cambridge, 1987), 70-71. An
important summary of European migration from an international perspective is J.
D. Gould, "European Inter-Continental Emigration, 1815-1914: Patterns and
Causes," *Journal of European Economic History* 8, (1979): 593-639. Also useful are
Aristide Zolberg, "International Migration in Political Perspective," and
Elizabeth McLean Petras, "The Global Labor Market in the Modern World-

Economy," both in Kritz, Keely, and Tomasi, eds., and Saskia Sassen, *The Mobility of Labor and Capital* (Cambridge, 1988), esp. 26-59. A noteworthy attempt to synthesize economic history with the waves of migration during modern history is Eric R. Wolf, *Europe and the People without a History* (Berkeley and Los Angeles, 1982). More limited in its scope than the "world economy" but still a fundamental work for the economic basis of international migration is Brinley Thomas, *Migration and Economic Growth: A Study of Great Britain and the Atlantic Economy* (Cambridge, 1954). Two other older, still useful works on the interaction of economic factors and migration are Richard Easterlin, "Influences in European Overseas Emigration before World War I," *Economic Development and Cultural Change* (April 1961), 331-48, and Charlotte Erickson, *American Industry and the European Immigrant, 1860-1885*, repr. ed. (New York, 1967). For a critique of Katznelson and Zolberg that draws on a world economy model, see John Laslett, "Challenging American Exceptionalism: 'Overlapping Diasporas' as a Model for Studying American Working Class Formation, 1810-1924," *Newberry Library Papers in Family and Community History* 87, 1 (April 1987), 7-10.

4. Klaus Bade, "German Emigration to the United States and Continental Immigration to Germany in the Late Nineteenth and Early Twentieth Centuries," and Robert Mikkelson, "Immigrants in Politics: Poles, Germans, and the Social Democratic Party of Milwaukee," both in *Labor Migration in the Atlantic Economies: The European and North American Working Classes during the Period of Industrialization*, ed. Dirk Hoerder, (Westport, Conn., and London, 1985). See also Karl Obermann and Heinz-Peter Thummler, "Allemagne: Les grand movements de l'emigration allemande vers les Etats-Unis d'Amerique au XIXe siècle," Wolfgang Kollman and Peter Marschalck, "Allemagne: German Overseas Emigration since 1815," and Celina Bobinska and Adam Galos, "Pologne: Poland: Land of Mass Emigration (XIXth and XXth Centuries)," all in *Les Migrations Internationales de la fin du XVIIIe siècle à nos jours* (Paris, 1980), 407-502.

5. Michael Piore, *Birds of Passage: Migrant Labor and Industrial Societies* (Cambridge, 1979).

6. Carl Solberg, "Mass Migration in Argentina, 1870-1970," in *Human Migration: Patterns and Policies*, ed. William McNeill and Ruth Adams (Bloomington, Ind., and London, 1978). See also Magnus Mörner, *Adventurers and Proletarians: The Story of Migrants in Latin America* (Pittsburgh and Paris, 1985), 35-66.

7. Mario Garcia, *Desert Immigrants: The Mexicans of El Paso, 1880-1920* (New Haven, 1981), 4-5, 35-37, and Lawrence, A. Cardoso, *Mexican Emigration to the United States, 1897-1931: Socio-Economic Patterns* (Tucson, 1980).

8. Kay Saunders, ed., *Indentured Labour in the British Empire: 1834-1920* (London, 1984); A. J. H. Latham, "Southeast Asia: A Preliminary Survey, 1800-1914," in *Migration across Time and Nations: Population Mobility in Historical Contexts*, ed. Ira Glazier and Luigi De Rosa (New York, 1986); Hugh Tinker, "Into Servitude: Indian Labour in the Sugar Industry, 1833-1970," and Pieter Emmer, "The Importation of British Indians into Surinam (Dutch Guiana), 1873-1916," both in *International Labour Migration: Historical Perspectives*, ed. Shula Marks and Peter Richardson (London, 1984); Yen Ching-Hwang, *Coolies and Mandarins: China's Protection of Overseas Chinese during the Late Ch'ing Period (18511922)* (Singapore, 1985), and P. C. Campbell, *Chinese Coolie Emigration to Countries within the British Empire* (London, 1923).

9. Besides Professor Bhana's essay in this volume, see Surendra Bhana, ed., *Essays on Natal's Indentured Indians* (Leeds, 1990), and Surendra Bhana and

J. B. Brain, *Setting Down Roots: Indian Migrants in South Africa, 1860-1911* (Johannesburg, 1990).

10. Philip Taylor, *The Distant Magnet: European Emigration to the USA* (New York, 1972), 44.

11. Thomas Archdeacon, *Becoming American: An Ethnic History* (New York, 1983), 43-49.

12. Centro de Estudios Puertorriquenos, *Labor Migration under Capitalism: The Puerto Rican Experience* (New York and London, 1979), 21-22, cited in Shula Marks and Peter Richardson, "Introduction," in Marks and Richardson, eds. See also Mary Kritz, "International Migration Patterns in the Caribbean Basin: An Overview," in Kritz, Keely, and Tomasi, eds.

13. Arthur Marwick, *The Deluge: British Society and the First World War* (New York, 1970), 71-72; W. R. Böhning, *Studies in International Labour Migration* (London, 1984), 274.

14. Klaus Bade, ed., *Population, Labor, and Migration in Nineteenth and Twentieth Century Germany* (London, 1986); Bade, "German Emigration," in Hoerder, ed., *Labor Migration;* Christoph Klessmann, *Polnische Bergarbeiter im Ruhrgebiet 1870-1945* (Göttingen, 1978), and the sources cited in note 4.

15. Robert Swierenga, "Dutch International Migration and Occupational Change: A Structural Analysis of Multinational Linked Files," in Glazier and De Rosa; Luc Schepens, *Van Vlaskutser tot Franschman* (Brugge, 1973); Jean Stengers, "Belgique," in *Les migrations internationales.* Between 1899 and 1910, Dutch immigrants came to the United States with an average of over $70, while most southern and eastern Europeans came with an average of less than $25. Taylor, 97.

16. Frank Thistlethwaite, "Migration from Europe Overseas in the Nineteenth and Twentieth Centuries," in *Population Movements in Modern European History*, ed. Herbert Moller (Boston, 1964), 75-77; Edmond Ronse, *L'emigration saisonnière belge* (Ghent, 1913), 23-27. In addition, perhaps as many as one-third of those who entered the United States during the nineteenth century left again. See also J. D. Gould, "European Inter-Continental Emigration—The Road Home: Return Migration from the U.S.A.," *Journal of European Economic History* 9 (1980): 41-122, and Dirk Hoerder, "Immigration and the Working Class: The Remigration Factor," *International Labor and Working Class History* 21 (Spring 1982): 28-41. On definitions of *circular* as opposed to other kinds of migration, Charles Tilly, "Migration in Modern European History," in McNeill and Adams.

17. Carl Solberg, *The Prairies and the Pampas: Agrarian Policy in Canada and Argentina, 1880-1930* (Stanford, 1987).

18. See the essays in this volume by Ruth Akamine and Surendra Bhana; Josef Barton, *Peasants and Strangers: Italians, Rumanians, and Slovaks in an American City, 1890-1950* (Cambridge, Mass., 1975), 28; Cardoso, 17; and Augustin Escobar, Mercedes Gonzalez, and Bryan Roberts, "Migration, Labour Markets, and the International Economy: Jalisco, Mexico, and the United States," in *Migrants, Workers, and the Social Order*, ed. Jeremy Eades (London and New York, 1986), 46-47. One of the coeditors of this volume, Camille Guerin-Gonzales, has completed a study of immigration and mining communities in southern Colorado, "Solidarity Is Not Enough: The Rise of the Working Class in Hispano Colorado," in *Regions of the Raza: Changing Interpretations of Mexican American Regional History and Culture*, ed. Antonio Rios-Bustamante (Encino, Calif., 1991), and is beginning a comparative study of immigrant and native-born coal mining families in Appalachia and northern England, "'A Living Wage': Community and Class Consciousness in the Coal Fields of Appalachia and Northern England, 1890-1946."

19. Sassen, 14-20.

20. Charles Tilly, "Transplanted Networks," Center for Studies of Social Change, New School for Social Research, The Working Papers Series, 35 (October 1986), 3.

21. Michael C. Lemay, *From Open Door to Dutch Door: An Analysis of United States Immigration Policy since 1820* (New York, 1987), 54-57, 82-86; John Higham, *Strangers in the Land: Patterns of American Nativism, 1860-1925*, 2nd ed. (New York, 1971), 300-324.

22. Gary Cross, *Immigrant Workers in Industrial France* (Philadelphia, 1983), 194-207; Frank Caestecker, "Het Vreemdelingenbeleid in de Tussenoorlogse Periode, 1922-1939 in België," *Belgisch Tijdschrift voor Nieuwste Geschiedenis/Revue Belge d'Histoire Contemporaine* 15, 3-4 (1984): 461-86; Camille Guerin-Gonzales, "Cycles of Immigration and Repatriation: Mexican Farm Workers in California Industrial Agriculture, 1900-1940," American Historical Association convention, 1985.

23. Bade, "German Emigration," 135, and Nancy L. Green, "'Filling the Void': Immigration to France before World War I," 148-49, both in Hoerder, ed., *Labour Migration*. West Germany reversed earlier restrictive German policies and, as a result, families of foreigners have, despite many problems with social discrimination, settled legally in the country since the 1950s. Despite the popular impression to the contrary, France has not been more restrictive toward guest workers' bringing in their families than have been West Germany, Belgium, and the Netherlands. See Böhning, *Studies*, 152-56.

24. Böhning, *Studies*, 140.

25. Edward Ruebens, "Low-level Work in Japan without Foreign Workers," *International Migration Review* 15, 5 (1981): 749-57; James Sterngold, "Japan Is Divided on Foreign Workers," *New York Times*, December 17, 1989, B-3.

26. Vaughn Robinson, "Bridging the Gulf: The Economic Significance of South Asian Migration to and from the Mideast," in *Return Migration and Regional Economic Problems*, ed. Russell King (London, 1986); Zafer H. Ecevit, "International Labor Migration in the Middle East and North Africa: Trends, Effects, and Policies," in Kritz, Keely, and Tomasi, eds.; and Roger Ballard, "The Political Economy of Migration: Pakistan, Britain, and the Middle East," in Eades, ed.

27. William McNeill, "Human Migration: An Historical Overview," in McNeill and Adams; Mack Walker, *German Home Towns: Community, State, and General Estate, 1648-1871* (Ithaca and London, 1971), 73-107.

28. McNeill, "Human Migration"; Jan deVries, *European Urbanization, 1500-1800* (Cambridge, Mass., 1984), 213; and James Lee, "Migration and Expansion in Chinese History," in McNeill and Adams.

29. Mack Walker, *Germany and the Emigration, 1816-1885* (Cambridge, Mass., 1964); Fermin Lentacker, *La frontière franco-belge* (Lille, 1974).

30. John J. Kulczycki, "The Prussian Authorities and the Poles of the Ruhr," *International History Review* 8, 4 (November, 1986): 599.

31. Jerome Blum, *The End of the Old Order in Rural Europe* (Princeton, 1978), 377-441; Barton, 28.

32. Cross, 99-119.

33. Robinson, 251; Kritz, "International Migration Patterns," 231.

34. James A. Sandos and Harry Cross, "National Development and International Labour Migration: Mexico 1940-1965," *Journal of Contemporary History* 18 (1983): 44. A helpful overview of the role of sending countries is Barbara Heisler, "Sending Countries and the Politics of Emigration and Destination," *International Migration Review* 19, 3 (1985): 469–84.

35. Stephen Castles and Godula Kosack, *Immigrant Workers and the Class Structure in Western Europe*, 2nd ed. (Oxford, 1985), 28-45; Böhning, *Studies*, 123-33; Jonathan Power, *Migrant Workers in Western Europe and the United States* (New York, 1979), 92-3, 107.

36. On the problems of indentured and contract labor migration, all the essays in Marks and Richardson, eds., *International Labour Migration*, are useful, but especially Charlotte Erickson, "Why Did Contract Labor Not Work in the Nineteenth Century United States?" The essays in Saunders are also helpful.

37. Mark Gibney, *Strangers or Friends: Principles for a New Alien Admissions Policy* (New York, 1986), provides a useful review of the clash between the notions of "community" and citizenship.

38. Higham, 35-104.

39. Joel Michael Halpern, "Yugoslav Migration Process and Employment in Western Europe: A Historical Perspective," in *Migrants in Europe: The Role of Family, Labor, and Politics*, ed. Hans Christian Buechler and Judith Marie Buechler (New York, Westport, Conn., and London, 1987), 107-9.

40. Samuel Baily, "The Adjustment of Italian Immigrants in Buenos Aires and New York, 1870-1914," *American Historical Review* 88, 2 (April 1983): 281-305; Herbert S. Klein, "The Integration of Italian Immigrants into the United States and Argentina: A Comparative Analysis," with comments and reply, ibid., 306-46. Two instructive overviews of ethnicity and the problem of immigrants' assimilation in the United States are Alan M. Kraut, *The Huddled Masses: The Immigrant in American Society, 1880-1921* (Arlington, Heights, Ill., 1982), and John Bodnar, *The Transplanted: A History of Immigrants in Urban America* (Bloomington, Ind., 1985).

41. John J. Kulczycki, "Nationalism over Class Solidarity: The German Trade Unions and Polish Coal Miners in the Ruhr to 1902," *Canadian Review of Studies in Nationalism* 14, 2 (Fall 1987).

42. See also Ruth Mandel, "Fragmenting Families, Mediating Piligrimages: Accounts of Turkish Migrants and Their Children" (unpublished paper, University College London, 1989).

43. Eric J. Hobsbawm, *Industry and Empire* [Economic History of Britain, Vol. 3, From 1750 to the present] (Harmondsworth, 1969), 309-12.

44. S. H. F. Hickey, *Workers in Imperial Germany: The Miners of the Ruhr* (Oxford, 1985), 82, 272. Hickey's citations unfortunately seem to be only to secondary sources. We would like to thank Prof. John J. Kulczycki for his help on this question.

45. Böhning, "Elements of a Theory of International Economic Migration to Industrial Nation States," 28; for a discussion of the role recruitment plays in initiating labor migration from developing to advanced industrial countries, see Piore, *Birds of Passage*, 19-24.

46. A wide range of models have been proposed to explain divided labor markets including "dual" labor markets and three or more segmented markets. For the purposes of explaining the discrimination and other problems that immigrants face in gaining better employment, here we are considering dual and segmented labor market theories together and contrasting them to the neoclassical model. See P. Doeringer and Michael J. Piore, *Internal Labour Markets and Manpower Analysis* (Lexington, Mass., 1971; Doeringer and Piore, "Unemployment and the Dual Labour Market," *Public Interest* (Winter 1975); David M. Gordon, *Theories of Poverty and Underemployment: Orthodox, Radical, and Dual Labour Market Perspectives* (Lexington, Mass., 1972); Richard Edwards, Michael Reich, and David M. Gordon, *Labour Market Segmentation* (Lexington, Mass., 1975; Gordon, Edwards, and Reich, *Segmented Work, Divided Workers; The Historical Transformation of Labor in the United States*

(Cambridge, Mass., 1982); Richard Edwards, *Contested Terrain: The Transformation of the Workplace in the Twentieth Century* (New York, 1979). Major studies of labor market segmentation on the basis of class and gender are Gordon, Edwards, and Reich, *Segmented Work, Divided Workers;* Natalie Sokoloff, *Between Money and Love: The Dialectics of Women's Home and Market Work* (New York, 1980); David Montgomery, *Fall of the House of Labor.* A recent study of Mexican immigrant workers in the United States that draws upon labor market segmentation and racial discrimination is James D. Cockroft, *Outlaws in the Promised Land: Mexican Immigrant Workers and America's Future* (New York, 1986).

47. Dual and segmented labor theories have, of course, provoked a major debate within economics and related subdisciplines that study labor. See Glen G. Cain, "The Challenge of Segmented Labor Market Theories to Orthodox Theory: A Survey," *Journal of Economic Literature* 14, 4 (December 1976): 1215-57; Barry R. Chiswick, "The Economic Progress of Immigrants: Some Apparently Universal Patterns," *Contemporary Economic Problems,* ed. William Fellner (Washington, 1979), 350, 359-99; and R. Loveridge and A. L. Mok, *Theories of Labour Market Segmentation: A Critique* (Boston and London, 1979), 47.

48. Gordon, Reich, and Edwards, *Segmented Work,* esp. 92-94, 116-21. For an excellent review of Gordon et al. as well as the work by Charles Sabel discussed below, see Jonathan Zeitlin, "Social Theory and the History of Work," *Social History,* 8, 3 (October 1983): 365-74. In some ways, Gordon, Edwards, and Reich's argument for the importance of craft workers in nineteenth-century industry resembles that for skilled workers in Britain: Eric J. Hobsbawm, *Workers: Worlds of Labor* (New York, 1984), chaps. 12-14, and Henry Pelling, "The Concept of the Labour Aristocracy," in his *Popular Politics and Society in Late Victorian Britain* (New York, 1968).

49. One weakness of Gordon, Reich, and Edwards' historical work on segmented labor is that they do not deal more substantially with immigrant workers. While they discuss "foreign-born" workers at several points, they have only one specific reference to an immigrant group, the Irish, 77-78.

50. The debate over the economic effect of immigration is, of course, enormous. See, in particular, George Borjas, *Friends or Strangers: The Impact of Immigrants on the U.S. Economy* (New York, 1990), and Böhning, *Studies in International Labour Migration.*

51. John Bodnar, *Immigration and Industrialization: Ethnicity in an American Milltown, 1870-1940* (Pittsburgh, 1972), 64-75, 132-37.

52. Peter R. Shergold, "'Reefs of Roast Beef': The American Worker's Standard of Living in Comparative Perspective," *American Labor and Immigration History, 1877-1920s: Recent European Research,* ed. Dirk Hoerder (Urbana and London, 1983).

53. David Montgomery, *Workers' Control in America* (Cambridge, 1979); Herbert Gutman, "Work, Culture, and Society in Industrializing America, 1815-1919," in his *Work, Culture, and Society* (New York, 1977), 47-54.

54. Business and economic historians have concentrated on explaining the bureaucratization of business and corporations, for example, but have been relatively silent on why labor markets should have been so resistant to formal, institutional controls. See, for example, Alfred D. Chandler, *The Visible Hand: The Managerial Revolution in American Business* (Cambridge, Mass., 1977), and Alfred D. Chandler and Herman Daems, eds., *Managerial Hierarchies: Comparative Perspectives on the Modern Industrial Enterprise* (Cambridge, Mass., and London, 1980). That labor markets in the United States resisted control by labor exchanges and employment bureaus seems to be demonstrated by Joshua Rosenbloom, "Institutional Innovation and Urban Labor Market

Adjustment in the Late Nineteenth Century," unpublished paper, University of Kansas, Department of Economics, 1988. This paper is based on Joshua Rosenbloom, "Labor Market Institutions and the Geographical Integration of Labor Markets in the Late Nineteenth Century United States," (Ph.D. diss., Economics, Stanford University, 1988). We would like to thank Professor Rosenbloom for permission to cite his unpublished paper.

55. Charles Sabel, *Work and Politics: The Division of Labor in Industry* (Cambridge, 1982), esp. chaps. 3 and 4, 78-193.

56. Lloyd H. Fisher, *The Harvest Labor Market in California* (Cambridge, Mass., 1953); Camille Guerin-Gonzales, "The International Migration of Labor and Segmented Labor: Mexican Immigrant Workers in California Industrial Agriculture, 1900-1940" (unpublished paper, September 1986). In craft or skilled trades in the United States, it appears tht large numbers of immigrants were allowed in by native workers, although these immigrants may have come disproportionately from certain groups, Robert Max Jackson, *The Formation of Craft Labor Markets* (London, 1984), 15, 125.

57. Montgomery, *Fall of the House of Labor*, 75-76. Rosenbloom's evidence that some employers, even those far from New York, were willing to hire groups of workers by contract for large projects also suggests that there was a need for "targeted" labor that the Italians could fill via the *padrone* system.

58. Paul Wormser, "Chinese Agricultural Labor in the Citrus Belt of Inland Southern California," in *Wong Ho Leun: An American Chinatown*, ed. Harry Lawton, (Riverside, Calif., 1987); Abel Chatelain, *Les migrants temporaires en France de 1800 à 1914*, 2 vols. (Villneuve d'Ascq, 1976), 2:705-10. The advantages workers gained by the straw boss or *padrone* system have to be weighed against the exploitation they often suffered at the hands of these bosses from their own ethnic groups. For the Italians, see Donna Gabaccia, "Neither Padrone Slaves nor Primitive Rebels: Sicilians on Two Continents," *Struggle a Hard Battle: Essays on Working Class Immigrants*, ed. Dirk Hoerder (Dekalb, Ill., 1986).

59. Chatelain, 1:236, 2:691; Dirk Hoerder, "An Introduction to Labor Migration in the Atlantic Economies," in Hoerder, ed., *Labor Migration*, 23.

60. Gill Burke, "The Cornish Diaspora of the Nineteenth Century," in Marks and Richardson, eds.; Hobsbawm, *Industry and Empire*, 309-12; David Katzman, *Seven Days a Week: Women and Domestic Service in Industrializing America* (Cambridge, 1978).

61. Scott Cummings, ed., *Self-Help in Urban America: Patterns of Minority Business Enterprise* (Port Washington, N.Y., 1980); Ivan H. Light, *Ethnic Enterprise in America* (Berkeley, 1972); on the Dutch as market gardeners and truck farmers, David Zandstra, "The Calumet Region," *Origins* 4, 2 (1986).

62. A. Ersan Yücel, "Turkish Migrant Workers in the Federal Republic of Germany: A Case Study," in Buechler and Buechler, eds., 134-39.

63. Frank Renkiewicz, "An Economy of Self-Help: Fraternal Capitalism and the Evolution of Polish America," and Karel D. Bicha, "Community or Cooperation? The Case of the Czech-Americans," both in *Studies in Ethnicity: The Eastern European Experience in America*, ed. Charles Ward, Philip Shashko, and Ronald Pienkos, (New York and Boulder, 1980); John Bodnar, Roger Simon, and Michael Weber, *Lives of Their Own: Blacks, Italians, and Poles in Pittsburgh, 1900-1960* (Urbana, 1982).

64. The strongest statement of the argument that immigrants undermined American labor solidarity is Gerald Rosenblum, *Immigrant Workers: Their Impact on American Labor Radicalism* (New York, 1973). See also Charles Leinenweber, "Socialism and Ethnicity," in *Failure of a Dream? Essays in the History of American Socialism*, ed. John Laslett and Seymour Martin Lipset, 2nd ed. (Berkeley, 1984), and C. T. Husbands, "Introduction," to Werner Sombart,

Why Is There No Socialism in the United States? (New York, 1976). An essential restatement of the whole debate on relations between native and immigrant workers in the United States is A. T. Lane, *Solidarity or Survival? American Labor and European Immigrants, 1830-1924* (Westport, Conn., 1987). On Brazil and Argentina, see Hobard A. Spalding, Jr., *Organized Labor in Latin America: Historical Case Studies of Urban Workers in Dependent Societies* (New York, 1977); Samuel Baily, "The Italians and the Development of Organized Labor in Argentina, Brazil, and the United States: 1880-1914," *Journal of Social History* 3, 2 (1969): 123-33; and Michael M. Hall, "Immigration and the Early São Paulo Working Class," *Jahrbuch für Geschichte von Staat, Wirtschaft und Gesellschaft Lateinamerikas* 12 (1975). Although much narrower than its title suggests, Donald Avery, *Dangerous Foreigners: European Immigrant Workers and Labor Radicalism in Canada, 1896-1932* (Toronto, 1980), is still useful for comparative purposes.

65. Immanuel C. Y. Hsu, *The Rise of Modern China*, 3rd ed. (New York, 1983), 454-70; Yen Ching-Hwang, *The Overseas Chinese and the 1911 Revolution* (Singapore, 1976).

66. Dirk Hoerder, ed., *Plutokraten und Sozialisten, Berichte deutscher Diplomaten und Agenten über die amerikanische Arbeiterbewegung, 1878-1917; Plutocrats and Socialists, Reports by German Diplomats and Agents on the American Labor Movement, 1878-1917* (London and Paris, 1981).

67. Archdeacon, 193.

68. Hideo Totsuka, "Japon: Koreans in Pre-War Japan," *Les migrations internationales.*

69. See Bhana's essay in this volume.

70. Robert Parmet, *Labor and Immigration in Industrial America* (Boston, 1981), 28-55. See also Alexander Saxon, *The Indispensable Enemy: Labor and the Anti-Chinese Movement in California* (Berkeley and Los Angeles, 1971), and Edna Bonacich and Lucie Cheng, eds., *Labor Migration under Capitalism: Asian Workers in the United States before World War II*, (Berkeley and Los Angeles, 1984).

71. Gwendolyn Mink, *Old Labor and New Immigrants in American Political Development: Union, Party, and State, 1875-1920* (Ithaca, 1986).

72. Hobsbawm, "What Is the Workers' Country?" in his *Workers: Worlds of Labor*, 59, 64. It is perhaps indicative of the silence among labor historians on the subject of ethnicity and nationalism that this rare word on the topic had been published three times: see Hobsbawm, "Afterword: Working Classes and Nations," in Hoerder, ed., *Labor Migration;* the essay originally appeared in *Saother* (Journal of the Irish Labour History Society) 8 (1982).

73. Castles and Kosack, 428-29.

74. Ibid., 152-79, the quotation is on 177. It is striking that the strongest statements on immigrants' effect on labor solidarity come in Castles and Kosack's introduction and conclusion, as in the previous note. The language in chapter 4 on "Trade Union Policies and Industrial Disputes," 116-179, is more cautious. Our criticisms of their work on labor should not be extended to their treatment of discrimination against immigrants in housing and social welfare. On the general problem of workers' discontent with West European unions, see Colin Crouch and Alessandro Pizzorno, eds., *The Resurgence of Class Conflict in Western Europe since 1968*, 2 vols. (London, 1978).

75. Constance Lever-Tracy, "Immigrant Workers and Postwar Capitalism: In Reserve or Core Troops in the Front-Lines?" *Politics and Society* 12, 2 (1983): 132-42.

76. Barbara Schmitter, "Trade Unions and Immigration Policies in West Germany and Switzerland," *Politics and Society* 10, 3 (1981): 317-34.

77. Rudolph Vecoli, "Comment on 'Socialism and Ethnicity,'" in Laslett and Lipset, eds.; David Montgomery, "Nationalism, American Patriotism, and Class Consciousness among Immigrant Workers in the United States in the Epoch of World War I," in Hoerder, ed., *Struggle a Hard Battle;* Victor Greene, *The Slavic Community on Strike: Immigrant Labor in Pennsylvania Anthracite* (New York, 1971); Michael Nash, *Conflict and Accommodation: Coal Miners, Steel Workers, and Socialism, 1890-1920* (Westport, Conn., 1982).

78. Gutman, "Work, Culture, and Society," 55-70.

79. John T. Cumbler, *Working-Class Community in Industrial America: Work, Leisure, and Struggle in Two Industrial Cities, 1880-1930* (Westport, Conn., 1979).

80. James R. Barrett, "Unity and Fragmentation: Class, Race, and Ethnicity on Chicago's South Side, 1900-1922," in Hoerder, *Struggle a Hard Battle,* 243.

81. See Mark Kesselman, ed., *The French Workers' Movement: Economic Crisis and Political Change* (London, 1984); Castles and Kosack, 130-37. Power, 55-57, sees the French unions in a more favorable light by comparison with the Germans, but he cites official policy statements rather than recruitment. An important study on a related topic is Gary Freeman, *Immigrant Labor and Racial Conflict in Industrial Societies: The French and British Experience, 1945-1975* (Princeton, 1979).

82. David Montgomery, "Nationalism, American Patriotism, and Class Consciousness," 327-51.

83. Allen Seager, "Class, Ethnicity, and Politics in the Alberta Coalfields, 1905-1945," in Hoerder, ed., *Struggle a Hard Battle,* 320.

84. Richard Oestreicher, *Solidarity and Fragmentation: Working People and Class Consciousness in Detroit, 1875-1900* (Urbana and Chicago, 1986), 111-12. A somewhat similar mixture of ethnic and ideological factors, in this case among Germans and East European Jews, is described in Hubert Perrier, "The Socialists and the Working Class in New York, 1890-1896," in Hoerder, ed., *American Labor and Immigration History.* For a similar argument for this position, looking at the case of the conflict between socialist ideology, Catholicism, and nationalism, see Carl Strikwerda, "The Divided Class: Catholics vs. Socialists in Belgium, 1880-1914," *Comparative Studies in Society and History* , 30, 2 (April 1988).

85. *Histoire des syndicats des ouvriers bronziers* (Ghent, 1906), 54; Sean Wilentz, *Chants Democratic: New York City and the Rise of the American Working Class, 1788-1850* (Oxford, 1984), 74, 77, 84.

86. Michael Anderson, *Family Structure in 19th Century Lancashire* (Cambridge, 1974); John Foster, *Class Struggle in the Industrial Revolution: Early Industrial Capitalism in Three English Towns* (London, 1974).

87. On cooperatives, Ellen Furlough, *The Politics of Consumption: The Consumer Cooperative Movement in France, 1834-1930* (Ithaca and London, 1991); Gerhard Huck, "Arbeiterkonsumverein und Verbraucher-organisation: Die Entwicklung der Konsumgenos-senschaften im Ruhrgebiet, 1860–1914," in *Fabrik, Familie, Feierabend: Beitrage zur Sozialgeschichte des Alltags im Industriezeitalter,* ed. Jürgen Reulecke and Wolfhard Weber (Wuppertal, 1978). One of the best studies of "workers' culture" during early industrialization is still William Sewell, "Social Change and the Rise of Working-Class Politics in Nineteenth Century Marseille," *Past and Present* 65 (1974). Studies of workers' culture in later industrialization include Vernon Lidtke, *The Alternative Culture: Socialist Labor in Imperial Germany* (New York, 1985), Standish Meacham, *A Life Apart: The English Working Class, 1890-1914* (New York, 1977); Donald Bell, *San Sesto Giovanni: Workers, Culture, and Politics in an Italian Town, 1880-1922* (New Brunswick, 1986), Donald Bell, "Worker Culture and Worker

Politics: The Experience of an Italian Town, 1880-1915," *Social History* 1,3 (1978); Roy Rosenzweig, *Eight Hours for What We Will: Workers and Leisure in an Industrial City, 1870-1920* (Cambridge, 1983); Gerhard Huck, ed., *Sozialgeschichte der Freizeit: Untersuchungen zum Wandel der Alltagskultur in Deutschland* (Wuppertal, 1980); and Peter Freidmann and Lisa Kosok, "Bibliographie 'Arbeiterkultur,'" in *Fahnen, Fauste, Korper: Symbolik und Kultur der Arbeiterbewegung*, ed. Dietmar Petzina (Essen, 1986).

88. Klaus Tenfelde, "Mining Festivals in the Nineteenth Century," *Journal of Contemporary History* 13, 2 (April 1978): 377-412. This entire issue of the journal is dedicated to the subject of workers' culture.

89. Edward D. Beechert, *Working in Hawaii: A Labor History* (Honolulu, 1985), 197-297; Ruth Akamine, "Ethnicity, Class, and the Changing World of Hawaiian Sugar Production, 1920-1946" (unpublished paper, Yale University, 1986), and her contribution below; Carl Strikwerda, "Regionalism and Internationalism: The Working Class Movement in the Nord and the Belgian Connection, 1870-1914," *Proceedings of the Western Society for French History*, ed. John Sweets, 12 (1985); Michel Perrot, *Les ouvriers en grève, 1870-1890*, 2 vols. (The Hague, 1974), 1:90, 169, 287, 325, 355. Although much less extensive than its title suggests, Jan Lucassen, *Migrant Labour in Europe, 1600-1900* (Bechenham, 1987), is still valuable for putting German, Dutch, and Belgian migration within Europe into context.

90. Eric Dorn Brose, *Christian Labor and the Politics of Frustration in Imperial Germany* (Washington, D.C., 1985); John Kulczycki, "Nationalism over Class Solidarity." On the Sikhs, see Castles and Kosack. On the Japanese, see Akamine's essay in this volume.

91. Neil Betten, *Catholic Activism and the Industrial Worker, 1919-1950* (Gainesville, Florida, 1976); Herbert Gutman, "Protestantism and the American Labor Movement: The Christian Spirit in the Gilded Age," in his *Work, Culture, and Society in Industrializing America*; Liston Pope, *Millhands and Preachers* (New Haven, 1942). An insightful study of the interaction of ethnicity and religion is Timothy Smith, "Religion and Ethnicity in America," *American Historical Review* 83, 5 (December 1978): 155-85. Just as labor history has often neglected ethnicity as a theoretical problem, so it has sometimes avoided religion. A positive sign of renewed interest is the "Special Issue: Religion and the Working Class," of the journal *International Labor and Working Class History* 34 (Fall 1988).

92. Donald Kinzer, *An Episode in Anti-Catholicism: The American Protective Association* (Seattle, 1964); Higham, 58-87; Eric J. Hobsbawm, "Religion and the Rise of Socialism," and "What Is the Workers' Country?" chaps. 3 and 4 in his *Workers*; Val Lorwin, "Labor Unions and Political Parties in Belgium," *Industrial and Labor Relations Review* 28, 2 (January 1975); Vernon Lidtke, "August Bebel and German Social Democracy's Relation to the Christian Churches," *Journal of the History of Ideas*, 27,2 (April-June 1966); John Boyer, *Political Radicalism in Late Imperial Vienna: Origins of the Christian Social Movement 1848-1897* (Chicago, 1981), 182; Charles Gulick, *Austria from Hapsburg to Hitler*, 2 vols. (Berkeley and Los Angeles, 1948), 1:27-31.

93. Taylor, 237-38; Archdeacon, 155-57; Barton, 117-63; Nathan Glazer and Daniel Moynihan, *Beyond the Melting Pot: The Negroes, Puerto Ricans, Jews, Italians, and Irish of New York City*, rev. ed. (Cambridge, 1970). As Glazer and Moynihan point out, by the 1960s, the political tendencies of the Catholics and Jews in New York had been completely reversed, the Jews giving up much of their loyalty to the Socialist and Liberal parties and uniting within the Democratic party, with the Catholic community increasingly split between the Republican, Democratic, and Conservative parties.

94. Hasia R. Diner, *Erin's Daughters in America: Irish Immigrant Women in the Nineteenth Century* (Baltimore and London, 1983), 70-102; Nancy Woloch, *Women and the American Experience* (New York, 1984), 231, 242; Carole Turbin, "And We Are Nothing but Women: Irish Working Women in Troy," *Women of America: A History*, ed. Carol Berkin and Mary Beth Norton (Boston, 1979), 203-20; Carl Strikwerda, "The Divided Class," and "Urban Structure, Religion, and Language: Belgian Workers, 1880-1914" (Ph.D. diss., University of Michigan, 1983), 111-12.

95. Böhning, "Statistical Survey of Economically Active Foreigners," chap. 2 in his *Studies in International Labour Migration;* L. Huan-Ming Ling, "East Asian Migration to the Middle East: Causes, Consequences, and Constraints," *International Migration Review* 18, 1 (1984): 19-36; Nasra Shah, "Pakistani Workers in the Middle East," *International Migration Review* 17, 3 (1983): 410-24; Solberg, "Mass Migration," 161; Adriana Marshall, "Structural Trends in International Labor Migration: The Southern Cone of Latin America," in Kritz, Keely, and Tomasi, eds.; Morner, 111; Hélène Carrère d'Encausse, *Decline of an Empire: The Soviet Socialist Republics in Revolt* (New York, 1979), 116.

96. Ralph Sell, "Egyptian International Labor Migration and Social Processes toward Regional Integration," *International Migration Review* 22, 3 (1988).

97. David Griffith, "Peasants in Reserve: Temporary West Indian Labor in the U.S. Farm Labor Market," *International Migration Review* 20, 4 (1986): 873-98; Theodore Friedman, "Israel's Arab Army of Migrant Workers," *New York Times*, Dec. 6, 1987, F1, F15-16; [Associated Press] "U.S. Jobs for Chinese Peasants?" *Kansas City Star*, Oct. 4, 1987, 7A; on Japanese and Filipinos, "Navy Workers Lose Out," *Kansas City Times*, Nov. 12, 1987, A-5. As pointed earlier, that these workers are employed does not mean the reliance on immigrant workers is inevitable. Instead, in these cases, the Israeli and U.S. governments have hesitated to bear the costs of restriction or expulsion. The Japanese and Filipino workers employed by the navy in the United States were eventually sent home, and the plans to supplement the Jamaican migrant workers with Chinese have so far not been approved. For a study of how Japan has consciously adopted policies to get undesirable work done without bringing in foreign workers, see Edward Ruebens, "Low-Level Work in Japan without Foreign Workers." On the recent changes in Japan, through which significant numbers of foreign workers have finally begun to appear, see Sterngold, "Japan Is Divided on Foreign Workers."

98. Larry Rohter, "Migrant Job Program Baffles Mexico," *New York Times*, Sept. 26, 1989, p. 1. The workers were considered "special agricultural workers" in 1988. It is not yet clear whether a new program, the "Replenishment Agricultural Worker" category, will result in continued immigration of Mexican workers, many of whom may move later from agriculture to other sections illegally, as did many *braceros* in the 1942-1964 Program.

99. David Binder, "Waves of Emigration Are Washing over Europe," *New York Times*, June 3, 1990, 10, and Judith Miller, "Strangers at the Gate: Europe's Immigration Crisis," *New York Times Magazine*, Sept. 15, 1991.

100. Barbara Crossette, "Shocks from Kuwait Hit the Third World," *New York Times*, Sept. 9, 1990, Section 4, 1-2.

EUROPEAN MIGRANTS IN THE UNITED STATES

2

The German Bakers of New York City: Between Ethnic Particularism and Working-Class Consciousness

Dorothee Schneider

Nineteenth-century immigration to the United States was part of a vast movement that sent people from many European countries overseas. German immigrants were an important part of this migratory flow to North America. Numerically, they made up the second largest group, after immigrants from the British Isles. German immigrants could be found in almost any occupation or region of the United States, although they tended to concentrate in skilled occupations and were numerous in America's industrializing cities.[1] Germans were welcome as workers who were well trained and had some experience working in an industrializing economy. Such a background, however, did not necessarily translate into economic advantages for the Germans. Especially in urban centers they had to compete with other immigrants for work that required fewer skills than at home and where low wage demands were often the only condition of employment.[2]

Even if their backgrounds did not translate into instant economic success, or bring higher pay, Germans nonetheless faced the exigencies of the New World better equipped than immigrants from many other countries. Though not united in a political or social sense, Germans were an extraordinarily well-organized group of immigrants who congregated in countless voluntary associations. Mutual benefit societies, cultural clubs, and leisure organizations, as well as political and trade organizations abounded within the German community. Framed by these organizations, Germans developed a lively literary and political culture. Helped by newspapers and a book-publishing industry, this culture served as a fertile soil for exploring, questioning, and shaping the American social and political system for new arrivals from Germany.[3] Their organizational and political activity made German immigrants particularly prominent in the nascent American labor movement during the late nineteenth century. But if organizing, writing, and speechmaking were part of an emancipatory German tradition, there were also parts of history that were not so liberating but rooted in century-old oppression and subservience. These traditions were difficult to overcome for some working-class immigrants as they struggled to link up with the American labor movement. Ironically, the strong sense of organizational cohesion among German workers made it more difficult to break out of traditional molds because it could lead to a degree of ethnic (and ideological) isolation from other immigrants and "American" workers. Ultimately, German Americans thus not only gave the American labor movement important positive impulses; they also contributed to an ethnic and ideological divisiveness that the labor movement had to overcome as it tried to unify on a nonethnic, "American" basis.

The following essay will examine the dual impact of the political and organizational tradition among the German bakers of New York City. Within the spectrum of United States labor history, bakers came from a trade with little impact on the North American labor movement at large during the nineteenth century. But beyond the confines of the institutional labor movement, German bakers (in New York as well as in most other large American cities) occupied a central place in the daily life of most neighborhoods. Their sheer numbers made them ubiquitous. At least twelve hundred could be found in Manhattan in 1880. There were 150 bakeries on the German Lower East Side alone in that same year. Altogether they made up over 50 percent of all bakers in the metropolis—far more than the 15 percent they represented in the general population. Thus the bakers were not just central to the life of German immigrants but were outposts of German immigrant culture in non-German neighborhoods.[4] Germans were also numerous in other food trades, bringing a special piece of their culinary traditions to the diverse population of New York City. But the bakers were in a peculiar situation because their status was less that of proud craftsmen than of sweatshop workers. Spread out into numerous small workshops, bakers toiled long hours under dismal conditions similar to those of cigar makers or garment workers—other typical sweatshop trades. In other ways, the trade was unique: its products were highly perishable and its hours were dictated by year-round consumer demand. Moreover, baking was deeply rooted in European customs and traditions, which could not be said of many other sweated trades.

The German Heritage of Baking

Bread baking was a very old craft with a history of being organized into guilds in medieval Europe. In premodern times, guilds cooperated with municipal authorities to enforce strict rules governing the education and licensing of bakers and the selling of bread, the quality of which was also closely monitored.[5] But the craft's regulations collapsed in the wake of the European wars of the sixteenth and seventeenth centuries. Despite efforts to revive the trade under the centralized rule of absolutist princes in the eighteenth and early nineteenth centuries, the bakers did not recover from the sudden loss of markets in the depopulated and impoverished areas of central Europe ravaged by two centuries of war. By the eighteenth century, access to the trade was no longer restricted. Europe was flooded with young men desperate to eke out a living as journeymen bakers. Prices fell under the competitive pressure of too many small shops. By the end of the nineteenth century, German bakers were among the most degraded workers in terms of workload and living and working conditions, not just in their homeland but all over northern and western Europe where they migrated in search of work. Long before the advent of mechanization, the trade had become badly impoverished. Mechanization was probably delayed substantially because of the continued availability of cheap labor in Europe and the United States throughout the nineteenth century.[6]

Work in German bakeries around 1900 followed fixed patterns that had changed very little over time. Before the regular shift began at 8:00 or 8:30 P.M., the starter dough was prepared by a journeyman. Workers on the regular shift then would mix the starter with flour and knead the dough; after fermentation, the dough was divided, put into forms, and left to rest. The baking itself was merely the last step in the process. Chopping firewood, tending fires in the bread ovens, and delivering bread were among the regular tasks that journeymen bakers had to perform before and after the baking.[7]

Despite such heavy reliance on manual labor, bakeries increased their productivity in nineteenth-century Germany. This was the result of a lengthening workday. Most German bakeries seem to have worked at least fourteen hours a day, seven days a week. The German socialist politician August Bebel found in his 1889 study *On the Situation of the Bakery Workers* (*Zur Lage der Arbeiter in den Bäckereien*) that bakers had the longest workday of any workers in central Europe. The study also uncovered that partly because of these inordinately long hours, most journeymen either lived directly with their employers (which meant a bed shared with another worker or even just a flour sack in the bakery) or in a bakers' hostel kept by the *Innung* (a guild-type organiza-

tion of the bakery masters). Meals were for the most part supplied but
were grossly inadequate, consisting of bread and watery soups. Wages
were meager: most journeymen made no more than about $2.00 a week
plus room and board, while apprentices labored for less than twenty-five
cents weekly.[8]

Despite low wages and miserable working conditions, the trade did
not lack apprentices during the nineteenth century. Laborers and small
farmers were eager to have their sons learn a trade that required no
apprenticeship fees—indeed it paid a small stipend and fed one's
offspring as well. But the trade had high turnover, even though
unemployment was usually not prolonged. Few bakers wanted to or
could survive the harsh living or working conditions for long, and almost
none were able to support families on their low wages. Almost all bakers
in Bebel's study were therefore bachelors. Few stayed in the trade into
middle age.[9]

The lowly position of journeymen was affirmed through certain
specific traditions that, in changed form, had survived in industrial
Germany. The *Innungen* were corporate institutions that existed, not as
part of a society of estates as in medieval times, but as part of a policy of
state protectionism of small businesses. The *Innungen* controlled
access to the trade by a variety of means. They thus secured the
livelihood of independent masters—though not of apprentices or
journeymen. Master bakers had to pass through years of training and
an examination by their peers in the *Innung* before they could train
apprentices or supervise journeymen. Apprentices and journeymen
were indispensable helpers in a shop of one's own. Journeymen were
dependent on the *Innung* in many ways: it conferred the status of
journeymen on the former apprentices, it alone could find work in town
for newly arrived bakers, and often enough the *Innung* assigned lodging
to all bakery workers who did not board with their masters. Journeymen
bakers thus were almost inevitably part of a hierarchical organization
that conferred few rights while greatly limiting their independence.[10]

This system, with its state-imposed domination by master bakers
and the dispersal of the journeymen in countless small shops,
confronted the German labor movement with an uphill struggle in
trying to organize the bakers. Since the 1870s the socialist labor
movement in Germany had made attempts to organize the bakery
workers, but it was not until 1885 that they had any success. Even as late
as 1895 the bakery workers' union in Germany had no more than 660
members.[11] Pressure for reform of the dismal conditions in the trade
came less from bakers' labor organizations than from middle-class
social reformers and legislators (some of them socialists) who
cooperated with the state to improve the conditions of the trade. In 1896
a government decree prohibited night and most Sunday work and

introduced the thirteen-hour workday. These measures did little to improve the economic status of most bakers and conferred no power on unions. No wonder journeymen bakers in very large numbers from the 1840s until after the turn of the century chose emigration to North America as a way out of their misery.[12]

The Trade in New York

But conditions in the New World were hardly more promising in the trade. Until the early nineteenth century New York's bakers prospered, sheltered from too much competition by limited immigration and municipal regulation of bread prices. But by the 1820s these barriers were crumbling. The regulation of bread prices had ceased, and growing numbers of immigrants lowered the economic status of the city's bakers, so that by the mid-nineteenth century many resembled their wretched colleagues in the Old World. In 1855 Manhattan had one baker for every 169 residents, an extraordinarily high number. By 1880, some of the thickly settled areas of the Lower East Side between Houston and Fourteenth Street, east of the Bowery, had two or three bakeries on one block. As the economic plight of the bakers worsened, the number of Germans in the trade rose; 54 percent were German immigrants as early as 1855, and by 1890 this percentage rose further to about 60 percent. Bakers also came from other European countries such as Switzerland, Austria, Bohemia, and France. Together with the Germans, these immigrants dominated a trade in which very few Anglo-Americans worked during the second half of the nineteenth century.[13]

Most immigrant bakers worked in the small bakeries that dotted the commercial landscape of greater Manhattan. In contrast to similar European establishments, almost all of the New York bakeries were cellar workshops with no separate retail store. Few bakery owners could afford the rent for a first-story shop or store. Cellar bakeries consisted of one room, usually eight feet high or less, with a dirt floor. Often sewage pipes for the entire tenement ran through the same cellar where the bakery shop was located. Coal and other fuels were stored next to the bread, and street dirt and vermin were unavoidable.[14] It was obvious to anybody who had seen New York's cellar bakeries that hygienic conditions in these workshops were terrible. Even the bakers themselves considered the New York baking trade "the dirtiest of trades, dirtier than in any other part of the world."[15]

Work was organized in a very traditional way, for the work divisions and hierarchies from the Old World persisted in most New York bakeries. The journeymen, called "first," "second," and "third" hands, worked under the supervision of the "bakery boss." Apprentices were rare.[16] As in Europe, most of the work took place at night. Preparations began in the late afternoon, and work lasted until the early morning hours of the next day. When the baking was done, journeymen had to deliver bread to neighborhood grocery stores where it was sold. Up to the 1880s fifteen to sixteen hours were a regular night's work. From Friday to Saturday bakers worked up to twenty-three hours, while five to six hours were the rule from Saturday to Sunday. Regular holidays did not exist.[17]

Despite these hours, German-American bakers were among the lowest-paid skilled workers in the city. According to a statistical report by the New York bakery workers' union, in 1881 journeymen bakers earned an average of $8.20 a week. Workers in large bakeries and foremen received $12 to $14.[18] This meant that most bakers were laboring for eight to ten cents an hour. Because unemployment was not an inevitable occurrence, bakers' yearly wages were higher than in some other trades, but this fact was more than offset by the exhausting work, which permitted few men to spend more than two decades or so in the trade before their health was ruined. Bakers were in notoriously bad health. Chronic overwork and the special stress of night work may also have contributed to a particularly high number of suicides among German bakers.[19]

As in Europe, the working hours and the small scale of most bakery businesses meant that bakers had to live at or very near their workshop. Most bakery owners lived in the tenement where the workshop was located, although the poorest of them camped out in the bakery itself. Journeymen and other helpers either slept in the cellar (on flour sacks or in the dough vat) or boarded with their employer in his apartment.[20] A sizable minority of bakery workers lived in bakers' boardinghouses, especially if they worked in larger establishments. The bakery hostels of the New World were managed by self-appointed entrepreneurs with good connections to the trade. Acting as contractor, the boardinghouse keeper would also run an informal employment service for his clients and would provide credit for temporarily unemployed bakers. As useful as this system was for the new immigrant who needed help in orienting himself and finding work, it was also open to abuses. Boardinghouse keepers had exclusive contracts with some employers, and workers were required to make use of the keepers' services if they wanted to have credit. In fact, the system resembled in many ways the strictures imposed by the *Innungen* in the Old World. Within the structure of the "free" market, the most oppressive features of a tightly supervised system had thus been preserved for the journeymen bakers.[21]

The social implications of these miserable living and working conditions for the journeymen bakers were fundamental: because of their low wages and long hours there were few alternatives to bachelorhood and life as a boarder. A weekly wage of $8.20 was not enough to feed even a small family in New York City during the 1880s and, therefore,

most employed bakers were unmarried. Only 36 percent of the journeymen bakers surveyed by the union in 1881 had families.[22] The fact
that journeymen bakers were not only poor but too poor to marry was
not lost on these immigrants. It was considered one of the greatest indignities bakers had to suffer, something that reminded the workers of
the order they had hoped to leave behind.[23]

One way to attempt to break this cycle of exploitation and poverty
was to set up one's own shop. Here the freewheeling capitalism of
North American cities treated all small entrepreneurs the same. In
contrast to Germany, the trade was open to anyone with the money and
energy to set up shop for oneself: no master's examination was
required, capital investment was low, and no fees had to be paid. But
since the status of the independent bakers was unprotected, the
competition among them, especially in Manhattan's lower-rent districts,
was fierce. Hours were no shorter for the "boss baker" than for his
employees (if he had any). The work was just as arduous. Like other
sweatshop operators, the owners of small bakeries led a precarious
existence, always in danger of slipping back into the ranks of the
journeymen.[24] Some differences remained, of course. For one thing,
independent bakers were more able to have families, not so much
because they earned more, but because they could organize their shop
as a family enterprise that stretched their income in various ways. They
could put their children to work as "apprentices" and take in their
employees as boarders, which was a way for their wives to add to the
household's income.[25]

The New York baking trade was not unique in many of the
conditions it presented to the late-nineteenth-century observer. But the
combination of factors that characterized it was somewhat unusual and
extreme. Unlike workers in other sweated industries who experienced
the same degree of overwork and exploitation, the roots of the bakers'
misery dated not to the beginning of the industrial age but back to the
past of central Europe. There were beneficial aspects of the history of
the baking trades—self-regulation and cooperation with the
government, for example—that did not become part of the craft in the
New World. In a sense, only the worst part of the European craft
traditions survived in late-nineteenth-century New York.

Early Attempts to Organize

New York's bakers had a relatively lively history of organizing in the
early and mid-nineteenth century, but little of that tradition had survived into the post–Civil War era, when the large majority of German-
American bakers arrived in the city. A few benevolent associations and
a singing society were all that existed by the late 1870s, at a time when
New York's working class was beginning to organize in large numbers.

The bakers were considered passive and of low intelligence, too isolated and unassimilated to participate successfully in organizing campaigns.[26] No one among New York's organized labor leaders therefore expected much of an attempt to launch a union of journeymen bakers in late 1880—at least the union press barely mentioned the initiative of the activist George Block to start a union of bakery workers. Block, a German-American socialist, was at the time a reporter for the *New Yorker Volkszeitung*. His background as a pocketbook maker who had once briefly worked in Shults's bread factory in Williamsburgh did not make him an insider in the bakery trade.[27] His organizational efforts, however, were immediately successful. At a mass meeting on April 12, 1880, the "Journeymen Bakers Union of New York and Vicinity" was officially launched, and within a few weeks the union had five sections with about six hundred bakers.[28]

While the membership at the beginning was exclusively German-speaking, other groups of bakers joined the union within its first year. In mid-1881, an English-speaking section was founded, and a few weeks later groups of Yiddish-speaking bakers and Bohemian bakers joined as well. A year after its founding date, the union had about three thousand members in metropolitan New York.[29] With its ethnically and geographically defined sections, the bakery workers' union reflected the divisions of the trade in many ways. Its leadership was largely anonymous and rotating and offered little central direction at the beginning. The union also had no system of financial support.[30] Nevertheless, enthusiasm ran high for the organization, particularly among bakers employed in larger shops. German immigrant bakers were all familiar with trade organizations, having been part of the *Innung* system in the Old World and having watched the rise of trade unionism in Germany during the 1870s. Even if they themselves had been on the sidelines of any labor movement so far, we can assume they had a knowledge of class-based independent unionism.

The union's goals were practical and immediate: a six-day workweek and a shorter workday, as well as "sufficient wages for the entire family," were core demands. Closely connected was the call for abolition of the mandatory boarding system.[31] These demands became more insistent as resistance to the union stiffened, especially from the owners of larger bakeries. In the spring of 1881 the union published an ultimatum to force employers to introduce the twelve-hour workday by May 2. On that day the organized bakers of the city went out on strike, publicizing their cause with a large parade and a mass meeting on the Lower East Side. Even though a number of smaller employers initially gave in to the union, the most important bakery bosses resisted. In the end the union lost not only the strike but most of its membership too. Within a year the organization had shrunk from three thousand to thirty-five members, and it ceased to exist entirely by 1882.[32] To a great extent, this swift failure of the union had to do with the impoverished and isolated conditions under which the bakers labored, part of a history they had hoped to leave behind in the old country. But history also meant a continuing patriarchal tradition that made it difficult to mobilize workers in small workshops against boss bakers as the class enemy. Inexperience and the absence of a strong umbrella organization of New York labor that could back the fledgling union added to the difficulties faced by the organization.

For the next three years, the New York labor movement would change in important ways, while the German bakers were without an organization. Between 1882 and 1885 New York's trade unions were united in the Central Labor Union, a powerful body encompassing tens of thousands of workers through their union representatives. Many of the member unions were also active in two national federations, the New York–based American Federation of Labor and the Knights of Labor. The Knights were dominant among Anglo-Irish workers in the city, while German Americans tended to affiliate with the AFL, although the two affiliations were not mutually exclusive. Under the auspices of the Knights, two local assemblies of English-speaking bakers, the Bakers Progressive Club and the Long Island Protective Association, were active between 1883 and 1886 in a number of ways. But they failed to improve the conditions in a trade that continued to be dominated by German immigrants who stayed outside these organizations.[33]

The Journeymen Bakers National Union

With the Knights not able or willing to venture among the German bakers and the AFL not yet strong enough to undertake organizing, it fell to individual activists among the German-American unionists (backed by the city's Central Labor Union) to attempt to revive a bakers' union in 1885. Once again, several mass meetings were held in January 1885 by George Block, and men who had remained faithful to the original union and other speakers extolled the virtue of unionization. That was enough to induce many German-American bakers to give the union another chance. The journeymen may have been among the most exploited workers in the city, but the value of a union had not escaped them. In the meantime circumstances had become somewhat more auspicious for a permanent union, with backing from a regional, or even national, labor movement.[34] Enthusiasm ran high, and within months hundreds of bakers were once again organized as members of a trade union. "The reorganization has surpassed our highest expectations," wrote the *New Yorker Volkszeitung*.[35] Three sections were again formed, all for German-speaking bakers.[36]

This time, George Block did not want to rely on the brushfire enthusiasm of the union's beginning, but wanted a more lasting organization. One step in giving the young union more of an air of permanence was for the union to issue its own paper, a daring, costly, and unusual step this early in the organizing campaign, as Block recognized. But he managed to raise the necessary funds and, in May 1885, exactly four years after the great strike of 1881, the first issue of the *Deutsch-Amerikanische Bäckerzeitung* appeared.[37] The paper soon proved to be an important organizing tool, much to the surprise of some unionists, and it helped the union to grow quickly during the summer of 1885. The journal was also instrumental in increasing the interest in unionization among German-American bakers nationwide. Under Block's auspices the Journeymen Bakers National Union (JBNU) was formed in January 1886. The New York German bakers' organization became Local 1 of the new organization and assumed a double role as the largest local in the country and headquarters for the National Union. By early 1886 the New York German bakers not only represented a well-organized trade in the city but also seemed poised for a national role in the movement to organize this long-neglected group of workers.[38]

While the bakers' general familiarity with labor organizations and the experience and backing of a regional and national labor movement were important, organizing on a neighborhood level remained the most crucial tool for the journeymen bakers' success. German bakers in New York were scattered throughout both the German and the non-German neighborhoods in the city, and therefore a community-centered approach was needed if the majority of German bakers were to be organized on a permanent basis. In order to organize the workers in the small bakeries of a neighborhood, the union would send out emissaries to some shops (usually those with more than one employee) who would speak with the journeymen about the purpose of the union and ask them to join the organization. In some cases the unionists were refused admittance by suspicious bosses or were forcibly thrown out. In other cases, the employer threatened to fire the workers if they joined the organization. Some journeymen, feeling threatened by their boss, refused to join the union or remained indifferent to the unionists' entreaties. When it met resistance, the union placed a boycott on the shop until the workers had changed their minds. Applied selectively and for distinct neighborhood businesses, this tactic seems to have worked quite well in many cases. Just the threat of a boycott moved most bakery owners to give in to the union.[39]

In some cases, however, the bosses proved more recalcitrant. The union's mobilization techniques in response to these extreme cases were an interesting example of neighborhood organization. The most publicized was the 1886 boycott of Mrs. Gray's bakery on Hudson Street in lower Manhattan, an area inhabited mostly by Irish immigrants at the time. Mrs. Gray, the proprietor, was Irish but the four bakers in her employ were German-born; they wanted to join the Journeymen Bakers Union but were forbidden to do so by her. The boycott, although initiated by the German-American union with few roots in the neighborhood, was supported by most of the largely working-class customers (who had ample alternatives to buying Mrs. Gray's bread). But the action also received unprecedented publicity in the city's middle-class press, which portrayed Mrs. Gray as a struggling widow trying to fend off the united forces of the New York labor movement. These stories induced wealthier patrons to venture down to Hudson Street from their uptown quarters in order to buy bread. The better-off sent their servants or gave cash. Despite such favorable attention, Mrs. Gray, being a neighborhood businesswoman, had to give in, and her four employees were eventually permitted to join the bakery workers' union.[40]

In this case the union clearly succeeded in enlisting working-class customers to its cause (even though they were not German) and fending off the employer (and her middle-class supporters). Such tactics were successfully used by other unions, too, mostly in small-scale industries that had a close connection with and a certain degree of dependence on their working-class neighborhoods. In those cases neighborhood organization could transcend ethnicity, but the tactic promised little success with large businesses that employed many dozens of bakers, most of whom were also members of the union. The union leaders, apparently aware of this problem, therefore began to make somewhat cautious attempts to find organizational strategies that would reach beyond neighborhood bakeries and bolster the position of factory bakers who labored much more anonymously. They introduced a label that was directly affixed to the bread made by union members. By the summer of 1886 the union contended that half of all bread in New York and Brooklyn was baked and labeled by union members.[41]

With fifteen hundred bakers organized and a large proportion of the bread production in union hands, the New York locals of the Journeymen Bakers National Union could finally try to achieve their long-sought goals: shorter hours (usually a cut to twelve hours), higher wages, and the abolition of compulsory room and board with the employers. In trying to achieve these goals the union again opted for a decentralized shop-centered approach, which involved only a few groups of workers at any given time. This was in marked contrast to the earlier tactic of the 1881 union and fit in well with the neighborhood-based strategy of the later union. Indeed, in most cases the organized bakers won their demands.[42] By the end of 1887, wages, working hours,

and working conditions had improved markedly for New York's German
bakers. "The bakers may be mentioned as a striking instance of specific
reforms effected.   They have been successful in obtaining great
reconstruction. Their hours ranging from fourteen to the whole of
twenty-four have been reduced from ten to fourteen," reported the
commissioner of labor for the state of New York.[43] A statistical study by
the bakery union confirms this statement. It also shows that weekly
wages had increased to $9.50 for second and up to $14.00 for first hands.
Except for "second-hand cockroach bosses," as the unionists called
them, employers no longer forced their workers to board with them.[44]

Crisis and Decline

In late 1887 it seemed clear that the German bakers' organization
had reached considerable power in the city's baking trade. It had
improved working conditions for the majority of those organized, who
numbered about three thousand in greater New York. Nevertheless,
some obstacles remained on the road to an organization that could
encompass all bakers in the city. The continuing ethnic division in the
trade needed to be overcome, which meant that the union needed to
reach more non-Germans in the trade. By the mid-1880s, the New York
social landscape had great ethnic complexity and a relatively high
degree of political organization. This meant bridging not only the gap of
language, leisure culture, and working habits but also of different forms
of organization and of views of working-class politics.

Nowhere was the gap in perceptions, status, and tactics clearer
than between the largely German Journeymen Bakers Union and the
English-speaking baker organizations that belonged to the Knights of
Labor. The Anglo-Irish workers were slightly better off than their
German colleagues, and the two English-speaking Local Assemblies, to
which the Anglo-Irish bakers belonged, saw to it that this remained the
case. Partly protected by the powerful District Assembly 49 of the
Knights of Labor, they managed to retain a certain privileged status
(working ten- to twelve-hour shifts, no mandatory boarding) and
campaigned for the prohibition of Sunday work and for the ten-hour
day. These activities focused on lobbying state and local politicians and
going to court. Otherwise the English-speaking bakers were not too
active in the New York labor movement at large. For the members of
the German bakers' union the goals of the English-speaking bakers
seemed utopian, their pressure politics compromising, and their
attitude toward their lesser-paid German colleagues elitist. For the
most part these differences in goals and styles simmered under the
surface, only breaking out into the open in Brooklyn over a shorter-hour
movement that dominated the agenda of both groups in 1885–86. John
Kelly, leader of the Brooklyn bakers in the Knights, bitterly complained

about the competition from the Germans and their union who, with their never-ending supply of "green" immigrants and their endorsement of the seventy-two-hour week, seemed to perpetuate the miserable state of the journeymen.[45] The German bakers, on the other hand, wanted to organize the maximum number of workers before mounting a major challenge to the length of the workday.

Because the English-speaking bakers were not very numerous, the German-speaking organization tried to ignore them and organized instead, the Yiddish-speaking and Bohemian bakers, who labored under conditions similar to those of the Germans and who were culturally much closer to the Germans as well.[46] In part, this tactic paid off; by the end of 1886, leaders of the English-speaking bakers became disenchanted with the internal squabbling in the Knights of Labor and were looking for a new affiliation. New York's leader of the English-speaking bakers, Michael McGrath, began to cooperate quietly with the German union, which he and his followers joined a year later as a separate local.[47] This did not fundamentally change the character of the union, however, which remained heavily German in its membership and political connections within the labor movement.

Closely connected to the ethnic character of the German bakers' union was its political direction. The leaders of the union had always been socialists, and as the New York labor movement grew in complexity during the mid-1880s, the German bakers could always be found on the side of the socialist wing. Nevertheless, union secretary Block also managed to keep a certain distance from the Socialist Labor party in order to keep the union out of the infighting that characterized the SLP during the second half of the 1880s. The cautious attitude could not prevent a serious conflict from erupting within the union over how "political" (that is, how closely involved with the Socialist Labor party) the union should be. At the end of 1887, both the local of the confectioners and that of the Vienna bakers (both relatively elite groups of workers within the trade) left the national union to start an independent Progressive Bakers Union, which was closer to the SLP than the National Union under Block's leadership.[48] The two locals eventually rejoined the National Union, but Block lost his office as national secretary and later as editor of the *Bäckerzeitung* in 1889.[49] This outbreak of internecine fighting among the German bakers, and especially the dismissal of the popular Block, did little to widen the appeal of the union to English-speaking bakers and to unorganized workers or to help build alliances with other labor organizations, which was what the bakers, still poor and relatively inexperienced, badly needed. Commenting on the convention that ousted Block, Michael McGrath exclaimed: "If that was a convention of bosses I would expect them to agree to put such a job on Block, but the possibility that a body which in all probability would not exist if it were not for him to go to work and stab the National Secretary in the back as the last convention did, I do not understand. Who is the Brutus?"[50]

The political crisis of the bakers' union underlined how much the organization was part of the German socialist movement rather than of a general, class-based labor movement in the city. By 1889 the union was internally paralyzed. Membership was declining, and its economic position was tenuous (it had a small treasury and no established benefit system). This weak position made the bakers' union once more vulnerable to worsening conditions in the trade and attacks from employers.

Change had crept steadily into the still largely traditional baking trade during the 1880s. By the end of the decade a large number of bread and pie factories, most of them situated in outlying areas like Brooklyn, had become prominent in the trade. These shops, which employed up to two hundred bakers each, now supplied an increasing share of bread to the city's consumers, mostly through grocery stores. The majority of those who worked in bread factories were German-born bakers, and most of them were members of the Journeymen Bakers Union.[51] The owners of these bread factories were usually of American or German background. But they had little in common with the old-fashioned bakery boss who labored with his journeymen in the basement and shared an apartment with them in the tenement upstairs. It was their recent success as businessmen that united these entrepreneurs in the late 1880s into an organization called the Bakers Association of New York and Vicinity. The fourteen members of this group represented virtually all the large shops in New York and Brooklyn. The association had a very different outlook from earlier groups of bakery bosses.[52] For one thing, it was not an ethnic organization but encompassed bakery owners of all large bakeries regardless of their background. It also had an unprecedented clarity of purpose: to break the hold of the union in the bread factories.[53]

An opportunity for united action against the union presented itself in the summer of 1889, after internal quarreling had left the bakers in a weakened state and at a time when the New York labor movement as a whole was split because of a quarrel between the Socialist Labor party and the American Federation of Labor. A seemingly trivial incident was the trigger event in July of 1889: the foreman at Rockwell's bakery had slapped a young journeyman during an altercation. The union representatives' prompt demand for the foreman's dismissal was rejected by the owner of the bakery. In response, the employees at Rockwell who were unionized went out on strike. The answer of the bakery owners' association seemed well prepared. All fourteen bakery owners who were members of the association forced their employees to sign a new list of rules that in effect prohibited union membership. The five hundred union members who refused to give in to this demand found themselves locked out of all fourteen "pool bakeries" at the end of August.[54]

This was not the first time such tactics were used against unionized workers: similar lockouts had occurred before among cigar makers and brewery workers in New York City. Some unions had been successful in holding their own, but in the bakers' case the pressure from unorganized workers willing to take the place of the locked-out bakers was great, and production in the fourteen pool bakeries was not seriously interrupted.[55]

Those workers who remained with the union were enlisted in organizing a bread boycott on all "pool bread." Organizing such an action was no small task. Grocers in the entire metropolitan area, through whom the wholesale bakeries sold their product, had to be induced to abandon their usual suppliers. If they refused to do so, they, in turn, were also placed under boycott by their neighborhood customers.[56] In addition to the locked-out unionists, neighborhood volunteers consisting of housewives, renters, grocers, and members of the Socialist Labor party canvassed their districts to enlist support for the bakers' cause. By and large their activity focused on German-American neighborhoods, a limited area that covered only a part of the wholesalers' market.[57] The bakers were not able to break out of the confines of ethnicity when it came to organizing support, whereas their employers had gone beyond the ethnically defined markets that once had bound all bakers closely to their neighborhoods. The situation was even more difficult because even if the neighborhood outlets (for example, in the German neighborhoods) were willing to switch their bread suppliers, there were few alternatives available. Neighborhood cellar bakeries were not able to take up all of the slack at once; the wholesalers were in fact nearly irreplaceable, having carved out a specific market for their products, which were of uniform quality and could be delivered in large, flexible quantities daily. A boycott of wholesale bread therefore proved to be nearly impossible.[58]

The situation was particularly difficult for the union because it was caught without any strike funds and had to rely on hastily imposed assessments to pay some support to the strikers.[59] Few of the local unions in the country proved willing or able to pay such extra assessments, however, so that even the most stalwart unionists could not get much in terms of financial support.[60] In desperation and to provide its supporters with an alternative source of income and its suppliers with "union-made" bread, the union started cooperative bakeshops in both Brooklyn and New York that employed about twenty bakers each and started in late September and early October. Although the cooperatives were a success from a business standpoint (before they dissolved a number of years later because of internal quarrels), they came too late to influence the outcome of the conflict with the pool bakers.[61] By the end of October the union conceded defeat by lifting the boycott on "pool bread," limiting itself (with little success) to a selective boycott in the following years.[62]

The defeat by the pool bakers threw the bakers' union into its most severe crisis since 1881. Local 1, which at the beginning of 1889 had had over one thousand members, shrank to fewer than thirty at the end of that year.[63] The Bohemian and English-speaking locals, whose members were not directly involved in the lockout (because they rarely worked in the pool bakeries), were less affected, but since they had always been on the periphery of the union, their stability did very little to help the union as a whole. In effect, the National Union had lost one of its most important and stable constituencies in the city: German bakers who worked in large bakeries.[64] With such an important core of the union membership gone, the existing personal, cultural, and political differences among the remaining union members broke out once more into the open. Some union locals split along political lines, while others left the National Union entirely.[65] This paralyzed any effective organizing within the New York baking trade for the next dozen or so years and weakened the National Union in general. Not until after the turn of the century did the New York bakers begin to recover from these internecine struggles. As late as 1911, on the twenty-fifth anniversary of the union, local officials were cautious in their assessment of the union's situation. It would take a lengthy change in the industry and the community to make the bakery and confectionery workers' union a force on the New York labor scene.[66]

While the leaders and some of the members in the bakery workers' unions fought about their ideological differences and personal preferences, the community around them changed as did the trade's organization and economy. While an all-time high of about thirty-five hundred German bakers toiled in the city's bakeshops in 1890, their numbers were declining slowly by the turn of the century and after. The proportion of German bakers decreased even more palpably as the places of the Germans were taken up by new immigrants, mostly eastern European Jews and Italians. Very little effort was made by any bakery workers' organization to reach out to these workers. They labored under conditions that were unchanged from the 1870s, in cellars with a minimum of machinery, hygiene, and personal freedom.[67] In fact, because of the absence of an effective organization, conditions in the city's bakeshops overall may have worsened in the 1890s after the gains of the late 1880s. Only the largest, most efficient bread factories could in fact compete with the overworked and underpaid "slaves" in the bakeshops. Middling bosses and large bakeries with a less efficient system of production were not able to keep up, as the union officials remarked when Hersemann's bakery, one of the original wholesale bakeries in Brooklyn, went bankrupt in 1895.[68]

When conditions did improve, it was not because of the union or because market forces made it more feasible or advantageous to rationalize and improve production conditions. Instead, improving conditions in the baking trades became one of the goals of progressive reformers from the mid-1890s on. After a report on the conditions in the cellar bakeries in the *New York Record*, the first of a number of official inquiries into the New York baking trade began. The shocking result of this inquiry prompted the New York state legislature to pass the law for which the union had for so long fought in vain. The union had no input into this legislation at all. The law limited the number of working hours for bakers to ten per day. The measure also prohibited sleeping in the bakeshop and set minimal hygiene standards. While it improved working conditions in the larger bakeries, in the small shops it remained unenforceable. A lasting and more wide-ranging improvement did not take place until, after World War I, the city's cellar bakeries were replaced by mechanized bread factories.[69]

Conclusion: Ethnicity and Organization

The history of the bakery workers and their organizations in New York illustrates more than the history of most other German-American workers the failed attempt to build a political entity out of an ethnic community. The example of the bakers also tells us something about the ambiguous nature of tradition in the role of union formation and community activism. Journeymen bakers had a rich tradition of craftsmanship, but the history of a self-governed guild trade had long deteriorated. By the late nineteenth century, only the most oppressive aspects of patriarchal labor relations had survived, punctuated by occasional outbursts of journeymen activism. Under the American free market system, building up a class-conscious union was doubly difficult. Not only was the social control of bosses over journeymen considerable; many journeymen also tolerated their employers' position because they were hoping to become "bosses" themselves one day. The social traditions that shaped the political expectations of journeymen bakers in the New World were thus not emancipatory but crippling in many respects.

Bakers had much in common with other workers. In addition, their experience differed significantly in ways that would make their attempts at organization still more problematic. Unlike other industries, the baking trade in much of New York remained in its preindustrial phase and did not make the transition to mechanization in the late nineteenth century as many other industries did. While factory labor thus did not threaten the bakers' skills significantly, the continuing sweatshop conditions and the isolation of workers in small shops made it more difficult to organize the bakers on an independent basis. Subdivision into ethnic branches was another important feature of the baking trade that made it extremely difficult to build a viable union movement. The German bakers, a majority of workers in the trade, were strongly rooted in their own ethnic community, which tended to isolate them from the sizable minority of bakers from other ethnic groups. Faced with the task not only of organizing their own ethnic groups but of building bridges to other immigrants in the trade and of connecting with the English-speaking labor movement, the representatives of the German bakers proved unable to do any of these tasks.

Political unity was elusive under these circumstances, and the bakers never came close to formulating their own political program. Unable to transcend ethnicity as their primary basis of solidarity, they were also unable to meet the challenge of labor reform in the long term when industrialization did come to the trade. It was the reform legislation of the Progressive era and the eventual mechanization of the trade that enabled the union to make the transition to industrial unionism during the first decades of the twentieth century.

Notes

1. The best survey of the demography of German immigration is Peter Marschalck and Wolfgang Köllman, "German Emigration to the United States," *Perspectives in American History* 7 (1973): 499-557.

2. Hartmut Keil, "Chicago's German Working Class in 1900," in *German Workers in Industrializing Chicago*, ed. H. Keil and J. Jentz (Dekalb, 1983), 26-28; Bruce Laurie, George Alter, and Theodore Hershberg, "Immigrants and Industry, the Philadelphia Experience, 1850-1880," in *Philadelphia: Work, Space, Family and Group Experience in the late 19th Century*, ed. Theodore Hershberg (New York, 1981), 93-119; Dorothee Schneider, "Gewerkschaft und Gemeinschaft: Drei deutsche Gewerkschaften in New York, 1870-1900" (Ph.D. diss., University of Munich, 1983), 43-46.

3. On the German-American propensity for organizations see Schneider, chap. 1, as well as Robert Ernst, *Immigrant Life in New York City* (New York, 1949), 112-34; and studies relating to Germans elsewhere, for example, Kathleen Conzen, *Immigrant Milwaukee* (Cambridge, 1976), 154-91; and Richard Oestereicher, *Solidarity and Fragmentation* (Urbana, Ill., 1986), 43-52.

4. Tenth Census of the United States, *Census of Population*, vol. 1 (Washington, D. C., 1882).

5. Karl Friedrich Wernet, *Wettbewerbs- und Absatzverhältnisse des Handwerks in historischer Sicht*, vol. 1, *Nahrung, Getränke, Genussmittel* (Berlin, 1967), 45-46, 67-88.

6. Johann Schwarz, *Das Handwerk der Bäcker in München* (Munich, 1899), 135; Walter Badke, *Zur Entwicklung des deutschen Bäckergewerbes* (Jena, 1906),

88-91, 94-95, 110-11; see also observations of Marx on the German bakers in London in *Capital*, vol. 1, edited by Friedrich Engels (London, 1906), 273.

7. Philipp Arnold, *Das Münchner Bäckergewerbe, eine wirtschaftliche, technische und soziale Studie* (Stuttgart, 1895), 28.

8. August Bebel, *Zur Lage der Arbeiter in den Bäckereien* (Stuttgart, 1895), 22-168 passim, and O. Allmann, *Geschichte der deutschen Bäcker und Konditorenbewegung*, vol. 1 (Hamburg, 1910), 155, 339-42.

9. Arnold, 67-68, 75; Bebel, 22-168 passim; Allmann, 80-82; Schwarz, 67.

10. Allmann, 81-86; Schwarz, 70-74.

11. Allmann, 12-15, 26-27, 74, 133, 250-399 passim; Schwarz, 51-53; Arnold, 79-81.

12. Allmann, 143, 144-55, 238-40, 256-57, 315, 334-39, 349; Wernet, 95-96; Friedrich Wolle, *Siebenhundert Jahre Bäckerhandwerk zu Erfurt* (Erfurt, 1928), 93; Paul Hischfeld, *Die freien Gewerkschaften in Deutschland: Ihre Verbreitung und Entwicklung, 1896-1906* (Jena, 1908), 110-11; Walter Troeltsch and Paul Hischfeld, *Die deutschen sozialdemokratischen Gewerkschaften* (Berlin, 1905) 104-05.

13. Ernst, 191, 213-14; Howard B. Rock, "The Perils of Laissez Faire," *Labor History* 17 (1973): 372-81; Sean Wilentz, *Chants Democratic* (New York, 1985), 139-40.

14. State of New York, *Preliminary Report of the Factory Investigation Commission*, 2 vols. (Albany, 1912) 1:209, 2:311, 315, 354, 406-608, 672, 741.

15. *Preliminary Report*, 2:212-17, 312-14.

16. *Preliminary Report*, 1:208, 2:323; *New Yorker Volkszeitung* [hereafter *NYVZ*], April 27, 1881.

17. *Slavery in the Bakeshops: A Pamphlet on the Condition of the Journeymen Bakers*, edited by the Journeymen Bakers Union of New York and Vicinity (New York , 1881), passim.

18. *Slavery in the Bakeshops*, 5-6.

19. *Preliminary Report*, 1:81, 227-29, 2:686-90; *Deutsch-Amerikanische Bäckerzeitung* [hereafter *DABZ*], 1886-92 passim, see esp. pp. 3 and 4 in each issue; for suicides see *NYVZ*, March 21 and 27, 1879.

20. *Preliminary Report*, 1:218, 2:324, *Slavery in the Bakeshops*, 5.

21. *NYVZ*, Sept. 20, 1880, Nov. 22, 1880, May 7, 1881; *Slavery in the Bakeshops* 5; New York, State Commissioner of Labor, *Tenth Annual Report* (New York, 1892), 443; United States Congress, Senate, Committee on Education and Labor, *Report of the Committee upon the Relations between Labor and Capital*, vol. 1 (Washington, D. C., 1885), 438.

22. *Slavery in the Bakeshops*, 6.

23. Ibid.

24. *John Swinton's Paper*, July 1885; *DABZ*, Nov. 16, 1887; *Slavery in the Bakeshops*, 8.

25. Census sample was taken from the Tenth Census, Population Schedules for New York County, Wards 10, 11, and 17.

26. *Relations between Labor and Capital*, 1:438-39.

27. Stuart Kaufman, *A Vision of Unity: The History of the Bakery and Confectionery Workers Union* (Kensington, 1986), 1.

28. Kaufman, 1-2, *NYVZ*, April 12, April 26, May 3, May 17, May 31, 1880.

29. *NYVZ*, April 4, April 16, April 24, Sept. 14, 1881.

30. *NYVZ*, April 26, May 3, May 31, 1880.

31. To buttress its demands, the union undertook a statistical survey of its members' wages and working hours which it published in 1881 under the title *Slavery in the Bakeshops*. The study (quoted earlier) made public the horrible working and living conditions in the trade. The union also started its own

(successful) hiring hall, to circumvent the boardinghouse keepers; see also *NYVZ*, March 7, April 11, 12, May 12, Aug. 9, 16, 18, and 25, 1881.

32. Kaufman, 2; *NYVZ*, April 10, 17, 18, 21, and 23, May 2, 3, 5, 6, 9-14, June 6, Aug. 18, Sept. 3, 1881, Jan. 23, Feb. 6, July 5, 1882; George Block, *A Concise History of the Bakers Union of New York and Vicinity*, passim.

33. Jonathan Garlock, ed., *A Guide to the Local Assemblies of the Knights of Labor* (Westport, Conn., 1982) 314, 322; *John Swinton's Paper*, Feb. 2, March 15, August 10, Nov. 18, 1884; April 5, 1885; *NYVZ*, June 20 and 21, and July 2, 1881; Jan. 11, Feb. 22, March 15, April 5, 1885.

34. *NYVZ*, Jan. 20 and 21, 1885.

35. *NYVZ*, Jan. 24, 1885.

36. *NYVZ*, Jan. 24, April 5, May 3, 1885.

37. In its three pages of text (a fourth page was filled with advertisements) readers were informed about politics, the labor movement, and scientific advances in all fields. The paper also published serialized novels and short stories. The *Bäckerzeitung* was not cheap at five cents an issue and Block, as its editor, made few concessions to the specialized interests of its readers (recipes and hints for the bakers workshop were rare). Block, 4; *NYVZ*, Feb. 23, May 10, 1885; *DABZ*, May 2, 1885 to Dec. 1889 passim; *Bakers Journal*, Jan. 11, 1911.

38. Kaufman, 508; Schneider, 343-47.

39. *DABZ*, Sept. 28, 1887; New York State Bureau of Labor Statistics, *Fourth Annual Report* (Albany, 1888), 738.

40. *Fourth Annual Report*, 748. See also Michael Gordon, "The Labor Boycott in New York City," *Labor History* 16, 4 (Summer 1975):213-19.

41. *Boycotter*, June 19, 1886; *John Swinton's Paper*, July 4, 1886.

42. *DABZ*, July 6, 1887; *Fourth Annual Report*, 420-421, 625.

43. Ibid. 659.

44. *DAVZ* Sept. 21, Nov. 30, Dec. 7, 1887.

45. For the situation of the English-speaking bakers and the attitude toward them of the German bakers' union, see *John Swinton's Paper*, Nov. 10, 1885, Feb. 2, March 15, Aug, 10, Nov. 18, 1884; *NYVZ*, Jan. 11, Feb. 22, March 15, April 5, 1885, for Kelly's complaints, see *NYVZ*, April 11, 1886.

46. *NYVZ*, April 5 and 12, 1886; *DABZ*, April 19, 1886.

47. Kaufman, 15-16; in Brooklyn the situation remained tense and conflict-ridden until after the turn of the century, *Bakers Journal*, Jan. 14, 1911.

48. *DABZ*, March 20, 1889.

49. *DABZ*, March 20, 1889, *Bakers Journal*, Jan. 14, 1911.

50. *Bakers Journal*, June 4, 1889.

51. *Bakers Journal*, Aug. 24, 1889.

52. *John Swinton's Paper*, May 23, 1886, Sept. 6, 1885; *DABZ*, May 12, May 18, 1886, June 30, Aug. 10, 1887; *NYVZ*, May 10, June 2, June 16, 1886, April 30, 1887; *Union*, April 30, 1886.

53. Ibid.

54. *NYVZ*, Aug. 21, 1889; *Bakers Journal*; Aug. 24, 1889, Jan. 14, 1911.

55. *Bakers Journal*, Aug. 31, 1889, Jan. 14, 1911; *NYVZ*, Aug. 23. 1889.

56. *NYVZ*, Aug. 26, 29, 30, 31, 1889, Sept. 11, and Oct. 2, 1889; *Bakers Journal*, Aug. 21, Sept. 14, and 21, 1889; *Paterson Labor Standard*, Nov. 2, 1889.

57. *NYVZ*, Aug. 30 and 31, 1881.

58. Schneider, 367-73.

59. Kaufman, chap. 3.

60. *NYVZ*, Sept. 11 and Oct. 2, 1889; *Bakers Journal*, Aug. 21, Sept. 14, and 21, 1889; *Paterson Labor Standard*, Nov. 2, 1889.

61. *NYVZ*, Sept. 16, 19, and 22, 1889; *Bakers Journal*, Sept. 23, 1889, Jan. 14, 1911.

62. *NYVZ*, Sept. 14 and 30, 1889.

63. *Bakers Journal*, Jan. 14, 1911.

64. Ibid.

65. *DABZ*, June 5 and 11, 1890; *Bakers Journal*, Jan. 14, 1911.

66. Ibid.

67. See for example, New York State Bureau of Labor Statistics, *Thirteenth Annual Report* (Albany, 1896), 6-7.

68. Ibid. and *Bakers Journal*, March 30, 1895.

69. *Bakers Journal*, March 30, 1895; New York State Bureau of Labor Statistics, 2:499-500; Hazel Kyrk, *The American Baking Industry, 1849-1923* (Stanford, 1929), 56-61.

3

Labour Party, Labor Lobbying, or Direct Action? Coal Miners, Immigrants, and Radical Politics in Scotland and the American Midwest, 1880–1924

John H. M. Laslett

In May 1908 the Miners Federation of Great Britain, and within it the thirty-thousand-strong Lanarkshire County Miners Union, in the West of Scotland, voted to affiliate with the British Labour party.[1] Since coal miners were, by the nature of their industry, geographically concentrated in specific areas, this was a momentous decision for Labour's political future. As a result of the 1908 decision, the MFGB exerted a paramount influence in more than thirty parliamentary seats not only in the West of Scotland but in England and Wales as well.[2] In fact it was the affiliation of the MFGB to the Labour party, more than anything else, that helped transform the party from a loosely knit group of Labour MPs into the majority party of the British working class. For ten months in 1924 the Labour party, which in 1906 had been described by Bernard Shaw as a "mere cork" floating on the Liberal party tide, became the official British government.[3]

I wish to thank the following for reading an earlier draft: Albion Urdank, Amy Z. Gottlieb, Stephanie Booth, Hamish Fraser, Alan Campbell, and the members of the Los Angeles Social History Study Group.

In much of Illinois, and particularly in the eight mining counties in the central and southern part of the state that will feature in this study, U.S. coal miners enjoyed comparable political influence to their British cousins. But they did not exercise their political influence in the same way. Illinois District 12 of the United Mine Workers of America had roughly the same number of colliers in it as the Lanarkshire County Miners Union. In June 1908, one month after the MFGB affiliated with the Labour party, the Illinois miners affiliated with the Illinois State Federation of Labor.[4] This, however, appeared to be contrary action to that taken by the Scottish miners. For, by affiliating their union with the ISFL, whose main function was to lobby the state legislature in Springfield on a nonpartisan basis, the miners of District 12 rejected the advice of those who urged it to support the Socialist party of America.[5] Between 1913 and 1924, they also rejected the pleas of those who urged it to affiliate with the Farmer Labor party, or with one of the other small independent labor parties that flourished in the period following World War I. By refusing to lend their support to such parties, the U.S. miners helped condemn them to political ineffectiveness.[6]

This essay deals with the causes and consequences of this political divergence and with the question of what significance should be attached to it. For the American labor historians, known as the Wisconsin school, led by John Commons, the different political tactics adopted by District 12 of the UMWA and the Lanarkshire County Miners Union symbolized a profound difference between the labor movements of the United States and Europe. This school posited a fundamental distinction between the economic and the political life of the working class. It argued that by shunning third-party politics the U.S. labor movement had, in Selig Perlman's words, discovered a unique form of "job-conscious unionism," which rejected socialist ideas and which set the American working class apart from the others in the industrial world.[7] Part of the reason for this, suggested Philip Taft, was the dominance of the antimercantilist tradition in America that made workers inordinately fearful of the power of the state. Instead, Taft argued, by limiting themselves to demands for union recognition in the economic sphere, U.S. workers elaborated a voluntarist philosophy that posed no fundamental challenge to the capitalist system.[8] "Unions in America have evolved in a very different fashion as compared with those of England and Western Europe," wrote Gerald Grob in 1961.[9] The reason was that "labor leaders, recognizing that the rank and file had not developed a . . . sense of class consciousness, . . . built their organizations in such a way as to bring them into harmony with the larger societal [i.e., capitalist] environment."[10]

The analysis presented here challenges the interpretation of Commons and his followers in several fundamental ways. It argues that

District 12, as part of the half-million-strong UMWA, used its political influence to secure legislative protection in the Illinois legislature in much the same manner as the British miners did vis-à-vis Parliament. It therefore rejects the notion that American workers always adopted a suspicious attitude toward the state. The essay also describes the hesitant manner in which the coal miners of the West of Scotland transferred their allegiance from the Liberal to the Labour party in the period of World War I. As a result, it disputes the assertion that British miners possessed an innately stronger sense of class consciousness than their American counterparts. By extension, my analysis brings into question the determinist view of the rise of the British Labour party that has been put forward by Keith Hutchison and other English historians. Hutchison argued that the extension of the franchise to an increasing proportion of the British working class, as a result of the 1884 and 1918 Ballot Reform Acts, virtually assured the success of the Labour party.[11] The evidence I shall put forward regarding the political behavior of the Scottish miners undermines that view. Instead, it upholds the position of Trevor Wilson and others that the British Liberal party remained a viable party of the Left at least up to 1914.[12] It was only World War I that brought about a fundamental change. In other words, at least as regards the workers analyzed here, in this early period the differences between the British and the American labor movements were far less marked than the Commons school assumed them to be.

I have chosen the Lanarkshire Miners and Illinois District 12 of the UMWA for this case study because of the strong cultural ties that existed between the two areas. Many of the northern European immigrants who laid the foundations for District 12 in southern Illinois before 1900 were Scottish colliers who had been trained in unionism by Alexander MacDonald. MacDonald was the dominant figure in the Scottish Miners Union between 1860 and the 1880; he visited Illinois three times between 1867 and 1876.[13] The Scots were never an actual majority in any of the Illinois mining towns, with the possible exception of Braidwood, in the northern part of the state in the 1870s, and Gillespie, in Macoupin County, after the turn of the century.[14] By 1917, Germans, Austro-Hungarians, and Italians, together with native-born whites, formed a majority of underground pit workers in most of the mining counties in the southern part of the state. This was particularly true in Franklin, Williamson, and Saline counties, which collectively constituted the area known as Little Egypt.[15]

Nevertheless, first- or second-generation Scottish, English, or Welsh immigrants played a disproportionately influential role within the elite of Anglo-Saxon pick miners, who dominated District 12 for much of its early history. For example, of the eleven miners elected to the Illinois General Assembly between 1874 and 1911, six were Scottish the Illinois General Assembly between 1874 and 1911, six were Scottish immigrants, three were English, one was Irish, and only a single member of the group was born in Illinois.[16] Two coal mine leaders of Scottish decent also played a disproportionately influential role in Illinois District 12 throughout much of its early history. These men were John H. Walker, who was born at Binnie Hill, ten miles from Glasgow, in 1872, and Duncan MacDonald. Although he was Illinois-born, Duncan MacDonald had been profoundly influenced by the tradition of Scottish mining radicalism.[17] Walker was president of the miners' union, District 12, between 1895 and 1908, and again between 1910 and 1912, before taking an even more influential post as president of the Illinois State Federation of Labor. He was thus in a critical position to influence the political direction of the Illinois labor movement. Duncan MacDonald was president of District 12 in 1909–10, and then secretary-treasurer between 1914 and 1917.[18]

Lobbying tactics, as well as the election of miners to legislative office, had played a role in securing mining legislation in Britain as well as in America in earlier decades. Beginning in the mid-1860s Alexander MacDonald had been paid by Lanarkshire colliers to travel to London when Parliament was in session to lobby before it for favorable laws.[19] Following suit, the Illinois miners retained Yorkshire-born lawyer John Hinchcliffe to represent them at the 1872 Illinois state constitutional convention. In the same year, partly as a result of Hinchcliffe's lobbying efforts, a package bill was passed by the Illinois General Assembly that provided for ventilation and escapement shafts in the mines and for the reporting and investigation of mine accidents.[20] Then, in 1874, Alexander MacDonald, along with Durham miners' leader Thomas Burt, became one of the first two working-class MPs to be elected to Parliament. They sat as de facto members of the Liberal party.[21] Once more following suit, at the turn of the century Illinois miners elected almost a dozen of their fellows as state assemblymen to Springfield.[22]

This mixture in both Britain and America of lobbying tactics and miners as political candidates was highly significant. It already tells us—contra Commons—that the Illinois miners were just as heavily engaged in political action to invoke the power of the state on their behalf as their British counterparts.[23] The difference, however, was that whereas the eleven miners elected to Springfield had been more or less evenly divided between Republicans and Democrats, the miners' MPs in Britain—whose numbers had increased by 1908 to fourteen—were all either Liberals, or so-called Lib/Labs, Labour party MPs who voted with the Liberals. That is, they occupied a transitional position between the welfare liberalism of Lloyd George and the 1906–15 Liberal government, and the putatively collectivist position of the infant Labour party.[24]

government, and the putatively collectivist position of the infant Labour party.[24]

This difference was, of course, not insignificant. By virtue of their association with the Labour party, the British miners' MPs found themselves—nominally at least—in political alliance with Fabians, with radical Independent Labour party activists, and even with a few Marxists in the Social Democratic Federation. All of these groups were also a part of the Labour party. No such institutional link existed between the trade unions and the political left in Illinois. The long-term effect of the affiliation of the MFGB with the Labour party was also to separate the miners from the cultural hegemony of the two main bourgeois parties, both Tory and Liberal. Nevertheless, as numerous commentators have pointed out and as the following narrative will confirm, the process of separating the Labour party from its two capitalist rivals was a slow and painful one, which was far from completed when the Labour party formally constituted itself as a separate political party in 1906. The process had still not been fully gone through when World War I began in 1914.[25]

In particular, the miners' MPs, whose parliamentary salaries were paid by the MFGB, not by the Labour party, were nearly all old-fashioned Liberals of the Gladstonian school who could not by any stretch of the imagination be described as Marxists. After the Miners Federation joined the Labour party in May 1908, three of them even refused to sign the Labour party's constitution. One of the nonsigners, Thomas Burt of Morpeth, stated in October 1909 that he would rather lose his seat in Parliament than "be handed over body and soul to the socialists."[26] Roy Gregory, the leading authority on the miners and British politics in this period, writes that even for those who did sign the Labour party constitution in the 1908–09 period, "their signatures made not a scrap of difference" to their rejection of collectivist ideas.[27] The same was true of the Liberal MPs who at this time represented most of the mining constituencies in Scotland. Let us now seek to demonstrate these similarities in outlook between the British and the American miners by examining in more detail their political fortunes in three Lanarkshire parliamentary constituencies, on the one hand, and in eight southern Illinois mining counties, on the other.

In the period between 1908 and World War I, the evidence seems at first to confirm the Commons view that the majority of miners in the eight Illinois counties showed little interest in radical politics. During these years several small Illinois mining towns did elect labor councilmen and mayors to office on the Socialist party of America ticket.[28] But these successes were not reproduced in elections to the state legislature, upon which the miners depended for needed safety legislation. In fact, after the turn of the century, the miners' earlier

practice of electing their own representatives to Springfield on either
the Republican or the Democratic ticket largely collapsed. In 1910 and
again in 1912 Adolph Germer, at that time secretary-treasurer of Sub-
District 5 and one of the best-known socialist miners' leaders in the
state, lost his bid to get elected to the General Assembly from
Macoupin County on the SPA ticket.[29] If we shift the focus to the two
major parties, we find that between 1908 and 1924, only two coal miners
were chosen out of sixty representatives elected to the state legislature
from the eight mining counties.[30]

Given this record, it seemed hardly surprising that the radical
element in District 12 failed to persuade their fellow miners to endorse
third-party action at the annual conventions of the union, despite the
rising SPA vote in other parts of the country. At the February 1910
miners' convention, several leading socialists registered their objections
to the 1908 decision of the district to affiliate with the State Federation of
Labor. They urged it to take independent political action instead.
Duncan MacDonald, who was president of District 12 that year, argued
that it was time for the miners to "employ another method than that of
begging at the State House door." Appealing directly to the British
immigrant miners in his audience, many of whom admired the English
Labour party and maintained contacts with fellow miners back home,
he urged the colliers to make "direct" use of the ballot, "as our brothers
across the ocean have been doing for some time past."[31] But District 12
refused to take MacDonald's advice.

In Lanarkshire at this time, by contrast, support for the Labour
party seemed to be already firmly established.   Since 1900 the
Lanarkshire Miners had been represented on the Scottish Workers
Representation Committee, whose purpose was to run independent
labor candidates for local and national office. It comprised elements
from the Scottish trade unions, from the ILP, from the cooperative
movement, and even from the Marxist Social Democratic Federation.
In the general election of 1906, the Lanarkshire County Miners Union
ran five of its officers as parliamentary candidates.[32] None of these
Labour party candidates won. But they alarmed the national leaders of
the Liberal party to such an extent that a secret memorandum drawn
up for their chief parliamentary whip in 1908 gloomily reported that the
alliance between Scottish trade union voters and the Labour party
posed a serious threat to the Liberals' future.[33]

Thus, in the general election of January 1910, it was widely expected
that all three of the seats for which the LCMU put up candidates in the
West of Scotland would fall to the Labour party. Standing on a platform
of mine nationalization, improved mine safety, amendments to the
Compensation Law, and Old Age Pensions, all three of the candidates
seemed to be in a strong position. Secretary William S. Small of the

LCMU, standing for Lanark North-West, had eight experienced subagents working for him in Shettleston, Tollcross, and Coatbridge, all of them substantial mining towns. His Liberal opponent W. M. R. Pringle appeared to court disaster by opposing votes for women, as well as a right-to-work bill favored by the Labour party. J. Sullivan, who stood for Lanark North-East, was a Catholic miners' leader who seemed well placed to capture the Irish vote in his constituency. And in the heart of the region, in Mid-Lanark, Labour ran the popular LCMU chief, Robert Smillie, who had served the Larkhall miners on and off for more than twenty years.[34] On the eve of the poll the ILP paper *Forward* asserted confidently: "Yes, friends, the tide of Democracy is rising. We are winning. We are going to see great changes in Scotland."[35]

Contrary to expectations, all three miners' candidates were defeated. Not only that, but in the December 1910 general election that followed ten months later, when only Mid-Lanark was contested, the LCMU's candidate, who was again Robert Smillie, did decidedly worse.[36] It is worth noting that these defeats in both Lanarkshire and southern Illinois took place in electoral districts where miners made up an estimated 18 percent to 34 percent of the vote.[37] Even in the British general election of December 1918, when the Labour party's popular vote throughout the country surged, only one miner was elected for a Lanarkshire seat. In fact, it was not until the general election of October 1922 that all six of Lanarkshire's industrial seats were won, and the great Labour party breakthrough—so long rumored to be inevitable— actually took place.[38]

Understandably, some of the reasons for these poor election results in Lanarkshire and southern Illinois reflected the different history of the Left in the two areas. In Scotland they derived, among other things, from the weakness of the ILP in the mining towns, from the failure of the Scottish Workers Representation Committee to maintain an effective political machine between elections,[39] and from the mutual suspicions that existed between politically moderate miners' leaders like John Robertson, David Graham, and David Gilmour, on the one hand, and firebrand Marxists like John McLean, on the other.[40] In Illinois, the poor showing derived from the generally weak political position of the Socialist party of America in the state, as well as from a long-standing commitment of most immigrant miners to vote for either the Republican or the Democratic party. Nevertheless, if we look beneath the surface, we find that there were at least two further reasons for this weakness that demonstrated the similarities, not the differences, between the political outlook of the miners in Britain and America. The first of these concerned the similar role that sectarian differences over culture and religion played, in both mining regions, in delaying the development of a politically united working class.

The lower half of the state of Illinois had originally been settled by southerners. Thus, ever since the Civil War, many of the eight mining counties where our focus lies had been dominated politically by poor, fundamentalist Protestant farmers who had come originally from Kentucky and Tennessee.[41] After 1900, the social conservatism of many of these Protestant voters was reinforced by hostility toward the large numbers of Slavic and Italian immigrants who had come to work in the mines. Their Catholic faith, their alien habits, and their heavy drinking offended the Baptist, prohibitionist outlook of the natives. Hence, even though solidarity across ethnic and religious lines was successfully inculcated by the local unions of District 12 in the workplace, no such class solidarity existed at the ballot box.[42] As a result, political contests in the area revolved around religious observance, nativist sentiment, and local option regarding liquor. Only rarely did they involve the economic issues of class. Besides this, only a small proportion of the eastern and southern European immigrants were American citizens and thus eligible to vote.[43]

In addition, many of the native Protestants of southern Illinois, and the hill regions of the upper South from which they came, maintained a tradition of private justice in which reliance on formal law enforcement procedures was more limited than it was in most other parts of the state. Thus, a resort to violence to settle disputes was easily mobilized when large numbers of foreign immigrants entered the region. The southern Italians among them brought a similar tradition of disregarding the law in settling disputes. from their homeland.[44] As a result, among the native-born Protestants, violent outbursts of anti-Catholic and anti-immigrant feeling, often originating in tavern brawls or strikebreaking activities, were not uncommon.[45]

Such ethnic and cultural divisions, and the problems that they created in impeding the growth of working-class solidarity at the ballot box, were thought by Selig Perlman to be one of the uniquely differentiating features of the American working class.[46] Yet when we look across the Atlantic to the Lanarkshire miners, with an allegedly greater sense of class cohesion, we find very similar sectarian differences. As early as the 1840s, Lanarkshire mine owners had imported unskilled Irish peasants in an attempt to prevent the native Scots from forming trade unions. In the years after 1886, the frequent drunken brawls, the marches and countermarches by supporters of the Protestant Irish Orangeites and the Catholic Irish Greens, and the religious disagreements between Catholics and the Protestants in the mining towns were exacerbated by the injection of Home Rule for Ireland as a national issue in British politics.[47]

Politically speaking, this meant that cultural and religious conflicts between native Scots and the incoming Irish in the Lanarkshire coalfield had very much the same effect on the politics of Clydeside that the cultural differences between native Illinoisans and southern and eastern European immigrants did on the politics of the mining towns in southern Illinois. That is, votes for local Republican and Democratic candidates were cast on the basis of ethnocultural predilections as much as they were on the basis of social class. What is more, in Lanarkshire the division between native Scots and Irish immigrant workers—in local steel towns such as Motherwell, as well as in mining villages like Blantyre—had become cemented in place by Liberal espousal of Irish Home Rule and by Tory opposition to it. Hence, although after 1906 the Labour party seemed to be the natural home for increasing numbers of miners, large numbers among those of them who could vote remained divided between Tory and Liberal. The Orangeite Protestant workers among them voted Conservative on patriotic grounds, while the Irish supported the Liberal government over Home Rule. Thus, in both of the 1910 elections, the United Irish League endorsed the Liberal rather than the Labour candidate in all three of the mining constituencies that the Labor party contested. By committing the Irish vote to the Liberals, the Irish League virtually doomed the Labour candidates to defeat. [48]

There was even an analogue in the Lanarkshire mining towns for the problem of low working-class turnout for elections that sidelined noncitizens among the Italian and Slavic miners in the coal towns of southern Illinois. A significant proportion of the Scottish miners who had been enfranchised by the British Reform Act of 1884 were young, single men who lived in boardinghouses. But their ability to vote had been restricted by the practice of political agents' registering to vote only those among them who lodged in residences with an annual rental of eighteen pounds or more. The effect of this was to exclude large numbers of working-class lodgers from the polls. Indeed, miners' political agent Duncan Graham claimed in 1910 that there was not a single mining village in the whole of Mid- and North-East Lanarkshire that had a lodger vote. Subsequently, he and his assistants successfully appealed a large proportion of these cases to the voting registration courts. The consequence was that by 1913 the number of miners on the electoral roll had increased thirteenfold.[49]

The second reason for the political weakness of the independent Left among the miners of both Lanarkshire and southern Illinois concerns the division of the more advanced sector of the working-class vote between the Liberal and the Labour parties, in the British case, and between the Progressive wings of both the Democratic and the Republican parties in the United States. As previously suggested, the determinist view of the rise of the Labour party in Britain assumes that after its impressive showing in the 1906 election, the party was destined to inexorable success. But this leaves out of account the Liberal party's revival in the period between 1906 and 1915, a revival that clearly exerted a major influence upon the Lanarkshire miners. This meant that the mining vote in the West of Scotland remained divided between the Labour and the Liberal parties for a longer period of time than the determinist case would allow.

The effect of the Liberal party revival in Lanarkshire was to divide the mining vote between Liberal and Labour candidates in much the same way that the mining vote was divided between the Progressives in both the Democratic and Republican parties in central and southern Illinois. Thus, in Lanarkshire many miners continued to vote Liberal because of the ongoing appeal of such traditional reform issues as free trade, temperance, hostility toward British imperialism, and limiting the power of the House of Lords.[50] An additional issue in both of the British general elections of 1910 was the rejection by the House of Lords of Chancellor of the Exchequer Lloyd George's 1909 budget. This budget proposed for the first time to tax wealthy landlords in order to release government revenue for socially desirable ends. The taxation issue enabled several "new Liberals" to win miners' votes and to divide the working class in the process. For example, in January 1910, Liberal MP W. M. R. Pringle won Lanark North-West with an election address praising the Liberal government for its legislative aid to the working classes. At Bridgeton, a Glasgow constituency bordering on Pringle's, Liberal MacCallum Scott won in December 1910, partly because he advocated a minimum standard in wages, and improved legislation in health, housing, education, and the poor law. Both improved housing and the idea of a minimum wage were of crucial importance to the miners.[51]

In addition, there were Liberal issues specific to Scotland that still had an ongoing, if somewhat indirect, appeal to the miners. Chief among these were land reform and Scottish Home Rule. Scottish Home Rule was a symbolic issue, rather than a compelling political objective.[52] On the other hand, land reform, in the sense of a land value taxation scheme such as was envisaged by Lloyd George's 1909 budget, was far from being merely symbolic. The idea of taxing wealthy landowners like the Duke of Hamilton, many of whom were also coal operators, was a significant vote catcher. So significant in fact, that in August 1911, ILP leader Joseph Duncan expressed concern that the Liberal land agitation "was completely overshadowing Labour's campaign for a minimum wage."[53]

Looking across the Atlantic, it soon becomes clear that, with the exception of the land issue, many of the social and political reforms that the British Liberal party was advocating in the 1906–14 period were very similar to those being advocated by Progressive Democrats and

Republicans in the American Midwest. In 1905, District 12 collaborated with the Illinois State Federation of Labor, the Chicago Federation of Labor, and a number of other trade unions in establishing the Joint Labor Conference Board. Its purpose was not only to lobby Springfield for legislation of immediate importance to trade unionists, but to pressure reformers in both the Republican and Democratic parties for measures that would benefit the Illinois working class as a whole. Partly as a result of such pressures, numerous pieces of reform legislation were enacted. They included the 1909 Health, Safety and Comfort Act for factory workers, new child labor laws, a Women's Ten Hour Law, and the Occupational Disease Act of 1911. In addition, the Illinois State Federation pressed repeatedly, if unsuccessfully, for an old age pension law very similar to the one that had been adopted by the Liberal government in Britain.[54]

Besides using lobbying tactics at Springfield, District 12 collaborated with the Illinois State Federation of Labor in employing two other methods to advance its legislative program. The first of these consisted of using the AFL's time-honored political method of endorsing particular candidates for state office because of their prolabor platforms. The second was reporting the voting records of individual state assemblymen to union members, with suggestions to vote accordingly. In accordance with the first of these two tactics, in 1908 District 12 President John H. Walker actively supported the Illinois State Federation's decision to endorse Progressive Republican Governor Charles Deneen because of his prolabor record. Walker did this even though, technically speaking, he violated District 12's constitution, which specified that members could not use the union's name to endorse any candidate for political office.[55]

Walker's actions caused a rumpus at the 1910 District 12 convention, both among conservatives who opposed this commitment to Progressive politics and among socialists who were dismayed by his willingness, as a member of the Socialist party, to endorse traditional party candidates.[56] Nevertheless, in making these endorsements Walker and others like him were following a path very similar to the Lib/Labist one being followed at this time by the miners of Great Britain: support for the Labour party where it seemed profitable, coupled with an ongoing commitment to socially conscious Liberals. In 1912 and again in 1916, Walker endorsed Democratic governor Edward F. Dunne because of his prolabor record, which included a washhouse law for miners, better safety legislation, and a law permitting women's suffrage in state elections. In 1916, Walker also endorsed President Woodrow Wilson's reelection as president.[57]

As we have already indicated, the core political issue for the miners, whether they lived in Illinois or in Lanarkshire, was the legislative mining code. And on this key issue, there is no evidence to suggest that the mining legislation that District 12 had secured by this time was inferior to what was on the books in Great Britain, despite its decision to opt for lobbying techniques, rather than for third-party action. In fact, the proximity of most Illinois coalfields to the state capital at Springfield, the large financial resources that the union could now command, and the freewheeling lobbying techniques that the miners had developed over the years probably gave them a greater ability to influence the political process than their British cousins. This fact is suggested by the alacrity with the Illinois Coal Operators Association entered into an agreement with District 12 to establish the Mining Investigation Commission in 1909. From this time on, this body provided the main avenue by which mining legislation was passed through the General Assembly.[58]

Three further developments revealed the degree of political influence that District 12 was able to exert over the subsequent operations of the Mining Investigation Commission. First, the General Assembly agreed to pay the salaries of the miners who were represented on the commission, for the duration of their work each year. This was not dissimilar to the British miners federation's practice of paying the salaries of their miners who were members of Parliament. Second, given the operators' natural antagonism to safety and other legislation, which would raise their costs of production, it is striking that they quickly agreed to join in the Investigation Commission's operation. In great measure this was due to the success that District 12 had enjoyed in convincing public opinion of the need for developing new mining laws.[59]

Third, and most remarkable of all, was the way in which the miners' representatives on the commission were able, often in the face of strong employer opposition, to preserve and enhance preexisting mine legislation so as to strengthen dramatically District 12's influence at the bargaining table. Two examples will suffice. One was the Shot-Firer Law of 1905, which was amended so as to make it the responsibility of the operators, not the union, to hire and to pay these men. The second was the strengthening of the Miners Qualification Act of 1907, which barred the use of untrained and uncertified labor in any Illinois coalfield. There is no evidence here to support Commons' view that U.S. workers were unwilling to enter the political field out of fear of legislative interference on the part of the state. To the contrary, District 12 did all it could to invoke the power of the state to advance its goals, much as the Lanarkshire miners did. It was small wonder, given these achievements, that the Illinois mining code should have been described by one expert in 1911 as "probably superior to . . . the mining code of any other state or country."[60]

In terms of independent labor politics, there is no doubt that World War I saw a widening of the gap between the Lanarkshire and the Illinois coal miners' movements. As we have already indicated, in the British general election of October 1922, all six of the local mining seats in the West of Scotland were won for the Labour party, five of them being taken by officers of the LCMU. The sixth MP to be selected, J. T. W. Newbold, was voted in by the mixed coal and steel town of Motherwell as a Communist.[61]

By contrast, at the close of the war the fortunes of the political Left in the United States moved in the opposite direction, downward. Under the onslaught of the 1919 Red Scare, the SPA vote for Illinois state treasurer, which had reached a high of 22 percent in 1912, fell to 9 percent in 1918, and to 7 percent in 1920.[62] Adolph Germer, who had become national secretary of the Socialist party in 1916, was indicted for opposing the draft, along with other leaders of the Illinois left.[63] By 1919, all of the Socialist administrations that had been elected in mining towns in the various parts of the state before World War I had been turned out of office.[64] John H. Walker, who was still president of the Illinois State Federation of Labor, ran for the Illinois governorship on the national Labor party ticket in the fall of 1920; and Duncan MacDonald was nominated by the Farmer-Labor party to run as its vice-presidential candidate in the same year. But neither of them came anywhere near to success.[65]

This bifurcation over the labor party question was important. The success of the British Labour party in the 1922 general election led ultimately to a fundamental restructuring of British politics. The absence of such a party in America helps explain why there was no similar political change in U.S. politics. But this difference should not lead us to believe, as it did the Commons school of historians, that U.S. workers showed no signs of comparable political and economic militancy in the period between 1917 and 1924. The Commons school unthinkingly assumed that the success or failure of a third political party was the sole criterion for socialist success. In doing this, it defined the meaning of labor politics far too narrowly, for it ignored syndicalism, cooperation, and numerous other strategies that labor movements all over the world, including the United States, have used in their efforts to advance an alternative to the capitalist order.

If we broaden the definition of labor politics in this way, a comparison between the political strategies followed by the Lanarkshire and the Illinois miners in the 1917–24 period also suggests a new, revisionist interpretation. For if we look beneath the surface of electoral politics in our two regions, we find that the Illinois miners not only suffered from many of the same postwar grievances as their Scottish fellows. We also find that their overall programs for postwar social reconstruction were remarkably similar. Moreover, at a time when radical ideas as a whole were thought to have been purged from the United States, we find that the syndicalist, or direct action, tactics that many rank-and-file Lanarkshire miners adopted as a means of achieving their goals in the postwar period were paralleled by similar direct action tactics on the part of the miners in Illinois.

Still more startling is the discovery that the intellectual inspiration for many of the syndicalist ideas that rank-and-file Scottish miners turned to in the post–World War I period came from the United States—from DeLeonism, from the American IWW, and from the industrial union traditions of the United Mine Workers of America.[66] This evidence directly contradicts the assumption of the Wisconsin school—as well as of historians who favor an exceptionalist interpretation of American history, generally—that radical ideas, to the extent to which they exerted an influence among American workers, derived from Europe and never took root in this country. In the case of the Scottish miners during this second period of our analysis, the traffic in radical ideas was partly the other way around.

Compared to the entire Glasgow region, it would be an exaggeration to say that the rank-and-file insurgency that swept across the coalfields of southern and central Illinois in the post–World War I period was as great as the one that developed on Clydeside. In the Glasgow region, the strike movement that culminated in raising the red flag in George Square on January 27, 1919, was the culmination of a deep and bitterly fought contest between the British government, on the one hand, and the militant workers of the Clyde region, on the other, that went back as far as 1915.[67] The strike movement also involved alliances between demobilized soldiers and shop stewards, between engineers and rent protesters, and between the Clyde Workers Committee and revolutionaries like Willie Gallacher and John MacLean, alliances for which there was no direct analogy in Illinois. The protest movement that developed in southern Illinois was also physically isolated from the strike wave that was then in progress elsewhere in the United States. Save for a few railroad workers, it was also a movement of miners alone.[68] Thus, it posed far less of a threat to the social order than did the upheaval on the Clyde.

Nevertheless, if we focus on the protest movement among the miners, and on the response that they made to the problems created by the question of who should control the coal industry, it is once again the similarities, not the differences in behavior, that stand out. In both places, maximum output had been demanded by the nation when World War I began; in both places the government had taken control of the coal industry (in Britain in December 1916, in America in October 1917); and in both places the authorities had exhorted the miners to work extra hours, with the promise of a "land fit for heroes" for them to return to once the conflict was over.[69]

In both Britain and America, however, the experience of the ordinary miner was far from what these promises presupposed. Despite wage increases, rampant inflation cut the average miner's spending power. In Britain, the index of retail food prices reached 323 in March 1920 (1914 = 100); in Illinois, the relative purchasing power of miner's wages fell from 100 in 1913 to 84.4 in 1920.[70] And with the rapid decline in demand for coal after the end of the war, wages began to fall, and unemployment grew rapidly. These trends accelerated with the termination of government control of the mines in each country, which in America took place in June 1919 and in Britain in March 1921. As a result, a bitter struggle took place in both Lanarkshire and southern Illinois between a conservative trade union bureaucracy on the one hand, and thousands of militant rank-and-file miners, on the other. The immediate issue was the terms on which the coal industry should be returned to private ownership. Behind this, however, lay much weightier political matters. They included mine nationalization, a "hands-off" policy toward Western intervention in Soviet Russia, further commitment to the idea of a labor party, and the freeing of political prisoners who had been jailed in both countries because of their opposition to World War I.

It was this list of political demands, in fact, that constituted the core of the miners' political program in both the United States and the United Kingdom in the period between 1917 and 1924.[71] With the sole exception of the idea of a labor party, which in Illinois was largely stillborn, these demands were advocated on both sides of the Atlantic with almost equal vigor. Sometimes they even fed off each other. In July 1919, for example, several thousand Illinois miners came out on unofficial strike in support of efforts to free the imprisoned labor radical Tom Mooney, who had been sent to jail for his alleged part in the bombing that took place during a July 1916 Preparedness Day parade in San Francisco. At a meeting of the Lanarkshire miners' Executive Council on December 28, 1918, the names of both Tom Mooney and Eugene Debs were linked with that of imprisoned revolutionary leader John MacLean, in a resolution that demanded the freeing of Scottish antiwar activists.[72]

But it was in their common use of the tactic of direct action to achieve their goals that the behavior of the rank and file in both Lanarkshire and Illinois was strikingly similar. This was true whether direct action was employed to protest the behavior of the government or the passivity of their own union officials in facing up to the problems of decontrol and unemployment. In January 1919, the Miners Federation of Great Britain put forward the so-called Southport proposals. These demanded a 30 percent raise in wages, a six-hour day, and full pay for recently demobilized miners.[73] On January 27, a rash of wildcat strikes broke out at Cambuslang, Uddingston, Hamilton, and Blantyre in order to stiffen the spine of MFGB officials in their negotiations with the British government over the Southport demands. Two days later, three thousand colliers converged on the LCMU's headquarters in Hamilton. They took over the building, hung a red flag from its balcony, and forced the Lanarkshire Executive Council to call an official "idle day" in support of the miners' demands. A couple of days later, another group of miners broke into the offices of Hamilton Palace colliery, damaged some property, and marched to Bellshill, where they were halted by a large police detachment.[74]

Five months later, on July 4, 1919, the Mooney strike, which we have already referred to, took place in various mining towns of southern and central Illinois. Although the protest against Mooney's imprisonment formed part of the motive for this strike, its most immediate cause was anger on the miners' part with the ongoing constraints of the Washington Agreement that had been signed by officials of the UMWA and the Federal Fuel Administration in October 1917. While conceding a wage increase, this agreement had contained a no-strike clause. It had also instituted a fine for striking, with the money to be deducted automatically from the colliers' pay packet.[75] Instead of backing up the workers' protest, District 12 leaders urged the miners to go back to work. As a result, early in August several thousand miners from Sub-District 5 held mass meetings in Priester Park in Belleville, near St. Louis. They demanded that the UMWA administration renegotiate the Washington Agreement or declare it nonbinding. The insurgents also resolved that the next UMWA national convention "issue a call to the workers of all industries to elect delegates to an industrial congress, there to demand of the capitalist class that all instruments of industries be turned over to the working class."[76]

At first glance, these examples of direct action on both sides of the Atlantic might be put down to frustration at the failure of union officials to stand up under government pressure. But as time went on, it became apparent that syndicalist ideas also played an important part in this upsurge. In Scotland, these ideas derived partly from the demands for the rank-and-file control of trade unions that the shop stewards' movement had pressed for in the Clyde Workers Committee during and just after the war. But they also derived, in an important sense, from imported American traditions of syndicalism and industrial unionism in which the UMWA, and within it District 12, also played a significant role.

Syndicalist ideas did not enter the consciousness of Scottish miners solely from the United States. Probably the most important source was the tradition of direct action that had been set going before World War I by the miners of South Wales. In 1912 a number of rank-and-filers there had issued a pamphlet known as *The Miners' Next Step*, which had rejected the parliamentary road to power favored by the Labour party, in favor of a syndicalist approach whereby the workers themselves would acquire control of the mines and carry out production on their own behalf.[77] Another possible source was the revolutionary syndicalist philosophy of French thinker George S. Sorel, which had been brought into Britain by trade union activist Tom Mann.[78] The South Wales miners themselves, however, were influenced in part by the DeLeonite wing of the American IWW. Furthermore, the idea of revolutionary industrial unionism, which had initially been advanced in the IWW concept of the "industrial department," had a presence of its own on Clydeside. One manifestation of this was the educational work carried out in 1903 by the Glasgow section of the British Socialist Labour party, which was an offshoot of the tiny U.S. political party of the same name.[79] Besides this, there was the Industrial Workers of Great Britain, a branch of the Chicago-based IWW, which had organized several hundred workers at the Singer Sewing Machine Works at Kilbowie, Clydebank, in 1911.[80] Both of these groups had also been influenced by a small group of internationally minded Irish militants, such as James Connolly, who was equally at home preaching the ideals of One Big Unionism whether he was addressing audiences in Chicago, Glasgow, or Belfast.[81]

In 1914 British syndicalists had also exercised an influence over the founding of the Triple Alliance of Miners, Railwaymen, and Transport Workers. The aim of this body was to coordinate the collective bargaining policies of these three giant British unions.[82] But none of these groups had hitherto succeeded in creating a truly integrated industrial union, in which all of the occupations associated with a trade would be united under one leadership. Indeed, it was the failure of the Triple Alliance to come out on strike in support of the MFGB's demands, in April 1921, that lent the syndicalist demand for trade union "amalgamation" much of its strength.[83]

It was here that the example of the UMWA came in. Although it allowed each district union a considerable degree of autonomy, the UMWA accorded a great deal more authority over the direction of union policy to its national office than did the MGFB, which was in essence a coalition of separate county unions.[84] In addition, the UMWA had, since its founding in 1890, pursued a policy of organizing all of the workers "in and around the mines." This included a higher proportion of skilled surface workers such as engineers, firemen, and carpenters than the MFGB had enrolled. Not only this, but some of the socialists in District 12, including Adolph Germer, displayed considerable enthusiasm for the integrated form of industrial unionism practiced by the IWW, despite their distaste for the IWW's dual unionist policies vis-à-vis the AFL. In fact, in 1912 a number of UMW radicals suggested that the UMWA withdraw from the American Federation of Labor and take the lead in setting up an "industrial organization of labor" that would aim at "the emancipation of the wage workers from the yoke of industrial slavery."[85]

All of this helps to explain why, in July 1917, when the Lanarkshire Miners Reform Committee was established at a delegate meeting held in Hamilton, reference was made to the more advanced industrial unionism of the UMWA. The Reform Committee's manifesto urged a reform of the MFGB, so that "a genuine British Miners' Industrial Union" would come into being, "with pooled resources, centralised direction, and a wide enough scope to embrace every worker of whatever craft, engaged in the industry."[86] "It is worthy of remark," added James D. MacDougall, a revolutionary syndicalist and protégé of John MacLean,[87] that "a prominent part was played in this conference by Lanarkshire men who had had experience as officials or members of the United Mineworkers' Union of America, either in Illinois or in British Columbia."[88]

After their respective foundings, the Lanarkshire Miners Reform Committee and the dissident body of militant rank-and-filers in Illinois District 12, which was known as the Committee of Fifty, followed paths that were in some ways different. The Lanarkshire Committee was overtly syndicalist. It rejected the commitment of the majority of union members to parliamentary action and to nationalization of the mines. Nationalization, the committee argued, would simply replace the present system of private ownership with ownership by the state.[89] Instead of negotiating with the government over the Southport demands, therefore, as a result of which the MFGB found itself outmaneuvered, the Reform Committee advocated a "down tools" policy, that is, strike action. Miners' MPs like John Robertson, Duncan Graham, and others, even though they represented the Labour party, were dismissed as trade union bureaucrats who had betrayed their class origins by compromising with the leaders of capital.

By contrast, District 12's insurgent Committee of Fifty, and the other dissident bodies that succeeded it, were less clearly committed to syndicalist theory than was the Lanarkshire Reform Committee. In some ways this was ironic, given the fact that Chicago was the international headquarters of the IWW. This did not necessarily mean, however, that there were no miners left in the state who believed in syndicalist ideas. It is likely that many of the Italians who lived in mining towns like Herrin or Marion, in Williamson County, remained sympathetic to the cause. A plausible explanation for the weakness of syndicalism is to be found in the impact of the 1919 Red Scare, which was far more virulent in the United States than it was in Great Britain. After 1919, the Red Scare prompted District 12 to expel IWW supporters from its ranks.[90] What emerged, instead, was widespread disillusionment at the outcome of World War I; rank-and-file anger at the switch from democratic procedures to bureaucracy in the running of the union; and an ongoing commitment to mine nationalization, old age pensions, and other social welfare programs.

Like thousands of other workers who took President Wilson's postwar declarations about industrial democracy seriously, Illinois miners wanted a share in the control of the industry to which they devoted their lives. At the February 1918 District 12 convention, therefore, a resolution was unanimously passed not simply expressing anger at the war profiteering of large corporations, but urging that the principle of conscription (i.e., of disappropriation) be applied to "surplus private incomes," as well as to labor.[91] The desire to retain, or increase, the amount of control they could exert at the workplace also helped motivate the Illinois miners to support the nationalization of the mines. The 1919 Convention of the UMWA as a whole instructed the union's officers to draw up a bill for presentation to Congress for government acquisition and control of all coal properties in the United States. This proposal was eventually scuttled by UMW president John L. Lewis.[92] But it was taken very seriously by large numbers of rank-and-file miners in Illinois, as it was in Pennsylvania and a number of other states.

Local unions in District 12 set aside special evening meetings to discuss the nationalization issue. The most frequent arguments put forward in favor of it were that coal was a natural resource that belonged to all of the people; that it should be mined for use and not for profit; and that collectivization under workers' supervision would enable the collier to escape from the bonds of the private employer.[93] Equally significant was District 12's campaign to secure an old age pension law, not simply for the miners themselves, but for the whole of the state's working class. In 1919, District 12's Legislative Committee collaborated with other unions in the Illinois State Federation to propose an old age pension bill to the state legislature.[94] Although it did not succeed, both it and the nationalization campaign provide further evidence of the inadequacy of the Commons argument about the unwillingness of U.S. unions to invoke the power of the state.

The most important evidence, however, of the Illinois miners' class-conscious desire to build an alternative model to the capitalist system was the network of cooperative stores that they established in the years between 1915 and 1923. Retail cooperative stores based on the Rochdale principle had long been a feature of the Lanarkshire mining towns.[95] Equally remarkable, however, was the system of more than ninety such stores that flourished under the joint control of Illinois District 12 and of the Central States Cooperative Society during the period of World War I. Like syndicalism and the use of strike action to assert miners' control at the workplace, cooperation represented a commitment to a form of collectivism that goes unnoticed if one confines one's analysis of radicalism to the role of political parties. Here also was another a direct link with Scotland. John H. Walker and Duncan MacDonald were both officers of the Central States Cooperative Society, in addition to their official roles in District 12; and several local cooperatives, including the ones at Gillespie and Glen Carbon, were founded by Scottish immigrants who had had experience in the cooperative movement at home. Robert McKechan, the first secretary of the Gillespie society, had worked as a baker in a Glasgow cooperative in earlier years.[96]

In addition to this, District 12 continued to improve the miners' legislative code during the World War I period, making use of the same lobbying tactics that had proved so effective before the conflict. Between 1917 and 1924, several important amendments were made in the laws concerning mine ventilation; the use of safety lamps and electricity; and the examination, certification, and duties of mine managers, mine examiners, and hoisting engineers.[97] Later in the 1920s, the activities of the Communists in the mines, as well as those of the Illinois branches of the insurgent miners' Progressive International Committee, strongly resembled those of the United Mine Workers of Scotland and the Miners Minority Movement in Great Britain, into which the Lanarkshire Miners Reform Committee was drawn.[98] Once again, although the methods used were different, the evidence suggests that as regards trade union democracy, miners' control over the work process, and the desire for far-reaching social change, the aims of the miners on both sides of the Atlantic were very similar.

My argument in this essay has not been that miners in the West of Scotland and in southern Illinois, many of whom came from the same ethnic roots, espoused an identical set of political beliefs The social crisis created by World War I cut deeper in Clydeside than it did in Illinois. And while solidarity at the workplace was equally strong in both places, the sources of cultural—and hence of political—division in the mining towns of southern Illinois remained greater than they did in Scotland.

The evidence presented here, however, suggests a number of important modifications to the traditional exceptionalist interpretation of U.S. labor politics and to the role that immigrant workers played within them. First of all, it seems clear that to judge the degree of class consciousness among workers solely by the extent to which they voted for a third political party, as the Commons school tended to do, is to wear the wrong set of glasses. It obscures similar traditions of militancy at the workplace on both sides of the Atlantic that were just as fundamental to raising political consciousness as the secondary question of how a ballot was cast.

Second, I have argued that the Illinois miners did not shun the political arena, as the Commons view implies. To the contrary, they sought to invoke the power of the state in enacting a mining code with just as much zeal as their Scottish counterparts. The difference lay in the means they used to secure this code. In Scotland, the first means used was the Liberal party, which was in no sense a collectivist body. Then, the Lanarkshire Miners made use of a Lib/Labist form of politics, which was articulated partly through the infant Labour party, but which mainly continued to depend on seeking to influence the Liberal party. This differed little from the lobbying methods that the Illinois miners used to secure needed legislation from the Progressives in both of the major parties at Springfield. Seen this way, the fact that around 1900 the Illinois miners abandoned electing their own representatives to the legislature in favor of the AFL's "reward-your-friends, punish-your-enemies" policy was testimony to the success of their involvement in the political process, not to their failure.

The sudden collapse of the British Liberal party during the period of World War I resulted from numerous factors affecting politics at the national level in Britain, which need not be gone into here. Basically, they stemmed from the fact that the philosophy of the party was ill suited to the coercive policies needed to fight a total war, and from a disastrous split that occurred between the followers of Prime Minister Herbert Asquith and these of his successor Lloyd George.[99] In Scotland, as elsewhere in Britain, this meant that the Labour party stepped into the gap created by the Liberal split, thereby becoming the "natural party of the Left" more quickly than the prewar strength of the Labour party had warranted. That meant that in both the 1918 and 1922 elections, large numbers of working-class voters went over to the Labour party not so much because they had changed their political opinions as because the Liberal party was no longer a viable option. In turn, this leads to my third major conclusion. This is to reject the excessively rigid assumptions about the superior political consciousness of European workers that lie behind the Commons model of the U.S. labor movement.

The collapse of the British Liberal party during the period of World War I did not mean that there was no genuine political swing to the left on the part of coal miners in the West of Scotland in the years from 1908 to 1924. What it did mean, however, is that in Lanarkshire and in southern Illinois it was the nature of the party system, and the different methods that the miners used to manipulate that system so as to secure their goals, that influenced their political choices. It had little to do with any fundamental difference in their respective levels of class consciousness.

Notes

1. Roy Gregory, *The Miners and British Politics, 1908–1914* (London, 1968), 31-32.
2. Ibid, 121-22.
3. Henry Pelling, *A Short History of the Labour Party* (London, 1974), 16.
4. Eugene Staley, *History of the Illinois State Federation of Labor* (Chicago, n.d.), 180.
5. A brief account of Socialist party influence in Illinois District 12 can be found in John H M. Laslett, *Labor and the Left: A Study of Socialist and Radical Influences in the American Labor Movement, 1881–1924* (New York, 1970), 205-7.
6. Charles R. Green, "The Labor Party Movement in Illinois, 1919–1924" (M.A. thesis, University of Illinois, 1959).
7. Selig Perlman, *A Theory of the Labor Movement* (New York, 1966), 276.
8. Philip Taft, *The A. F. of L. in the Time of Gompers* (New York, 1957), xvii-xviii.
9. Gerald R. Grob, *Workers and Utopia, A Study of Ideological Conflict in the American Labor Movement, 1865–1900* (Evanston, Ill., 1961), vii.
10. Ibid., 189.
11. Keith Hutchison, *The Decline and Fall of British Capitalism* (Hamden, 1966), xii-xiii, 74-96, 230-35.
12. Trevor Wilson, *The Downfall of the Liberal Party, 1914–1935* (London, 1966), 15-17. See also Samuel H. Beer, *Modern British Politics* (London, 1965), 109-12, 124-25; Neal Blewitt, *The Peers, the Parties and the People: The General Elections of 1910* (London, 1972), chap. 18.
13. For the career of Alexander MacDonald, see Gordon Wilson, *Alexander MacDonald* (Aberdeen, 1982).
14. For the Scottish miners in Braidwood, see Amy Z. Gottlieb, "A Demographic Study of Braidwood and Streator, Illinois," *Journal of the Illinois State Historical Society* (August 1979): 179-186. On the Scottish miners in Gillespie, see Victor Hicken, "Mine Union Radicalism in Macoupin and Montgomery Counties," *Western Illinois Regional Studies* 13, 2 (Fall 1980): 180-81.
15. Daniel J. Prosser, "Coal Towns in Egypt, Portrait of an Illinois Mining Region: 1890-1930" (Ph.D. diss., Northwestern University, 1973), chap. 2.
16. Gottlieb, 189.
17. For biographical material on Walker and MacDonald, see John H. Keiser, "John H. Walker, Labor Leader from Illinois," *Essays in Illinois History, in Honor of Glen H. Seymour*, ed. Donald F. Tingley (Carbondale, 1968), 75-89; Duncan MacDonald, "Early Experience" (autobiographical notes in Duncan MacDonald Collection, Illinois State Library, Springfield, Ill.).
18. Keiser, 78-79; MacDonald, "Early Experience," 31-32.
19. Wilson, chap. 9.
20. Earl R. Beckner, *A History of Labor Legislation in Illinois* (Chicago, 1929), 292.

21. Henry Pelling, *The Origins of the Labour Party, 1880–1900* (London, 1954), 4.

22. Gottlieb, 189.

23. This point is not intended to challenge the general argument that both the American and the British labor movements were more suspicious of state power, and less willing to undertake revolutionary action to secure control of it than the labor movements of the European continent. It merely suggests that the political behavior of the UMWA (which like the MFGB was the largest union in its nation's labor movement) did not correspond to the Commons stereotype. For further discussion, see Henry Pelling, *Popular Politics and Society in Late Victorian Britain* (London, 1968), chap. 4; Michael Rogin, "Voluntarism: The Political Functions of an Anti-Political Doctrine," *Industrial and Labor Relations Review* 15 (July 1962): 521-25; and Adolph Sturmthal, *Unity and Diversity in European Labor* (Glencoe, 1953).

24. For a discussion of Lib/Lab MPs in the British Parliament, including miners, see Frank Bealey and Henry Pelling, *Labour and Politics, 1900–1906* (London, 1958), chap. 9.

25. On this point, see Wilson.

26. Quoted in Blewitt, 250.

27. Gregory, 42.

28. The towns in which these successes were secured included Glen Carbon (1910) and Granite City (1911, 1913, 1917) in Madison County; O'Fallon (1911), Phelps (1915), and Mascoutah (1918) in St. Clair County; Buckner (1917) in Franklin County; and Herrin (1910) in Williamson County. See James Weinstein, *The Decline of American Socialism, 1912–1925* (New York, 1967), 116-18. See also Errol W. Stevens, "The Socialist Party of America in Municipal Politics: Canton, Illinois, 1911–1920," *Journal of the Illinois State Historical Society* 72, 4 (November 1952): 345-46, n. 60; and Robert F. Hoxie, "The Rising Tide of Socialism," *Journal of Political Economy* (October 1968): 613, 618.

29. Lee L. Cary, "Adolph Germer: From Labor Agitator to Labor Professional" (Ph.D. diss., University of Wisconsin, 1968), 10-11, 24.

30. In 1914 William T. Morris, a British-born miner, was elected for a two-year term from Duquoin, in Perry County, on the Democratic ticket. And from 1914 through 1924 William J. Sneed, president of Sub-District 10, was elected as Republican from Herrin, in Williamson County. See *Blue Book* (1916) 155; (1922) 270.

31. *Proceedings of the Twenty-First Annual Convention of the United Mine Workers of America, District 12,* (Peoria, 1910), 15-16.

32. I. G. C. Hutchison, *A Political History of Scotland, 1832–1924; Parties, Elections and Issues* (Edinburgh, 1986), 246; David Howell, *British Workers and the Independent Labor Party, 1888–1906* (New York, 1983), 32-39; Hamish Fraser, "The Labour Party in Scotland," in *The First Labour Party, 1906–1914,* ed. K. D. Brown (London, 1985), 46-47.

33. Hutchison, 246.

34. *Forward* 4, 4 (Oct. 20, 1909): 4; 4, 13 (Jan. 1, 1910): 5; 4, 14 (Jan. 8, 1910): 2; 4, 15 (Jan. 15, 1910): 5; Gregory, 94. For Robert Smillie, see his autobiography *My Life for Labour* (London, 1924).

35. Quoted in Hutchison, 246.

36. In December 1910. Robert Smillie polled fewer votes in Mid-Lanark than he had in January. See Hutchison, 257.

36. This estimate is based upon data recorded in Stephanie E. Booth, "The Relationship between Radicalism and Ethnicity in Southern Illinois Coal Fields, 1870–1940" (Ph.D. diss., Illinois State University, 1983), 240; and in F. W. S. Craig, *British Parliamentary Election Results, 1918–1949* (London, 1977), 647.

38. Craig, 630-36.
39. For example, in a special report made to the Labour party headquarters in London on the defeat of John Robertson as Labour candidate in a by-election held in Lanark North-East in March 1911. Arthur Peters, the party's national agent, stated that no proper canvassing had been done during the campaign, that the political agent hired by the LCMU had been ineffective, and that few nationally known Labor party leaders had been invited to speak in the constituency. See Arthur Peters to Executive of Parliamentary Labour Party, April 21, 1911 (Infancy of Labour Party Collection, London School of Economics, Folios 1-345).
40. Hutchison, 246-56; Fraser, 48-52.
41. James T. Przybylski, "Twentieth Century Elections in Illinois: Patterns of Change" (Ph.D. diss., University of Illinois, 1974), 26-41.
42. Ibid. 26-28; Prosser, chap. 2.
43. In a survey taken in 1920, it was found that in Williamson and Franklin counties, only 19 percent of the eastern and southern European immigrants had certificates of naturalization. See Grace Abbott, "The Immigrant and Coal Mining Communities in Illinois," *Bulletin of the Immigrants Commission* 2 (1920): 26.
44. Booth, 282.
45. Prosser, 70-75, 98-113.
46. "Next to the abundant economic opportunities available to workers of this country," Perlman wrote in his *Theory*, "immigration has been the factor most guilty of the incohesiveness of American labor," Perlman, 168.
47. For the Irish in the west of Scotland generally, as well as the conflicts between Protestant Scotish and Irish Catholic miners that frequently occurred in the Lanarkshire mining towns, see J. E. Handley, *The Irish in Modern Scotland* (1943), and Alan B. Campbell, *The Lanarkshire Miners: A Social History of Their Trade Unions, 1775-1874* (Edinburgh, 1979), chap. 7.
48. Sectarian conflict between Catholic and Protestant miners in the December 1910 election was particularly acute in Lanark North-West where LCMU leader Robert Small came at the bottom of the poll in a bitter, three-way contest between himself, Liberal Home Ruler W. M. R. Pringle, and the fanatical Orangeite Conservative, W. Mitchell-Thomson. See Fraser, 52; *Observer*, Jan. 8, 1910, 5.
49. Fraser, 57-58.
50. For example, Thomas F. Wilson, Liberal candidate for Lanark North-East in December 1910, issued an election manifesto that emphasized ending the power of the House of Lords to veto financial legislation, temperance reform, and Home Rule for Ireland, Scotland, and Wales. See *Letterbooks* containing "Candidates Election Manifestos," Scottish Liberal Association Collection (University of Edinburgh Library).
51. Fraser, 59; Hutchison, 239-40.
52. Michael Keating and David Bleiman, *Labour and Scottish Nationalism* (London, 1979), 48-58.
53. Quoted in Hutchison, 245.
54. Staley, 264-80.
55. Donald F. Tingley, *The Structuring of a State: The History of Illinois 1899-1928* (Urbana, 1980), 172-73.
56. The Socialist minority also opposed Walker's willingness to support the lobbying activities of the JLCB rather than endorsing the SPA's statewide tickets. For example, in August 1908, District 12 Secretary-Treasurer Frank Hayes wrote to Duncan MacDonald criticizing Walker's political tactics. He could not understand, wrote Hayes, how Walker "as an avowed socialist" could

support such a nonpartisan approach. Frank Hayes to Duncan MacDonald, August 30, 1908 (Duncan MacDonald Collection), Box I, Folder I. See also *Proceedings of the Special Convention of District 12, U.M.W. of A.* (Peoria, 1916), 235-41.

57. In 1916, Walker was expelled from the SPA because of his endorsement of Dunne and President Wilson. See Tingley, *Structuring of a State*, 164; Staley, 418.

58. Beckner, 298-99.

59. The miners were aided in this task by the public sympathy that had been generated for the union by the Cherry mine disaster of 1910. See Amy Z. Gottlieb, "The Regulation of the Coal Mining Industry in Illinois with Special Reference to the Influence of British Miners and British Precedents, 1870–1911" (Ph.D. diss., University of London, 1975), 291; *Proceedings of the Twenty-Second Annual Convention of the United Mine Workers of America, District 12* (Peoria, 1910), 69-74.

60. Beckner, 347.

61. Craig, 630-36.

62. Lee M. Wolfle, "Radical Third-Party Voting among Coal Miners, 1896-1940" (Ph.D. diss., University of Michigan, 1976), 74.

63. Cary, 41-42.

64. Stevens, 259-60.

65. Green, 91-97.

66. One of the few to recognize this transatlantic connection is James D. Young in his article "Daniel DeLeon and Anglo-American Socialism," *Labor History* 17, 3 (Summer 1976): 329-50.

67. For a general account of the so-called "Red Clyde" phenomenon, see Robert Keith Middlemas, *The Clydesiders: A Left Wing Struggle for Parliamentary Power* (London, 1965). See also James Hinton, *The First Shop Stewards Movement* (London, 1973), chaps. 3, 4, 10; Harry McShane, *Glasgow 1919: The Story of 40 Hours Strike* (Kirkintilloch, n.d.).

68. The most extended accounts of the post–World War I Illinois miners' insurgency are in Sylvia Kopald, *Rebellion in Labor Unions* (New York, 1924), chaps. 2-3; Harold W. Perrigo, "Factional Fights in District No. 12, United Mine Workers of American 1919 to 1933" (Ph.D. diss., University of Wisconsin, 1933); and in John H. M. Laslett, "Swan Song or New Social Movement? Socialism and Illinois District, 12, United Mine Workers of America, 1919–1926," *Socialism in the Heartland: The Midwestern Experience, 1900–1925*, ed. Donald T. Critchlow (Notre Dame, Ind., 1986), 167-214.

69. G. D. H. Cole, *Labour in the Coal Mining Industry (1914–1921)* (Oxford, 1923), chaps. 1-3; McAlister Coleman, *Men and Coal* (New York, 1969), 89-91.

70. Charles Mowat, *Britain between the Wars, 1918–1940* (London, 1956), 27; Isador Lubin, *Miners' Wages and the Cost of Coal* (New York, 1924), 230.

71. For the Illinois miners' political demands, see Harold W. Perrigo, 122. For the demands of the British miners, see Cole, 70-72, and LCMU *Council Minutes*, Feb. 14, 1919. The LCMU *Council Minutes* are cited with the permission of the National Union of Mine Workers, Scottish Region.

72. Kopald, 69-70; LCMU *Council Minutes*, Dec. 28, 1918. In May 1919 John MacLean himself, who was imprisoned several times for his antiwar activity, wrote an open letter to Eugene Debs on the anniversary of Debs's conviction under the U.S. 1917 Espionage Act. "To-day on Glasgow's famous 'Green,'" MacLean wrote, "I announced a demonstration for Sunday, May 25, to demand your release," along with that of Tom Mooney, Bill Haywood of the IWW, and SPA leader Victor Berger. See *The Worker*, May 17, 1919, p. 3.

73. Cole, 71-72.

74. *Hamilton Advertiser*, Jan. 27, 1919, p. 4.

75. Perrigo, 51-55.

75. Kopald, 75.

77. Henry Pelling, *A History of British Trade Unionism* (Harmondsworth, 1963), 140.

78. Jonathan Schneer, *Ben Tillet: Portrait of a Labour Leader* (London, 1982), 149.

79. Walter Kendall, *The Revolutionary Movement in Britain, 1900–21: The Origins of British Communism* (London, 1969), chap. 4.

80. Patrick Renshaw, *The Wobblies: The Story of Syndicalism in the United States* (New York, 1968), 222-23.

81. For the career of James Connolly, and his connections with the IWW, see R. D. Edwards, *James Connolly* (Dublin, 1981).

82. P. S. Bagwell, "The Triple Industrial Alliance, 1913–1922," *Essays in Labour History, 1886–1923* ed. Asa Briggs and John Saville (London, 1971), 96-128.

83. For this incident, which more than anything else doomed the MFGB's postwar struggle for social justice in the mines, see Bagwell, 118-21; Cole, 199-220.

84. A more centralizing tendency was given to the MFGB in 1918 by transferring the central office from Manchester to London, by the election of a full-time president and secretary, and by the national negotiations that took place under state control as a result of the war. But it still remained less centralized than the UMWA. See Cole, 66-67.

85. For the character of the UMWA's industrial unionism, and its relations with the IWW, see Laslett, *Labor and the Left*, 207-17.

86. J. D. MacDougall, "The Scottish Coalminer," *The Nineteenth Century* 102 (July–December 1927), 767.

87. For biographical material on James D. MacDougall, and for further insight into his role as sponsor of the Lanarkshire Miners Reform Committee, see the entry under his name in William Knox, *Scottish Labour Leaders, 1918–1939: A Biographical Dictionary* (Edinburgh, 1984), 170-75.

88. MacDougall, 767.

89. Instead of nationalization, wrote McDougall in *The Worker*, which was the official organ of the Scottish Workers Committee Movement, the focus should be on the election of pit committees, in which underground workers would be represented along with surface workers, craftsmen and clerical workers who were employed at the pithead. These pit committees would then form the basis of a new, democratic structure in the MFGB that would create the "necessary means towards the establishment of self government in industry." See *The Worker*, Oct. 14, 1920, 4.

90. For example, the March 1918 District 12 convention refused to support an appeal for funds on behalf of Severine Oberdan, an Italian miner who had been arraigned under the 1917 Espionage Act because of his antiwar speeches, on the ground that he was a member of the IWW. See *Proceedings of the Twenty-Seventh Consecutive and Second Biennial of the United Mine Workers, District 12* (Peoria, 1918), 219-24. For an overall account of the Red Scare in Illinois, see Tingley, *The Structuring of a State*, chap. 7.

91. *Proceedings of the Twenty-Seventh Convention*, 124-25.

92. For accounts of how President John L. Lewis of the UMWA sabotaged rank-and-file demands for the nationalization of the American coal mines, see John Brophy, *A Miner's Life* (Madison, 1964), 152-75; and Melvyn Dubofsky and Warren Van Tyne, *John L. Lewis: A Biography* (New York, 1977), 92-94.

93. *Proceedings of the Thirtieth Consecutive and Fifth Biennial Convention of the U.M.W. of A., District 12* (Peoria, 1924), 91-99.

94. Beckner, 486; *Proceedings of the Twenty-Ninth Consecutive and Fourth Biennial Convention of the United Mine Workers of America, District 12* (Peoria, 1921), 589-95.

95. Hutchison, 288; *Council Minutes,* May 18, 1921.

96. Colston E. Warne, *The Consumers Cooperative Movement in Illinois* (Chicago, 1926), 342-44. For more on the relationship between District 12 and the cooperative movement, see Warne, chaps. 5-6; and Laslett, "Swan Song or New Social Movement?" 193-97.

97. Beckner, 308-9.

98. For analyses of the Progressive International Committee and other Illinois miners' reform movements such as the Reorganized United Mine Workers of America, the National Miners Union, and the Progressive Mine Workers of America, see Booths 98–142; Brophy, chap. 5; Dubofsky and Van Tyne, chaps. 6-8; and Theodore Draper, "Communists and Miners, 1923–1933," *Dissent* (Spring 1972), 371-92. For the role of the United Mine Workers of Scotland and the Miners Minority Movement, see R. Page Arnot, *A History of the Scottish Miners from the Earliest Times* (London, 1955), chap. 9; Hywel Francis and David Smith, *The Fed: A History of the South Wales Miners in the Twentieth Century* (London, 1980), chap. 5; and Martin Sime, "The United Mineworkers of Scotland," unpublished paper (Edinburgh, n.d.).

99. An excellent summary of the reasons for the decline of the British Liberal Party, and of how far this was due to changes in the political allegiance of the working class and how far to other factors, can be found in J. A. Thompson, *The Collapse of the British Liberal Party: Fate or Self-Destruction?* (Lexington, 1969).

MIGRATION WITHIN EUROPE
IN THE
NINETEENTH CENTURY

4

France and the Belgian Immigration of the Nineteenth Century

Carl Strikwerda

The Belgian migration to France, one of the largest migratory movements between European countries in the nineteenth century, remains one of the least understood. Because France's population grew slowly, foreign labor was essential to its industrialization. During the nineteenth century, France received more immigrants than any other European country, and Belgians, numbering over 400,000, were the largest group of foreigners in France during all that time. Belgians were especially important in the department of the Nord, the most industrialized region of France. Sixty percent of the Belgians in France lived in the Nord, where they made up over one-fourth of the industrial work force.[1] While sheer numbers alone argue for the importance of the Belgians in France, the group also plays an important role in the debate over labor militancy and the presence of immigrant workers. The case of the Belgians has usually been cited as one more example of how exploitative employers manipulated politically passive immigrants and thereby undercut the attempts of native workers to organize successfully. A second but largely ignored view, however, has suggested that far from hindering a fledgling labor movement, Belgian immigrants played a central role in organizing unions and supporting strikes. The

Research for this article was supported, in part, by the Belgian American Educational Foundation and the National Endowment for the Humanities. For helpful comments and bibliographical suggestions, thanks are owed to Joan Coffey, Michael Foley, Camille Guerin-Gonzales, John Vincent Nye, Donald Reid, and the members of the University of Kansas Social and Economic History Seminar.

case of the Belgians, therefore, provides a controversial arena in which to test general interpretations of immigrant workers. Evidence about the Belgians, this essay will argue, challenges the common picture of the naive and powerless immigrant worker and suggests a far more dynamic picture with implications for general models.

Most historical scholarship on the Belgian immigrant workers in France follows the line begun in the immediate pre–World War I era. According to this interpretation, the Belgians were a conservative work force whose migration into France was deliberately encouraged by employers and the state to undercut French workers' militancy, break strikes, and hold down French wages. Victor Renard, the socialist president of the French national textile workers' union, denounced the Belgians in 1904:

> The bosses favor their immigration because they find them a passive and docile element against whom they are strongly armed with decrees of expulsion they can get from the government, to use against those foreigners brave enough to demand their rights in a strike. The bosses set these exotic workers against the native workers and profit from this by lowering the cost of labor.[2]

This view has been echoed by French, British, and, especially, American historians. According to David Landes, the textile manufacturers of Roubaix, in the Nord,

> were able to draw on an abundant supply of cheap, sometimes desperate, always docile labor, which offered the inestimable advantage of being disposable. . . . Belgians could be shipped back across the border at little or no political cost. And if French labor got difficult, the Belgians were always ready to serve as scabs.[3]

Gary Cross argues that French employers recruited Belgians in the late nineteenth century in order to create a "secondary labor market," that is, a group of workers who had to take jobs at whatever wage they were offered. Employers did this in order to undercut native French workers who might protest through strikes or unions: "While French citizens," Cross argues, "began to use the political process to find alternatives to the private labor market, politically powerless foreigners took their place."[4] The Belgian immigrants hurt the position of French workers, these historians argue, because the two groups found it difficult to work together. One historian, for example, has claimed that in the Nord

> the Belgians initially weakened French textile workers' solidarity by offering convenient scapegoats for native-born

workers' wrath at the growing rate of unemployment in the
1880's. . . . native-born workers complained that the Belgians
were "naturally more docile"—willing to accept the worst jobs
at the lowest wages without protest.[5]

As a result, according to another historian, in the city of Roubaix, the
leading textile city in the Nord, "a barrier of hostility" separated French
and Belgian workers.[6]

Although their material on Belgian workers has usually been
ignored, two French scholars have pointed out that, far from being
passive and conservative, some Belgian immigrants were at the
forefront in creating labor unions and socialist parties and in organizing
strikes in the Nord. In her book on strikes, Michelle Perrot found that
Belgian migrants led the first large strike in the Nord, which broke out in
1880. Firmin Lentacker, writing about the Franco-Belgian border,
pointed out that Belgians in the Nord helped found consumer
cooperatives and the Socialist party in the region.[7]

Unfortunately, neither Perrot's nor Lentacker's insights on the
Belgian migrants have been noted by most historians working on
France. Perrot's great work has been seen as dealing with strikes, not
migration, while Lentacker's book has been seen as primarily an
economic and geographic study, rather than a study of labor. Some
recent scholarship has acknowledged that the Belgians could be
militant, and not just conservative, yet these scholars cannot account for
this apparent contradiction. The same historian who argued that French
and Belgians were separated by hostility also wrote that "Some Belgians
were unwilling to strike and worked as strikebreakers, while others were
willing to be participants and even leaders of strikes in Roubaix."[8]
Laurent Marty, in a study of workers' culture in the Nord, wrote,
"Roubaix was submerged in a tidal wave of immigrants, who brought
with them at the same time competition and new ideas."[9]

How accurate then is the portrait of the Belgians in France as
passive, docile, and underpaid? Can the examples of Belgian militancy
pointed out by Lentacker and Perrot be reconciled with the more
widespread view of Belgian conservatism and passivity? Were Belgian
migrants militant sometimes and conservative at other times? And if so,
why?

Waves of Migration

Belgian migrants came to France in several distinct waves. The
difference between these waves accounts in part for the mis-
understanding in the historical literature. From the 1840s through the
1860s, several hundred thousand Belgians settled in France, most of
them employed either in the textile industry in the Nord region or in

skilled trades in Paris. From the 1880s to 1914, three smaller movements of Belgian migration took place: some forty thousand lived near the Franco-Belgian border and commuted into the Nord to work; another group of approximately forty thousand came to France temporarily each year to work in agriculture or brick making; and finally, a group of Belgian miners labored more or less permanently in the Pas-de-Calais coalfields near the Nord.

The largest wave of Belgian migrants to France came during the period of the 1840s through the 1860s. Workers had moved back and forth between the two countries for centuries, and already in 1819 there had been enough Belgian workers in the Nord for French workers to stage riots against them.[10] The migration beginning in the 1840s, however, represented a new phase both because it was larger and because it was more closely tied to the process of industrialization. Belgium was the first country to industrialize after Britain, yet the very foundations upon which it industrialized—its dense population and extensive rural industry—meant that parts of its economy had to undergo enormous change in the process. Factory production forced workers out of rural industry, and, at the same time, industrialization could not produce jobs quickly enough to provide employment in such a densely populated country. The majority of migrants to France came from the Belgian provinces of West and East Flanders, driven by the collapse of the rural industry in linen textiles. In 1843, almost one-third of the population of West Flanders, for example, depended on spinning or weaving linen in their homes, yet machine-made cotton and linen from both Britain and Belgium were rapidly replacing cloth made in homes.[11] Simultaneously, in a tragedy second only to that of Ireland, the Flemish rural workers were devastated by the potato blight, poor grain harvests, and epidemics of the 1840s. The death rate and out-migration from rural Flanders in the mid-nineteenth century was so great that, despite a high birth rate, Flanders' population fell 3 percent within five years.[12]

Initially, only a minority of the migrants from Flanders went to France; the majority went to large urban and industrializing areas of Belgium—the cities of Antwerp and Brussels and the coal and metallurgical regions in the southern provinces of Hainaut and Liège.[13] During the 1850s and 1860s, as poverty and the decline of rural industry continued to grip Flanders, however, more of the migrants went to France, especially to the Nord. Between 1851 and 1871, the number of Belgians in France went from 128,000 to 375,000, easily making the Belgians the largest group of foreigners in the country. Up to 1901, Belgians usually represented about 40 percent of all the foreigners in France; their numbers reached a peak in 1886 at 489,000 people.[14]

The Belgian immigration had by far the greatest effect in the Nord, the French department bordering on Belgian Flanders. Out of the eighty-eight departments in France, the Nord department alone had 60 percent of the Belgians in the country. With its rich agricultural base, long history of textile production, and accessible coal, the Nord became the one area of France whose explosive economic growth resembled that of the industrialized regions of Britain, Germany, Belgium, and the United States. The textile city of Roubaix, in the Nord, for example, grew from 8,000 people in 1800 to 124,000 in 1896, making it the most rapidly growing city in France. Contemporaries never tired of calling Roubaix an "American city," because of its raw, fast-growing character, or of referring to Roubaix and its sister cities of Lille and Tourcoing as the "French Manchester."[15] The Belgians were essential to this growth. By 1872, 55 percent of Roubaix's population was Belgian, many of them born in Roubaix of Belgian parents. During the second half of the nineteenth century, in the *arrondissement* or county of Lille as a whole, one-fifth of the population was Belgian.[16]

The Belgian population in the Nord was especially important because it formed a distinctive community in the area, whereas the Belgian workers in other areas in France blended in with their French neighbors. After the Nord, the next largest Belgian community in France was in Paris, where about 10 percent of the Belgians in France lived during most of the nineteenth century. The Belgians in Paris formed few societies or clubs and often went unnoticed by contemporaries. In a city of over a million, the fifty thousand Belgians formed only a small group. In addition, in contrast to the Nord, many of the Belgians in Paris were skilled workers—glove makers, printers, and hatters. With higher incomes and greater job security, they had less need to gather in close-knit working-class neighborhoods than did the textile workers in the Nord. Finally, whereas the Belgians in the Nord were overwhelmingly Flemish, that is Dutch-speaking, many more of the Parisian Belgians spoke French or were fully bilingual and spoke both French and Dutch easily. What was true of the Parisian Belgians applied as well as to the Belgian migrants in other northern French cities outside of Paris and the Nord: the roughly one hundred thousand Belgians found scattered in places such as Rouen, Nancy, Reims, and Arras rarely formed identifiable communities. The one other large group of Belgian workers were miners from the French-speaking southern Belgian province of Hainaut who occasionally found work in the mines in the Nord and the neighboring department of Pas-de-Calais. Again, a common language and small numbers meant that they rarely were a major presence in France.[17]

The large Belgian community in the Nord was composed of two groups: those who came from declining rural industry areas and who settled more or less permanently in the Nord, and a smaller group of experienced factory workers from cities such as Ghent who moved back and forth between the Nord and Flanders in response to the business cycle. Those from rural areas had fewer financial resources and skills and could rarely afford to return to their place of origin. The factory workers from places such as Ghent, on the other hand, more often had savings to finance journeys back and had enough skills to help them find work in different cities more easily. During the early 1860s, for example, Belgians flooded into the Nord when the "cotton famine" caused by the American Civil War weakened the Flemish cotton industry and sparked a boom in the woolen and linen industry in the Nord.[18] Between 1861 and 1865, some two thousand workers from Ghent, out of an industrial work force of about forty-five thousand, left the city. A police survey in Ghent in 1862 found that out of 189 inhabitants leaving the city during a three-month period, 159 or almost 80 percent, went to the Nord. After the textile industry in the Nord suffered its own recession in the late 1860s with the end of the American Civil War, a newspaper in Ghent reported, "Flemish factory workers are still coming out of France to our city. Fortunately, there is now enough work among us to keep them all busy."[19]

The frequency with which many migrants went back and forth to Belgium may also have encouraged the Flemish in the Nord to form a separate community.[20] Almost all the Belgians in the Nord, in fact, remained Belgian citizens, even when they had lived in France for decades and had raised children there. Becoming a citizen in France was, until 1889, a lengthy, often expensive process. Retaining Belgian citizenship allowed migrants to escape French military service and eased the possibility of returning to Belgium. Until the expansion of social welfare in France around 1900, acquiring French citizenship brought few benefits.[21] Many Flemish workers saw themselves as only temporarily in France. As a Flemish worker in Armentières in the Nord wrote in a socialist newspaper, "If we want a rest, then we go to Belgium, there we have our own house."[22]

Together, the permanent and temporary migration of Belgians had a profound effect in the Nord. While much of France experienced only modest industrial growth, the abundant labor provided by the Belgians helped to make the Nord the premier industrial region in the country. At the same time, the Belgian migration gave a distinct cultural cast to much of the Nord. In Roubaix, the city government and many businesses and political campaigns had to print notices in both Dutch and French to ensure that their message got through. Belgian newspapers and Flemish singing groups and clubs all flourished in this French department.[23]

The Belgian migration to the Nord and the rest of France, however, underwent a crucial, and often misunderstood, change between 1870s and 1900. During the economic recession of the early 1870s, Belgian migration to France dropped significantly. Although it revived slightly in the late 1870s, it fell again during the hard times of the mid-1880s. Only briefly, right before World War I, did Belgian migration to France ever approach the levels of the 1850s and 1860s again.[24] In 1889 and 1893, new French laws made it easier for immigrants to become French citizens. They could now simply request citizenship to be granted after only three years of residence, rather than undergoing numerous formalities after ten years of residence, as had previously been the case. For foreign spouses and children of French citizens, citizenship became virtually automatic. As a result, the number of Belgian citizens in the Nord dropped while the number of naturalized French citizens grew for the first time.[25]

Most important, the textile industry in the Nord no longer grew in the same robust, continually upward fashion that it had in midcentury. Recessions were frequent, and expansionary phases less vigorous. Protected by high tariff walls, the French textile industry survived the late-nineteenth-century period of intense foreign competition, but it rarely sold large amounts in world markets.[26] In the late 1890s, Roubaix's woolen industry, in particular, nearly collapsed owing to high prices of raw wool and to increased foreign competition.[27] The Nord as a whole became less of a textile region and, in part because of the expansion of the nearby Pas-de-Calais coalfields, turned more toward metallurgy.[28] As a result, the Nord provided many fewer readily available unskilled jobs in the textile industry, and what jobs it did have were more insecure. Because of the decline in immigration and the increase in naturalization, the number of Belgians in the Nord went from 289,000 in 1891 to only 169,000 in 1911.[29]

Rural poverty still drove Flemish laborers to France, but fewer of them migrated and settled in the Nord. Instead, around 1900, they more often lived inside Belgium just on the border with the Nord and commuted daily or weekly into France. Or they took up migrating into France for only part of the year and worked in agriculture or brick making. Previously the availability of jobs in France had been the main factor affecting migration between the two countries. By 1900, French wages and cost of living had risen well above the Belgian levels. By working in France, but living in Belgium, these commuting and temporary seasonal workers could take advantage of high French wages but avoid high French prices. Because they did not live in France, however, these Belgian workers had a much different relationship with French co-workers than did the Belgian migrants of an earlier period.

A major reason for the cost of living's becoming significantly higher in France than in Belgium was that, especially after 1892, France adopted high tariffs on foreign goods and foods. The high tariffs on foreign goods allowed French producers to charge higher prices. Meanwhile, Belgium kept its tariffs low, particularly on manufactured goods. Whereas the French cost of living had been about 10 percent higher during the mid-nineteenth century, by 1900, it was more than 20 percent higher. The difference in rents was even greater: an international study of the cost of living in European countries found that rents in France were one-third higher than those of Belgium.[30] Living in France was also more expensive than in Belgium because of the two countries' differing tax policies: French cities still generated much of their tax revenue from the *octrois*, tolls that had to be paid on merchandise going in and out of the city. Belgium had abolished its *octrois* in 1867. Since the workers and the poor naturally paid proportionately more *octrois* that did the rich, Roubaix's socialist government in the 1890s tried to abolish the *octrois* but was overruled by the national government.[31]

As a result, the late nineteenth century saw a huge increase in the number of *frontaliers*, or border workers, who lived in Belgium but commuted to work in France. While the population of Roubaix and Lille fell after 1896, the Belgian towns along the border boomed, and their economies became almost completely tied to France. In 1902, the Belgian socialist leader Auguste DeWinne estimated that in Mouscron, a town on the border that lay only 5 kilometers from Roubaix, almost three thousand workers or roughly half the work force was employed in France.[32] By 1908, perhaps as many as forty thousand Belgians crossed daily or weekly to jobs in the Nord.[33] The Belgian government's transportation policy aided this shift of population. To help the impoverished rural workers without forcing them to move to the cities and give up their cherished plots of land, the Belgian government in the late nineteenth century built an enormous system of "light railroads," really tramways, and provided cheap workmen's tickets on the national railroads. The tramways and inexpensive rail tickets allowed workers to commute daily or weekly to cities to work and still keep their families and farmland in the small towns or countryside. Incidentally, these policies also attempted to keep workers out of the cities where they might swell the ranks of the Socialist party and labor unions. The number of workmen's tickets issued yearly went from 14,223 in 1870 to over a million in 1890 and over 4.5 million by 1900. In the region bordering France, these policies did not keep workers out of the cities so much as keep them out of France. The trams and inexpensive tickets allowed Flemish workers to get to the border quickly and thus get more quickly to factories in the Nord, which were usually only several kilometers inside France.[34] In 1901, the Belgian government even gave a special reduced rate on workmen's tickets that applied only to workers commuting into France.[35]

Many French people—with the exception of employers—resented the Belgian border workers, arguing that they depressed wages, undermined a sense of community in the Nord, and contributed little to France except their labor. French workers and shopkeepers often called the Belgians who commuted "butter pots" because the Belgians brought much of their food along with them while coming to work in France.[36]

The other new kind of Belgian immigration to France by the late nineteenth century was the movement of thousands of Flemish laborers to work on farms and in brickyards for several months of the year and then return to Belgium. The growth in the numbers of these *"Franschmans,"* or "Frenchmen," as the Flemish called them, came as a result of economic and demographic changes in both France and Belgium. Hit hard by the decline in grain prices, and unable to compete with cheaper North American and Russian grain, some French farmers switched to growing sugar beets. Rising incomes allowed urban dwellers to buy sugar, while the expansion of railroads and cheaper coal permitted sugar-processing factories to be located almost anywhere. Thinning out sugar beets in the spring and harvesting and chopping them in the fall, however, were labor-intensive, demanding, and unattractive jobs. Furthermore, there was little need for workers except at planting and harvesting times, both of which lasted only a matter of weeks on any given farm. Consequently, French farmers preferred to hire workers on the basis of the job to be done, rather than to hire them for a year or the entire season.[37]

Flemish farm workers came to fill the needs of French farmers both because the Flemish had special skills in working with sugar beets and because, as explained below, the agricultural situations in France and Belgium tended to create a demand for labor in France and an oversupply of workers in Belgium. The Belgian farmers had begun producing sugar beets in large numbers earlier than the French, and the large-scale production of sugar beets may, in fact, have spread to France from Belgium. Large-scale growing of sugar beets began in France in the Nord, on the Belgian border, and spread south to the rest of the country during the second half of the nineteenth century.[38]

It has often been argued that the demand for agricultural laborers like the Belgians came because France's population grew so slowly. This is only partly true. The drop in the birth rate in France was great enough that, by 1901, no less than fifty-nine French departments had more deaths than births as opposed to only twenty-eight that had more births than deaths. Yet many of the French departments in which the Belgians worked, most of which were in northeastern France, were not losing population or were losing population only slowly. Equally important was that so many young people and laborers in the French countryside left for the cities and that those who remained refused to take positions as agricultural workers.[39] The high French tariffs on agriculture, too, protected many small farmers. This prevented a situation from developing where small farmers had to sell out and become laborers or hire out themselves or their children part-time to support their own farms.

Not only the demand for farm labor in France but also the lack of opportunities in Belgium encouraged Flemish rural workers to migrate. In the late nineteenth century, shoe production, one of the traditional rural industries, was being displaced by shoe production done in urban factories.[40] Meanwhile, the demand for day laborers in Flemish agriculture dropped as large landowners bought up more and more farmland. Because free trade kept grain prices low in Belgium, the large landholders preferred to take advantage of the Flemish peasants' hunger for land as security and status rather than to use capitalist methods and work the land themselves with farm laborers. The large landowners rented out land to tenants who competed with each other and hardly could afford to pay good wages to farm hands. In 1911, the pioneer British sociologist B. Seebohm Rowntree found that agricultural rents in Belgium were nearly twice as high as in Britain, while farm wages were only one-half of British wages. With Belgium's industrial employment growing slowly in the late nineteenth century, a large pool of impoverished laborers collected in the Flemish countryside.[41]

At the same time, the sheer growth of population in Flanders led to an enormous increase in the number of very small plots of farmland. Around 1900, the average size of farms (excluding those of less than one acre) was 63 acres in Great Britain, 33.5 in Prussia, 24 in France, and only 14.5 in Belgium. Including the plots of under one acre, the average size of a farm in Belgium was only 5.7 acres.[42] The owners of the little plots could not support themselves as farmers. Instead, they took jobs as hired hands on rented farmland, commuted each day or each week to work in the cities, or increasingly, migrated each season as farm hands to France. As another observer wrote in 1906:

> Walk through any Flemish village on a winter day, and you will find outside the numerous bars, as also outside the railway station, a great number of miserably-dressed sinister-looking men on the lookout for a job which may give them a penny or two. These are the poor coolies of Northern Europe, birds of passage, who with the first breath of spring spread out their poor ragged wings and fly away to France to find the work and earn the bread which social conditions deny them in their own country.[43]

By 1900, at least forty thousand of Flanders' two hundred thousand farm workers migrated to France each spring. Some estimates even run as high as sixty thousand.[44] As a result, as Rowntree noted, "It is not an uncommon occurrence in the summer time to visit a village in Flanders from which almost every able-bodied man has departed, the work at home being carried on by the women, children, and old men."[45]

Militant or Conservative?

How conservative, then, were the Belgians who came to France in these different waves of migration—the semipermanent migrants, the border workers, and the seasonal agricultural workers? The evidence clearly points to the semipermanent migrants to the Nord being more militant than conservative, and, indeed, being major contributors to the creation of the French working-class movement in the Nord. Although the border workers and seasonal workers were not nearly as militant, in their case, too, their conservatism has probably been exaggerated.

Well before the rise of socialism, the textile workers who came to the Nord in the middle of the nineteenth century had a long history of strikes and union activity. In Ghent, the hometown of many of the migrants to the Nord, weavers in the cotton mills had established one of the first successful industrial unions on the Continent already in the 1850s. Between 1868 and 1871, the Ghent members of the International Association of Workingmen, the association that Karl Marx helped organize, sent funds collected in Belgium to Roubaix, and, on several occasions in the 1860s and 1870s, striking workers in Ghent sought work in the Nord.[46] In the mid-1870s in Ghent, the former members of the First International were already converted to a kind of socialism akin to that of Marx through their contacts with German and Dutch socialists.[47] The Ghent socialists played an important role in spreading socialist ideas beyond the German-speaking world when, in 1877, they organized an international socialist congress that was attended by thirty foreign delegates from eight European countries, including Wilhelm Liebknecht of Germany and Paul Brousse of France. Liebknecht concluded his address to the congress by calling Ghent the strongest citadel of socialism outside Germany.[48]

Historians have usually attributed the introduction of socialist ideas into the Nord to Jules Guesde, the leader of the most orthodox Marxist faction of the French working-class movement. The Nord, in turn, became one of the strongholds of socialism in France. Socialism, in fact, put down such deep roots in the Nord that most workers there stayed with the socialists even after the rise of communism following World War I. Yet the Belgian socialists from Flanders, particularly Eduard Anseele and Edmond VanBeveren, had an influence at least as great as

Guesde in the early years when the working-class movement in the Nord began. Guesde's first visit to the Nord was in June 1881, and the first major recognition of his influence came in 1882 when he was invited to give a speech at the anniversary celebration of the Commune of Paris.[49] The Ghent socialists, however, had been holding meetings along the border with Flemish and French workers from the Nord since 1877. Already in February 1880, Anseele—referred to as "Anselme" by the French police—distributed a translation of the German socialists' Gotha Program, at the time the best short summary of Marxist ideas. Anseele, VanBeveren, and other leaders from Belgium held meetings almost monthly along the border, sometimes attracting as many as three hundred workers from Roubaix. They constantly urged their listeners to reject both the liberalism and the simple revolutionary fervor that had been popular among French workers and instead to adopt the "collectivist" program derived from Marx and the German socialists. This meant having a workers' government and the nationalization of private property as ultimate goals and building strong labor unions, political leagues, and consumer cooperatives as the foundations of a socialist movement.[50] The French police noted that "although having received only an elementary education, VanBeveren reads and translates German perfectly, which has permitted him to distribute socialist pamphlets from across the Rhine among the Ghent workers."[51] Because of his popularity in the Nord, Anseele was invited to give the speech at the anniversary of the Commune in 1881. When Guesde came the following year to the same event, Anseele helped to introduce him to the workers in the Nord.[52]

It was also Belgian leaders, who, even before Guesde came to the Nord, advised workers in the Nord during the first major strike there. In 1880, almost thirty-five thousand textile workers in the Nord went on strike, in one of the largest strikes in French history up to that time.[53] Although the strike failed to achieve its immediate objective of a wage hike, it transformed the union movement in Roubaix. Many of the leaders of the strike were young recent immigrants from Belgium. The native French strikers included many workers who later became famous socialist leaders in the Nord: Gustave Delory, the "boss" of the Nord socialist federation before World War I, and Henri Carette, later mayor of Roubaix, both received their first socialist experience during the strike of 1880. The strikers got assistance from Belgium, despite the police, by going over the border and carrying back supplies and by holding strike meetings in Belgium, some of them presided over by Anseele of Ghent. The Belgians, as Michelle Perrot says, "were the teachers of socialism in the north of France; if after 1880, Guesdist propaganda developed rapidly and successfully, it was the Belgians who tilled and prepared the terrain."[54]

Even Michelle Perrot, however, overlooks the real contribution of the Belgians to the development of the working-class movement in the Nord. Perrot uses the presence of the Belgians to demonstrate that strikes in the 1880s were most often led by those less open to bourgeois influence—the young, foreign-born recent immigrants to the city—and thus that strikes before 1890 represent a more authentic kind of spontaneous working-class action than the dull bureaucratic unions that came later. In fact, Belgian participation in the 1880 strike, which Perrot cites five times in her book, led French workers away from the spontaneity that Perrot emphasizes. The Ghent socialists incessantly preached the value of organized unions, with regular strike funds and a disciplined membership. Indeed, as a result of the strike of 1880, eight new unions were formed in Lille and Roubaix.[55]

The Ghent socialists also called for the creation of socialist consumer cooperatives. They had been among the first socialists in Europe to create such institutions. One of the distinguishing features of the working class in the Nord was the strength of socialist cooperatives modeled on those of Belgium. Of the twenty-six founding members of La Paix, the most important working-class cooperative in Roubaix, nineteen had been born in Belgium, thirteen of them in Ghent.[56] As a recent historian of French cooperatives points out, "By 1898, La Paix had a membership of 5,000 families, sold bread, coal, and groceries, and housed the local textile workers union and the Roubaix section of the POF," the Guesdist Socialist party.[57] The union cooperative in Lille, founded in 1892, began among French workers who had visited the cooperatives in Ghent and Brussels and who modeled their organization on La Paix. The union went on to become the largest and most successful socialist consumer cooperative in the Nord, with eight thousand families as members by 1912.[58]

The Belgian stress on organization—cooperatives and strong labor unions—is crucial because it was probably as important a factor as Guesdism in forming a working-class identity in the Nord. Although the socialist federation of the Nord was described as "Guesdist," the socialist movement there actually developed in some markedly different directions from those Guesde wanted. Guesde opposed consumer cooperatives because he believed that by lowering the cost of food they merely allowed employers to pay workers less. He was also suspicious of labor unions because he feared that their purely economic action might divert workers from socialist activity. Most of all, Guesde wanted the socialist political party to be the centerpiece of the entire working-class movement. Instead, what happened in the Nord was that the socialists developed a movement resembling the one in Ghent, with consumer cooperatives, labor unions, and political clubs all playing important roles.[59] While many historians have pointed to the Nord as the one

region of France where socialism succeeded as a mass movement
before World War I, few of them have acknowledged that this was in
part due to the influence of immigrant workers from Belgium. Eduard
Anseele was exaggerating only slightly when he said, in response to
proposals in 1910 to limit Belgian migration to France:

> They want to attack the immigration of the Flemish. But, it
> is the only revolutionary immigration into France! It is the
> Ghent socialists who, by their tireless effort, created in the
> Nord the nucleus of militants from which the French socialist
> party today has grown.[60]

The Belgians could influence the development of the working-class
movement in the Nord because natives and immigrants often
succeeded in working together, despite the cultural differences and
economic competition between French and Belgian workers. In general,
many historians writing on the Nord have exaggerated both the
unfortunate economic effects caused by the Belgian immigrants and
the divisions between Belgian and French workers.

Gary Cross, for example, argues that the French employers gained
special advantages by using foreign laborers such as the Belgians.
"Expanding the labor market supply through immigration," he writes,
"doubtless worked against wage increases."[61] The argument that the
Belgians depressed wages or created a disadvantaged secondary labor
market, however, has numerous problems. As a member of the French
parliamentary commission investigating the Nord textile industry in
1904, the famous socialist leader Jean Jaurès criticized French union
leaders for saying that Belgians took work at lower wages. In fact, he
pointed out, Belgian and French workers doing the same job were paid
the same. Jaurès instead suggested that wages as a whole were lower in
the Nord because the Belgians flooded the labor market.[62] But even the
argument that the Belgians depressed the general level of wages for all
workers in the Nord is doubtful. Wages in the Nord, including those in
the textile industry, were among the highest in France.[63] In addition,
wages in Roubaix and Tourcoing were hardly lower than those in Lille
even though there were many more Belgians in Roubaix and
Tourcoing.[64]

The argument that the Belgian immigrants to the Nord depressed
wages, furthermore, focuses too narrowly on the way in which a growing
supply of labor exerts a downward pressure on wages. In general, of
course, a growing labor supply tends to increase competition between
job seekers and strengthen the ability of employers to offer lower wages
or to defer wage increases. This effect can be partially offset, however, if
the growth in the supply of labor is largely a response to increasing
demand for labor, which seems to have been the case in the Nord.

Unemployment in the Nord during the second half of the nineteenth century appears to have been the same as or even less than in other areas of France, and instead, the growth in the demand for labor and the growth of the labor supply through immigration appear to have been relatively closely matched.[65] Belgian migration into the Nord closely followed rising wages. When wages and emplyment dropped in the recession of the late 1860s, for example, Belgians stopped migrating to France, and many already in France left the country.[66] In addition, the downward pressure on wages which the Belgian immigrants exerted could be reversed by the beneficial effects that they brought as "human capital." Many of the Belgians were skilled or at least experienced workers who gave a tremendous boost to industry in the Nord. Indeed, productivity in the textile industry in the Nord was as high as that in the United States, despite less capital investment and less utilization of electricity.[67]

The French complaints about the Belgian workers in the Nord are a bit ironic when one realizes how crucial the availability of labor and the proximity to Belgium may have been as the causes of economic growth in the Nord. The French geographer Raoul Blanchard, writing in 1906, actually reversed the argument of the labor leaders and asserted that the Nord owed its prosperity largely to its geographical proximity to Belgium and other foreign countries. Protected by tariff walls from British and Belgian competition, the Nord nonetheless brought in most of its imports and sent out its exports through lower-cost Belgian and British ports. Belgian and British capitalists invested in the Nord, sold the French their machinery, and acted as middlemen in selling French textiles on the international market. Further, Blanchard added, the availability of Belgian labor was one other critical advantage that the Nord enjoyed over other textile regions in France and, in fact, was one key to its prosperity.[68]

The Belgian migrants in the Nord were able to contribute to shaping the French working-class movement in the Nord because, from 1848 until the late nineteenth century, few barriers separated French and Flemish workers and there was little open hostility between the two groups. Within the working class in Roubaix, for example, Belgians were found in all occupations and at all levels of skill. Only in certain skilled occupations and, paradoxically, in the most unskilled jobs were Belgians found in disproportionate numbers. Even a writer who tried to argue that economic differences separated Belgian and French workers in Roubaix found, for example, that "In the 'semi-skilled category,' into which most of the textile jobs fell, the Belgians were neither under- nor over-represented in proportion to their distribution in the labor force." Outside of industrial jobs in textiles, the French dominated managerial, professional, and clerical jobs, while the Belgians were overrepresented in skilled, artisanal jobs.[69]

Although it has been claimed that a "barrier of hostility" separated French workers "from this important migrant group," the Belgians, there is little evidence between 1848 and 1900 that this was the case.[70] Louis Reybaud, a well-known observer of French industry, wrote in 1867 that French workers in Roubaix had few friendships with Belgian workers but that there were no instances of open hostility.[71] In her study of strikes, Michelle Perrot found that violence by French workers against the employment of foreigners was much less frequent in the Nord than in other areas of France where foreigners were common. And violence against the Belgians was much less frequent than against other groups. Although accounting for almost half the foreign workers in the country, the Belgians had only eleven incidents of violence directed against them, while the Italians had no less than sixty-seven, and the Germans, only one-fifth as numerous as the Belgians, were the target of seven incidents.[72]

After an outburst of antiforeign conflict among workers in the early 1890s, the French Ministry of the Interior did a nationwide survey of relations between native and foreign workers. The police chief in Roubaix responded that there were no incidents of anti-Belgian conflict in his city.[73] It is true that a fight between French and Belgian workers, which left several people wounded, had occurred just months before the police chief's report. Interestingly, however, the fight was between French workers and French-speaking Belgians from Verviers, a city located at the extreme other end of Belgium from Flanders, where the large majority of Belgians came from. The immigration of Verviétois to the Nord was quite unusual, and it seems probable that these Belgian workers, unlike the Flemish, did not fit into the either the native French or the Flemish Belgian working-class communities in the Nord.[74]

The lack of hostility between the French and Flemish in the Nord in the late nineteenth century is illustrated by the career of Alphonse Merrheim, one of the major leaders of the French national labor union federation, the CGT. One of the key turning points in Merrheim's career came between 1905 and 1914 when he witnessed the hostility of French workers toward their Italian co-workers in the metallurgical industry in Lorraine, in eastern France. Such divisions between workers eroded Merrheim's faith in the working class's potential to be a united, revolutionary force. In giving up his faith in workers' revolutionary potential, Merrheim turned increasingly to reformism. Yet Merrheim, who had begun his working life in Roubaix, was the leader of the coppersmiths' union of Roubaix and Tourcoing between 1893 and 1903. All Merrheim's years living in a French city that was over a third Belgian never made him question the ability of workers of different nationalities to unite. Only after leaving the Nord in 1903 did his doubts arise. None of the biographers of Merrheim mentions incidents in Roubaix, where he was troubled by any hostility he witnessed between French and Belgian workers. Indeed, the impact that being a union leader in Roubaix had on Merrheim seems to have been the reverse: the relations between Belgians and French made him believe workers could feel a solidarity between nationalities.[75]

The assertions that the Belgian migrants "were used by Roubaisien employers to threaten labor militancy" and that the Belgians "could be, and were strikebreakers" are also weak.[76] It is true, of course, that employers in Roubaix and elsewhere in the Nord were eager to hire Belgians. When Jean Jaurès suggested that France could force Belgium to lower its hours of work to the French level by refusing to hire Belgian workers, employers from the Nord all responded: "It's absolutely impossible: foreign labor is absolutely necessary for us."[77] This eagerness to hire the Belgians and the natural desire of employers to avoid strikes does not mean, however, that employers seriously tried to undercut labor militancy by hiring Belgians or, if they did try, that they succeeded in doing so. The claim that the Belgians were strikebreakers, in particular, appears to be exaggerated. The one clear example of Belgians' continuing to work and thus helping to break a strike occurred in 1903 and 1904 when the frontier workers continued to work in Armentières, Roubaix, and Lille.[78] Before this, there are almost no documented cases. The police reports on forty-five strikes in the Nord between 1880 and 1883 and another series of reports on twenty-two strikes in 1895 reveals only two cases where "foreign workers" took strikers' jobs. In only one of these two cases is the nationality of the workers mentioned, and they were British workers.[79] Furthermore, the employers, if they were deliberately trying to undercut labor militancy in the Nord by bringing in Belgians, appear to have failed miserably. The Nord was almost always one of the most strike-prone areas of France, despite over seventy-five years of Belgian migration. Referring to the time when Roubaix was over 50 percent Belgian, Michelle Perrot says, "The France of strikers is, first of all, the France of textiles, its capital is Roubaix."[80] Even after the turn of the century, when the increasing number of border workers did present a grave new problem for working-class militancy in the Nord, workers in the region vigorously organized strikes. During the period of 1910 to 1914, Roubaix had an annual strike rate of over thirty strikes per 100,000 workers—one of the highest of any industrial area in France and, indeed, a high rate even by world standards.[81]

One of the most widely known incidents where French workers protested against the hiring of Belgians ironically reveals that in the late nineteenth century relations between the two groups were not, in fact, deeply hostile. In the summer of 1892, French miners in the department of Pas-de-Calais, next door to the Nord, went on strike to force their employers to lay off approximately six hundred Belgian miners who had just been hired. The French miners accused the Belgians of having taken jobs at wages below the level at which the French worked. Aided by socialist-run local governments who sympathized with them, and by the central government authorities who did little to protect the Belgians, the French miners were able to force the Belgians to return to their home country. The entire incident was treated by the press as an example of the failure of international solidarity among workers. The national leaders of both French and Belgian socialist movements and the national miners' union federations even organized a kind of summit meeting, held appropriately in Roubaix, to ease tensions between workers in the two countries.[82]

On close examination, however, the incident did not indicate a high level of hostility toward the Belgians among French miners. The French miners reacted only after their employers had laid off miners who were involved in union activities and had indicated their intention to undercut the strong position that the miners' unions had won in the region. While it does not appear that the Belgians knowingly took jobs at lower wages, they nonetheless accepted work conditions, such as longer hours and night work, that were typical in Belgium but not in France. Yet the French miners did not act against all Belgians, but only those brought in by their employers. Between four and five thousand Belgians worked in mines in the Pas-de-Calais, amounting to almost 12 percent of all miners in the region. As the one historian who studied the incident carefully noted, "It was not against the Belgian worker population that the anger of the French was unleashed, but against the new arrivals. Until then, the populations of the two countries lived together without difficulty, but the Belgians who arrived in 1892 had the misfortune to come when the French workers who had been laid off for union activity were still without work."[83]

Seasonal and Border Workers

At first glance, the Belgian seasonal workers in French agriculture would appear to fit better the stereotype of the exploited immigrant laborer—unable to speak the language, forced to move from one temporary employer to another every few weeks, and at the mercy of foreign employers and government officials. The Belgian "Franschmans" often lived in squalid conditions on French farms, isolated, except for occasional brawls, from the native population. Belgian consular officials and Catholic priests collected numerous complaints from seasonal workers about French farmers cheating Belgians out of part of their wages.[84] Indeed, the Belgians and other foreign agricultural workers in France have been described as classic examples of a "secondary," that is, disadvantaged, labor market.[85] But a close look reveals a much more complicated picture. The seasonal workers, aided by sympathetic priests and government officials, fought back against employers by organizing unions, boycotts, and strikes and by making full use of the bargaining power they possessed against their employers.

By 1905, Belgian Catholics had organized "Committees of Protection" in all three of the dioceses that sent seasonal workers to France. The Catholic priests employed by these committees offered counseling, loans, and legal advice to the "Franschmans" and, most important, organized associations of workers that soon became, in all but name, labor unions. By 1911, the priests and their lay sympathizers had organized over fifteen thousand of the estimated forty thousand seasonal workers into associations—a large proportion of the work force by the standards of the pre–World War I era. The associations provided model contracts that French farmers should sign with the Belgian workers, obtained the aid of Belgian consular officials and other Belgians residing in France to help the farm laborers, and helped the workers put forth demands to the French farmers. So impressive was the work of these Belgian labor organizers that French Catholics who organized native farm laborers modeled their associations after the Belgian ones.[86]

The French farmers reacted to the Belgian workers' organizations with a variety of tactics: they tried to introduce machines to replace some of the work done by migrants and tried to hire both native French workers and Polish migrants as substitutes. The Belgian workers, however, had a number of stratagems to counter these tactics and made full use of the advantages they possessed. The machines for cutting sugar beets were still not fully reliable and often depended on good weather conditions to function properly. Frequently, farmers found they had to use both machines and migrant workers. As a result, the Belgians, at times, could boycott certain farmers to keep them from making extensive use of machines. In addition, the Belgians kept moving to more distant agricultural areas in France to take advantage of the scarcity of labor and the high wages in those areas. This had the additional effect of keeping wages up in the areas where the Belgians had first come in.[87] The French farmers also found it difficult to substitute Polish or native French workers for the Belgians. The Poles were accustomed to labor markets in Germany where strict regulations were in force, and many of them refused to work in France. The Polish and French workers, furthermore, did not possess the tightly knit work gangs with experienced straw bosses as did the Belgians.[88]

Despite the farmers' desire to cut down the employment of Belgians, they found that working with the Belgian straw bosses was often indispensable. Only these straw bosses could easily produce the necessary number of experienced workers quickly. One famous Flemish boss, Felix van Winne, was reputed to have been able to produce up to eight hundred workers in variously sized gangs.[89] At the same time, the straw-boss system among the Belgians was usually not constructed to exploit the average worker: the straw boss represented the workers and helped negotiate a contract with the farmer; he did not get the wages from the farmer to divide among the workers. French farmers who tried to sue straw bosses, because they were dissatisfied with the work the Belgians had done, found that the straw bosses were not considered legally liable. In this, the Belgian system differed from the subcontracting systems typical of some migratory worker situations where the workers were at the mercy of the bosses of their own nationality.[90]

Because the Flemish workers could often choose to work for the farmers who paid the most and because they were paid by the task, they could, by working extremely long hours, return to Belgium with relatively large sums. In some cases, they could, after several favorable years, buy farms in Belgium with their accumulated earnings. One reporter on the "Franschmans" encountered a farmer in Zedelgem in Flanders who showed off his farm and said, "All that you see, it's from French money!"[91] It is also important to note that Belgians increasingly had a number of alternative areas of employment to choose between: Germany, partly for nationalistic reasons, tried to lure Flemish workers to replace Polish migrants, while, both in France and in Belgium, employers in construction, brick making, and coal mining offered jobs to seasonal workers.[92]

Thus, it does not seem correct to say that the seasonal workers formed an unusually exploited or passive labor force. Although the number of Belgians employed as seasonal workers had begun to decline in the last years before World War I, this was less because of the French employers' attempts to replace them than because the Belgian economy had begun to revive and draw off more of the potential work force.[93]

The situation of the border workers in the Nord who commuted into France daily or weekly would appear to be a more typical case of the foreigners who undermine the situation of native workers. It seems clear that few of the border workers in the largest textile towns in the Nord— Lille, Roubaix, and Tourcoing—joined French labor unions or participated in strikes in the Nord. The clearest instance of how the Belgian border workers hurt the situation of French workers came during strikes in 1903 and 1904, when the border workers continued to work and helped cause the defeat of the strikes in Lille and Roubaix. It is also possible that French workers were more likely to see the border workers as weakening working-class solidarity because more of them after 1890 were single women who typically did not join unions as frequently. More of the workers who immigrated between the 1850s and 1880s had been single men or members of families that immigrated.[94]

The negative impact of the border workers, however, can be easily exaggerated. The failure of the strikes of 1903 and 1904 resulted from a number of factors, and it is not clear that the border workers' continuing to work was the major cause of the strikes' failure. Some of the most detailed accounts of the labor movement in the Nord during the period give it only minor significance. The more important cause, according to Robert Baker, was the splits between two groups of socialists, the Guesdist socialists in Lille and Roubaix and the independent socialists in Armentières. The Lille and Roubaix leaders had been preparing for a major strike in 1903 when, without their approval, the workers in Armentières launched a strike and pressed many of the workers in Lille and Roubaix to join them. The failure of this strike helped to defeat the attempt at a strike the following year in the same cities. Indeed, the whole socialist movement in the Nord nearly fell apart during these years. The socialists lost control of the city government of Roubaix in 1902 and of Lille in 1904, while rival socialist factions established themselves in the coal-mining regions, in Dunkerque along the coast, and in Armentières. The failure of the socialist union leaders to organize the border workers was probably as much a result of the problems of the French labor movement as it was a result of the border workers' special situation.[95]

When French and Belgian union leaders recognized the new situation created by the growing number of border workers, these Belgian workers did join unions and support strikes. What was necessary to mobilize the border workers was alliances between unions on both the French and Belgian sides of the border and alliances between socialists and Catholics. Alliances with the Catholics were crucial because the Belgian Catholics, along with organizing seasonal workers, had created unions among the border workers. During a 1910 strike in the French town of Halluin, right on the border with Belgium, for example, Catholic and socialist unions in Halluin and Catholic and socialist unions in the Belgian town of Meneen formed a joint strike committee. The help of the Belgian organizations, in fact, was crucial to the French workers in towns such as Halluin where many of the workers were commuting border workers.[96] After the failure of the 1903 strike, which had affected Halluin as well as Armentières, Roubaix, and Lille, French workers in Halluin broke their ties with the socialist textile union in Roubaix in part because the Belgian unions had helped them more than had the Roubaix union.[97]

It cannot be argued that the growth of Catholic unionism among the Belgian border workers and on both sides of the border were minor developments alongside the growth of French unionism in the Nord. Instead, in the period between the two world wars, the Belgians became much more well organized than the French workers' unions, and the links between the French and Belgian Catholic unions proved critical. In the largest textile strike in the Nord in the 1930s, the coalition of Belgian Catholic, Belgian socialist, and French Catholic unions was able to control the direction of the strike more than were the French communist and socialist unions.[98]

A natural question is why the Belgians' role in French labor history has so often been misunderstood. One major cause is that the hypernationalism of the period around 1900 led certain groups to emphasize the differences between the workers of the two countries. Until the late nineteenth century, the cooperation as well as the conflict between Belgians and French had been noted. The new nationalism obliterated the image of the militant Belgian cooperating with French workers and emphasized the Belgian as the conservative enemy of the French. The isolation and conservatism typical of many border and seasonal workers was taken to be the norm, the memory of the militants of the 1870s and 1880s was erased, and any militancy among border and seasonal workers was discounted. In 1882, the French socialists still defended the Belgians from those who accused foreigners of undermining the position of native workers: "In all strike and wage demands, the majority of Belgians whom one can find never weaken; they always keep to the end the energy necessary for success of the demands."[99] Aggressive nationalism and antiforeign prejudice in France, however, continued to grow, especially as Flemish Belgians were seen as part of the "Germanic" threat.[100] In 1910, the French Socialists supported a bill to levy a special tax on border workers to discourage their being hired, a bill that all Belgians bitterly attacked.[101] Like their French counterparts, the Belgian Socialists initially supported international solidarity. They criticized Flemish Belgians who resented having to use French: "The more languages a people knows, the more the borders shall disappear and the brotherhood of peoples shall be strengthened."[102] By the 1890s, however, a vehement Flemish nationalist movement tried to undermine the dominance of French-speaking Belgians over Flanders and to turn Belgian workers against French culture.[103] Flemish nationalists, who were usually Catholic, tried to smear the Socialists with being pro-French and antipatriotic: "the [Belgian] socialists are for internationalism, no more borders, and the French socialists throw out with disgust the Belgian workers who go to France to earn their bread."[104] When August Debunne, the socialist leader of the border workers, ran for reelection to Parliament in 1910, his supporters described the Catholics' propaganda against him as "nothing but attacks against France and great insults against deputy De-bunne."[105] The simultaneous rise of Flemish linguistic nationalism and of a dynamic Catholic labor movement in Belgium especially divided French and Belgians and made the two societies less alike. More and more literature and political discourse among Flemish Belgians went on in Dutch, which almost no educated French people understood, while French Catholics, unlike their Belgian counterparts, remained largely reactionary and without organized support among workers. The strength of the Catholic labor movement forced Belgian socialists to cooperate with the Catholics, something almost unthinkable between French socialists and Catholics.[106] The results were two societies that had become, despite their economic ties, estranged from each other and, as well, a host of scholars unable to believe French and Belgians had at one time had quite a different relationship.

Ethnicity and Labor

In conclusion, the case of the Belgians in France points up the persistence of the stereotype of the immigrant worker. Historians' use of the more theoretical, social scientific literature on contemporary Western European migration, has, if anything, reinforced the older tendencies among historians to see immigrants as passive and exploited and to see the cultural divisions between natives and immigrants as necessarily undermining labor solidarity.[107] Although the Belgians came to France from a country with higher unemployment and lower wages, they were sometimes more militant than French workers. Nor did the cultural divisions between natives and immigrants necessarily undermine solidarity between workers: where Catholic organizers and socialist leaders along the border took the initiative, even the difficult-to-organize border workers and seasonal agricultural workers formed unions.

The case of the Belgians also points out the dangers in overlooking the differences between immigrants of the same nationality. The differences between the militant Belgian strike leaders of the 1880 strike and the more conservative border workers of 1904 could be quite important. Both long-run economic changes and the crucial importance of leadership have to be taken into account to understand these differences between immigrant groups. Belgian migration shifted in the late nineteenth century from the settled textile workers to the temporary border workers and seasonal agricultural workers in response to declines in Belgian agriculture, a rise in French tariffs and prices, and changes in both French farming and textile production. As a result, new ways had to be found to organize Belgian immigrant workers in France. Where leaders found new ways, these workers could be organized;

where the French unions and socialist movements had to contend with
their own internal divisions and lack of leadership, this challenge was not
met.

The case of the Belgians in France and the literature on contemporary Western European immigration also suggest the continuing
question that immigration and ethnicity pose for labor mobilization. The
tendency, both among social scientists working on contemporary
Western European migration and among historians working on groups
such as the Belgians in the nineteenth century, has been to argue that
immigrants will fail to act in strikes and in unions because they are
especially exploited and socially isolated. Yet another trend in the
literature on labor, a trend going back to Marx, suggests that it is just
because they are exploited and isolated that workers are more likely to
be militant. Much of the social scientific literature on labor has failed to
resolve the paradox between these two points of view. Some labor
scholars, though not usually those working on migration, have suggested
that organization is a critical variable in determining whether an
exploited group becomes militant.[108] The case of the Belgians suggests
that ethnic or religious identity may help a group of workers organize
themselves. The Belgian migrants in France helped introduce socialism
and distinctive kinds of association such as consumer cooperatives
because their connection to Flemish comrades gave them ideas that
French workers lacked. Similarly, that so many of the border workers
and seasonal farm workers were Catholic meant that they could be
organized into distinctive Catholic workers' associations.

In short, the case of the Belgians in France seems to offer several
lessons: a healthy mistrust of any portrayal of immigrants as the
scapegoats for native workers' exploitation or lack of organization, an
openness to the long-run trends in population and political economy
that explain shifts in migration, and an increased awareness of the
complex ways in which workers mobilize themselves—drawing variously
on ethnicity, religion, or ideology.

Notes

1. Jean Stengers, "Les mouvements migratoires en Belgique aux XIXe et
XXe siècles," *Les migrations internationales de la fin du XVIIIe siècle à nos jours*
(Paris, 1980), 293; Firmin Lentacker, *La frontière franco-belge: Étude
géographique des effets d'une frontier internationale sur la vie de relations*
(Lille, 1974), 219, 238; Nancy L. Green, "'Filling the Void': Immigration to France
before World War I," *Labor Migration in the Atlantic Economies: The European
and North American Working Classes during the Period of Industrialization*, ed.
Dirk Hoerder (Westport, Conn., and London, 1984), 150.

2. [France, Chambre des Deputés,] *Enquête sur l'état de l'industrie textile et la condition des ouvriers tisseurs* [hereafter *Enquête*], 5 vols. (Paris, 1906), 2:289.

3. David Landes, "Religion and Enterprise: The Case of the French Textile Industry," *Enterprise and Entrepreneurs in Nineteenth- and Twentieth-Century France*, ed. Edward Carter et al., (Baltimore, 1976), 48. Landes's evidence is the conflicts between Belgian and French workers in 1819 and around 1848. The article by Franchomme that he cites on the later period actually points out the contribution of the Belgians to worker militancy. While citing an article by Lentacker on 1848, Landes overlooks his book, which contains information on the Belgians' militancy. Lentacker, *La frontière*, 250-51; G. Franchomme, "L'evolution démographique et èconomique de Roubaix dans le dernier tiers du XIX siècle," *Revue du Nord* 51, 201 (1969): 211-12.

4. Gary S. Cross, *Immigrant Workers in Industrial France: The Making of a New Laboring Class* (Philadelphia, 1983), 10.

5. Patricia Hilden, *Working Women and Socialist Politics in France, 1880–1914: A Regional Study* (Oxford, 1986), 19-20, also 65.

6. Leslie Page Moch, "Urban Structure, Migration, and Worker Militancy: A Comparative Study of French Urbanization," *Proletarians and Protest: The Roots of Class Formation in an Industrializing World*, ed. Michael Hanagan and Charles Stephenson (Westport, Conn, 1986), 117.

7. Michelle Perrot, *Les ouvriers en grève: France 1871–1890*, 2 vols. (Paris and The Hague, 1974), 1:169; Lentacker, *La frontière*, 250-51, 271-72.

8. Moch, 121. Moch's major source on the Belgians is Nicole Quillien, "La S.F.I.O. à Roubaix de 1905 à 1914," *Revue du Nord* 51 (1969): 277. Quillien cites no sources on the Belgians.

9. Laurent Marty, *Chanter pour survivre: Culture ouvrière, travail et techniques dans le textile Roubaix 1850–1914* (Lille, 1982), 115.

10. Lentacker, *La frontière*, 197, 227; P. Reboul, "Troubles sociaux à Roubaix en juillet 1819," *Revue du Nord* 36 (1954): 339-50.

11. Julian Theys and O. Vanneste, *Een analyse van de Grensarbeiders in Noord-Frankrijk* (Brugge, 1969), 27-30; Joel Mokyr, *Industrialization in the Low Countries, 1790–1850* (New Haven and London, 1976), 252-58.

12. Mokyr, 238-47.

13. Benoît Verhaegen, *Contribution à l'histoire économique des Flandres*, 2 vols. (Louvain and Paris, 1960), 1:73-77; Mokyr, 246; Lentacker, *La frontière*, 226.

14. Stengers, 293; Green, 150. "Belgians" were defined as Belgian citizens, both those born in Belgium and those born in France of Belgian citizens.

15. Franchomme, 202; *Enquête*, 2:166.

16. Lentacker, *La frontière*, 224.

17. Lentacker, *La frontière*, 228-29, 253-55; Stengers, 293-97; Jean Vidalenc, "Les belges dans l'agglomeration rouennaise en 1921," *Mélanges offerts à G. Jacquemyns* (Brussels, 1968), 646-59. The famous Catholic industrialist and progressive employer Leon Harmel, the "French Robert Owen," employed a large number of Belgians at his establishments at Val-du-Bois near Warmériville in northeastern France: in 1886, over 15 percent of Warmériville's population was Belgian. Almost all of these appear to come from the French-speaking provinces of Belgian Luxembourg and Liège. Pierre Trimouille, *Leon Harmel et l'usine chrétienne du Val du Bois, 1840–1914* (Lyon, 1974). I owe this reference to Joan Coffey.

18. Claude Fohlen, "Crise textile et troubles sociaux: Le Nord à la fin du Second Empire," *Revue du Nord* 35, 138 (1953): 107-23; Claude Zarka, "Un exemple de pole de croissance: L'Industrie textile du Nord de la France, 1830–1870," *Revue économique* 9, 1 (1958): 65-103.

19. Denise DeWeerdt, *De Gentse Textielbewerkers en Arbeidersbeweging tussen 1866 en 1881* (Leuven and Paris, 1959), 150-51; "Etat numerique des ouvriers qui ont quitté la ville pour aller travailler dans autres localités," Stadsarchief Gent, R7U, Ghent. In 1869, in Halluin near Lille, the outflow of Belgians left the "workshops deserted," Dominique Vermander, *Un siècle d'histoire ouvrier à Halluin, 1840–1940* (Halluin, 1978), 20. In addition, F. Lentacker, "Un épisode de la Révolution industrielle: Ouvriers à demeure, ouvriers immigrés dans l'industrie cotonnière de Roubaix de 1857 à 1864," *Revue du Nord* 69, 275 (1987): 767-75.

20. Luc Schepens, *Van Vlaskuter tot Franschman: Bijdrage tot de Geschiedenis van de Westvlaamse Plattelandsbevolkings in de negentiende eeuw* (Brugge, 1973), 125.

21. Franchomme, 211; Lentacker, *La frontière*, 232, 236-37, 251.

22. "Strijdpenning," *De Toekomst*, 2-3 Juni, 1883, 4.

23. Marty, 77; Franchomme, 211; Lentacker, *La frontière*, 249.

24. Lentacker, *La frontière*, 405; Stengers, 293; Schepens, 130.

25. Lentacker, *La frontière*, 237-38.

26. R. E. Tyson, "The Cotton Industry," in *The Development of British Industry and Foreign Competition, 1875–1914*, ed. Derek Aldcroft (Toronto, 1968), 115-17; E. M. Sigsworth and J. M. Blackman, "The Woolen and Worsteds Industries," in Aldcroft, 139-43.

27. Georges Eeckhout, "La crise lainière de Roubaix-Tourcoing," *Revue sociale catholique* 4 (1899–1900): 393-37; Franchomme, 239-40; *Enquête*, 2:214.

28. E. A. Wrigley, *Industrial Growth and Population Change: A Regional Study of the Coalfield Areas of North-West Europe in the Late Nineteenth Century* (Cambridge, 1962), 74; Norman G. Pounds and William N. Parker, *Coal and Steel in Western Europe* (Bloomington, Ind., 1957), 172-77; Marcel Gillet, "The Coal Age and the Rise of Coalfields in the Nord and Pas-de-Calais," *Essays in European Economic History*, ed. W. H. Chaloner et al. (London, 1969), 179-202.

29. Lentacker, *La frontière*, 238.

30. "Cost of Living of the Working Classes in the Principal Industrial Towns of Belgium," [United States] *Bulletin of the Bureau of Labor* 87 (1910): 612; *Enquête*, 2:382.

31. *Enquête*, 2:184; Robert P. Baker, "A Regional Study of Working-Class Organization in France: Socialism in the Nord, 1870–1920" (Ph.D. diss., Stanford, 1967), 113.

32. Auguste DeWinne, *A travers les Flandres* (Brussels, 1902), 109-10.

33. Theys and Vanneste, 36. Workers who commute across national borders are still an interesting group that is not taken into account by many scholars. One of the few studies is Charles Ricq, *Les travailleurs frontaliers en Europe* (Paris, 1981).

34. *Enquête*, 2:444-45; Emile Vandervelde, *L'exode rural et le retour aux champs* (Paris, 1903), 143; E. Mahaim, *Les abonnements d'ouvriers* (Brussels, 1910). The effect of French tariffs was also to encourage some French companies to establish factories in Belgium, often in the border region. Thus, border workers, by living in Belgium, could more easily take advantage of the possibility of working in either France or Belgium, especially with the aid of the Belgian government's transportation policy, *Enquête*, 2:191, 382.

35. "Les ouvriers travaillant hors frontiers," *L'union ouvrière*, 1 juin, 1901, 3.

36. *Enquête*, 2:448; Marty, 77-79.

37. Edmond Ronse, *L'émigration saisonnière belge* (Ghent, 1913), 35, 115-17, 136; U. Guffens, "L'émigration saisonnière de nos 'Franschmannen,'" *L'expansion belge* 4, 11 (1911): 308-11.

38. Abel Chatelain, *Les migrants temporaires en France de 1800 à 1914*, 2 vols. (Villeneuve d'Ascq, 1976), 2:682-87.

39. M. Lair, "Les ouvriers étrangers dans l'agriculture française," *Revue économique internationale* 4 (1907): 531-35.

40. Louis Banneaux, "L'industrie de la cordonnerie en pays flamand," *Revue sociale catholique* 4 (1899-1900): 375-80.

41. Benoît Bouché, *Les ouvriers agricoles en Belgique* (Brussels, 1913), 31-43, 139-48; B. Seebohm Rowntree, *Land and Labour: Lessons from Belgium* (London, 1911), 537; Jan Craeybeckx, "De Agrarische Depressie van het Einde der XIXe eeuw en de Politieke Strijd om de Boeren," *Belgisch Tijdschrift voor Nieuwste Geschiedenis/Revue belge d'histoire contemporaine [BTNG/RBHC]* 4, 1-2 (1973): 191-230, and 5, 1-2 (1974): 181-225. Belgian landholding patterns were complex: ownership was very widespread, with one of every ten people owning land and only twenty-seven people owning estates of 5,000 acres or more; on the other hand, most farmers did not own enough land to support themselves, since two-thirds of Belgian farmland was worked by tenants. See Rowntree, 543; Craeybeckx (1973), 195-96, 204-6. In contrast to Belgium, Britain, which also had free trade policies in agriculture, entered the late-nineteenth-century period of falling grain prices with much of its land already in the hands of large landowners and much more of its "surplus" agricultural population already moved to the cities. Only slowly, after 1900, did Belgium imitate Denmark and, through cooperatives, get its farmers and tenants to switch to poultry, dairying, and truck farming. E. J. Hobsbawm, *Industry and Empire* (London, 1968), 196-201; Abel Varzim, *Le Boerenbond Belge* (Paris, 1934).

42. Rowntree, 106-9.

43. Erik Griskov, "Home-Industry and Peasant Farming in Belgium. I," *The Contemporary Review* 90 (September 1906): 401.

44. Guffens, 311; Schepens, 215-24; Lentacker, *La frontière*, 194-95; Verhaegen, 1:314-16.

45. Rowntree, 205.

46. Hubert Wouters, *Documenten betreffende de Geschiedenis de Arbeidersbeweging ten tijde van de Ie Internationale (1866–1880)*, 2 vols. (Leuven, Paris, 1970-71), 1:198; DeWeerdt, *De Gentse*, 150-54; S. H. Scholl, *Bijdragen tot de Geschiedenis der Gentse Arbeidersbeweging (1815–1875)* (Brussels, 1957), 148-50, 156, 164, 169; Lentacker, *La frontière*, 227; Lentacker, "Un episode," 767-75.

47. Paul Kenis, *Het Leven van Edward Anseele* (Ghent, 1948), 86-95; Denise DeWeerdt, *De Belgische Socialistische Arbeidersbeweging op zoek naar een eigen vorm 1872–1880* (Antwerp, 1972), 81-97; DeWeerdt, *De Gentse*, 182-90.

48. Wouters, 2:1166-74; DeWeerdt, *De Belgische*, 85-87; Samuel Bernstein, *The Beginnings of Marxian Socialism in France* (New York, 1965), 116-63; Carl Strikwerda, "Regionalism and Internationalism: The Working Class Movement in the Nord and the Belgian Connection, 1871–1914," *Proceedings of the Western Society for French History*, ed. John Sweets, 12 (1984): 221-30.

49. Commissaire en Chef de Police de Tourcoing, to Prefect, 27 juin, 1881, and Victor Capart to Commissaire en Chef de Police de Tourcoing, 18 mars, 1882, M162,6, Archives Departementales du Nord, Lille [hereafter A.D.N.].

50. S. H. Scholl, *De Geschiedenis van de Arbeidersbeweging in West-Vlaanderen (1875–1914)* (Brussels, 1953), 55-56; "Meenen," "Kortrijk," *De Volkswil*, 28 December, 1879, 4; "Wervik," *De Volkswil*, February 29, 1880, 2; Commissaire en Chef de Police de Roubaix to Prefect, 29 décembre, 1879 and 1 mars, 1880, M 162,6, A.D.N.; Lentacker, *La frontière*, 240-1. The French

authorities noted that the Belgians had been organizing workers in the Nord since 1878, Reseau du Nord, Commissaire Special de Tourcoing, 28 janvier, 1884, A.D.N. Good examples of how recent historians on the Nord ignore the role of the Belgians are Bernard Simler, "Gustave Delory et les débuts du mouvement socialiste à Lille et dans la region du Nord sous la troisième Republique," *Les Pays-Bas Français. Annales/De Franse Nederlanden. Jaarboek* (1982), 117–19, where Simler never mentions the Belgians, although he points out that there were probably only a dozen "Guesdists" in the Nord in 1880, and William Reddy, *The Rise of Market Culture: The Textile Trade and French Society, 1750–1900* (Cambridge, 1984), 302-5, where he ignores the Belgians completely in his discussion of the 1880 strikes. Hilden, 139-44, also ignores the Belgians' role. The clearest example of dismissing the Belgians, however, is probably David Landes, see note 3.

51. "No. 6. Le socialisme en Belgique," 1886, M 162,5, A.D.N.

52. See note 48. It should also be pointed out that one of the earliest editions of Guesde's *Essai de catechisme socialiste* was published in Brussels in 1878.

53. Gendarmerie, Roubaix, 22 avril, 1880, F12 4660, Archives Nationales, Paris; Commissaire en Chef de Police de Tourcoing, 31 mars, M 162,6 A.D.N.; France, Office du travail, *Les associations professionnelles ouvrières*, 4 vols. (Paris, 1901), 2:385; Baker, 27-28; Perrot, 1:90.

54. Perrot, 1:169. On the strikes and the Belgians, Capart to Commissaire en Chef de Police de Roubaix, 31 mai, 1880, and Commissaire Special sur les Chemins de fer, Tourcoing, 7 mai, 1880, M162,6, A.D.N.; Prefect du Nord, Lille, 10 mai, 1880, F12 4660, Archives Nationales, Paris; *Enquête*, 2:227, 2:388; Jacques Marseille and Martine Sassier, "*Si ne veulent point nous rinquérir in va bientôt tout démolir!*" *Le Nord en grève, avril/mai 1880* (Paris, 1980), 80-81, 92-97, 116, 125-29. A good overview of the Belgians' relations with the Nord is Herman Balthazar and Nicole de Ryckere, "Betrekkingen tussen het socialisme in Vlaanderen en Noord-Frankrijk (1870–1914)," *De Franse Nederlanden. Jaarboek/Les Pay-Bas francais. Annales, 1979,* 11-29, although they underestimate the influence of Ghent on the Nord in the late 1870s and early 1880s.

55. Perrot, 1:90, 169, 287, 325, 355. On the unions: Office du travail, *Les associations*, 1:417-19, 2:386-88; Office du travail, *Annuaire des syndicats* (Paris, 1890), 178-80; Alexandre Zevaes, *Le syndicalisme contemporaine* (Paris, 1911?), 103; Baker, 33; Felix-Paul Codaccioni, "Développement d'une nebuleuse urbaine, 1851–1914," *Histoire d'une metropole: Lille-Roubaix-Tourcoing*, ed. Louis Trenard (Toulouse, 1977), 392-93. Charles Lefebvre, "Socialistes belges et française de la fin de l'empire au debut de la IIIe Republique," *Revue du Nord* 37 (1955): 191-98 provides a rather sketchy account of the role of the Belgians.

56. Ellen Furlough, "The Politics of Consumption: The Consumer Cooperative Movement in France, 1834–1930" (Ph.D. diss., Brown University, 1987), 179. I thank Professor Furlough for making her unpublished work available to me.

57. Furlough, 179. The role of the cooperatives in working-class life is described in Louise A. Tilly, "Rich and Poor in a French Textile City," *Essays on the Family and Historical Change*, ed. Leslie Page Moch and Gary Stark (College Station, Tex., 1983), 65-90.

58. Furlough, 180; *Enquête*, 2:316; Paul Descamps, "La Flandre française: L'ouvrier de l'industrie textile," *La science sociale* 24, 59 (June, 1909): 76-80.

59. Jean Gaumont, *Histoire générale de la cooperation en France*, 2 vols. (Paris, 1924), 2:274; Claude Willard, *Le mouvement socialiste en France (1893–*

1905) Les Guesdistes (Paris, 1965), 33, 138; Gustave Delory, *Aperçu historique sur la fédération de Nord 1876–1920* (Lille, 1921), 169; Baker, 56-62.

60. Lentacker, *La frontière*, 272. In many ways, socialists in Ghent were the key to the development of the entire Belgian socialist movement just as the Catholics in Ghent were for the Belgian Catholic labor movement. Carl Strikwerda, "The Divided Class: Catholics vs. Socialists in Belgium, 1880–1914," *Comparative Studies in Society and History* 30, 2 (1988): 333-59. Studying the connections between the Flemish and the Nord may also help illumine some unexplained developments among the socialists in the Nord. Hilden, for example, puzzles over the decline of an autonomous women's movment in the Nord in the 1890s. This was the same period when the Flemish socialists suppressed the same kind of movement in Ghent. Philip van Praag, "Emilie Claeys, 1855–1943," *Tijdschrift voor sociale geschiedenis* 4, 11 (1978): 190-92.

61. Cross, 12.

62. *Enquête*, 2:304-6.

63. *Enquête*, 2:285; Landes, 48-49.

64. *Enquête*, 2:468-69, 5:271-303.

65. Lentacker, 273; *Enquête*, 2:189. Wrigley makes a good case for considering Belgian migration to the Nord as a response to the demand for labor. Wrigley, 166.

66. Reardon argues that "during the latter part of the Second Empire with the flood of immigration from Belgium and from other parts of France, wages stagnated in Roubaix." She draws on the wage figures in the mayor's reports for the years 1864-71, the same years that saw a slump in Belgian migration to the Nord and an exodus of Belgians from France because of the recession following the end of the American Civil War. Reardon, 171, 182 and above, n. 19.

67. Jean-Pierre Daviet, "Le complexe industriel de Roubaix-Tourcoing et le marché de la laine (1840–1950)," *Revue du Nord* 69, 275 (October-December, 1987): 805-6.

68. Raoul Blanchard, *La flandre: Étude géographique de la pleine flamande en France, Belgique, et Hollande* (Dunkerque, 1906), 395-450, 457-59; Lentacker, *La frontière*, 72, 83; Franchomme, 217-18; *Enquête*, 2:381, 449, 465. The latest research on the textile industry in the Nord emphasizes the crucial importance of the markets and *entrepôts* of London, Liverpool, and Antwerp for the manufactures in the Nord Daviet, 793-94, 798-99.

69. Reardon, 172.

70. Moch, 117.

71. Louis Reybaud, *La Laine* (Paris, 1867), 212-13. Reardon cites this remark but discounts its importance.

72. Perrot, 1:164-76. Moch, 107, Reardon, 168-69, and Cross, 30, 233 n. 35, all cite Perrot's section on antiforeign violence but ignore the distinctions Perrot makes between the Nord and other regions and between the Belgians and other groups.

73. Lentacker, *La frontière*, 235. Reardon, 167, cites this report but discounts its importance.

74. Reardon, 171.

75. Nicholas Papayanis, *Alphonse Merrheim: The Emergence of Reformism in Revolutionary Syndicalism, 1871–1925* (Dordrecht, Neth., 1985), 3–19; Christian Gras, "La Fédération des Métaux en 1913-14 et l'évolution du syndicalisme revolutionaire française," *Le Mouvement social*, 77 (1971): 85-111; *Dictionnaire biographique du mouvement ouvrier français*, 17 vols. (Paris, 1973), 14:70-73. On the Italians in Lorraine, R. P. Serge Bonnet, "Political Alignments and Religious Attitudes within the Italian Immigration to the Metallurgical

Districts of Lorraine," *Journal of Social History* 2, 2 (1968):   123-55, is useful, although it concentrates on a later period.

76. Moch, 117.

77. *Enquête*, 2:240.

78. Lentacker, *La frontière*, 34, 268. Even after the strikes in 1903 and 1904, the chamber of commerce of Lille said that the "Belgians often take the lead in workers' movements in Halluin, Lille, and Armentières," which, as Lentacker points out, "should not be surprising since unionism is more powerful in Belgium than in France." Lentacker, *La frontière*, 273.

79. Reports, Prefect du Nord, 1880-83, F12 4660 and 1895, F12 4677, Archives Nationales, Paris.

80. Perrot, 1:352.

81. Edward Shorter and Charles Tilly, *Strikes in France, 1830-1968* (Cambridge, Mass., 1974), 276-77. Moch cites this statistic as well as Perrot's comment on Roubaix's high strike rate but nonetheless asserts that Belgians were important as strikebreakers. Her only examples are 1903 and 1904. Shorter and Tilly also found that between 1890 and 1914, the Nord had the second highest strike rate (strikes/100,000 workers) and striker rate (strikers/100,000) among the six most urbanized departments in France, 268.

82. [France, Direction du travail] *Statistique des grèves survenues en France pendant l'année 1892* (Paris, 1893), 87-92; Alain Dantoing, "Une manifestation de defense ouvrière contre le travail étrange dans les mines du Pas-de-Calais en 1892," *BTNG/RBHC* 4, 3-4 (1974): 427-45; Lentacker, *La frontière*, 34, 234.

83. Dantoing, 436. Also, *Statistique*, 90-92. Other incidents of hostility against Belgians by miners were reported, but it is not clear what the circumstances were or how typical they were. Cross, 30.

84. Ronse, 162-63.

85. Cross, 9-10, 20-22.

86. Lentacker, *La frontière*, 209-10, 255; G.-C. Rutten, *Algemeen Verslag over den Toestand des Christene Vakbeweging* (Ghent, 1911), 23; Chatelain 2:709, 713; Scholl, *De Geschiedenis*, 20-24; Ronse, 175-76, 193-99, 242-47. Cross only cites the French authorities having thrown out a team of Belgians who were organizing unions among the migrant workers. Cross, 31.

87. Chatelain, 1:220-27, 2:708, 718-20; Ronse, 52.

88. Lentacker, *La frontière* 211; Chatelain, 2:709-10, 720-22. Although Cross does not cite Chatelain's book or discuss the organizations and straw-boss system among the Belgian migrants, he does note that only 5,000 of the 20,000 Poles recruited to work in France continued to work there by 1914. Cross, 24-25. This appears to confirm the argument that the Belgians' straw-boss system worked to their advantage over the Poles.

89. Ronse, 127.

90. Ronse, 129, 177-9. Contrast this with the *padrone* system among Italian workers as summarized by David Montgomery, *The Fall of the House of Labor: The Workplace, the State, and American Labor Activism, 1865-1925* (New York, 1987), 75-77, 94-95.

91. Ronse, 58.

92. Blanchard, 515; Ronse, 150-51; Lentacker, *La frontière*, 211; Dirk Hoerder, "An Introduction to Labor Migration in the Atlantic Economies, 1815-1914," in *Labor Migration in the Atlantic Economies*, ed. Hoerder, 23, although Hoerder's reference to sources is unclear.

93. In 1890, fifteen Flemish arrondissements had work forces over 40 percent agricultural; by 1910, only nine did. The number of arrondissements where the work force was less than 30 percent agricultural went from three to nine. Ron

J. Lesthaeghe, *The Decline of Belgian Fertility, 1800–1970* (Princeton, N.J., 1977), 32.

94. In 1896, 4,000 of the 9,000 workers commuting from the Kortrijk and Ieper areas to Roubaix were women. Verhaegen, 1:316. Strictly comparable figures are unavailable from the earlier period, but it appears more of them were families or single males Balthazar, "Betrekkingen," 14.

95. Baker, 100-38, 207-10; Lentacker, *La frontière*, 271; Codaccioni, 397-401. It seems clear, furthermore, that socialist unionism around Lille grew significantly only *after* the failure of the 1903 and 1904 strikes, while the number of border workers continued to climb. The number of unionists in Lille went from 5,437 in 1904 to 14,922 in 1908; in Roubaix from 2,327 to 12,200 although the number there had been about 5,000 in the late 1890s. Codaccioni, 399.

96. Lentacker, *La frontière*, 272; Vermander, 27, 46-49, 53; Marinus DeRijcke, *August Debunne en de Werkersbeweging in het arrondissement Kortrijk* (Brussels, 1931), 68-69, 143.

97. DeRijcke, 98-100; Vermander, 44; Baker, 214; *Dictionnaire*, 1:324-25; Scholl, *De Geschiedenis*, 77-78; Lentacker, *La frontière*, 271.

98. Michel Launay, "Le syndicalisme chrétien dans un grand conflit du travail," *Le mouvement social* (1970): 39-78; Jean-Yves Derville, "Les débuts de la C.F.T.C. du l'arrondissement de Lille (1919–1931)," *Revue du Nord* 51, 203 (1969): 603-28; Lentacker, *La frontière*, 277-79. Cross points out the superiority of the Belgian unions, 145, but does not take this into account in his discussion of the earlier period.

99. "Une reponse," *Le forcat*, 22 octobre, 1882, 1 (Perrot 1:175 incorrectly cites this as 1885).

100. Baker, 84-85, 97, 158-60; Lentacker, *La frontière*, 165, 209, 211.

101. Lentacker, *La frontière*, 208, 270. Belgian Catholics used the French socialists' position to smear both countries' socialists, "Uit Ruyen," *De Textilebewerker* (1910), 43.

102. "Willemfonds," *De Toekomst*, 27 November, 1881, 3.

103. Shepherd B. Clough, *The History of the Flemish Movement in Belgium* (New York, 1930); Carl Strikwerda, "Language and Class Consciousness: Netherlandic Culture and the Flemish Working Class," *Papers from the First Interdisciplinary Conference on Netherlandic Studies*, ed. William Fletcher (Lanham, Md., and London, 1985).

104. "Socialistische Kluchtspelers," *De Vrije Kiezer* 12 October, 1899, 3; Lentacker, *La frontière*, 274.

105. "L'insulté," *L'avenir* (avril 1910), 2; DeRijcke, 137.

106. On French Catholicism's conservatism, Pierre Pierrard, *L'église et les ouvriers en France* (Paris, 1984); on the Western European context, Carl Strikwerda, "Catholic Working Class Movements in Western Europe," *International Labor and Working Class History* 34 (1988): 70-85. It is true that the Nord was one area of France where the Catholic community eventually developed an important labor organizations, but in doing so it was at least a generation behind much of Belgium and was, in fact, heavily influenced by the Belgians. Y.-M. Hilaire, "Les ouvriers du Nord devant l'Eglise catholique (XIXe et XXe siècles)," *Le mouvement social* 57 (1966): 181-201.

107. Reardon, 173; Cross, 1-5, 213-25.

108. Shorter and Tilly, commenting appropriately on the Nord among other examples, 255-83; Craig Calhoun, "Community," in *History and Class*, ed. R. S. Neale (Oxford, 1982), 108-9.

5

Scapegoating the Foreign Worker: Job Turnover, Accidents, and Diseases among Polish Coal Miners in the German Ruhr, 1871–1914

John J. Kulczycki

The expansion of the coal-mining industry in the Ruhr region of the Rhineland and Westphalia in the second half of the nineteenth century resulted in an enormous increase in the demand for labor. Between 1850 and 1913 the work force in the mines multiplied more than thirty times, from 12,741 workers to 394,569.[1] This demand exceeded the capacity of the local population and drew migrants into the region from increasingly greater distances. In the 1870s these, for the first time, included groups of Polish-speaking inhabitants of eastern Prussia, that is, Upper Silesia (the Opole [Oppeln] regency or subprovince of Silesia) and the provinces of East Prussia, West Prussia, and Poznania (Posen)—a legacy, in part, of Prussia's participation in the partitioning of the Polish-Lithuanian Commonwealth in the eighteenth century.

This article was made possible by a travel grant from the Campus Research Board of the University of Illinois at Chicago and by a research grant from the Joint Committee on Eastern Europe of the American Council of Learned Societies and the Social Science Research Council, financed in part by the National Endowment for the Humanities and the Ford Foundation. An earlier version of this article appeared in *Polish American Studies* 46, 1 (1989): 42–60, and has been reprinted here with permission.

Already in 1893 a survey found that about 14 percent of the work force in the mines spoke Polish or the closely related Masurian language.[2] By 1897, those whose mother tongue was Polish—excluding noncitizen, Masurian, or bilingual miners—amounted to 18.6 percent of the Ruhr's miners.[3] Later surveys of the work force of the Ruhr's mines took no account of language, but the portion born in the Prussian East grew virtually every year, from 25.5 percent in 1898 until it peaked in 1908 at 37.9 percent. Because the percentage of eastern migrants from Poznania, Germany's sole province with a Polish-speaking majority, similarly increased from 35.6 percent in 1898 to 41.9 in 1914, one can assume that the portion of the work force that spoke Polish as its native language also continued to expand.[4]

Thus, as the industrialization of the Ruhr progressed, the work force of its mines took on an increasingly alien character. Though Prussian subjects and German citizens, many of the migrants from the East spoke a foreign language previously not heard in the Ruhr. Most of them also were new to mining and even to industrial labor. Whereas initially the Ruhr mines sent agents to recruit Polish-speaking miners in Upper Silesia, migrants from the predominantly agricultural regions of the East soon overwhelmed them. In 1898 the migrants born in Upper Silesia amounted to only 10 percent of the Ruhr's miners from the East and by 1910 declined to a low of 7 percent.[5]

Furthermore, this doubly "foreign" population heightened its impact by concentrating in the northern part of the Ruhr, where new mines were being sunk, rather than around the older, southern mines. The very process of migration also led to a denser population of migrants in certain areas. Agents sent to the East recruited for a particular mining company. Once a migrant established himself, he drew relatives and acquaintances from his home village to the same locale. As a result, certain mines came to be known as "Polish" mines: those where over half the work force came from the East. In 1900 there were already a dozen such mines or shafts, with Ewald I/II, 88.65 percent of whose work force had been born in the East, heading the list.[6] This led to jokes about an entire work force of a mine having the same Polish grandmother; it also led to cries of alarm about a "Polish peril."[7]

The expansion of the Ruhr's coal-mining industry that brought about the influx of migrants from the Prussian East stemmed from a number of technological, economic, and legal developments that transformed the very character of the industry in the second half of the nineteenth century. Initially, mining in the region confined itself to the area along the Ruhr River, where the coal lay near the surface. Only in the 1840s did technical advances permit the exploitation of the richer, but increasingly deeper, coal deposits further north. The coming of the railroads further facilitated this process of expanding production at the same time as it opened up new markets for the Ruhr's coal. Increased demand for coal made possible the greater capital investment required by these new mines, which by the 1860s often began operations as large-scale enterprises with several hundred workers, in contrast to the family-run operations of the early part of the century.[8] Meanwhile, seeking to promote production, the Prussian government issued a series of laws between 1851 and 1865 by which the state abandoned direct management of the mines within its territory, including the Ruhr, turning this function over to the private owners and retaining for itself only a regulatory role.[9]

These developments had profound consequences for the miners of the Ruhr as well as for the region's population as a whole. As a result of the legal changes, miners lost the special privileges that had given them the status of a corporate body. The creation of large-scale enterprises also affected working conditions. The spread of these enterprises northward into rural areas fundamentally altered these areas' social and economic character and introduced the ills of modern industrialism into a formerly isolated agrarian society. All this occurred while a growing number of eastern migrants came into the region. Although part of the transformation of the Ruhr, the Polish-speaking miners seem more rightly viewed as an effect rather than a cause of many of the changes in question. Yet the coincidence of their arrival with these changes and their vulnerability led to their becoming scapegoats for many of the negative repercussions of these developments. It was easier to blame the foreign migrants than to challenge the abstract and concrete forces behind the transformation of the Ruhr. Even recent accounts of the history of the Ruhr perpetuate stereotypes of the migrants that lack general validity.

The conditions and attitudes that the migrants from the East encountered in the Ruhr combined with the attitudes that they brought with them. From this mix came their response, which in turn became an ingredient in the changing conditions in the Ruhr. Central to these dynamics was the mine, the workplace to which most of the male migrants came to the Ruhr to seek employment. Life in the mines and the relations there between the migrant and his fellow workers, as well as between him and his employers and their representatives, stood at the heart of his life and that of the Ruhr's working class.[10] Thus, in our examination of the Polish-speaking miners as scapegoats, we will focus on the stereotypes of the migrants that relate to their role in the mines.

Job Turnover

A high rate of job turnover in all large-scale enterprises characterized the period of rapid industrialization after about 1880, but it apparently affected the Ruhr mining industry more than others.[11]

According to mine inspector reports, in 1898 as many as 40 to 110 men left an individual mine each month.[12] In 1913, when the mines had an average work force of 409,271 workers, the mines hired a total of 318,719 miners while 282,518 left work. In the years 1896 through 1913, the annual average turnover rate varied from 89 percent to 147 percent of the work force.[13] (Turnover is all new hirees plus those leaving.) Some miners took up work and quit at more than one mine per year and thereby inflated the total turnover, but a considerable number of miners must still have participated in the practice.

This high turnover rate could have negative consequences for both the mine owners and their workers. According to a report of a mine inspector in Bochum in 1897, "The accident rate is highest at those mines at which there is a higher turnover of workers and lowest at mines with a permanent work force."[14] Besides supposedly impairing safety, the turnover rate took the blame for raising the industry's administrative costs, encumbering planning, causing competition for workers, requiring constant training periods, and thereby lowering productivity.[15] Trade unionists might also regard frequent job changing as a hindrance to the organization of the workers in defense of their interests at a particular mine or in a particular community.[16]

Observers commonly connected the rise in the job turnover rate with the increase in migrants from the East, even more specifically with the Polish-speaking migrants. A widely noted account issued by the anti-Polish Pan-German League in 1901 put it this way: "Among the Poles there are many 'runners,' who are not long satisfied at any mine and quit at the least excuse, tie up their bundle after fourteen days, and go to work at another mine."[17] Another contemporary, more sympathetic to the migrants, noted, "Job turnover is especially high among unmarried workers and the Poles."[18] Indeed, the turnover rate in the mines in the northern part of the Ruhr, which drew the bulk of the migrants from the East, considerably exceeded the rate in the southern part of the Ruhr.[19] In a dissertation written in 1910, a mine official attributed this disparity to the rapid development of mining in the northern Ruhr region, which prevented mines there, unlike those in the southern Ruhr, from creating a stable work force that grew with the mines. Yet he added that the foreign migrants had no great interest in remaining in one place and their negative traits, especially "their unsteady [*unsteter*] character," often influenced native miners to be untrue to their traditions.[20] A leading German social historian of the Ruhr miners, Klaus Tenfelde, also claimed that the Poles exhibited greater geographic mobility in the Ruhr than their fellow migrants from the East, the Masurians.[21] He apparently accepted the charge against the Poles of being the "birds of passage" of the region and attributed this trait to their strong will to improve their situation.[22]

A closer examination of the statistics on job turnover in the Ruhr's mines, however, indicates that the migrants from the East had no more to do with its increase than other miners and probably even less than others. Although job changing in the mines reached its prewar peak in 1913, it did not rise steadily.[23] Its ups and downs do not parallel those of the proportion of eastern migrants among the Ruhr's miners. Interruptions in the rise of the turnover rate in 1901 and 1908 suggest that it derived from the state of the economy rather than the number of eastern migrants. Job turnover had its source more in demand for laborers than in their place of origin. Periods of economic expansion and labor shortage offered opportunities, or at least seemed to offer opportunities, for better pay that led many miners to quit their jobs at one mine and seek employment at another. Thus we might see job turnover as part of the workers' struggle against employers for higher wages.[24]

In 1900, the job turnover rate equaled 120 percent of the Ruhr's total work force (68 percent of the total having taken up employment and 52 percent having left employment at a particular mine that year), a level that was not exceeded until 1907.[25] A breakdown of the turnover rate by mining district in that year shows that the highest rate, 149 percent of the work force, occurred in two districts: Recklinghausen East and Oberhausen.[26] According to a survey on January 1, 1900, the first of these ranked third highest among the seventeen mining districts in the percentage of miners born in the East, but Oberhausen had only two-thirds of the average percentage of eastern migrants for the entire Ruhr among its miners.[27] Moreover, of the seven districts with above average turnover rates, only one other besides Recklinghausen East had an above average percentage of miners from the East. Indeed, one of the seven, Werden, had the lowest percentage (4.57 percent) of miners from the East of all the Ruhr's districts!

Of course, even Werden had enough miners born in Germany's eastern provinces for them to account for, or be blamed for, all of the district's job turnover in 1900. But this seems even less likely if we focus our attention on the districts most heavily populated with eastern migrants. Of the seven mining districts with above average percentages of eastern migrants among their miners, five had below average turnover rates. Gelsenkirchen, which had the highest percentage (52.48 percent) of eastern migrants among its miners, actually had a turnover rate 5 percentage points below average. Since Gelsenkirchen had the largest number of migrants from East Prussia of all the Ruhr's mining districts, one might be tempted to take this as a reflection of a low turnover rate among Masurians, who came from that province, as compared with Poles. But the Herne mining district, which had the highest percentage of migrants from *Polish* Poznania and the second highest percentage of all migrants from the East among its miners, had a lower turnover rate (111 percent) than Gelsenkirchen.

The limited data on turnover rates at individual mines confirm the conclusion that the stereotypical image of the eastern migrant as chiefly responsible for the high turnover rate had no basis in reality. In a study that gives the turnover rates for 122 mines in 1900, of the 9 "Polish" mines (those where migrants from the East constituted a majority of the work force), only 3 had a rate above the average.[28] A list of 35 mines with above average rates of turnover in 1899 includes only 2 mines, Unser Fritz and König Ludwig, out of 11 "Polish" mines on January 1, 1900.[29] Even at Unser Fritz, the turnover rate exceeded the average (114 percent in 1899) only at one of its two shafts (where it stood at 120 percent) and not at the other (100 percent), or for the mine as a whole (110 percent). (It is noteworthy that at the former shaft, an absolute majority of migrants from the East came from East Prussia and therefore probably included many Masurians, while at the latter shaft with the lower turnover rate the number from Poznania approaches that of the plurality from East Prussia.) As for König Ludwig, its high number of miners who left the mine in 1899 resulted in part from a wildcat strike that occurred in June of that year at König Ludwig and several other nearby mines.

The mine with the highest turnover rate in the list from 1899 was the Neumühl mine in Hamborn with a rate of 213 percent, yet on January 1, 1900, only 12.39 percent of its work force stemmed from the East.[30] The mine with the second highest turnover rate, Concordia I with 203 percent, had a percentage of miners from the East significantly above average, 38.99 percent as compared to 29.95 percent for the Ruhr as a whole, but its high turnover rate came at least in part from conditions specific to the mine.[31] Over all, at the six mines or shafts with the highest turnover rates, each with rates greater than 150 percent of the average rate in 1899, migrants constituted only 26.55 percent of the work force, although very nearly half of them came from Poznania.

Another list of fifteen mines or shafts with above average turnover rates in 1903 includes none of the "Polish" mines or shafts of 1900 or 1906.[32] Indeed, only one of them, König Ludwig IV/V with the fourth highest turnover rate, had an above average proportion of eastern migrants in its work force two years later.[33] Concordia IV/V, which had the highest turnover rate of all, over three times the average rate, in 1905 still had less than two-thirds the average percentage of eastern migrants.

The most complete information on the turnover rate at individual mines dates from 1906.[34] Out of 172 mines or shafts, 14 had a turnover rate over 150 percent of the average for the Ruhr as a whole but at only 4 of these 14 did the percentage of eastern migrants exceed the average, at only 1 by more than 2 percentage points. Of the 29 "Polish" mines or shafts in the list, only 7 had above average turnover rates. At some mines a significantly higher percentage of eastern migrants employed at one shaft than at another of the same mine correlated with a lower turnover rate. Perhaps the most striking example of this occurred at the General Blumenthal mine, where shafts III/IV, nearly a quarter of whose work force came from the East, had a turnover rate of 99 percent, while shafts I/II with nearly double the portion of eastern migrants had a turnover rate more than a third lower.[35]

These data for individual mining districts and mines cover only a limited period of time, but one of high migration from the East, and they therefore should reflect the behavior of the many new arrivals. The Duisburg district, for which we have statistics for all except two years from 1897 through 1908, had a turnover rate far higher than the Ruhr as a whole, yet it had few migrants from the East.[36] Significantly, Duisburg also had many new mines, as did the Oberhausen and Recklinghausen East mining districts. This may take us further toward explaining a higher turnover rate than the number of migrants. The Neumühl mine began to produce coal only in 1897.[37] Both the König Ludwig IV/V and the Concordia IV/V pits opened after 1900. The same was true of the four mines of the Hamm mining district, which in 1906 had a turnover rate of 221 percent, more than twice as high as the Ruhr as a whole, but just over half the average percentage of miners born in the East.[38] Without a settled, experienced work force, new mines had to offer higher pay to attract workers, who then may have found conditions worse than in the older, well-established mines, which resulted in a high number of both new arrivals and departures.

In choosing to migrate from the Prussian East to the Ruhr, an individual showed a willingness to move in search of higher pay and better working conditions. One Polish miner from Upper Silesia who migrated to the Ruhr in 1889 later addressed in his memoirs the question of why so many were willing to leave home, and noted that the pay was much better in the Ruhr—five to six marks per shift for a hewer in the Ruhr compared with two to three marks in Upper Silesia.[39] In addition, he claimed workers encountered better treatment in the Ruhr than in the mines of Upper Silesia. But proof is lacking that the Polish-speaking miners deserved the sobriquet of "birds of passage."

A study of the attitudes of the Polish immigrant of peasant origin in America indicated that the greater importance he attached to income did not necessarily result in frequent job changing and could even have led to considerable stability. "The peasant begins to search, not only for the best possible remuneration for a given amount of work, but for the opportunity to do as much work as possible. No efforts are spared, no sacrifice is too great, when the absolute amount of income can be increased."[40] Such an individual accepts hardship and bad treatment as part of the price of a higher income.[41] He sees work as an undesirable but necessary means of obtaining the money he seeks. Instead of changing jobs at the "slightest hope of immediate improvement, and without regard to the future (as expressed in contract-breaking and wandering from place to place), the peasant now begins to appreciate more and more the importance of a steady job."[42]

Unlike the miner from Upper Silesia to the Ruhr, most migrants from the East did not find employment in their old line of work, and the work was harder and more monotonous than that which they had been used to. Devoid of attraction in and of itself, the job also offered no security and therefore prevented the making of long-term plans. At the same time, the migrant had no great fear of losing a job because of the belief that he would sooner or later find another one.

> This whole set of conditions—to which must be added, as the first disturbing influence, the very fact of leaving the old economic status in search of new opportunities—acts upon the former tendency acquired from tradition and early experience to regard economic situations as essentially permanent and future possibilities as limited to a certain narrow field. The effect is the opposite tendency to live as if economic life were devoid of any general and stable schemes or principles, "from hand to mouth." This effect is, however, usually counteracted by other causes. The most important of these is the desire of the immigrant to acquire property by saving. . . . If the conditions are propitious for the satisfaction of this desire, i.e., if the immigrant earns enough to increase his savings continuously and he feels himself advancing to the status of a property owner, a new kind of economic life-organization, resulting from a permanent economic ideal, substitutes itself for the old one, which was a matter of habit due to the stability of external conditions.[43]

Polish organizations in the Ruhr could reinforce this tendency toward stability. "The immigrant who comes to an older, coherent community finds certain already established social schemes of economic life which, though they differ from those he knew and followed in the old country, are relatively easily understood and imitated."[44]

Accidents

The principal calamity that could befall a worker was the loss of his capacity to earn a living, which alone allowed him any autonomy.[45] Miners, in fact, suffered from a higher and earlier rate of disability than those in other occupations: in 1907, 14 percent of those in their thirties, over a third of those in their forties, and 65 percent of those over fifty were invalids.[46] Consequently, they had an overriding concern for safety and health in the mine. The miners' unions reflected this concern by publicizing in alarmist tones the annual statistics on accidents: in this connection, in 1903 one union declared, "The sea of blood is rising."[47] This was not sheer demagoguery. In Germany more accidents occurred in mining than in any other occupation, and it ranked second highest on a per capita basis.[48] Worse, its rate of accidental fatalities significantly exceeded that of the mining industry in France, Belgium, or England.[49]

While concern for their common safety could unite the miners in solidarity, it could divide them if one group widely viewed another within its own ranks as the chief culprit in a rising tide of accidents. This was indeed the case, with the Polish-speaking migrants again serving as the scapegoats, diverting attention from factors and agents that contributed more to an increase in accidents than did the migrants. As early as 1882, a newly formed miners' association in Gelsenkirchen opposed the hiring of Polish workers for reasons of safety.[50] Both Christian social and socialist elements in the labor movement, as well as contemporary commentators and even modern scholars blamed the eastern migrants, especially the Polish-speaking ones, for a growth in mining accidents that accompanied their arrival in the Ruhr.[51] Officials also voiced the same opinion. Thus, for example, in a report in 1896, the *Bergamt,* or state mining office of the Herne district, attributed an increase in accidents "in large part to ineptitude, especially of the Polish worker," though it also noted that the work force had grown in size and some workers involved in small accidents reported them simply out of a desire for a pension.[52]

In addition to the appeal of attributing negative developments to outsiders, this conclusion had its logic. The migrants from the East generally lacked mining experience and German-language ability, which hindered communication. Both Poles and Germans saw the language difference as of primary importance for the question of safety in the mines. Stanislaw Wachowiak, an activist in the Polish labor movement in the Ruhr before 1914, implicitly acknowledged the responsibility of Polish-speaking migrants for the high accident rate by insisting that "the sole means of preventing accidents" would be to post mine safety regulations in the Polish language.[53] A contemporary German observer similarly believed the lack of a knowledge of German together with the absence of translations of mining regulations bore "a large part of the guilt."[54] In fact, German unions joined Poles in demanding such translations, similar to those that existed at that time in the mines of Pennsylvania.[55]

The Prussian authorities, however, drew the opposite conclusion and attempted to exclude from the mines those who did not understand German while, for political reasons, refusing to permit the posting of regulations in Polish.[56] After the nationalist Pan-German League published its study of the Poles in the Ruhr in 1901 that linked them with the high accident rate, the head of the Prussian mining authority in the Ruhr, Otto Taeglichsbeck, sent copies to all district mine officials and insistently directed them to oversee the strict enforcement of ordinances, including ones dating from 1899 that prohibited the employment of Poles from outside of Germany in the mines of the Ruhr and that restricted the employment of Polish-speaking German citizens to those who demonstrated a sufficient knowledge of German.[57] Only at the end of this directive did he ask that the officials gather information on whether in fact, as seemed obvious to him, migrants ignorant of the German language and of local conditions contributed to the rise in accidents.

Accidents also allegedly stemmed from certain practices linked with eastern migrants. A desire for the highest possible earnings supposedly led Poles to ignore safety regulations.[58] Moreover, the assumption that they engaged in frequent job changing, which supposedly contributed to a growth in accidents, again put the onus on the eastern migrants.[59]

Just what the statistical evidence suggests with regard to a connection between an increase in accidents in the mines of the Ruhr and the migrants from the Prussian East or Polish-speaking miners obviously depends on what statistics one chooses. As usual the available statistics are incomplete and vary in their bases. In itself even a correlation between an increase in accidents and migrants proves nothing unless one assumes there were no other relevant variables, which hardly seems likely considering the changes occurring in the Ruhr's mining industry at this time. But a search for suitable scapegoats has no need to take such considerations into account.

Accidental fatalities in the mines of the Ruhr actually began to exceed those in France and Belgium by a significant margin already after 1869, well before the arrival of any Polish-speaking migrants.[60] Of course, the Ruhr then drew other migrants, often just as inexperienced in mining. The leading historian of the miners of the Ruhr in this period connects increases in fatal accidents with peaks in migration into the Ruhr in 1856-57, the 1860s, 1868-71, and 1880-83, only the last of which included a large number of migrants from the Prussian East.[61]

Between 1886 and 1907, the number of fatal accidents per thousand miners actually fell substantially, but no commentator has connected this to the high rate of migration from the Prussian East during the same two decades.[62] After the turn of the century, fluctuation in the number of accidental deaths in the Ruhr mines seems to have had no relation to the rate of migration.[63] Even the proportion of victims from the East does not differ greatly from their proportion in the work force.

The rate of certain other serious accidents also declined between 1886 and 1907. The rate of accidents resulting in a miner's permanent complete incapacity to work actually diminished by 50 percent.[64] The rate of accidents resulting in permanent partial incapacity rose until 1892, just before the flood of migrants from the East began, and then declined. Indeed, only the rate of the least serious accidents, those resulting in a temporary incapacity to work, rose with the increase in the number of eastern migrants in the Ruhr work force.

The main statistical argument made for linking eastern migrants to mining accidents focuses on statistics from the early twentieth century that indicate that more eastern migrants than other German citizens suffered injuries in the mines that rendered them temporarily unable to work.[65] This argument takes no account of the differences in employment between the migrants and other German citizens although, according to the testimony of the head of the foremen's association, Poles worked at more dangerous, deeper mines while the statistics on other German citizens include those who filled the ranks of the safer positions of mine officials.[66] Moreover, those who use these statistics ignore others from after 1907 that show the accident rate among eastern migrants to be equal to, and in some years even lower than, their proportion in the work force.[67] Yet the number of eastern migrants among Ruhr miners peaked only in 1913, at a level 27.6 percent above that of 1907.

The only extensive statistics on the accident rate at individual mines and shafts, covering 172 of them in 1906, cast further doubt on any link between accidents and the eastern migrants.[68] Of the 8 mines or shafts with at least one and a half times the average accident rate, only 3 had a work force with an above average percentage of eastern migrants—by only 1 percent. At the same time, the "Polish" mines or shafts had a below average accident rate in 18 cases and an above average rate in only 9 cases, with 2 exactly average rates.

Observers and historians blithely cite other cases that at least indirectly link the rise in accidents to the eastern migrants. Thus we find repeated, without comment, the report of a mine inspector of the Bochum district of 1897 in which he claimed that accident rates were highest at the mines with a high turnover of laborers and lowest at those with stable work forces like the Hannover and Hannibal mines.[69] As we have seen, the high turnover of workers in the mines of the Ruhr was widely attributed to the eastern migrants and Poles, in particular. But no one citing this report noted that in 1897 both of the mines referred to as having low accident rates had substantial numbers of Polish-speaking miners: 406 at Hannover and 240 at Hannibal.[70] While in 1900 only one pit of these two mines had an above average percentage of miners born in the Prussian East, the migrants nevertheless constituted a sufficiently large portion of the work force at the other pits at these mines to adversely affect the accident rate if they were particularly accident prone: 40.56 percent of the work force at Hannover I/II, 22.83 percent at Hannover III, 24.55 percent at Hannibal I, and 18.53 percent at Hannibal II compared to 29.95 percent for the Ruhr as a whole.[71] One must conclude on the basis of this and other evidence that stigmatizing the eastern migrants with responsibility for accidents seems unwarranted.

Diseases

Disease posed an even greater threat of incapacitating miners than accidents. For example, in the Ruhr in 1903, accidents rendered 15.7 percent of them temporarily unable to work, whereas illness similarly affected 61.3 percent.[72] This rate of illness considerably exceeded that of all German workers and even all German miners in the same year: 36 percent for the former and 52 percent for the latter.[73] Both accidents and illness could impose heavy financial burdens on the victims and their dependents. The *Knappschaft*, the miners' pension and insurance fund, did not compensate workers for the first three days of sick leave and thereafter only at about a quarter (after 1903 about a half) the level of the average wage.[74]

As with the rise in mining accidents, many observers found a convenient explanation for the contagion of diseases among miners in the migrants from the Prussian East along with other "foreigners." August Brust, the leader of the Christian miners' union, in a speech in 1897 blamed the spread of illnesses such as hookworm on "foreign or Galician [Austrian] workers," apparently referring as well to the migrants from the East who, like most Galicians, spoke Polish.[75] In 1904 the annual report of the Medical Department of the Prussian Ministry of Religion and Education mentioned Poles together with "Russians and Galicians"—probably meaning the Polish-speaking citizens of Russia and Austria—as propagators of several diseases including smallpox, typhus, and trachoma.[76] Trachoma, which can result in blindness, and hookworm, which brings on severe incapacitating symptoms, even death, spread among miners in the late nineteenth and early twentieth centuries. In blaming the eastern migrants for the spread of disease in the Ruhr, observers claimed that the migrants brought it with them from their homeland, where allegedly it was endemic.[77] The migrants' daily habits and their lack of understanding supposedly hindered any progress against the diseases by medical means.[78] Observers also cited a propensity to drink, but above all a "frightful lack of cleanliness" as the source of the migrants' ills.[79]

Certain statistics from these years do indicate a greater prevalence of these diseases among the Ruhr miners born in the Prussian East: in

1905, for example, 5.2 percent of them as opposed to 2.2 percent of other German citizens and 3.8 percent of foreign citizens could not work because of trachoma, and 2.4 percent as opposed to 1.5 and 2.0 percent, respectively, suffered from hookworm.[80] Such statistics have led some to conclude that the mines with the fewest migrants had the best health situation.[81]

Diseases like hookworm, however, spread quite sporadically. According to a police report on its prevalence at eleven mines in 1903, when hookworm reached epidemic proportions, all four of the mines on the list where 10 percent or more of the work force had come down with the illness had less than an average percentage of eastern migrants. The two mines on the list that in 1905 had a majority of eastern migrants reported only 6 cases among 725 workers at one mine and none among 1,500 at the other.[82] A ministerial report in November 1903 on hookworm in the various mining districts of the Ruhr further contradicts the assumption of a particular concentration in those with a large portion of eastern migrants among their miners.[83] Of 380 cases, in 1912, nearly half occurred in the Oberhausen district, which had a slightly less than average proportion of eastern migrants among its miners, and over a quarter of the cases occurred in the Herne district, where almost half the miners were eastern migrants, while the Gelsenkirchen district, which had the highest proportion of miners from the East, had only 4 cases of hookworm.[84]

A different picture of the relationship between eastern migrants and diseases among the Ruhr's miners emerges from other statistics. In 1903, of 18 mines where on average over 100 percent of the work force missed work for three days or more due to illness, only 7 mines had a larger portion of eastern migrants than average and only 4 had work forces that two years later had a majority of miners born in the East.[85] In 1906, out of 12 mines or shafts (in a list of 172) that had an illness rate a third or more above average, 5 exceeded the average percentage of eastern migrants for the Ruhr, but only 2 by more than 3 percentage points.[86] That same year the "Polish" mines and shafts had a lower than average illness rate in nineteen cases and exceeded the average in only nine instances.

In 1903 and 1904 the eastern migrants' rate of illness from diseases other than hookworm was lower than that of other German citizens among the Ruhr's miners.[87] It exceeded the latter in 1905 and 1906 but fell below it again in the following years, when the absolute number of eastern migrants among Ruhr miners peaked. Statistics for 1910 and later years indicate a significantly lower rate of illness, including hookworm, among Ruhr miners born in the Prussian East than among those miners who were German citizens born elsewhere.[88] In 1912, the Dortmund district doctor even attributed an especially low number of cases of tuberculosis and a relatively low infant mortality in areas of the Ruhr with concentrations of population born in the East to the large migration of "healthy elite-material" among them.[89] Foreign citizens, however, had by far the worst rate of illness among Ruhr miners, and this tainted the Polish-speaking eastern migrants in the eyes of the German public, which often identified the latter as "foreigners" despite their German citizenship.[90]

As with the accident rate, any attempt to associate Polish-speaking miners with a high rate of illness must take into account the degree to which their working conditions differed from those of other miners. The contemporary Polish observer Wachowiak claimed that they were employed at the most unhealthy enterprises, citing as evidence their undoubted preponderance among coke oven workers.[91] Polish-speaking miners also formed a larger portion of the underground workers than of the surface workers. In 1911, almost 75 percent of the underground workers took sick leave for an average of twenty-four days, while only 53 percent of the surface workers were too ill to work.[92] In 1906, among mine officials, who constituted nearly 3 percent of the total work force and included very few eastern migrants, the illness rate stood at 32.4 percent in contrast to 47 percent for the whole work force.[93] Mine management blamed the spread of hookworm on the high turnover of miners, changing jobs from one mine to another.[94] But working conditions seem more significant. The heat and the humidity of the deeper pits, to the point that miners preferred to work half naked and in the course of a shift could wring buckets of water from the few clothes that they wore, provided ideal conditions for the hookworm larvae to incubate in and then penetrate the skin of miners.[95] Management's neglect of elementary sanitation compounded the problem. It failed to provide sufficient toilet facilities for the underground workers, and miners infected with hookworm transmitted the disease through their feces.[96] Sump water filled with slime was often used to hose down the coal dust, spreading contamination.[97] Miners even turned to sump water to satisfy their thirst if the management failed to provide sufficient drinking water.[98] Above ground, management did not always do better, only gradually introducing more hygienic showers to replace the large tubs in which twenty workers at once washed themselves after work.[99] In fact, as management took measures to improve sanitation, the illness rate dropped. With the obligatory use of toilets underground, hookworm no longer posed a threat.[100]

Conclusion

Job turnover, accidents, and disease greatly affected the lives of the Ruhr coal miners. For many miners, as well as for officials, mine owners, union leaders, contemporary social and political commentators, and recent historians, all three trends went together and all seemed connected with the simultaneous increase in migration from the Prussian East. In fact, among thirty-nine selected mines and shafts from 1899, almost all those with the highest turnover rates also had above average illness rates among their miners.[101] In 1906, the two mining districts with the highest turnover rates also had the highest accident and illness rates.[102] But bad conditions at a mine could motivate a miner to quit and move, just as much as could the promise of higher wages. Excessive dirt and moisture, neglect of sanitation, especially in the washrooms, made work at one mine less attractive than at another. A former foreman at Neumühl, which had the highest turnover rate in 1899, referred to the mine as the "Wild-West," with gun-toting foremen and at least one murder a month.[103] This suggests that the causality in a correlation between a high turnover rate and high accident and illness rates might run in the direction opposite to the one usually supposed, putting greater responsibility on the mine owners rather than the victims—miners who quit mines with unsafe and unsanitary conditions.

Poor working conditions in the mines led one Polish migrant, who arrived in the Ruhr in 1890, to abandon it for the United States in 1895.[104] But the evidence indicates that the eastern migrants did not generally quit their jobs as often as other miners. Doubly "foreign," these migrants were doubly victimized. Along with other miners, they suffered the consequences of changes that had their source in the development of the mining industry of the Ruhr. Yet, instead of this serving to unite both native and migrant against their common foes, stereotypes of the migrants made them scapegoats for these changes and for their consequences. This stigma could only reinforce existing differences of origin and culture. It served to justify a hostility toward the migrant that manifested itself in an official policy of the state directed against the migrants, in inadequate efforts by the German miners' unions to recruit the migrants, and in a lack of solidarity on the part of the native miners when a strike broke out, initiated primarily by Polish-speaking miners in 1899.[105] These in turn strengthened tendencies among the migrants to organize among themselves, resulting most importantly in the creation of a separate Polish trade union in 1902 that succeeded in winning over the overwhelming majority of the organized Polish-speaking miners of the Ruhr. Differences of culture and origin among the Ruhr's coal miners did not divide them as much as did their response to these differences.

Notes

1. Max Jürgen Koch, *Die Bergarbeiterbewegung im Ruhrgebiet zur Zeit Wilhlems II* (Düsseldorf, 1954), 139.
2. O. Taeglichsbeck, *Die Belegschaft der Bergwerke und Salinen im Oberbergamtsbezirk Dortmund nach der Zählung vom 16. Dezember 1893*, 2 vols. (Dortmund, 1895 and 1896), 2:xiii. The Polish-speaking population of Russia and Austria (primarily in the province of Galicia) far exceeded that of Prussia's eastern provinces, but the Prussian authorities effectively barred the employment of large numbers of Polish-speaking noncitizens in the industries of the Ruhr. Thus, the Polish-speaking migrants to the Ruhr came mainly from Upper Silesia and Poznania, both of which had a Polish-speaking majority, while the Masurian-speaking migrants came mostly from East Prussia.
3. *Die Polen im rheinisch-westfälischen Steinkohlen-Bezirk* (Munich, 1901), 13. This pamphlet was put out by the "Gau Ruhr und Lippe" of the Alldeutscher Verband, the Pan-German League.
4. Statistics on eastern migrants in the work force and from each eastern region are given by Christoph Klessmann, *Polnische Bergarbeiter im Ruhrgebiet 1870-1945* (Göttingen, 1978), 265-66, and Krystyna Murzynowska, *Polskie wychodzstwo zarobkowe w Zaglebiu Ruhry w latach 1880-1914* (Wroclaw, 1972), annex, tables 1 and 2.
5. Klessmann, 266.
6. Oberpräsidium [hereafter OP] 2748 Bd. 3, ff. 214-25, Staatsarchiv Münster [hereafter STAM], corrects statistics in *Die Polen*, 120-31. For a discussion of these statistics and a listing of "Polish" mines, see my "Polscy górnicy w Zaglebiu Ruhry: Próba charakterystyki statystycznej na podstawie nieznanego zródla (1 stycznia 1900)," *Przeglad Polonijny* 13,3 (1987): 21-26.
7. On the "Polish peril," see, for example, *Die Polen*, which as noted above even inflated the percentage of eastern migrants, and Johannes Altkemper, *Deutschetum und Polentum in politisch-konfessioneller Bedeutung* (Leipzig, 1910), esp. 59-95.
8. Helmuth Croon, "Die Einwirkungen der Industrialisierung auf die gesellschaftliche Schichtung der Bevölkerung im rheinisch-westfälischen Industriegebiet," *Rheinische Vierteljahrsblätter* 20 (1955): 302-5.
9. Klaus Tenfelde, *Sozialgeschichte der Bergarbeiterschaft an der Ruhr im 19. Jahrhundert* (Bonn-Bad Godesberg, 1977), 177-90; Koch, 13-16.
10. Richard J. Evans, "Introduction: The Sociological Interpretation of German Labour History," *The German Working Class 1888-1933*, ed. Richard J. Evans (London, 1982), 32-33, urged closer attention to the workplace for a better understanding of the working class.
11. Tenfelde, *Sozialgeschichte*, 230-31.
12. Lorenz Pieper, *Die Lage der Bergarbeiter im Ruhrrevier* (Stuttgart, 1903), 125.
13. Gerhard Adelmann, "Die soziale Betriebsverfassung des Ruhrbergbaus vom Anfang des 19. Jahrhunderts bis zum Ersten Weltkrieg," *Rheinisches Archiv* 56 (1962): 155; Koch, 24.
14. Quoted in Hermann Hilbert, "Die Zusammensetzung der Grubenbelegschaft des Ruhrkohlengebietes um die Jahrhundertwende und ihre Probleme" (Ph.D. diss., Cologne, 1955), 75.
15. Franz J. Brüggemeier and Lutz Niethammer, "Schlafgänger, Schnapskasinos und schwerindustrielle Kolonie," in *Fabrik, Familie, Feierabend,*

ed. Jürgen Reulecke and Wolfhard Weber (Wuppertal, 1978), 168; Adelmann, "Die soziale," 157; Pieper, 125; Stephen Hickey, "The Shaping of the German Labour Movement: Miners in the Ruhr," in *Society and Politics in Wilhelmine Germany*, ed. Richard J. Evans (London, 1978), 225.

16. Albin Gladen, "Die Ruhrbergarbeiterstreik von 1889—ein sozialer Konflikt aus konservativer Motivation," in *Soziale Innovation und sozialen Konflikt*, ed. Otto Neuloh (Göttingen, 1977), 107, among others, presumed this effect of job turnover.

17. *Die Polen*, 100. Miners had to give two weeks' notice before quitting or suffer a loss in pay.

18. Pieper, 126.

19. Tenfelde, *Sozialgeschichte*, 299.

20. Ewald Oberschuir, *Die Heranziehung und Sesshaftmachung von Bergarbeitern im Ruhrkohlenbecken* (Düsseldorf, 1910), 13-14.

21. Tenfelde, *Sozialgeschichte*, 240.

22. Ibid., 246. Klessmann, 48, more cautiously suggested that a large portion of the Poles probably engaged in job changing.

23. Adelmann, 155, and Koch, 24, gave the turnover rate for 1896-1914; Klessmann, 48, described it as a rising tendency with considerable variations.

24. H. Seidl, "Der Arbeitsplatzwechsel als eine frühe Form des Klassenkampfes der mittel- und ostdeutschen Braunkohlen-bergarbeiter in der Zeit von 1870 bis 1900," *Jahrbuch für Wirtschaftsgeschichte* 4 (1965): 102-24, cited in David F. Crew, *Town in the Ruhr* (New York, 1979), 255.

25. Koch, 24.

26. Pieper, 126. Apparently, no previous historian has undertaken the following comparative statistical analysis.

27. See note 6 above.

28. Calculated on the basis of statistics in Robert Hundt, *Arbeiter-Wohnungen im Ruhrrevier* (Berlin, 1902), 33-38; these statistics do not seem comparable to those in Koch, 24. See also, Klessmann, 209.

29. Pieper, 128.

30. Ibid.

31. Adelmann, 154, noted these conditions at Concordia.

32. Anton Erkelenz, *Kraftprobe im Ruhrgebiet* (Düsseldorf, 1905), 32. See Georg Werner, *Unfälle und Erkrankungen im Ruhrbergbau* (Essen, 1908), 12-21, for "Polish" mines and shafts in 1906.

33. See Franz Schulze, *Die polnische Zuwanderung im Ruhrrevier und ihre Wirkung* (Munich, 1909), 94-102, for the portion of eastern migrants at each mine in 1905.

34. Werner, *Unfälle*, 12-21.

35. Ibid., 14; the opposite correlation also occurred but less often.

36. Brüggemeier and Niethammer, "Schlafgänger," 151.

37. Erhard Lucas, *Zwei Formen von Radikalismus in der deutschen Arbeiterbewegung* (Frankfurt, 1976), 27.

38. Werner, *Unfälle*, 21.

39. Franciszek Polomski, "Ze wspomnien, stargeo 'Westfalaka'—A. Podeszwy," *Studia Slaskie* 1 (1958): 257.

40. William I. Thomas and Florian Znaniecki, *The Polish Peasant in Europe and America*, 2 vols., 2d ed. (New York: 1927), 1: 199.

41. Dieter Langewiesche and Klaus Schönhoven, "Einleitung," *Arbeiter in Deutschland: Studien zur Lebenweise der Arbeiterschaft im Zeitalter der Industrialisierung*, ed. Dieter Langwiesche and Klaus Schönhoven (Paderborn, 1981), 12, saw this attitude as inhibiting solidarity with protest actions without noting any effect on job turnover.

42. Thomas and Znaniecki, 1:199.

43. Ibid., 2:1656-57.

44. Ibid., 2:1657-58.

45. Barrington Moore, *Injustice: The Social Bases of Obedience and Revolt* (White Plains, N.Y., 1978), 197.

46. Werner Berg, *Wirtschaft und Gesellschaft in Deutschland und Grossbritannien im Übergang zum "organisierten Kapitalismus"* (Berlin, 1984), 247.

47. Quoted in Klaus Tenfelde, "Der bergmännische Arbeitsplatz während der Hochindustrialisierung (1890 bis 1914)," *Arbeiter im Industrialisierungsprozess,* ed. Werner Conze and Ulrich Engelhardt (Stuttgart, 1979), 334.

48. Klessmann, 52; Koch, 145; Friedrich-Wilhelm Henning, "Humanisierung und Technisierung der Arbeitswelt," *Fabrik, Familie, Feierabend,* ed. Reulecke and Weber, 86.

49. Erkelenz, *Kraftprobe,* 17.

50. Tenfelde, *Sozialgeschichte,* 537.

51. Lambert Lensing, *Der grosse Bergarbeiter-Streik des Jahres 1889 im Rheinisch-Westfälischen Kohlenrevier* (Dortmund, 1889), 18; August Siegel, "Mein Lebenkampf" (typewritten), 110, Industrie-gewerkschaft Bergbau und Energie Archiv, Bochum; *Dziennik Poznanski,* Oct. 9, 1908, no. 232, cited the "socialist" *Bergarbeiter Zeitung,* Oct. 3, 1908, no. 40, as linking Poles with accidents, clipping, Biblioteka Raczynska (Poznan) Ms. 800, f. 29; Schulze, 74-75; Heinrich Münz, *Die Lage der Bergarbeiter im Ruhrrevier* (Essen, 1909), 102; among more recent observers, see, for example, Hans Georg Kirchhoff, *Die Staatliche Sozialpolitik im Ruhrbergbau 1871-1914* (Cologne, 1958), 171, who blamed "especially foreigners and Poles," uncritically citing an archival source; other examples are cited below.

52. Bergamt Herne A8 nr. 27, Draft to Royal Oberbergamt Dortmund [hereafter OBAD], 29 July 1896, STAM.

53. Stanislaw Wachowiak, *Polacy w Nadrenii i Westfalii* (Poznan, 1917), 67. He also accepted the popular view connnecting Poles with accidents, 63-4.

54. Schulze, 91.

55. Pieper, 148.

56. See my "The Prussian Authorities and the Poles of the Ruhr," *The International History Review* 8, 4 (1986): 593-603.

57. Bergamt Lünen AIII-63, OBAD letter, Jan. 9, 1901, STAM OBAD Hauptmann Taeglichsbeck recommended recognition of the authors of *Die Polen* to the minister of commerce and industry, OP 2748 Bd. 3, Nov. 29, 1900, copy, STAM.

58. Hilbert, 48, claimed Poles above all were known for this.

59. Oberschuir, 15, argued that, though difficult to prove, the connection between job turnover and accidents stood to reason; Schulze, 75, tied Poles to job turnover and then to accidents.

60. Tenfelde, *Sozialgeschichte,* 225.

61. Ibid., 228, but based on logic rather than additional evidence; he also assumed the language difference after 1880-81 adversely affected safety.

62. Münz, 111; also see, S. H. F. Hickey, *Workers in Imperial Germany* (Oxford, 1985), 120; Kirchhof, 127.

63. Klessmann, 52, 272.

64. Münz, 111.

65. Variations of the same statistics are cited by Münz, 102; Hickey, 121; Koch, 82; Wilhelm Brepohl, *Der Aufbau des Ruhrvolkes in Zuge der Ost-West-Wanderung* (Recklinghausen, 1948), 197; Hilbert, 76.

66. Werner, *Unfälle*, 24. Hickey cited this source but disregarded this point.

67. Klessmann, 52, 272. For other statistics suggesting the same conclusion, see Hans Schaefer, "Die Polenfrage im rheinisch-westfälischen Industrierevier während des Krieges und nach dem Krieg" (Ph.D. diss., Universität Würzburg, 1921), 26; Murzynowska, annex, table 3.

68. Werner, *Unfälle*, 12-21.

69. Schulze, 75, explicitly linked a high job-turnover rate to the Poles; among recent historians, see Hickey, 122, who also implied a connection with the Poles.

70. *Die Polen*, 110; these figures included all Polish-speaking miners, whether born in the Prussian East or the Ruhr, but not Masurian, bilingual, or noncitizen miners.

71. OP 2748 Bd. 3, ff. 220, 225, STAM; this survey on Jan. 1, 1900, is the first allowing calculation of percentages after 1897; it is noteworthy that Poznanians formed a majority of the migrants at Hannover I/II and a plurality at III.

72. Koch, 82-83.

73. Ibid.

74. Franz-Josef Brüggemeier, *Leben vor Ort* (Munich, 1983), 171; Hickey, 125, 127.

75. Regierung Münster VII-52, Bd. 6, Landrat Recklinghausen, Sept. 29, 1897, STAM; Amtmann Herten, Sept. 26, 1897; in 1893 only 1.21 percent of the Ruhr's miners came from all of Austria-Hungary. J. V. Bredt, *Die Polenfrage im Ruhrkohlengebiet* (Leipzig, 1909), 13.

76. Schulze, 75.

77. Ibid., 76.

78. Ibid., 75.

79. Hilbert, 49, 86-87; Oberschuir, 39.

80. Schulze, 76-77.

81. Hilbert, 87-88; Koch, 84, also cited Schulze's statistics without his general conclusion that eastern migrants were healthier than other miners except for these two diseases, Schulze, 77.

82. Royal District Police Commissioner, Essen, Aug. 29, 1903, to Regierungpräsident Düsseldorf, Regierung Düsseldorf Polizei, 30411, f. 92, Hauptstaatsarchiv Düsseldorf. See Schulze, 94-102, for the percentage of migrants at each mine in 1905.

83. Klessmann, 53.

84. Wachowiak, 43, 73. This suggests that a link between hookworm and migrants from Poznania, since the Herne and Ober-hausen mining districts had the densest population of miners from that province among their eastern migrants, whereas East Prussians predominated among the migrants in the mines of the Gelsenkirchen district. Wachowiak, 51-52, ignored his own evidence in claiming that hookworm was not related to migration, 74. Since Poznanians, however, had gradually been increasing their share among eastern migrants and actually surpassed that of East Prussians in 1913, the link may be between hookworm and the more recent migrants.

85. Erkelenz, 16. These statistics probably combine injuries due to accidents with illness.

86. Werner, *Unfälle*, 12-21.

87. Münz, 117.

88. Schaefer, 24; Wachowiak, 69; Murzynowska, annex, table 4.

89. Quoted by Klessmann, 54. In Hamborn, however, respiratory illnesses were the primary cause of death between 1900 and 1910, Lucas, 67.

90. Wachowiak, 69.

91. Ibid., 72. Wachowiak also argued that work at these ovens understandably fostered alcoholism. According to Schulze, 77, Poles chose higher-paying jobs, including at the coke ovens.

92. Klessmann, 53, connected Poles with underground work. See Brüggemeier, *Leben*, 171, 329, on the rate of illness.

93. Calculations based on data in Werner, *Unfälle*, 21, 24.

94. Koch, 84.

95. Hickey, 112, 124; Pieper, 155.

96. Hickey, 124; Pieper, 158; Wolfhard Weber, "Der Arbeitsplatz in einem expandierenden Wirtschaftszweig: Der Bergmann," in *Fabrik, Familie, Feierabend*, ed. Reulecke and Weber, 110.

97. Tenfelde, "Der bergmännische," 323.

98. Hickey, 124; Pieper, 158.

99. Weber, 110.

100. Carl Jantke, ed., *Bergmann und Zeche* (Tübingen, 1953), 187; Hickey, 125.

101. Pieper, 127-29.

102. Werner, *Unfälle*, 21. Werner, *Unfälle*, 28–29, made a causal connection similar to the following.

103. Georg Werner, *Ein Kumpel* (Berlin, 1930), 124, quoted by Lucas, 114.

104. Janina Dziembowska, ed., *Pamietniki emigrantów—Stany Zjednoczone*, 2 vols. (Warsaw, 1977), 2:601-2, brief registry, no. 77.

105. See my "Nationalism over Class Solidarity: The German Trade Unions and Polish Coal Miners in the Ruhr to 1902," *Canadian Review of Studies in Nationalism* 14, 2 (1987): 261-76.

LATIN AMERICAN AND ASIAN MIGRATION TO THE UNITED STATES

6

The International Migration of Workers and Segmented Labor: Mexican Immigrant Workers in California Industrial Agriculture, 1900–1940

Camille Guerin-Gonzales

Between 1870 and 1940, California agriculture underwent a fundamental change in the kind of crops farmers concentrated on and in the structure of agricultural production. The pivotal period in California agriculture proved to be the 1870s, when large-scale wheat farmers began to shift to fruit and vegetable farming. By the turn of the century, the state was well on its way to becoming one of the leading agricultural producers in the nation. In 1900, California stood in eleventh place in value of farm commodities produced nationally. Within only thirty years, California had moved to second place, behind Texas and ahead of Iowa.[1] Excellent soil conditions, irrigation projects, improved transportation networks, the use of ice in railroad cars, and a factory system of farming contributed to the rapid development of California agriculture.

The research for this essay was made possible by a University of California President's Postdoctoral Fellowship and a National Endowment for the Humanities Grant. For their comments and suggestions on earlier versions of this essay, the author would like to thank Carlos Cortes, Martha Olney, Carl Strikwerda, and the members of the Labor Colloquium of the Department of Economics at the University of Massachusetts, Amherst.

Of these, the industrialization of agriculture was most important in the spectacular growth of California agriculture. The factory system of farming developed from a combination of several elements, including crop specialization, large-scale production, high capital investment, a close relationship with financial institutions and other complementary industries, and the acquisition of a large, low-wage labor force. The cost of producing crops decreased proportionately as the scale of production increased. Therefore, crop specialization and large-scale production allowed California farmers to increase their profits.

California agriculture is characterized only in part by large-scale farming and corporate structure. Far more important to the uniqueness of California are specialization in labor-intensive crops and the resulting intense demand for seasonal workers.[2] In order to have a dependable supply of low-wage labor, California farmers experimented with various types of workers and developed a labor system that was segmented according to nationality and ethnicity, and based on the manipulation of immigrant workers.[3] The formation of a segmented labor market in California agriculture was closely tied to the development of large-scale specialty-crop farming.

By far the most crucial element in the large-scale production of fruits and vegetables in California was the supply of labor.[4] In highly specialized fruit and vegetable farming, where one or two crops constitute a farmer's entire production, farmers needed large numbers of workers for one or two months of harvesting, during which farmers paid four times the national average for wages.[5] But during the rest of the year, agricultural production required only a fraction of that work force.[6] Faced with high fixed costs for irrigation, transportation, fertilizer, and land, farmers sought to control labor costs. The labor factor presented farmers with three major questions. First, how could farmers secure a sufficient number of workers at harvest time? Second, how could farmers keep wages low? Finally, where would workers go when farmers no longer needed their labor?

California fruit and vegetable growers addressed the first problem, that of finding enough workers to harvest their crops, in a variety of ways. From nearby towns and cities, they hired part-time workers who could leave their jobs for a few hours each day. They also employed housewives and schoolchildren, who contributed to their families' income by working on farms. In addition, farmers recruited native white and black migrant workers, disparagingly referred to as hoboes and bindle stiffs. These were mostly single men who had previously worked in the wheat fields. But farmers learned they could not find enough part-time farm workers and domestic migrant workers to satisfy their labor needs. One option was to pay wages high enough to draw workers permanently away from other occupations. Instead, California fruit and vegetable farmers turned to foreign labor, finding they could recruit large numbers of workers from countries that had lower wage rates. Thus, California farmers resolved their problem of securing an ample supply of labor by using a combination of part-time workers, including women, children, and domestic migrant workers, to supplement their foreign work force.

Second, farmers addressed the question of how to keep labor costs to a minimum. By hiring part-time workers they could pay low wages on the grounds that agricultural work merely supplemented other income. Employers justified paying women and children lower wages by arguing that they believed women and children did substandard work and were merely earning "pocket money."[7] The transiency of domestic migrant workers made it difficult for them to develop the financial security or organization from which to press for higher wages.[8]

In addition, farmers controlled wages by hiring foreign workers. Many foreign workers planned to stay in California only temporarily, while they earned enough money to buy land or otherwise better their economic condition in their home country. As a result, they tended to evaluate their wages on the basis of what they could buy at home. Foreign farm workers joined the migrant work force and, as in the case of domestic migrant workers, their transiency restricted their ability to secure higher wages. Of all the groups used for agricultural labor, farmers found they could most easily control the labor costs of foreign workers.

The farmers' final problem was what to do with workers once the harvest season was over. Local seasonal workers usually returned to their jobs in towns and cities. Women and children returned to other endeavors, such as housework and school, in nearby communities. Because the California growing and harvesting seasons were long, owing to the warm climate and extensive irrigation system, migrant workers could find farm employment for six to eight months of the year by moving from crop to crop. During the four to six months when no farm work was available, migrant workers entered towns and cities, where they sought temporary employment or aid from charitable organizations. Foreign workers in the migrant stream did the same or, in some cases, returned to their home country.

Foreign Agricultural Labor in California

Throughout the 1880–1930 period, California farmers experimented with several types of labor and concluded that a certain type of foreign worker best satisfied their labor requirements. In their search for a low-wage foreign labor force, growers came to prefer four characteristics in their workers. They favored workers who (1) were newly arrived immigrants; (2) would accept low wages; (3) were set apart from the rest of American society by religion, language, or preferably color; and (4) planned to return to their home country.

Of these four factors, the key to labor control in California agriculture was maintaining a large labor force of newly arrived immigrants. As the years passed, foreign labor increasingly became central to the success of California specialty-crop agriculture. Throughout the 1880–1930 period of transition and development of industrialized agriculture in California, farmers relied primarily on three foreign groups for agricultural labor: Chinese, Japanese, and Mexicans. In addition, Hindustani and Filipino workers labored in California's fields in large numbers during this period. Growers ultimately realized that many Chinese, Japanese, Hindustani, and Filipino workers did not return home as hoped. The distance between the United States and the home countries of these immigrants discouraged seasonal return migration. After a period of time in the United States, immigrants tended to organize for higher wages, buy property, and move out of wage-labor agricultural work into other occupations. Moreover, their presence as a settled immigrant population aroused nativists and many American workers to agitate for legislation restricting immigration from these countries. By the 1920s, as a result of their dissatisfaction with other foreign groups, California growers came to rely on Mexican immigrant workers as their major source of labor for industrial agriculture.

Mexican Immigrant Workers in California Agriculture

Mexican immigrants worked in California agriculture throughout the second half of the nineteenth and the twentieth century. Immigration that had begun in the nineteenth century gained momentum after 1910, so that Mexicans in California increased from 8 percent of the Mexican population of the United States in 1910 to approximately 25 percent in 1930.[9] While Mexican workers continued to work in mines, on railroads, and in other industries, an increasing number worked on California farms after 1910.

By 1920, Mexicans formed the largest single ethnic group among farm workers in California, and during the 1920s they became the mainstay of California large-scale, specialty-crop agriculture. Mexican immigrant workers had the four characteristics growers sought in an ideal low-wage labor force. First, they were set apart from the dominant cultural group in the United States by physical appearance, religion, and language. Second, Mexican workers immigrated in large numbers so that employers could use them to replenish their labor force. Third, because Mexican workers judged their wages in terms of purchasing power in Mexico and not the United States, they accepted low wages. Finally, many planned to return to Mexico within a short period of time.

The latter factor was particularly vital to California agriculture. The proximity of the Mexican border provided farmers with what they hoped would be a built-in solution to their problem of maintaining a labor system based on temporary immigrants. Mexican workers could return to their home country during the winter and migrate back to the United States when harvesting began again in late spring and early summer. The possibility of Mexican workers' leaving the United States each year also provided an argument that could be used to minimize opposition from residents of towns and cities, who resented unemployed immigrant farm workers' settling in their communities during the winter. In response to expressions of fear that Mexican immigrants would settle permanently, farmers argued that they were "homing pigeons" who returned to Mexico each year.

Between 1910 and 1917, Mexican immigration to California increased at a steady rate. That rate leaped with the 1917 entry of the United States into World War I, which created a shortage of agricultural labor as black and native white workers left farm work for jobs in war-related industries and for military service. Growers turned increasingly to Mexican workers to fill their labor needs, and Mexican immigration increased dramatically.[10] Growers were able to persuade the secretary of labor to exempt Mexican immigrants from the head tax and literacy restrictions of the 1917 Immigration Act, as a wartime measure, so that they could recruit Mexican workers under a temporary worker program to satisfy their need for sufficient labor to harvest their crops.[11]

Over seventy-two thousand Mexican workers took part in that program between 1917 and 1921. Most engaged in agricultural work, primarily in the Southwest. A small number worked in other industries. In addition, a large number of Mexican immigrants entered the United States without registering with authorities, in response to reports of war-related labor shortages.[12] The secretary of labor extended the wartime waiver until March 1921, primarily because of grower pressure. The temporary worker program was called into question when an economic recession in 1920 led unemployed American workers to protest the employment of Mexican workers, and the secretary of labor responded by rescinding the waiver and ordering the return of all temporary workers.

Temporary program workers and other unemployed Mexican immigrant workers, including seasonal workers returning home for the winter, joined in a mass return migration to Mexico, which lasted approximately six months. But an upturn in the U.S. economy in the spring of 1922 and the promise of employment led to renewed immigration to the United States, although the temporary worker program was not extended.[13] During the 1920s, the Mexican-born

population in California doubled as many Mexicans, seeking to escape
the ravages of eleven years of revolutionary war and the 1926 Cristero
Rebellion, responded to the promise of jobs and left their country for
the United States.

Labor Control in California Industrial Agriculture

Agricultural workers in California constituted a divided and
increasingly segmented secondary labor force by the 1920s, when
Mexican immigrants entered in large numbers. Agricultural employers
sought to maintain these divisions and control their workers through
four principal strategies: overrecruitment of workers for harvesting
crops; the pitting of ethnic groups against each other; repatriation
programs; and manipulation of agrarian mythology to gain community
support for undermining worker organizations and breaking strikes.

First, California large-scale farmers, in order to ensure a sufficient
number of workers who would accept low wages, consistently recruited
more workers than were needed to harvest crops. Even during the times
of actual agricultural labor surpluses, growers continued to complain of
shortages. In 1918 and 1919, there were more agricultural laborers in
California than there were jobs. Nevertheless, farmers succeeded in
convincing the secretary of labor to extend the wartime waiver of
Mexican immigration restriction.[14] According to the Department of
Agriculture, the supply of agricultural workers exceeded demand
throughout the 1920s.[15] Nevertheless, farmers continued, throughout
the decade, to complain of an insufficient supply of workers. But, in
fact, there was no shortage of workers willing to engage in agricultural
work; rather it was a shortage of workers willing to accept low wages.
During 1922 and 1923, farmers complained that they were forced to pay
workers wage rates that were too high.[16] Because of this desire to lower
wages, growers overrecruited workers.

There were an estimated one hundred fifty thousand Mexican agricultural workers in California in the 1920s.[17] During the same period, a
work force of approximately ninety thousand workers was sufficient to
harvest California's crops. Even allowing for maldistribution, this excess
of Mexican workers, added to others seeking agricultural employment,
contributed to the low wage rates paid to workers.[18]

A second method used to try to ensure low wages and encourage
divisions among workers was to pit ethnic groups against each other.
Farmers established separate wage rates for different ethnic groups.
This put different groups in competition with each other, led to
antagonism among workers, and fostered racism.[19] In addition, growers
assigned work tasks based on the ethnicity of workers. On farms in the
Sacramento Delta islands, for example, Chinese farm workers planted
potatoes, onions, and asparagus on one island, then moved on to

moved on to another island. Italian workers followed behind, planting barley and beans. Portuguese farm workers then planted vegetables. Japanese, Hindustani, Filipino, and Mexican workers also participated in rotation planting, each group responsible for a different crop.[20]

At the ten-thousand-acre Giffen Ranch, located seven miles southwest of Mendota, native white, Japanese, Mexican, Filipino, and Armenian farm workers labored in the fields. In addition, Hindustani farmers worked on seventeen hundred acres that they leased from Wiley B. Giffen, the owner. Native white workers drove tractors for wages of fifty-five cents per hour. Japanese workers picked melons, while Mexican laborers worked in the cotton field, along with a few Filipinos and native whites. Armenians picked pomegranates. Of these groups, only Mexican workers worked in family units.[21]

In addition to segregation of workers, different languages and customs isolated groups and militated against the development of solidarity among farm workers. Workers spoke five different languages on one ranch in the San Joaquin Valley.[22] H. W. Owen, a dried fruit producer, reported that his Spanish (light-skinned Mexicans), Mexican, and Filipino workers did not "like each other" and so he kept them apart.[23]

Since different ethnic groups were hired to do particular tasks, groups competing for the same task often underbid each other. Juan Estrada, vice-president of the Asociación Mutual Mexicana del Valle Imperial, in El Centro, complained that Filipinos worked for lower wages than Mexican workers. "They work for less in lettuce thinning. When we work for $7 an acre, they will go to the farmer and work for $6.50 or even as low as $5.50. We do not talk much with either Filipinos or Hindus."[24] One Mexican grape picker disliked Filipinos because he had lost a job as a result of underbidding by a group of Filipino workers. "The Filipinos are bad people. They take contracts for less than we do. Two years ago in Imperial Valley they took contracts for thinning lettuce for seven dollars per acre when we were getting more. So the farmers gave the contract to the Filipinos and let us go."[25]

Third, growers used the threat of deportation to maintain low-wage labor. Mexican workers greatly feared deportation. Ernesto Galarza, a labor organizer and historian, reported that "the fear of deportation often takes the proportions of a community psychosis, affecting even those who have legal status as resident aliens."[26] During the 1928 cantaloupe workers' strike in the Imperial Valley, growers and their supporters threatened Mexican workers with deportation if they did not return to work.[27] Imperial County District Attorney Elmer Heald stated, "it would be better if we picked a whole lot of Mexicans and sent them back to Mexico."[28] The secretary of the Brawley Chamber of Commerce told Paul S. Taylor, an economist from the University of

California, that a number of Brawley's leading citizens had been able to have the organizers of the cantaloupe workers' strike deported: "They [*sic*] was three men from Mexico stayed here as organizers whom we deported. We did not like them holding meetings. No, we did not fear violence, but they was going to tie up the cantaloupe industry. Cantaloupes are perishable and we couldn't let them have a strike."[29] Workers, intimidated, gave up the strike and returned to work on their employers' terms.[30]

Finally, growers succeeded in gaining the support of their communities and local, state, and federal agencies in wage disputes with their workers by manipulating the myth of the family farm. According to that myth, the farm laborer and laboring farmer were nearly synonymous.[31] The farmer worked alongside his hired hands, of which there were usually only one or two. The hired hand was male, young, single, native born, and considered to be a part of the family.[32] He was expected to work as a hired hand for a few years and then to move up the agricultural ladder to the position of farm owner or operator. Economically, the hired hand prospered or suffered along with the farm owner. Because he was a member of the farm family, it was incongruous for a hired hand to demand higher wages.[33] The myth of the family farm drew its power by recalling one of the ideals upon which the nation was founded, that America was to be a republic of small farmers, each having the goal of producing enough to support family, church, and government rather than of making large profits.[34] By appealing to the myth of the family farm, growers gained the sympathy and support of other members of the community and often of the state and federal government.

Living Conditions of Mexican Farm Workers

Employers also used housing as a means of dividing and controlling their workers. Mexican migrant farm workers either lived in employer-owned housing or provided their own shelter. For a brief period after 1935, a few lived in federally owned and run labor camps. Most employers allowed workers to camp on their land during harvesting and sometimes provided tents or cabins, then evicted workers if they failed to move on after the harvest. Often growers did not provide workers with water or sanitary facilities.

Employer camps ranged from adequate to very bad in the quality of housing provided workers in the years for which the Commission of Immigration and Housing conducted inspections of camps. Such inspections originated as a result of hearings held to determine the cause of the riot in Wheatland at the Durst Hop Ranch in 1913. Camps on farms that required large numbers of workers for long seasons of cultivation and harvesting generally provided the best housing for workers. Those camps located on farms specializing in the production of peas, tomatoes, prunes, and potatoes and requiring large numbers of workers for short periods of time had the worst record with the commission.[35] According to one employer, whom the commission prosecuted for operating an unsanitary camp, once his workers "have finished harvesting my crops, I will kick them on the county road. My obligation is ended."[36]

In contrast, citrus and sugar beet farmers experimented with building permanent housing for workers, in an attempt to ensure a year-round supply of skilled labor. Citrus and sugar beet farms provided probably the best housing for their workers. Citrus growers, fearful that they would not be able to secure enough low-wage workers, became interested in building permanent housing for Mexican workers during World War I, when white native workers were in scarce supply and farmers were making the transition from Japanese to Mexican farm workers. A. D. Shamel, the United States Department of Agriculture farm adviser in the Riverside–San Bernardino–Corona area in the late 1910s and 1920s, wrote that "most citrus employers are agreed that, for the present at any rate, the most practical source of additional labor is Mexico. Through the efforts of the American Latin League, and other organizations, the immigration restrictions for Mexican laborers has [sic] been so modified that it now seems likely that citrus growers will be able to secure enough labor to care for their orchards, pick, pack and market their crops. The problem of housing these laborers is one that needs the earnest and thoughtful attention of everyone concerned."

Citrus growers requested advice from sugar beet farmers on the most practical and economic housing for Mexican workers, since sugar beet companies provided permanent housing for their workers.[37] During the World War I period, citrus and sugar beet growers experimented with permanent housing for their Mexican farm workers in an attempt to guarantee that an adequate number of skilled workers would be available. The housing projects the growers built during this period were superior to housing that agricultural workers on other farms in California lived in after World War I.

On the Chase Plantation in Corona, in 1918, citrus growers built thirty-six adobe structures, which housed Mexican families who handled lemons and oranges. Each house consisted of a room ten feet square and a screened porch, in front, that was six feet by ten feet in dimension. The grower also provided barns and other buildings for workers' animals, which included horses and chickens. Chase Plantation packing shed workers lived in houses made of adobe bricks. Two of the houses had two bedrooms each, with a bathroom between, and included a dining room, parlor, kitchen, back screened porch, and front porch. Two of the houses had four rooms and were twenty feet by twenty feet, with screened back and front porches. Mexican families lived apart from native white workers, most of whom were single men who lived in dormitories.[38]

On the Sespe Ranch in Ventura, citrus growers provided Mexican workers and their families with land, but the workers had to build their own houses. The owner of the ranch lent money to those who did not have the funds with which to purchase construction materials and deducted $10 a month from their wages. Families who left the employ of the Sespe Ranch had the option of selling their equity in the house to another Mexican family or to the owner of the ranch.[39]

One hundred cottages housed five hundred Mexicans in "villages," on the Limoneira Ranch, in Santa Paula, located in Ventura County. Each cottage occupied a plot of ground forty feet by one hundred feet. Cottages were eighteen feet by twenty-two feet in dimension and had piped-in water. Some had shower baths. Growers paid $250 to $275 to construct each cottage and provided them rent-free to their workers. Workers paid no rent. The cottages consisted of three rooms; one served as a large combined kitchen and living room, and two were smaller bedrooms. Workers did most of their cooking outdoors, although the kitchen contained a stove, dish closet, and water faucet. Native white workers with families lived in houses with attached garages for their automobiles, which attests to the higher standard of living white workers were able to achieve.[40]

The conclusion of World War I allayed growers' fears of a shortage of low-wage farm labor. This and increased immigration from Mexico during the 1920s led growers to abandon their plans to expand housing projects for Mexican farm workers. Their efforts during the war years to build adequate permanent housing give an indication of the type of housing and living conditions Mexican farm workers might have had available if growers had continued to perceive that they had a limited supply of low-wage workers. Instead, partially reflecting the surplus labor, a generally low standard of farm worker housing prevailed throughout the 1920s.

The housing that workers provided for themselves in the 1920s and 1930s consisted of makeshift shelters on land owned by growers, automobiles or trailers in auto camps, and houses bought on rented land. In the Imperial Valley, workers usually lived in lean-to shacks or tents in "ditch-bank camps," located on the bank of an irrigation canal.[41] Housing sometimes consisted only of canvas, or some other material, stretched across branches for sun and wind protection. Permanent camps included a number of these structures, as well as houses made of rough lumber.[42] Many of the camps in the Imperial Valley were squatter camps, set up during the harvest season and abandoned once the season was over. Workers found that growers did not charge rent for the use of land for camping during harvesting but imposed a $2.50 monthly fee per family once the season was over.[43]

Workers in Fresno often camped along irrigation canals, which provided water for bathing and washing clothing and dishes. In one camp, Mexican families camped along an irrigation ditch under a group of eucalyptus trees northeast of Fresno. The families obtained their drinking water from a well some distance from the camp. Since there were no sanitary facilities, the area was fly-infested.[44] Such conditions discouraged the settlement of workers and encouraged migrancy.

In September 1928, the Martinez family, consisting of a mother, father, and five children, lived in a tent under some trees near Clovis between the highway and the railroad tracks, because their employer provided no housing for seasonal farm workers. Martinez complained about the absence of toilets and the fact that for water he had to pay fifty cents a week to the owner of a boardinghouse for single workers. He, his wife, and their children had to bathe in an irrigation canal.[45]

Nine other Mexican farm worker families lived in a camp nearby, making a total of one hundred workers. Mr. Martinez, and his five children all worked picking grapes. Mrs. Martinez cooked for the family and kept the family's camp area clean. The family followed the crops from ranch to ranch, never spending more than four days in one place. A labor contractor found employment for the family in return for 5 percent of the family's earnings. In addition, the contractor occasionally earned fifty cents an hour from a grower for Martinez's labor. Martinez and his children picked from 300 to 350 boxes of grapes a day and earned up to $7 per day.[46] The Martinez family also worked in the citrus industry, picking navel oranges in the spring and Valencia oranges in the autumn.[47]

Another Mexican farm worker supervised four Mexican families for a Japanese labor contractor, on a three-hundred-acre Fresno-area farm owned by an Armenian. He had no permanent home: "I move, after the grapes, to Imperial Valley for work in planting and thinning lettuce. Then I may work in oranges around Anaheim and Pomona. Then I come to the grapes in Fresno."[48] Moving from crop to crop was expensive. If a worker did not have an automobile, expenses could easily exceed earnings. Most newly arrived immigrants from Mexico worked for the railroads until they were able to save enough money to buy a car or truck.[49] By following the crops, a Mexican farm worker family might earn enough money to subsist through the summer and cover a portion of expenses for the winter, when employment opportunities for Mexican workers were scarce. The margin for saving above yearly expenses was very small, if it existed at all.

The worst living conditions prevailed in squatters' camps. Workers camped in fields, along river bottoms, on irrigation ditch banks, and along roadsides. They had no sanitary facilities and usually had to carry their water over long distances. Workers either slept out in the open or in tents made of strips of cloth or canvas stretched across branches of a tree or pieces of wood placed in the ground.

The State Relief Administration found that conditions in a squatter camp it inspected in 1936 had changed little from conditions in squatter camps of the previous decade. The camp was situated in the Santa Ana Wash between San Bernardino and Redlands. A group of farm workers' families camped in a one-half-square-mile area and lived in houses made of paper boxes and/or tin, in automobiles, and in trailers. Another writer described a squatter camp as being the worst type of housing in California. Workers had to walk to a filling station and purchase water at five cents a bucket.[50] The absence of safe drinking water greatly increased the danger of disease in squatter camps.[51]

Mexican farm workers also lived in auto camps and provided their own shelter in automobiles or trailers. The camps often had a grocery store and filling station. Since most of the auto camps were designed for stays of short duration, sanitation and health measures typically were inadequate.[52]

The State Emergency Relief Administration (SERA) described a farm worker community in Sacramento in 1935 that had changed little since the 1920s. This particular community consisted of 539 households. Residents built their houses out of scrap collected from dump heaps. "The outside appearance of most dwellings is repellent," the SERA reported. "Decay has rotted scrap construction material, and the overflow piles of sodden junk help prepare the visitor for a sordid look within the household." Thirty-five of the houses had no beds.[53] The problems farm workers encountered in acquiring adequate housing militated against the formation of settled communities. As a result, Mexican agricultural workers found it very difficult to establish an economic and social base from which to demand better working and living conditions.

Education and Labor of Mexican Immigrant Children

Mexican immigrants also found their access to another avenue to economic and social power, education, limited because of ethnic discrimination. Residents of communities in farming areas often complained if Mexican farm worker children attended their schools. For this reason, the owner of the Giffen Ranch, near Mendota, established schools for farm worker children on his ranch. According to Giffen, "the Mendota school people got alarmed lest they be flooded with more Mexican than white children." The grower bused white children on the ranch into Mendota to attend school while the Mexican children went to ranch schools.[54] Edwin B. Tilton, assistant superintendent of schools in San Diego, told Paul Taylor that he believed the Mexican student to be inferior. "He is inferior; an inferior race, no doubt. The Japs and Chinese shoot past him. They are superior. The Mexicans are slow to learn." He claimed that "the Mexicans at Sherman school have bad social habits and are not clean."

Mexican children who lived on citrus farms either went to schools located on the farms or traveled to schools in nearby communities by bus, operated at the expense of the grower. Most Mexican children, however, also worked alongside their parents on farms. They attended school for several months during the winter and usually did not go beyond the sixth or seventh grade. Many only had one or two years of school. Although parents had hopes that their children would be able to move out of agricultural work through education, the necessities of providing an income to support the family forced them to enlist the aid of their children during the school year.

A Mexican farmer picking grapes in Fresno told an interviewer in 1928 that he looked forward to the day when his children would be old enough to help him work. "Boys and girls can help pack grapes from about eight years of age on. They are an expense; after that they can help you." Without family labor, farm workers barely made a subsistence living.[55]

The children of another grape picker went to school in Whittier. The farm worker told an interviewer that his children "like school very much and I like them to go. I do not like to see them do the hard work I have had to do since I was young. I want them to get an education and have nice jobs when they grow up." The family picked grapes near Clovis during the summer and fall, so he planned to send his children to school in Clovis until the grape-picking season was over.[56] Another boy, who picked fruit in southern California and lived in Burbank during the winter, attended junior high school in Burbank, which went from seventh to tenth grade, and expected to be able to complete junior high school. He did not believe he would attend high school because, as he told an interviewer, "it costs too much money and anyway I have to help my father."[57]

Luz Romero hoped she would somehow escape a future of low-wage, farm labor. A high school sophomore in Brawley in 1928, Luz planned to go to business school after high school. She worked with her family picking grapes during the summer but managed to stay in school. In order to achieve her ambition, Luz associated with few friends. Friends, she felt, only wanted to go dancing and have fun. She did not care to marry early, either, because she felt that would prevent her from finishing school.[58]

Education, for both children and adults, offered the hope of economic and social advancement for Mexican immigrants and their children. The little education that they did experience raised their expectations for the kind of life they could have in the United States. Despite the efforts of employers to control Mexican labor, some immigrants succeeded in establishing homes and sending their children to school. In order to do this, Mexican immigrant agricultural workers endured great hardships and struggled against prejudicial treatment. Yet low wages, migration, and racial prejudice thwarted the attempts of all but a few to advance economically.[59]

During the 1920s, Mexican immigrant workers became the primary work force within California agriculture's segmented labor system. The success of agricultural employers in controlling their labor force prevented the formation of a strong labor organization through which Mexican immigrant farm workers could establish higher wage rates. The low wages that Mexican immigrant farm workers continued to earn throughout the 1920s required that all able farm worker family members work in order to support the family. This and racial prejudice prevented most Mexican farm worker children from obtaining an education, which would have provided them with skills to enter higher-paying occupations. In addition, low wages forced farm workers to supplement their income by working in other industries between harvests. Competition from Mexican immigrant workers generated resentment among native white workers. As a result, when the country experienced a severe economic depression in the 1930s, Mexican immigrant families found themselves with few resources and became the objects of agitation for their expulsion from the United States.

Mexican Immigrants in the United States during the 1930s

Over one-half million Mexican immigrants and Mexican-American's left the United States during the Great Depression. An unknown number of Mexicans had come into the country illegally and returned on their own to Mexico when they could not find employment. Others were deported, while many Mexican-descent American citizens, legal immigrants, and children born in the United States of immigrant parents (and therefore eligible for U.S. citizenship) took part in repatriation programs organized by county relief agencies. A still greater number left the country out of fear that they either would be deported or would be denied relief. Repatriation of Mexican workers and their families by government agencies in the United States between 1931 and 1934 became the most extensive organized program to remove a foreign population ever undertaken in the country up to that time.

Repatriation affected both Mexican-Americans and Mexican immigrants who participated in the program and those who remained in the United States. Those who stayed behind found their economic and social position in the United States even more precarious than before. Enrique A. Gonzales, a Mexican consular inspector, visited the Southwest in 1932 to determine the impact of the Depression on Mexican workers in the United States. He found that at least 20 percent, and in some locales as many as 50 percent, of all Mexican workers in the Southwest had no jobs.[60] One contemporary writer noted that Anglo workers threatened violence to employers "who hired Mexicans rather than unemployed Americans."[61]

Competition for farm jobs became especially severe as unemployed city workers moved to the countryside in search of farm jobs. Nationally, over 1,540,000 left cities for farms in 1932, while 468,000 migrated from farms to cities. As a result, the 1933 farm population of 32,000,000 was the largest in history, as two workers competed for each farm job during that year.[62]

Working and living conditions for all farm workers deteriorated as the Depression deepened, but for Mexican workers, who were the objects of racism and nativism, the Depression was especially disastrous.[63] Mexican families earned one-sixth of the national average of $1,784 in 1935. The California State Relief Administration reported that, in 1935, a family required a minimum of $780 to provide for food, utilities, and rent. The Heller Committee for Research in Social Economics at the University of California established $972 for what it termed a "health and decency" budget for an average family, in 1935. Yet a study of 775 Mexican families in California conducted that year revealed an average annual income of only $289.[64]

Wages for agricultural workers in California fell dramatically between 1930 and 1933. Farm workers, who had been earning a monthly salary of $60.75 in 1930, earned only $30.12 in 1933. Daily wages dropped from an average of $2.55 per day in 1930 to $1.40 a day in 1933, so that some workers were earning only 15 to 16 cents an hour.[65]

The year 1933 marked the low point in farm wages. It also marked the beginning of a rise in prices for California crops. The demand for fruits and vegetables increased in 1933, and total shipments were up from the previous year.[66] The Department of Agriculture reported that "the sharp advance in the prices of nearly all farm products since February 1933 is likely to increase farmers' gross income for production in 1933 over the unusually low income of 1932."[67] Although California farmers received higher prices for their crops in 1933 and their gross income increased over the previous year, they did not raise their workers' wages. Workers responded in 1933 by participating in the largest number of strikes in California agricultural history.[68] Although the popular perception of migrant workers during the Depression is of native white refugees from the dust bowl, until 1935 Mexican workers continued to provide the majority of agricultural labor in California and took part in nearly every strike in the state.

Despite farmers' efforts to maintain a foreign force, by 1936, Anglo workers comprised over 80 percent of farm labor. The most successful union organizing of migrant workers occurred in 1937, when native whites predominated among agricultural workers in California. Employers found that a large number of Anglo farm workers, who could not be repatriated or deported, jeopardized their control over wages. Farmers wanted a return to a predominantly Mexican worker force. And, in the 1940s, they were able again to initiate the large-scale recruitment of Mexican workers.

The entry of the United States into World War II generated increased industrial activity, which brought an end to the Depression. Anglo workers left low-paying unskilled and semiskilled agricultural jobs, which they associated with Mexican labor, for higher-paying employment in war-related industries. Employers were once again able to convince the U.S. government to waive immigration restrictions in order to allow Mexican workers to enter the United States and provide low-wage labor for agriculture. As a result, the United States and Mexico entered into a bilateral agreement, the Bracero Program, to supply workers to agricultural employers, and large-scale immigration to the United States resumed.

Conclusion

The recruitment of Mexican agricultural workers reveals what Michael Piore has called a basic contradiction in industrial societies. "How is it that industrial economies seem not only able to absorb, but in fact are actively seeking out uneducated, illiterate workers from the very types of societies to which they are, in the conventional view of what industrialization is all about, generally contrasted?" In an effort to maximize profits, employers in the Southwest recruited, for certain low-paying, low-skilled jobs, foreign workers with characteristics that differed sharply from, and were viewed negatively by, native white Americans. These characteristics included color, language, religion, or a combination of the three. The presence of such a work force in certain occupations degraded the status of those particular occupations in the view of Anglo society. Native white workers shunned jobs that foreign workers held, thereby contributing to the development of a segmented secondary labor market that featured the maintenance of an army of low-wage workers, divided along market lines of ethnicity and race.

Thus, Mexican immigrant workers first contributed to and later became essential to the industrial development of agriculture in California. The qualities that made Mexican immigrants attractive to California agricultural employers relegated them to a secondary labor market and severely limited their access, and the access of second- and third-generation Mexican Americans, to better paying, more secure jobs in the primary labor market.

Notes

1. U. S. Bureau of the Census, Twelfth Census, 1900, 20 vols., 5:703; Fifteenth Census, 1930, Statistics of Agriculture, 3: 9-10.
2. Lloyd H. Fisher, *The Harvest Labor Market in California* (Cambridge, Mass., 1953), 2.
3. See Richard C. Edwards, Michael Reich, and David M. Gordon, *Labor Market Segmentation* (Lexington, Mass., 1975); David M. Gordon, Richard Edwards, and Michael Reich, *Segmented Work, Divided Workers: The Historical Transformation of Labor in the United States* (Cambridge, 1982); Sam Rosenberg, "A Survey of Empirical Work on Labor Market Segmentation," Working Paper no. 138, Department of Economics, University of California, Davis.
4. U. S. Bureau of the Census, Twelfth Census, 1900, Statistics of Agriculture, 6:305.
5. Ibid., 307.
6. Ibid.
7. LaWanda Cox, "Agricultural Labor in the United States, 1865-1900; with Special Reference to the South" (Ph.D. diss., University of California, Berkeley, 1942), 12, 13, 34, 37, 38.
8. Carey McWilliams, *Factories in the Field* (Boston, 1939; reprint ed., Santa Barbara and Salt Lake City, 1971), 56-57.
9. State of California, Mexican Fact-Finding Committee, *Mexicans in California: Report of Governor C. C. Young's Mexican Fact-Finding Committee* (hereafter cited as *Governor Young Report)* (San Francisco, 1930; reprint ed., San Francisco, 1970), 33-34; Varden Fuller, "The Supply of Agricultural Labor as a Factor in the Evolution of Farm Organization in California," La Follette Committee *Hearings*, pt. 54, 19852.
10. Lawrence A. Cardoso, "Labor Emigration to the Southwest, 1916-1920," in *Mexican Workers in the United States*, ed. George C. Kiser and Martha Woody Kiser (Albuquerque, 1979), 16.
11. Fuller, 19852; Cardoso, "Labor Emigration," 18.
12. Arthur F. Corwin and Lawrence A. Cardoso, "Vamos el Norte," in *Immigrants—and Immigrants: Perspectives on Mexican Labor Migration to the United States*, ed. Arthur F. Corwin (Westport, Conn., 1978), 52.
13. Lawrence A. Cardoso, *Mexican Emigration to the United States, 1897-1931* (Tucson, 1980), 98-103.
14. Fuller, 19860.
15. Ibid.
16. Ibid, 19860-61.

17. McWilliams, 125. The census estimated that Mexican workers comprised only 21 percent of the total farm labor force, while farmers claimed they constituted over 80 percent of their workers. The lower census estimates result from the fact that the census was taken during the early spring, during the low point of agricultural employment. It is probable that many Mexican farm workers were not counted in the census because some had returned to Mexico and because a number had taken jobs in other industries, thus listing those industries as their occupation. See also Fuller, 19859-60.

18. Ibid, 19859.

19. McWilliams, 117-18.

20. Lawrence J. Jelinek, *Harvest Empire: A History of California Agriculture* (San Francisco, 1979), 53.

21. Interview, son of Wiley B. Giffen, owner of the Giffen Ranch, Mendota, California, Sept. 7, 1928, "Field Notes for *Mexican Labor in the United States,*" Paul S. Taylor Collection, Bancroft Library, University of California, Berkeley. [Hereafter cited as "Field Notes," Taylor.] Captain Y. L. Harvill, Employment Manager of the Columbia Steel Corporation in Pittsburg, California, reported that the steel industry gave the better-paying jobs to whites, just as employers of farm workers did. "We don't pay the Mexicans different rates for the same work but we give the better jobs with tonnage pay and higher earnings generally to the whites." Interview, Captain Y. L. Harvill, "Field Notes," Taylor.

22. McWilliams, 118.

23. Interview, H. W. Owen, Brentwood, California, Sept. 4, 1928, "Field Notes," Taylor.

24. Interview, Juan Estrada, in San Luis Pool Hall, El Centro, California, Oct. 14, 1928, "Field Notes," Taylor.

25. Interview, Mexican grape picker northeast of Fresno, Sept. 5, 1928, "Field Notes," Taylor.

26. Ernesto Galarza, U.S. Select Committee to Investigate the Interstate Migration of Destitute Citizens. *Hearings. Interstate Migration.* 76th Cong., 3rd sess., 1941-1942, pt. 10, 3884, cited by Mark Reisler, *By the Sweat of Their Brow: Mexican Immigrant Labor in the United States: 1900-1940* (Westport, Conn., 1976), 113-14.

27. Charles Wollenberg, "Huelga, 1928 Style: The Imperial Valley Cantaloupe Workers' Strike," *Pacific Historical Review* (February 1969): 48; Rudolph Acuna, *Occupied America: A History of Chicanos*, 2nd ed. (New York, 1981), 213.

28. Interview, Elmer Heald, District Attorney, Imperial County, 1928, "Field Notes," Taylor.

29. Interview, Brawley, California, 1928, "Field Notes," Taylor.

30. Wollenberg, 48; Reisler, 234-36; Cletus Daniel, *Bitter Harvest: A History of California Farm Workers, 1870-1941* (Berkeley, 1941), 108-9.

31. Cox, "Agricultural Labor," i, ii.

32. Ibid., 1.

33. Ibid., i, iii, 1, 14.

34. Leo Marx, *The Machine in the Garden: Technology and the Pastoral Ideal in America* (London and New York, 1964), 3-4, 353; see also Thomas Jefferson, *Notes on Virginia* (1785).

35. Department of Industrial Relations, Division of Housing, *Biennial Report, 1945-46*, 47-48; Commission of Immigration and Housing, *Annual Report, 1926*, 17, cited in Albert Croutch, "Housing for Migratory Agricultural Workers in California" (M. A. thesis, Univ. of California, 1948), 23, 25-26.

36. Commission of Immigration and Housing, *Annual Report, 1926*, 17, cited in Croutch, 26.

37. A. D. Shamel, "Housing Employees of California's Citrus Ranches," *California Citrograph*, February 1918, 71.

38. Ibid., February 1918, 71.

39. Ibid., March 1918, 96.

40. Ibid., May 1918, 150-51.

41. Paul S. Taylor, *Mexican Labor in the United States: Imperial Valley* (Berkeley, 1934), 55.

42. Ibid.

43. Paul S. Taylor, Visit to Imperial Valley, Aug. 30, 1928, "Field Notes," Taylor.

44. Interview at Mexican camp underneath eucalyptus trees, northeast of Fresno, "Field Notes," Taylor.

45. Interview, Mr. Martinez, Clovis, California, Sept. 5, 1928, "Field Notes," Taylor.

46. Ibid.

47. Ibid., 3.

48. Interview, Mexican grape picker Northeast of Fresno, Sept. 5, 1928, 1, "Field Notes," Taylor.

49. Interview, Mr. Martinez, Clovis, California, Sept. 5, 1928, 6, "Field Notes," Taylor.

50. Carleton Beals, *American Earth*, 395, cited by Croutch, 17-18.

51. Omer Mills, *Health Problems among Migratory Workers*, Farm Security Administration, 1939, 3; State Rural Resettlement Administration, Resettlement Administration, Statement Support of Project to Establish Camps for Migrants in California, 1935, Croutch, 18.

52. Carey McWilliams, *Testimony before the Tolan Committee*, part 6, 2542, Croutch, 19.

53. California State Emergency Relief Administration, 1935, 38, Croutch, 19-20.

54. Interview, Giffen (son of Wiley B. Giffen), Giffen Ranch, Mendota, Sept. 7, 1928, "Field Notes," Taylor.

55. Interview, Mexican grape picker Northeast of Fresno, Sept. 5, 1928, "Field Notes," Taylor.

56. Interview, Mr. Martinez, Clovis, California, Sept. 5, 1928, "Field Notes," Taylor.

57. Interview on the road from Fresno, Burbank school boy, Sept. 5, 1928, "Field Notes," Taylor.

58. Interview, Luz Romero, Brawley, California, 1928, "Field Notes," Taylor.

59. *Governor Young Report*, 177-78. In a 1928 survey of several Mexican districts in the Los Angeles area, researchers found that average annual income for a Mexican family in one district was $795 and between $600 and $800 in another. Since this was a house-to-house survey, researchers did not include the incomes of agricultural workers living in farm camps, and therefore even these figures are misleadingly high.

60. Gonzales to Secretary Tellez, Jan. 1, 1932, Archivo de Relaciones Exteriores de Mexico, Mexico, D.F., file 41-26-139; Santibanez to all consuls Oct. 17, 1930, ibid., file 73-84-1; Gonzales to Ortiz Rubio, April 4, Ortiz Rubio papers, 250; all cited by Cardoso, *Mexican Emigration to the United States*, 145.

61. Harold Fields, "Where Shall the Alien Work?" *Social Forces* 12 (December 1933): 213-14, cited by Ricardo Romo, *East Los Angeles: A History of a Barrio* (Austin, 1983), 164.

62. United States Department of Agriculture (USDA), Bureau of Agricultural Economics, "The Agricultural Situation" 17, 5 (May 1, 1933): 1-3.

63. Reisler, 228.

64. California, State Relief Administration, *Migratory Labor in California* (San Francisco, 1936), 109, 123; U.S. Bureau of Labor Statistics, *Monthly Labor Review* 49 (July 1939): 69; U.S. Bureau of Census, *Historical Statistics of the United States* (Washington, D.C., 1960), 166, cited by Reisler, 228-29.

65. Fuller, table 37, 19890; Stuart Jamieson, *Labor Unionism in American Agriculture* (Washington, D.C., 1945), 80.

66. USDA, Bureau of Agricultural Economics, "The Agricultural Situation" 17, 6 (June 1, 1933): 13; ibid., 17, 7 (July 1, 1933): 2.

67. USDA, Bureau of Agricultural Economics, "The Agricultural Situation" 17, 9 (September 1933): 2.

68. Jamieson, 80.

7

Class, Ethnicity, and the Transformation of Hawaii's Sugar Workers, 1920–1946

Ruth Akamine

The establishment of Hawaii's sugar industry in the mid-nineteenth century brought about the confluence of many national experiences within the boundaries of a tiny island chain. In the attempt to supply the industry's enormous labor demands, early planters drew workers from every part of the world—including China, Russia, Scandinavia, Korea, Puerto Rico, and Portugal and the Madeiras—in the hope of finding an ideal labor force to tend their fields.[1] Immigrant workers naturally brought with them perspectives of work, authority, and their rights as workers that were rooted within the social frameworks of the countries they had left. This often resulted in conflicts not only with their new employers but with their fellow workers as well. Hawaii's planters, organized into the powerful Hawaiian Sugar Planters' Association (HSPA), capitalized on such divisive forces: with the strategy of "divide and rule," they became astute players of cultural antagonisms in their efforts to sustain a large and compliant work force.[2]

In 1920, Japanese and Filipino union leaders on Oahu organized separate walkouts by their constituents and negotiated the possibility of striking in a joint effort; no joint effort occurred, however, and the strikes failed. But, twenty-six years later, a Territory-wide, multiethnic strike by sugar transport workers crippled Hawaii's economy, and the workers gained major concessions from their employers. What made such a transformation possible? How did the largely immigrant work force overcome barriers created by the strength of ethnic affiliations to unite together as a single force?

Examination of the workers' success in 1946 first requires an understanding of their roots in homeland societies, and of how differences in those social backgrounds and national histories created the potential for conflict between groups of workers. One must investigate how workers from different countries structured their communities together with, and apart from, each other and determine what paths early resistance took. Further, one must acknowledge the changes taking place in the relationship between the planters in the HSPA and their workers throughout the interwar years, the importance of political changes on Territorial and national life, and, finally, recognition of the breakdown of Hawaii's isolation from the mainland labor movement. Only then can the significance of the 1946 strike become truly apparent.

Influence of Homelands

Filipino and Japanese immigrants formed the largest ethnic bloc on Hawaii's "Big Five"–owned plantations.[3] While in 1915 Filipinos constituted 19 percent of the work force and the Japanese 54 percent, by 1931 the Japanese majority had dwindled to 28 percent, and the Filipino percentage had risen to 57. Sixty-three percent of the Filipinos came from the regions of Ilocos Norte, Ilocos Sur, and Cebu—regions heavily overpopulated and containing rapidly growing textile and sugar industries. Japanese immigrants also left overpopulated and developing provinces in southwestern Japan, such as Yamaguchi, Hiroshima, and Kumamoto.[4]

While many of the new arrivals from Japan came from landowning peasant families, the vast majority of Filipino migrants came from tenant families. In the Philippines, peasants participated in an agricultural system in which an elite class of Spanish- and-English speaking landowners hired, or made sharecropping arrangements with, an ethnically distinct work force. As an "internally class homogeneous unit," the Philippine village held "a potential for unity against the economically and culturally distinct landowners in town."[5] In Japan, on the other hand, most villages consisted of a hierarchy of landowners, with a smaller group of tenant farmers at its base. Disruption of Japanese peasants' lives accelerated in the 1880s with the skyrocketing of land taxes. Coupled with deflation, thousands of peasants were forced to default on payments, stripping them of land that had been family-owned for generations.[6] In the Philippines, late-nineteenth-century efforts by landlords to increase their share in international markets created severe upheaval in tenants' lives, especially as landlords shifted from a fixed-rent to a sharecropping system.[7]

The Philippines' centuries-long history of colonization—culminating in the defeat of Spain in 1898, the brief existence of an independent republic that was defeated by the United States in 1901, and the imposition of American colonial rule—made an indelible impact on its people's perception of rights and authority. So too did the colonial linkage of power with race and nationality. Ethnic heterogeneity formed an integral part of the archipelago's social fabric, and in fact the intermingling of Spanish and Chinese with the number of indigenous ethnic groups in that country created a mosaic not unlike that found on a smaller scale in Hawaii. Japan's history of sovereignty and ethnic homogeneity produced a very different social landscape. In Hawaii, Japanese immigrants would be confronted with adapting to the workings of a complex, heterogeneous social structure for the first time.

Despite such differences, however, many Filipino and Japanese immigrants were united by a common desire to accumulate savings abroad to aid difficult financial circumstances at home.[8] Upon arrival in Hawaii, both faced an agricultural environment that exhibited familiar components of work housed in an unfamiliar framework of production: a world regulated by the clock, a workplace that subordinated personhood to productivity.[9] In such an environment, community played a crucial role for the new arrivals.

New World Interaction

Tsuru Yamauchi arrived from Okinawa at the turn of the century as a "picture bride," overwhelmed by the challenges of new life in an alien culture. Fortunately, a cousin who lived near her began to teach her pidgin English, and neighbors with whom she shared an outdoor stove taught her other practical skills. Yamauchi reciprocated once she had a family of her own. "Many picture brides came . . . and lived near me," she attested. "Since they did not know as many things, I taught them what to do as I had been taught earlier." Furthermore, she reminisced, "everyone was just like brothers and sisters. When I was sick and couldn't do things, people came to help me after finishing their own work and doing their own chores." Members of each community gave, and received, help in times of difficulty.[10]

In contrast to the Japanese, Filipino camps were characterized by relative transiency—a perpetual concern of the planters' association, the HSPA.[11] This is hardly surprising, considering that over 90 percent of the Filipino work force came to Hawaii on three-year contracts. Nonetheless, the male communities also welcomed and oriented newly arrived recruits. When Faustino Baysa first arrived on Oahu in 1927, for example, he and his uncles learned the essentials of barracks cooking from new roommates. "The environment" in Hawaii "was a little different," Baysa recalled; "but some of the people in our neighborhood were someone I could talk to. And whenever I felt homesick I could go to the neighbors and play cards, tell stories about the old homes, and talk about their own families. And soon, the time was up to go to sleep."[12] In such ways, Filipino men passed some of the time they had committed to service in Hawaii.[13]

Although the first Japanese also worked as contract laborers in the 1880s, as the years passed many established families in the islands. By the 1920s, many contract workers had left the sugar fields to establish businesses or small farms, and many of those who remained on the plantations advanced through the plantation hierarchy of labor. As the largest ethnic bloc in the islands, the Japanese community soon formed a large and thriving presence in the Territory. Cultural activities proliferated in the islands. Buddhist associations flourished, banding together to form a loose interisland confederation; four newspapers reported events taking place in Japan as well as in the islands; 174 language schools instructed second-generation children, promoting character building in addition to language acquisition. The Imperial Department of Education in Japan authorized teaching materials for Hawaii. Teachers stressed veneration of the emperor, and on Saturdays girls learned customary Japanese sewing techniques. Virtually every child attended the schools, for there was a "good deal of social censure within the Japanese community if a child was not sent."[14] In 1931, 99 percent of the Japanese children were American citizens, but in the culturally diverse environment that surrounded them, parents determined to instill in their children a loyalty to their ethnic heritage.[15]

Such loyalty insulated ethnic communities from each other. For Japanese parents, it was not enough "to marry just a Japanese; he must belong to the same prefecture and be of equal rank, and of course so much the better if his family [was] from the same community in Japan"; marriage to a non-Japanese was almost inconceivable to some *issei* (first-generation immigrants). When one woman announced that she was going to marry a non-Japanese, for example, conflict ensued: while her parents retained a framework of social status rooted in Japanese life, she represented a social environment in which ethnic heterogeneity was a norm—a world with expanded rules governing interaction and belonging.[16]

Interaction between workers from different countries changed the ethnically homogeneous perspectives of some immigrants, however. In one instance, a parent used such a friendship to teach his son about diversity and camaraderie. The young Chinese boy was frightened by the plantation's sole black worker, so his father gave him a "good lesson. One day he invite that Negro to come and sit on our back porch," he recalled. "They slap each other and laugh . . . and get a good time out of it, that he was joking with him. And then after that, I was cured. I had no more fear of any Negroes." The same father spanked his son "without asking any question" when he fought with Japanese children.[17]

Holiday celebrations created bonds of community spirit that transcended ethnic loyalties. On Rizal Day—a holiday feting José Rizal, who initiated the Philippine nationalist movement against Spanish rule—Filipinos on Ohau's Waialua plantation pooled their resources and held a feast for everyone in their camp, regardless of background. Puerto Rican communities held annual church bazaars for general attendance; at Haleiwa, friends celebrating a Japanese wedding drove around the plantation beating a drum, signaling everyone to join in the celebration. At such festivities, observance of homeland traditions also served the joint function of celebrating Hawaii's ethnically diverse community life as well.[18]

Planters' Strategies of Control: "Divide and Rule" and Paternalism

Since the 1860s, when Chinese workers were first brought in to offset an increasingly restive work force made up of native Hawaiians, "divide and rule" formed a cornerstone of managerial operations in the industry's early years. "Anglo-Saxons" ruled the plantations; Portuguese and Puerto Rican immigrants worked as overseers or mechanics; and beneath them, Asian laborers worked the fields. Anti-Chinese sentiment on the mainland United States resulted in legislation that severely restricted Chinese immigration in 1881. In 1904, added legislation cut off further migration from Japan. The planters then turned to the Philippines to supply their labor requirements and capitalized on the U.S. possession's exemption from exclusion laws. They accelerated their recruitment campaigns markedly following the defeat of a strike by Japanese workers in 1920. As the newest participants in Hawaiian industry, Filipinos entered as the bottom of the plantation hierarchy of labor.

Entry of yet another ethnic component to the industry's work force deterred development of organized solidarity, and managers exploited such ethnic division during simultaneous but separate strikes by Japanese and Filipino workers in 1920. The HSPA's accelerated recruitment drives in the Philippines were intended to counter not only Japanese strikers' efforts but those of the Filipinos as well. Most of the Filipino work force came either from Ilocos Norte Province or the Visayan Islands—two very different regions, both culturally and linguistically. In Hawaii, conflict between Ilocanos and Visayans was common, and, in 1920, strike participation was limited largely to Visayans.[19] James Campsie, manager of the Hawaiian Agricultural Company, evidently exploited this tension during the strike. A reply from the HSPA head office informed him, "We have for acknowledgement your Labor

Requirement from March requesting fifty laborers, Ilocanos preferred. We are at present assigning all new arrivals to the plantations on [Oahu] to take the place of the strikers."[20]

To a large extent, job classification followed ethnic lines. Caucasians occupied top managerial positions, as well as those related to engineering, mill work, and railroad work. Japanese men occupied some positions in the mills, as well as upper-echelon field work. Finally, women and Filipinos performed the unskilled field tasks.[21] This exacerbated divisions among the plantation work force, and in at least one instance ethnicity became the prism through which a wage dispute was viewed. In 1930, a Filipino field worker and four friends wrote to HSPA headquarters requesting the removal of a Japanese *luna* (overseer), asserting that he had cheated them of bonus pay:

> Really the officers of this Pahala Plantation are here watching us everyday, but I know already that they are infavor to those LUNAS CONTRAC-BOOS or Japanies. I tell you the truth that all CONTRACTORS here are Japanies and we the Filipinos who are working to them feel very very sorry because the LUNAS OR CONTRACTORS are not doing right. I say they are not doing right because they are stealling the Plantation too.

Clearly, the petitioner framed his anger over the wage conflict in racial terms.[22]

Housing patterns reinforced occupational and ethnic stratification.[23] In the nineteenth century, planters had maintained a policy of segregated housing, but by the 1920s, the separation resulted from workers' preference as well as managerial planning. Workers banded together in crews made up of fellow nationals, and because housing camps were built near work sites, which spread several miles on the average, plantation separation resulted. On the one-hundred-thousand-acre domain of the Hawaiian Agricultural Company, for example, Filipino gangs secured long-term contracts to cultivate those fields located at higher altitudes, requiring up to an extra year's tending to reach maturity. Their camps were distant from other field workers and farther still from those who lived in town and worked at the mill. Nine miles away, a longshore crew consisting mainly of native Hawaiians operated the company's shipping terminal.[24]

Hawaiian employers, like many of those on the mainland, adopted a new paternalistic relationship with their workers beginning in the 1920s. In what became known as the perquisite system, employers provided housing, entertainment, and other benefits. Perquisites, they hoped, would offset the increasing strength of immigrant union movements. In 1920, Japanese strikes demanded improvements in housing conditions and "provisions for health and amusement of laborers."[25] Three months after the strike's end, HSPA plantations raised wages and revised the "bonus" system.[26] At the same time, congressional legislation limiting Asian immigration made employers fear that they could no longer rely on new waves of docile laborers. Instead, perquisites might ensure labor peace. By the end of 1921, a new HSPA bureau, formed to monitor living conditions, reported expenditures of $2 million to upgrade living conditions. By 1922, the Hawaiian Agricultural Company began to screen weekly movies, construct new housing, and install playing fields. During the 1920s, HSPA plantations also installed indoor plumbing and kitchens and improved medical care.

HSPA plantations also began to make official allowance for the observance of ethnic holidays. In 1927, Japanese workers were excused from work to observe the emperor's funeral; likewise, Filipinos gained exemption to celebrate Rizal Day.[27] Until 1941, managers also allowed the operation of Japanese schools, in part because having children in the schools freed women to work in the fields. In 1922, when Caucasian Territorial legislators feared Japanese domination of the islands and passed new regulations on the Japanese schools, the HSPA's determination to "safeguard the [existence] of *wahine* [women's] labor in the field" resulted in its vote to subsidize the schools.[28] At the same time, however, managers promoted the development of Americanism within communities. Company Christmas parties were yearly highlights for plantation children. Some companies sponsored Fourth of July gatherings, and one company sponsored a week-long festival celebrating American music.[29] Public school education also played a crucial role in exposing immigrant families to American culture and ideals.[30]

Despite the improvement in living and working conditions, however, no substantial changes were made in wages throughout the 1920s. The most common excuse was that the higher value of workers' perquisites functioned as a de facto wage increase. With the onset of the Depression, wages for a skilled male day laborer (including bonus) dropped between 1930 and 1933 from $1.66 per day to $1.40.[31]

To eliminate dissent among its work force, the HSPA maintained a surveillance network and blacklist throughout the Territory. In the early 1920s one IWW organizer was expelled from a plantation when he began to speak with its workers. The association closely monitored efforts among the Japanese and Filipino communities to raise money for the defense of Pablo Manlapit, an organizer of the 1920 and 1924 Filipino strikes.[32] Representatives of foreign organizations were scrutinized for "inflammatory" messages. One representative was cleared with the following memo:

> So far as can be learned there is nothing harmful to the
> interests of the Association. . . . The organizer has expressed
> himself as being in favor of quiet and orderly work among the
> Filipinos . . . and has advised the members to disregard any
> thoughts of disturbance, strikes or organizations pointed the
> way. This organization is not regarded as conflicting with the
> interests of the plantations, and it is even thought that if the
> Filipinos will think along the lines of such an association,
> they will probably be less susceptible to pleas from Union
> Organizations.[33]

The HSPA had good reason to fear the possibilities of organization, for
in 1920 and 1924, Japanese and Filipino strikes dealt major blows to
HSPA productivity.

Early Workers' Movements

In 1920, the Federation of Japanese Labor (FJL) and the Filipino
Labor Union (FLU) led twelve thousand Oahu workers—77 percent of
the island's total labor force—in separate strikes for similar demands.
At issue were raises in daily wages from 77 cents to $1.25 for unskilled
male laborers and from 59 to 93 cents for women workers, an eight-hour
day, and restructuring of the bonus system. The FJL also demanded
overtime and maternity leaves.

Despite efforts to consolidate the strikes, both groups retained the
interests of fellow nationals as their top priority: each group considered
alliance only as a means to achieve those objectives. In December
1919, both unions had submitted grievances to the HSPA. Both were
rejected. The FLU then called for a strike but extended its deadline as
its leader, Pablo Manlapit, made last-minute attempts to gain FJL
support.[34]

FJL leaders were reluctant to ally themselves with the FLU. Newly
arrived Filipino recruits constituted the bulk of the FLU's membership,
along with a small number of Spanish, Portuguese, and Hawaiian
workers. While the FLU was newly formed and loosely organized, the
FJL had strong grass-roots foundations in community groups such as
the Buddhist associations. Furthermore, the FJL received support from
the nonplantation Japanese community, which organized a "Plantation
Laborers Supporters Association."[35] In a meeting with Manlapit, FJL
leaders indicated that they would cooperate with the FLU on the
condition that Manlapit and his followers agreed to submit to FJL
leadership.[36] Manlapit refused, and ordered the FLU walkout to begin
on January 20.

Japanese intellectuals called for community support of the FLU
effort. Most vocal were the editors of three newspapers, all of whom had
played a role in a strike by Japanese workers in 1909. One editor urged

workers to remember that the FLU's "righteous indignation is our righteous indignation . . . their problem is your problem."[37] Within the ranks of FJL leadership itself, Takashi Tsutsumi extolled the advantages of a united effort and accurately predicted the consequences of separatist action:

> Form a labor organization and admit all nationalities into membership! The capitalists would not be able to raise a finger of opposition. If instead, an organization of Japanese alone is formed, the capitalists would take advantage of an excellent pretext, and would incite a racial disturbance, pitting one race against another.[38]

Although Japanese union leaders called for a day-long "general layoff" on January 23 in sympathy with the FLU, it was only when HSPA officials rejected a third petition that FJL leaders called for their own walkout, to begin February 2.

As Tsutsumi had forewarned, planters capitalized on the disagreements between the two unions to regain control. A company president wrote to the manager of Hawaiian Agricultural:

> We are inclined to think that the best prospect, in connection with this strike, is the fact that two organizations, not entirely in harmony with each other, are connected with it, and if either of them falls out of line, the end will be in sight.[39]

Accordingly, HSPA officials began to sabotage the strikes. It subsidized an antistrike newspaper. An HSPA attorney met with Manlapit in the hope of bribing him to end the FLU strike. Whether or not because of this offer, Manlapit rescinded his walkout order on February 8, one week into the walkout by Japanese; at the same time, he accused the Japanese of striking in order to "cripple the industries of the Territory of Hawaii," leaving it open for takeover "by an unscrupulous alien race." Adding to the chaos, he reissued his order to strike six days later. With such leadership, it is hardly surprising that FLU members steadily returned to work through the duration of the Japanese walkout.[40]

As in the past, the HSPA management evicted the striking workers from plantation-owned housing and closed off their accounts at company stores. Nonplantation community members provided many strikers with housing and food; yet the duration of the strike, coupled with the debilitating effects of a severe influenza epidemic, sapped the FJL's strength. On July 1, FJL union leaders met with HSPA representatives and agreed to return to work. The union disbanded—after changing its name to the Hawaii Laborers' Association[41] —marking the end of unionism among the Japanese until the mid-1930s.

Examination of the language used by both unions reveals the extent to which homeland perceptions of authority and rights structured the logic for taking collective action in Hawaii. In a pamphlet published by the Japanese union, traces of the Confucian ideal of family seem to be adapted to the industrial setting—with labor and capital as joint members in a family unit, each member having its "place" within the whole, and equilibrium the desired ideal. The writer suggested that the relationship between planters and laborers historically had been one of mutual dependence; but an "undesirable element" within the planter class had violated that relationship by mistreating the workers, causing divisions between the partners and "compelling" a strike.[42] He stressed

> [t]he separation of capital and labor was only a variation of
> the moment; the co-operation of the two is the natural state of
> condition. It is for the maintenance of this normal condition
> that we should strive.[43]

The confrontational stance of European and American workers repelled the writer. They seemed to embark on "strike after strike with little or no thought for the progress of the industrial world or the peace of society": individual gain was placed above the well-being of the collective.[44] As far as Japanese labor's role was concerned, the writer, speaking for the Japanese union as a whole, expressed "regret" for the conflict caused by the strike and voiced a willingness to "do our part toward Hawaii's production and welfare the best we know how . . . endeavoring to safeguard justice and humanity as members of the great human family."[45]

Manifestly different was the attitude held by Filipino leader Manlapit in April 1924, when he again led workers—this time throughout the islands—on a year-long series of strikes. In this instance the strike movement was essentially an all-Filipino effort, since its aim was to better conditions for unskilled field workers.[46] At issue were wage increases from $1 to $2 per day; abolition of the bonus system; overtime payment; and wage equity between male and female co-workers. The HSPA responded with more brutality than it had displayed in 1920. At Hanapepe, a violent confrontation left sixteen strikers and four policeman dead. The National Guard surrounded strike camps with machine guns to prohibit movement, and in May 1925, its arrest of the remaining strikers on Kauai ended the strike. Manlapit and others were tried for perjury, and he was deported to the Philippines.

Manlapit defended the Filipino strike by asserting that the terms of HSPA work contracts violated their holders' rights as citizens. The contracts "conflict[ed] with the provisions of the Constitution of the United States." Moreover, the HSPA—by paying "an un-American wage" and creating "intolerable conditions"—was guilty of violating the wage" and creating "intolerable conditions"—was guilty of violating the fundamental principles of the American dream promised each new participant. He elaborated:

> The keynote of Americanism, for the laborer, is the opportunity to advance—to better his condition. It is one of the cherished American ideals that each generation shall stand in advance of the preceding one, better physically, mentally, spiritually. And America demands for her workers this opportunity for development. If the opportunity is lacking in any industry, that industry must remold its methods and conform to the demands of society, or it must be eliminated.[47]

In Manlapit's opinion, Filipinos' labor contributions and partial participation in the American political system guaranteed "inalienable rights" that were being denied them—giving them the right to suspend contractual obligations to their employer. Manlapit also asserted:

> Instead of a "living wage" American labor demands a "saving wage"! And it demands it not only for itself but for all the strangers within its gates. It cannot tolerate conditions that lower the standards of living for any considerable portion of its population, whether native or foreign birth, for it is a maxim that the lowest paid worker sets the standard for all the rest.[48]

In this argument, Manlapit acknowledged that, because Filipinos were not full citizens under the American Constitution, they were to some extent "strangers";[49] nevertheless, as participants in America's labor system, Filipinos were entitled to the living standard accorded mainland workers.[50]

In 1932, Manlapit returned to Hawaii and formed a new Filipino Labor Union with other workers; shortly after its founding, however, one of his cohorts was jailed for organizing, and in 1935 Manlapit himself was banished permanently from the Territory. The one leader remaining transformed the union into a secret society, Vibora Luviminda, and in 1937 the society led a walkout of cane cutters on Maui plantation. Before calling for the walkout, however, it called on representatives of the mainland-based longshoremen's unions working in Honolulu to help organize the field workers. At the three-month strike's end, the cane cutters had won a 15 percent raise through negotiated settlement: the first such victory in the Territory's history.

Breakdown of Hawaiian Isolation

Success in the 1937 strike was aided by developments that were rapidly transforming Hawaii's political and social environment. First,

New Deal legislation generated a frenzy of unionization in the United States that carried over into the Pacific. Sailors returned home to Hawaii changed by what they had experienced in San Francisco and other parts of the West Coast.[51] Hawaiian labor linked up with the mainland movement when longshoremen in Honolulu and Hilo organized under the International Longshoremen's and Warehousemen's Union (ILWU) in 1937. ILWU members soon spread their beliefs by speaking with members of Vibora Luviminda and by organizing mill workers under the United Cannery, Agricultural, Packing & Allied Workers Union.

Second, New Deal legislation forced HSPA corporations to be more accountable for their labor policies. In 1937, the National Labor Relations Board (NLRB) began an investigation of labor conditions in the islands, which resulted in one of the Big Five corporation's being convicted on charges of unfair labor practices. In part because of this conviction, HSPA counsel advised the manager on Maui to settle with the Vibora Luviminda when it struck his plantation.[52]

Also a factor in the lessening of HSPA dominance was the escalation in the number of workers who could vote. In 1900, almost three-fourths of the Territory's male population had been ineligible to vote. Between 1931 and 1944, however, the percentage of Japanese male workers who were eligible to vote rose from 19 percent to 54 percent, and for women from 19 percent to 52 percent. In 1930, only 12 percent of the industry's work force were American citizens, but by 1939 the figure had risen to 45 percent.[53] Nevertheless, all Filipinos continued to be denied voting rights until the Philippines became a sovereign nation in 1946. The ILWU organized a voting drive in 1938 to elect candidates to the territorial legislature, and three months into the campaign the drive succeeded in electing its first candidate.

The bombing of Pearl Harbor and America's entry into World War II forced workers to reconsider their ethnic heritages, along with their ties to other workers in their communities—a relationship that became more complex as sons enlisted in the American military, and as U.S. forces fought Japanese forces to regain control of the Philippines.[54] Tension often resulted between Filipino and Japanese workers; others, however, tried to subordinate ethnic differences in favor of the maintenance of camaraderie between co-workers. One Filipino worker who volunteered in a civilian defense squad recounted:

> there were some situations where the thinking was, "How can I fight my Japanese neighbors when I eat with them all the time?" . . . . Most of my friends working together, with whom we eat at work, were Japanese. So, we tried to avoid telling, "You are Japanese" or "You're Filipinos." We just worked.[55]

One issue that united all workers, however, was the issue of wages. The job and wage freezes set by martial law laid bare the contrast between plantation wages and those of other workplaces. This was especially true when managers acted as labor contractors for Defense Department projects, making a profit when they lent workers for an average wage of sixty-two cents per hour to the projects while still paying workers their plantation wages of less than twenty cents an hour. The collective resentment against this practice would help to fuel the ILWU's phenomenally quick and successful unionization drives beginning early in 1944.

Mobilization

With the partial removal of martial law in 1943, the ILWU resumed its drive full force. Perhaps the most influential union figure at the time was Jack Kawano, who persuaded the union to diversify inland to the plantations.[56] President of the ILWU's Honolulu local, Kawano was himself a child of the plantations. Dissatisfied with plantation work, Kawano had moved on to the docks after working as a trucker. In February 1944, Kawano's local voted to appropriate $5,000 for the organization of mill workers, thereby initiating the ILWU's Hawaiian "march inland."[57]

ILWU recruiters' ties to plantation communities served as swift conduits of the union's message. By March 1945, the ILWU had won NLRB elections in all the mills on Maui and Hawaii (with the exception of one AFL affiliate), and only seven had yet to hold elections on Oahu and Kauai. It secured a one-year contract for these mills through August 1946.

Ethnic conflicts reemerged in the process of unionization. At one plantation, Filipinos resented the fact that most of the local's offices were occupied by Japanese, even though Filipinos dominated the work force. To counteract ethnic resentment, Frank Thompson—sent by mainland headquarters from his work with California field workers—ignored normal union procedures, unilaterally incorporated the locals, and installed a representative board consisting of a Portuguese president, Japanese and Filipino vice-presidents, and a Hawaiian secretary-treasurer. To him, organizational representation of the union's ethnic diversity took priority, "with the qualifications of the officers being secondary."[58]

The mainland ILWU office supported Thompson's move, stating: "The importance of racial unity in the islands makes it imperative that steps be taken to put Filipinos, Hawaiians, Portuguese and others into prominent positions, even though in some cases they might not be as qualified or capable as the Japanese."[59] The union also strove to maintain equality among its members by conducting all local meetings in English, Ilocano, and Japanese. Finally, actions taken by the ILWU on the mainland on behalf of its Japanese members affirmed its commitment to equality among all workers: in 1942, the ILWU was the only union to protest Japanese-American incarceration at administrative hearings in California, and in 1945 the head office expelled a Stockton local for refusing to readmit Japanese-American workers to their former jobs.

The union finished its vertical organization of the sugar industry following passage of the Territory's "Little Wagner Act" on May 21, 1945, which sanctioned organization of agricultural workers. Mill workers recruited field workers. Members of a sailors union recruited 90 percent of the Filipinos aboard the SS *Maunawili*—the final shipful of Filipino workers from U.S.-occupied Philippines—before it had even docked in Honolulu in January 1946.[60] By November 1945, locals had been established on all thirty-three HSPA plantations; by mid-1946, signup of field workers was complete. By June 1946, over 20,000 workers had become ILWU members.

The Strike of 1946

Contract negotiations began in the summer of 1946, but insufficient progress was made before all the mill workers' contracts expired. Consequently, on September 1, the ILWU led thirty-three thousand workers and their families on a 79-day strike for a union shop, abolition of the perquisite system, a minimum-wage increase as well as a raise in general wages, an eight-hour day, a job classification system, and a ban on discrimination based on race, political belief, or union membership. In a prior arrangement with the ILWU, the HSPA agreed not to evict strikers from their homes.[61]

The walkout by field, mill, and transport workers belonging to the union—bolstered by sympathy strikes by other unions—paralyzed Hawaii's economy. Ships carrying goods could not be unloaded, nor could they take on added cargo. Goods already on the docks remained. And thousands of tons of cane rotted in the fields as negotiations stalled. The strike caused divisions in families split by management and union affiliation. Conflict resulted between parents and children— some fathers pointing out the benefits of the security that came from free housing and a steady job, while their children rebutted that workers paid for such perquisites with their cheap wages. Yet the strike bonded participants together. Picket lines and strike kitchens provided environments where all could congregate "just for fellowship."[62]

On November 18, the union won a minimum-wage raise to twenty-seven cents per hour, a job classification system, and abolition of the perquisite system. The victory signified a momentous occasion for the Territory's workers. First, abolition of the perquisite system signified the end of induced dependence on the HSPA and the beginning of control by workers over the daily framework of their lives. Second, a minimum-wage increase secured Pablo Manlapit and the Filipino Labor Union's ambition to gain equity for unskilled field workers. Third, the acquisition of negotiated contracts for all the industry's workers practically and symbolically emphasized the new element of equality between workers and employers: a relationship that permitted workers an official voice. Finally, the method of achieving that voice—that is, through multiethnic unity and action—signified the fundamental transformation of the workers' perceptions of themselves as a whole.

In many respects, 1946 marks the end of Hawaiian sugar's status as a neocolonial industry: one in which, through monopoly of capital and power in an isolated region, the HSPA was able to select and mold the composition of its work force to its best advantage. Throughout its early decades and into the twentieth century, it had been possible for the industry to maintain hegemony through its reliance on a steady influx of immigrant labor that remained divided along ethnic lines. Filipinos and Japanese had remained divided by occupational stratification within the plantations as well as by political, economic, and cultural differences that extended outside the plantations. As each group established itself in its new land, it began to assert its claims for just treatment and wages—the Japanese in 1909 with their first strike, and the Filipinos in 1920. This, combined with the passage of mainland legislation restricting immigration, a steady outflow of workers from the plantations, New Deal labor legislation, and increased competition between beet and cane sugar interests within the international marketplace, forced HSPA leaders to reshape their relationship with their workers. Yet the impetus to change created by workers' collective action became most forceful only after the ethnically diverse work force united together through and with the mainland American union movement. By uniting under the ILWU in 1946, Hawaii's workers found a powerful vehicle through which to express their newly found collective voice and set a precedent for Hawaii's relationship with the rest of the United States that would find political affirmation in 1958.

Notes

1. Sugar production is a labor- and capital-intensive endeavor. Sugar production requires a semitropical environment, a long cultivation period with constant tending, access to an enormous amount of water (one ton per pound of refined sugar), and efficient transportation networks to convey cut cane immediately to a mill for processing, since cane spoils quickly. Hawaiian planters balanced the demands of labor and mill efficiency by staggering cultivation to permit year-round mill operation and employment. Each aspect of

cultivation was divided among work crews, which rotated among fields as they reached particular stages of growth. This eliminated seasonal employment, contributing an unusual element of stability to agricultural labor in the islands. Unskilled field labor took up about one-third of the industry's work force; women worked in all aspects of field work, and made up 6 to 8 percent of the entire work force. A smaller group of mill workers processed the cane into raw sugar, which was then shipped to California for refinement. For a more detailed breakdown of production, see U.S. Department of Labor, "Labor Conditions in the Territory of Hawaii, 1929-1930," *Bulletin* 534 (March 1931). See also Ronald Takaki, *Pau Hana: Plantation Life and Labor in Hawaii* (Honolulu, 1983), and John M. Liu, "Race, Ethnicity, and the Sugar Plantation System: Asian Labor in Hawaii, 1850 to 1900," in *Labor Immigration under Capitalism: Asian Workers in the United States before World War II*, ed., Lucie Cheng and Edna Bonacich (Berkeley, 1984), 186-210.

2. In 1895, Hawaiian planters consolidated their resources into a voluntary and unincorporated organization that came to maintain research and development facilities, a recruitment office in Manila, a bureau to monitor living conditions and labor conflict throughout the islands, and a lobby in Washington to promote Hawaiian sugar interests against those of Louisiana and other mainland sugar-producing regions and to secure appointment of its gubernatorial candidates. By 1920, 80 percent of the Territory's fifty-two plantations belonged to the HSPA.

3. By 1933, the so-called Big Five corporations controlled 96 percent of the Territory's sugar production and controlled most the rest of the Hawaiian economy as well. Big Five members controlled the Hawaiian Pineapple Company, which at the time produced half of the world's pineapples; owned two newspapers, several banks, public utilities, and insurance companies; and controlled the stevedoring and shipping firms that transported Big Five sugar to the California & Hawaii (C & H) Sugar refinery in California, also owned by the Big Five.

4. Bruno Lasker, *Filipino Immigration* (New York: Arno, 1969), Appendix C; Alan Moriyama, "The Causes of Emigration: The Background of Japanese Emigration to Hawaii, 1885 to 1894," in Cheng and Bonacich; Robert C. Schmidt, *Historical Statistics of Hawaii* (Honolulu, 1977), 25. See also John Bodnar, *The Transplanted: A History of Immigrants in Urban America* (Bloomington, 1987), especially chapter 1, "The Homeland and Capitalism."

5. Brian Fegan, "The Social Life of a Central Luzon Barrio," in *Philippine Social History*, ed. Alfred W. McCoy and Ed. C. de Jesus (Honolulu, 1981), 94-103.

6. Between 1882 and 1892, the Japanese government derived 85.6 percent of its revenue from land taxes; between 1880 and 1883 alone, land taxes rose 39 percent. Not surprisingly, defaults and dispossessions skyrocketed during the decade. Over 360,000 peasants defaulted on payments; land sales more than doubled, from 680,000 sales in 1887 to 1.7 million in 1891. Mikiso Hane, *Peasants, Rebels and Outcasts* (New York, 1982), 17; Roger W. Bowen, *Rebellion and Democracy in Meiji Japan* (Berkeley, 1980), 92-99; E. H. Norman, *Origins of the Modern Japanese State* (New York, 1975), 251-54.

7. Miriam Sharma, "The Philippines: A Case of Migration to Hawaii, 1906-1946," in Cheng and Bonacich, 337-58; Alfred W. McCoy and Ed. C. de Jesus, "Introduction," in McCoy and de Jesus.

8. For Filipino and Japanese peasants, American wages offered a way to secure capital for their families at home. In the Philippines, agricultural wages averaged less than a peso per day for men and just over half a peso for women, while the cost of living could reach 1.25 pesos per day (2 pesos equal $1). In Japan, a tenant family earned an average of 4.5 yen per month, while an urban

laborer averaged 10 yen per month (2 yen equal $1). Hawaii's average wage of $1 a day for unskilled male laborers created a small margin of surplus that often found its way back to homelands. In 1904, a Japanese official reported that money sent home from Hawaii exceeded 100 million yen; that year, too, Hawaiian workers contributed 90,000 yen to support the nation's war with Russia, and "showed interest" in buying bonds totaling 3 million yen. Letter from Makoto Morioka to Baron Komura Jutaro, quoted in Wayne Patterson, "Japanese Imperialism in Korea: A Study of Immigration Foreign Policy," in *Japan in Transition*, ed. Hilary Conroy et al. (Rutherford, N.J., 1974), 296.

9. As in any industrial workplace, plantation life and work was regulated by the whistle. One contemporary sociologist recorded the following schedule: "At 5 a.m. the first whistle warned those living some distance away to be ready for the bus or train. . . . At 5:20 a second whistle was the signal for the assignments for the day; latecomers missed their assignments and were not permitted to work that day. At 5:40 a third whistle was the signal for the truck or train to take the workers to the fields, and at 6 o'clock the day's work began." Quoted by Robert N. Anderson et al., *Filipinos in Rural Hawaii* (Honolulu, 1984), 49-50. See also Herbert Gutman, *Work, Culture, and Society in Industrializing America* (New York, 1976), 5-41; David Montgomery, "Immigrant Workers and Managerial Reform," in his *Workers' Control in America* (New York, 1979), 32-47; and especially Sidney W. Mintz, *Sweetness and Power* (New York, 1985), 52, for an analysis of labor in the sugar industry as an agricultural counterpart to industrial labor.

10. *Uchinanchu*, 498.

11. Miriam Sharma, "Labor Migration and Class Formation among the Filipinos in Hawaii, 1906-1946," in Cheng and Bonacich, 582-86, 609. One author has found that in 1910 HSPA recruiters negotiated to transport an entire Filipino village, complete with priest and village leaders, to Hawaii "as an ideal community on one of the plantations. It was hoped that such a community would have a stabilizing influence on the Filipino men" and would encourage them to establish roots in the Territory. The plan never materialized, but it well illustrates the lengths to which the HSPA would go to secure a stable work force. Sister Mary Dorita, B.V.M., "Filipino Immigration to Hawaii" (master's thesis, University of Hawaii, 1975), 19.

12. Ethnic Studies Oral History Project, *Waialua and Haleiwa* (Honolulu, 1981), 3:26 (hereafter referred to as *W&H*).

13. See also Sharma, "Labor Migration," 586-94. For a contemporary sociological analysis of the impact of homeland social structure on organization in Hawaii, see Roman R. Cariaga, *The Filipinos in Hawaii: Economic and Social Conditions, 1906-1936* (Honolulu, 1937).

14. Charles Katsumu Tanimoto, *Return to Mahaulepu* (Honolulu, 1982), 34; Takashi Shinoda, written reply to this writer's questionnaire, March 1986.

15. "Census of Hawaiian Sugar Plantations. Total Employees and Families, including Planters. Summary—All Islands," June 10, 1931, HSPA.

16. Emi Yoshizawa, "A Japanese Family in Rural Hawaii," *Social Process* 3 (May 1937): 59; *W&H*, 3:82.

17. *W&H*, 1:137-38.

18. Ibid., 3:87.

19. Ibid., 1:137, 2:82, 3:87, 110.

20. Memo, HSPA Secretary R. Mead to the Hawaiian Agricultural Co. (hereafter Hn. Ag.), March 1920. Microfilm records of Hn. Ag. correspondence are housed at University of Hawaii, Manoa campus. All documents of Hn. Ag. cited in this paper have been taken from reel 11.

21. Sharma, "Labor Migration," 601-2; *W&H*, 3:12. In 1929, the HSPA reported that it employed nearly 1,500 women—only about 10 percent of the total female plantation population. The 90 percent unaccounted for were certainly not idle. The money they raised from cooking and cleaning for 35, 000 single men or from sales of vegetables or meats that they raised themselves constituted an essential component of each family's economy. See Bodnar, 71-83, on the immigrant family economy.

22. Typed letter, Benjamin Acasio to HSPA headquarters, Honolulu, copy sent to Hn. Ag., Jan. 29, 1930. In response to the HSPA headquarters' questions regarding the complaint, Hn. Ag.'s manager asserted that Acasio had been overpaid the previous month and hence the extra sum had been deducted from his next check, Hn. Ag., General Manager, June 19, 1931.

23. Memo, HSPA to Hn. Ag., May 22, 1922; Memo, HSPA Director of Industrial Services Bureau to Hn. Ag., Sept. 1, 1924. In a memo to all plantation managers in 1924, an HSPA director suggested that Japanese families residing in cramped duplexes be moved into new single-family homes. "Many of the old homes," he concluded, "with some remodelling, could then be occupied by new Filipino families."

24. Honolulu *Star-Bulletin* 1920 Centenary Issue, June 25, 1935; *Advertiser*, May 3, 1932, June 7, 1941.

25. Hawaii Laborers Association, *Facts about the Strike on Sugar Plantations* (Honolulu, 1920), 7. For an essay on the rise of paternalism as a strategy, see David Brody, "The Rise and Decline of Welfare Capitalism," in his *Workers in Industrial America: Essays on the Twentieth-Century Struggle* (New York, 1980), 44-81.

26. Bonuses constituted part of an incentive system in which those who worked over a set number of days per month were given an extra sum. Although called "bonuses," they were in fact indispensable components of subsistence budgets.

27. Memo, HSPA to Hn. Ag., Jan. 19, 1927.

28. Letter, HSPA Secretary J. Butler to Hn. Ag., Aug. 15, 1922. The letter detailed HSPA concerns about the impending elimination of lower grades from the Japanese schools. Butler reported, "This situation would result in a number of these children becoming a problem [in] the plantation camps, with the result that the plantations [would lose] the benefit of the labor of a number of Japanese women who would stay at home to take care of the children rather than be fit for labor." He suggested that each plantation hire a "suitable school teacher," which "would result in merely an extension of [the] policy calling for the establishment of the Day Nurseries." (Bracketed material appears where manuscript is obscured.)

29. In 1924, the director of the HSPA's bureau that monitored living conditions promoted "music week," asserting: "Music plays an important part in our national life and it is a great factor in promoting Americanism." Furthermore, he added, "[i]t is a well established fact that music improves morals." D. S. Bowman to Hn. Ag., April 22, 1924.

30. *Uchinanchu*, 419. Public schools played a crucial role in exposing immigrants' children to Hawaii's multiethnic society. In 1924, 56,000 children from more than eight countries enrolled in Hawaii's public schools. That year, the Board of Education set its goals: (1) to train children to speak standard English instead of "pidgin"; and (2) to set "high ideals of democracy and right living through the [Boy] Scout movement and inter-school athletics." Department of Public Instruction, Territory of Hawaii, *1923-24 Biennial Report*, 18.

Schools were the first to emphasize the significance of American citizenship. By emphasizing democratic ideals, however, schools also highlighted the disparity between the rhetoric and reality of equal rights in the minds of their students. One plantation student later commented: "The public school system perhaps without realizing it created unrest and disorganization. Here the children learn[ed] about democracy or at least the theory of it. Democracy is a vague word, but as the people on the plantation see it, there are outward manifestations like economic, political, racial, social and religious equality. . . . But we only learned the theory of economic and social equality, for after graduation the inequalities showed themselves. Learning that honest labor was a virtue in school we saw that it wasn't so on the plantation. If you were a *haole* [Caucasian] applying for a job, you didn't have to worry too much. But if you were of any other color, we had to be 'smart with the mouths.' . . . Moral values of fair play and industriousness were also reiterated by the school. But too many times, the disparity between practice and theory was wide." Quoted by Curtis Aller, in *Labor Relations in the Hawaiian Sugar Industry* (Berkeley, 1957), 39.

31. Bruno Hartung, "A Study of Changes in Employment Conditions among the Sugar Workers of Hawaii" (master's thesis, University of Hawaii, 1948), 83.

32. Letter to all plantation managers from HSPA Secretary J. Butler, May 13, 1927: "For your personal information and in order that you may be able to answer any questions asked by your Filipino employees . . . I give you the following: I am informed that two separate moves have been instituted in Honolulu to raise funds on behalf of Pablo Manlapit, such funds to be raised by Filipinos. The Hawaii Hochi, through its Japanese paper of this same name and through the English section which is called the "Bee" has recently put out articles asking Filipinos to contribute money to hire a good lawyer to fight the case of Manlapit. The 'Bee' or Hochi indicates it will receive funds for this purpose. . . . My report in this connection states that collectors attempt to get money from Filipinos on plantations for Rizal's [Birth]day, Rizal Day or other misrepresentation. This is for your information." Manlapit had been convicted of perjury in 1924 and deported.

33. Memo, HSPA to Hn. Ag., Dec. 12, 1921.

34. Hawaii Laborers Association, 7; Yayoi Kurita, "Labor Movements among the Japanese Plantation Workers in Hawaii" (master's thesis, University of Hawaii, 1948), 27.

35. Kurita, 24, footnote. At the association's inaugural meeting in October 1919, at least four unions sent representatives; the four Japanese newspapers dispatched thirteen representatives; and two Japanese school principals were elected chairman and secretary.

36. Ibid., 28.

37. Quoted by Takaki, 166.

38. Quoted by Koji Ariyoshi, in "Plantation Struggles in Hawaii," *Counterpoints*, ed. Emma Gee (Los Angeles, 1976), 389. For an account of Japanese strikes before 1920, see Takaki, 145-64.

39. Quoted by Takaki, 170.

40. Ariyoshi, 388; Takaki, 170; Kurita, 35. For a more detailed description of conflict within the Filipino movement, and of Manlapit himself, see Sharma, "Labor Migration," 595-600.

41. From this writer's viewpoint, the change represents not so much an attempt to emphasize a "class thrust of the new organization" (Takaki, 174) as a pragmatic attempt by the FJL to remove the focus of press attacks on the organization (i.e., the FJL as a subversive Japanese nationalist group), and to encourage its members to identify with Hawaii rather than Japan.

42. Hawaii Laborers Association, 13.
43. Ibid., 27.
44. Ibid., 17.
45. Ibid., 2.
46. Pablo Manlapit, *Filipinos Fight for Justice: Case of the Filipino Laborers in the Big Strike of 1924* (Honolulu, 1933), 64.
47. Ibid., 13, 23, 26.
48. Ibid., 26.
49. Filipinos faced a no-win situation concerning their citizenship throughout the period of American colonial rule. The Supreme Court ruled that they were neither aliens (since aliens must be born outside American jurisdiction and not yet have been naturalized); nor were they American citizens, nor could they naturalize, since they did not qualify for alien status.   Eligibility to naturalize came only after service in the American armed forces.
50. Manlapit, 17-18.
51. Several Hawaiian sailors had participated in San Francisco's maritime strike in 1934 and returned home to proselytize their fellow workers. Maxie Weisbarth, a Hawaiian-German, returned to open a Sailor's Union of the Pacific (SUP) hall in his hometown of Honolulu.   Harry Kamoku, a Hawaiian-Chinese, began to organize Hilo's docks for the International Longshoremen's Association, which later became the ILWU in Hawaii.
52. Sanford Zalburg, *A Spark Is Struck!* (Honolulu, 1979), 21.
53. "Census of Hawaiian Sugar Plantations," 1931; "Census of Hawaiian Sugar Plantations," June 30, 1944, HSPA.
54. For Takashi Shinoda, son of Hilo's Japanese school principal, "the traditional Japanese values instilled by [his] family, language school, and the Japanese community coexisted with American values instilled in school and the larger community without any sense of clash or conflict." In the mid-1930s, for example, he and his grade-school friends idolized the *Sanyushi*—three suicidal bomber pilots who died during the Sino-Japanese War. Yet when kamikaze attacked Pearl Harbor, the "unsettling thoughts" about his dual heritage began. Shinoda reply to the writer's questionnaire.
55. *W&H*, 3:44-45.
56. While mainland unions warred among themselves over jurisdictional rights to various workplaces, Hawaii's small size and the linkage between its workplaces permitted extraordinary cooperation between union leaders. For example, Jack Hall, the ILWU's most influential postwar figure, organized for the ILWU even though he came the islands as an SUP representative, and despite conflict between the two unions on the mainland. The mainland SUP office suspended him when it learned of his activities, and soon thereafter he made his affiliation with the ILWU official. For a detailed account of union politics and the logistics of organizing Hawaiian labor, see Edward D. Beechert, *Racial Divisions and Agricultural Labor Organizing in Hawaii* (Honolulu, 1977).
57. For an account of ILWU diversification in California, see Harvey Schwartz, *The March Inland: Origins of the ILWU Warehouse Division, 1934-1938* (Los Angeles, 1978).
58. Quoted by Zalburg, 126.
59. Ibid., 86.
60. *W&H*, 3:126-27.   Immediately after the ship's landing, ILWU representatives appointed some of the new members aboard to become stewards of newly created crews.
61. For a breezy rendition of the ILWU organizing effort and a blow-by-blow narrative of the 1946 strike, see Zalburg, *supra.*

62. Robert Hirayama, "Student Evaluations of Unionization in Plantation Communities," *Social Process* 13 (1949): 24-25; Kiyoshi Ikeda, "Unionization and the Plantation," *Social Process* 15 (1951): 17; *W&H*, 3:40.

ASIAN MIGRANTS IN AFRICA
AND IN ASIA

8

Indentured Labor Migration: Indian Migrants to Natal, South Africa, 1860–1902

Surendra Bhana

A total of 152,184 indentured laborers migrated from India to Natal between 1860 and 1911. This figure constitutes part of the over 1.3 million indentured Indians who migrated mainly to parts of the British Empire in the nineteenth and early twentieth centuries. Indian indentured migration is small compared to the 50 million Europeans who emigrated to the New World between 1800 and 1914. Yet, as Eric Wolf has reminded us, both categories of migration are the consequence of the growth and expansion of a capitalist mode of production and the development of a world market.[1]

In seeking to explain indentured migration this paper takes the position that it cannot be fully understood in terms of hypotheses that stress demography, ethnicity, or economics. Dualistic models use equilibrium in explaining the movement of individuals from "traditional" (preindustrial) to the "modern" (capitalistic) economy in which market mechanisms are regarded as primarily the causes; and those who advance neoclassical models highlight migration in terms of individualistic rational decision making. However useful these models may be in explaining individual migrations, they are not adequate in defining the circumstances that saw the migration of indentured Indians. Large-scale migrations require analyses that go beyond the individual psyche and the immediate social and economic environment of the migrant. The models ignore the nature of the fundamental structural changes that occurred in Indian society following the implementation of British policies in the nineteenth century. These changes altered social relations of production, introducing mechanisms by which the powerful exercised control and manipulation over vast sections of the population. In essence, they constituted "structural preconditions," as Marks and Richardson explain, by which displaced individuals created waves of internal migrations. Where surplus labor could be expended, the colonial state built structures for its export abroad. State instrumentality in generating indentured labor was maintained from its source to its destination, where the recipient states exercised strict controls until the contract ended.[2]

In arguing this position, this paper will focus on three areas. First, it will discuss the circumstances that gave rise to the indenture system, and the role played by the government of India in devising the details to ensure its success; second, it will examine the extent to which British policies were instrumental in generating migrations; and third, it will highlight the backgrounds of ninety-five thousand indentured Indians who went to Natal between 1860 and 1902, and their status as immigrant laborers in this South African British colony.

The indenture system came in the wake of the 1834 abolition of slavery in the British Empire. This immediately brought a crisis among planters in the sugar-producing colonies, whose major source of labor was slavery. The planters in British Guiana (known then as Demarara and today as Guyana), Trinidad, and Jamaica agreed to an apprentice system by which freed slaves could continue to work on plantations as free laborers. But the manumitted slaves viewed the system with suspicion, and most of them refused to be associated with it. For the planters the labor problem remained unresolved, and they searched for alternative sources of labor. They considered a variety of options, and indeed British Guiana introduced white laborers from England, Ireland, Portugal, and Brazil. Trinidad imported a few Chinese. In the end, however, they settled for India as a source of large-scale immigration.[3] The idea of India as a source appealed to the West Indian planters mainly because as part of the British Empire, this country already had colonial structures that could facilitate the transfer of labor migrants recruited from among its masses. The selection of India was no accident. The machinery for transferring laborers from one part of the empire to another already existed. Mauritius, a British insular possession in the Indian Ocean, had already experimented with the importation of indentured workers from India. When slavery ended in Mauritius, the planters had imported slaves illegally and convicts from India; and it had introduced contract laborers in the 1820s. Thereafter, the Colonial Office in London had agreed to Mauritius's importation of indentured laborers from Chota Nagpur, and the first batch of Dhangers ("Hill Coolies") arrived in 1834. In the West Indies, British Guiana was the first to import indentured Indians. In 1838, this colony received its first consignment of 396 laborers, known as "Gladstone's coolies." The Colonial Office stopped the traffic in 1839 because of abuses but allowed resumption in 1842 for Mauritius and in 1844 for the British West Indian colonies after stricter regulations had been introduced to protect the emigrants.

Thereafter the traffic in indentured labor migration continued virtually uninterrupted until it was abolished in 1917. Natal joined in 1860 and Fiji in 1879. By 1917, at least 1.3 million Indians had gone abroad as indentured laborers, as table 1 shows.[4] Indentured labor was preferred over free labor because it was available. Five-year contracts ensured a steady supply of reliable laborers relatively free from the fluctuation of sugar prices on the international market. Besides, the strict terms under which the indentures operated and the foreign status of the workers made the laborers easier to control. They could be returned home. Laws governing indentured immigration provided the option of subsidized repatriation of the workers after their contracts expired. Local colonial legislatures either honored or subverted this provision. In Natal at any rate, coercive taxation was used in the 1900s to drive home those not willing to remain in indentures. Table 1 shows that more than 440,828 returned to India. The government of India was not quite as solicitous about reintegrating the returnees as it was about recruiting and sending them abroad.

In addition to the officially established indenture system, there was privately organized recruitment known as the *kangany* system, named after "kankani," a Tamil headman who organized the recruitment. The sources of this much larger outward migration, officially approved by the colonial government, are to be located in circumstances that are similar to those of indentured migration. However, it operated quite separately from the indenture system and will not be incorporated in the discussion in this paper. Operating mainly from South India, the *kangany* system saw the migration of some 4.25 million Indians to Burma, Ceylon (Sri Lanka), and Malaya between 1834 and 1938.[5]

The population of British India in 1901 was just under 232 million, and the departure of over 1.3 million Indians over eighty years had no impact on India's economy or its population. Most of the emigrants were recruited in the United Provinces and Bihar except in Natal's case, where two-thirds of the Indians were drawn from the Madras Presidency and one-third in the northeastern part of India. The government of India recognized that indentured migration was of little consequence to India itself, but it took a fairly protective attitude toward the migrants from the inception of the system. It was sensitive to the criticism of antislavery groups in Britain, more specifically the Aborigines Protection Society (f. 1837), which kept a vigilant eye on the indentured traffic in

Table 1
Indentured Migrations, 1830s–1917

COLONIES		TOTAL	RETURNED
A WEST INDIES		534,109	49,054
British Guiana	238,909		
Trinidad	143,939		
amaica	86,412		
Surinam	34,304		
Grenada, St. Vincent,			
and St. Lucia	10,026		
Martinique	25,519		
Guadeloupe	45,000		
B INDIAN OCEAN ISLANDS		584,018	
Mauritius	466,018		168,774
Reunion	118,000		8,000
			(1835–1900)
C NATAL		152,184	35,000
			(1860–1911)
D FIJI		60,533	Unknown
		1,330,844	440,828

SOURCE: Author's calculations, based on sources listed in note 4.

the early days. Hence, the conditions under which emigration was allowed were revised from time to time as and when abuses occurred. The government of India used the threat of suspension or suspension itself to extract compliance from offending colonies.

How did the system operate?[6] Calcutta, Madras, and until 1865 Bombay were designated as ports of embarkation. Karikal and Pondicherry served as ports for the emigrants to the French colonies. Each of the importing colonies was required to have an emigration agent, although often one agent served several colonies. The recruits had to be properly housed at officially designated emigration depots with due regard for local customs and habits. They underwent thorough medical examination first by an Indian doctor and then by a white depot surgeon to screen out those who were mentally or medically unfit. The successful recruits were then placed on ships that were to transport them to their destinations. The government of India stipulated cubic footage for individual passengers; it also provided for precise instructions to be followed with regard to the emigrants' medical care on the journey, rationing, cleanliness, and so on. In the early days when sailboats were in use, a voyage to the West Indies could take up to 120 days. Mortality rates were high. But once steamships came into operation, the duration of the journey was almost halved, and mortality rates dropped dramatically. In all of this, the government of India was eager to discourage comparison between slavery and indenture.

However, the aspect of the indenture system that remained controversial throughout its existence was the way in which the recruits were procured. It is this aspect that separates the indentured migrant from other types of migrants who rationally decide to emigrate. Recruitment procedures were established in the late 1830s and were revised early in the 1860s to eliminate abuses. Yet the abuses persisted. The emigration agents were responsible for the recruitment of laborers. They appointed subagents in large district towns who were usually Jews, Armenians, Indian Christians, Eurasians, and even Europeans. The subagents in turn hired licensed recruiters, who were expected to bring the recruits before local magistrates to ensure that they had willingly entered into the indentured contracts. Those who agreed then undertook the "chalan," a journey from the subdepots to the emigration depots.

But it was not the licensed recruiters who were the most important agents in the recruitment process. It was the *arkatis* (also *arkatias*) in the North and the petty *maistris* in the South who made up the backbone of the whole system. They had a good knowledge of the local people and were usually well informed about individuals who might be in financial distress. They frequented markets, bazaars, caravanserais, railway stations, temples, and so on to prey upon people in distress. While the *arkatis* and petty *maistris* were legally answerable to nobody, they were pivotally important in the vast recruitment machinery. The whole operation had to succeed or fail with them.

It is at this level of recruitment that abuses occurred most frequently. Charges against these operators ranged from kidnapping to misrepresentation of the facts. The credulity of many of the recruits no doubt contributed to the widespread prevalence of fraud and deception. They believed; and they often agreed to nod understanding before the local magistrates upon the instruction of recruiting agents. Men who agreed to go to distant lands to fulfill vague promises cannot be said to have understood the coercive nature of the contract they had entered. It was a fact never fully revealed to any of the recruits, from the lowest levels of recruitment to the highest. The recruit learned about it only when he began his term of industrial residence, the term used to describe the duration of the contract.

As benevolent as its interest was in the indentured emigrants, the government of India was aware of the coercive nature of the contracts. Its primary objective was to promote British imperial interests. It was therefore open to pressures from plantation lobbies in other colonies which exercised powerful influence on the Colonial Office. It often stated that indentured emigration was of little benefit to India as a whole. Yet it argued that imperial exigencies required it to act in a larger context. Lord Salisbury, secretary of state, made the point in 1875 that "it [was] desirable to afford an outlet from these redundant regions into the tropical and subtropical dominions of Her Majesty, where people, who hardly earn a decent subsistence in their own country, may obtain more lucrative employment and better homes."[7]

But the government of India was responsible in a much more fundamental way for creating circumstances that saw the exacerbation of internal and external migration. Scholars are divided on the extent to which the implementation of British policies in India dislocated the population from their traditional moorings. An enormous literature has grown up on the extent and nature of the dislocation, and indeed whether it was significant at all in some regions. The classical view starts out from the assumption that the basic preconditions of an industrial revolution existed in India in 1800, and that nineteenth-century British policies had the effect of dampening it and preventing it from taking place. Whether or not British policies retarded growth, the point is that major industrial and agricultural changes occurred as a consequence of those policies; and likely many forms of the changes have their roots in the period before 1800. Dharma Kumar found that the class of landless agricultural laborers in the Madras Presidency was not wholly created during the British period, but that its conditions likely deteriorated in the nineteenth century. We turn briefly to the impact of British policies to determine their role in indentured migration.[8]

India enjoyed a thriving indigenous handicraft industry at the beginning of the nineteenth century. The free and unfettered access of British goods into India, especially textiles, devastated the local handicraft cotton industry. British imports rose from £100,000 in 1813 to £18.4 million in 1896. The availability of cheaper yarn imports dealt a severe blow to the spinning sector in the cotton industry. The Bengal Presidency was especially hard hit by Western commercialism as European manufactured goods, most importantly Lancashire cotton products, flooded the local market. In addition, the introduction of English mill operations in the presidency had the effect of deindustrializing the indigenous economy. The Bombay Presidency did not suffer to the same extent because the handicraft industry was dispersed here, and the local market strong. But even in this region the penetration of foreign-made goods was evident, thanks to the rapid construction of the railroad in India. As Charlesworth points out, British policies reflected the "subordination of Indian to wider imperial needs, providing too sharp a contrast with government policy in continental Europe, where tariff barriers were steadily erected."[9]

The impact was severely if unevenly felt throughout India. Thousands of weavers, spinners, tanners, and smelters became unemployed as the indigenous industries collapsed. Modest public and private enterprises in railway construction, tea plantations in Assam, jute mills and coal mines in Bengal created some employment, in the process of which internal migrations occurred. But such economic enterprises were far too limited to take up the employment deficit. Indeed, most of the unemployed were forced into agriculture, which was already crowded. Between 1891 and 1901, the percentage of those who were dependent upon agriculture increased from 61 percent to 66 percent.[10]

In agriculture, the British introduced a land revenue system based upon proprietory ownership. This created rent-receiving interests that were ultimately responsible for changes in ownership. Except for the Madras Presidency, the last forty years in the nineteenth century saw land in British India pass from agricultural classes to nonagricultural moneylenders. In the *zamindari* and *ryotwari* systems of land revenue, the British policies had the effect of displacing peasant farmers from their land and of creating debt peonage. In the first system, the *zamindar* (landlord), who could be a moneylending nonoccupant, collected the taxes from the peasant farmers, paid the state's portion, and kept the balance for himself. In the second system, the *ryot* (peasant) paid the taxes direct to the state. Even though there were no middlemen, the effect was, as Saha points out, to extract more revenue from the peasant than under the first system. The two systems created peasant farmers who were hopelessly in debt with little or no prospect of recovering, and farm laborers who could be employed only seasonally. In the context of the growth of a cash economy and the increasing commercialization of agriculture, large-scale alienation of peasant holdings occurred. Most peasant farmers continued to eke out a precarious existence in a stagnating agricultural sector. The pace of internal migrations increased. And some migrated abroad.[11]

One cannot, of course, ignore the impact of natural disasters like famines, droughts, and scarcities, which occurred with regular frequency. Thousands of individuals were uprooted. But, as Bhatia points out, the British policy of encouraging farmers to grow exportable commercial crops in place of food crops made the masses more vulnerable to food shortages during periods of calamities. This policy benefited a few urban-based traders and rural capitalists.[12]

The implementation of British policies had a dramatic effect upon social relationships. While some individuals became rich and powerful as a consequence, others became marginalized. Craftsmen and artisans were forced to seek other means of livelihood; peasant farmers suffered under the burdens of the new land revenue system and sank deeper into debt; and farm laborers felt the intolerable pressures of underemployment. All of this exacerbated internal migrations. Lal in his study on Fiji's indentured Indians found that in the United Provinces, nearly 1.5 million migrants were from other parts of India. He found, however, no correlation between internal migration and indentured emigration.[13] Yet the causes in both instances were more than likely the same.

It is the peasant population that predominates in our Natal sample of indentured immigrants, which reflects the segments of the population most seriously affected by the upheavals in nineteenth-century India. Intense poverty and dense populations characterized the districts from which indentured Indians were recruited for all the colonies, including Natal. If they contributed unequally to the pool of indentured laborers it was partly because colonial requirements fluctuated with the demand for sugar on the international market and partly because socioeconomic conditions varied somewhat from district to district. Only a district-by-district investigation into the socioeconomic backgrounds in relation to the fluctuations in the colonial political economies will yield a proper answer. In the process one might learn more precisely the nature and extent of the impact of British policies in each district.

Natal, having discovered in the 1850s that its soil and climate were ideal for sugar cultivation, debated about where it was to procure laborers to work on the plantations. The question is why Natal, with its reservoir of Zulu labor, opted for indentured immigrants. The Department of Native Affairs, constituting an *imperium in imperio,* was able to thwart settlers' attempts to draw upon Natal's African population for a regular supply of labor. It developed a system to shore up the traditional economy of Zulu pastoralists and farmers who saw no need to become wage earners. The planters were able to get the colonial state to subsidize the importation of *Amatonga* migrant laborers from neighboring Portuguese Mozambique even in the face of opposition from up-country colonial farmers who did not benefit directly from the venture. However, these coastal planters were unable to develop the *Amatonga* and other foreign African workers into a permanent labor force. After 1893, when responsible government was introduced, newer elements began having greater say. The pressure to end public money for foreign African labor would mount. The demand for greater use of African labor in Natal would increase.[14] In time, Zululand would be gradually absorbed into a capitalist relationship with the colony of Natal, and the Zulus would become proletarianized.

Meanwhile, the problem of labor on the plantations was immediate. Hence, the planters followed the lead of their counterparts in Mauritius and the West Indies by turning to India for labor. A three-way agreement was reached among the British government, the government of India, and the colonial government of Natal by which the planters were allowed to import indentured laborers from India. The first batch of Indians arrived in November 1860, and, after a brief suspension between 1866 and 1873 because of an economic depression in Natal, importation was continued between 1874 and 1911. By July 1911, a total of 152,184 indentured Indians had arrived in the colony.

Natal did not enjoy a full-blown plantation system as Mauritius, for example, did. Its economy was fairly diversified so that sugar production did not dominate colonial politics. There were competing factions in the ruling class. In contrast, the colonial state of Mauritius worked closely with the plantocracy because it considered the island's prosperity synonymous with the sugar industry. And this planter hegemony in Mauritius went unchallenged until 1948. In Natal the planters were not quite as politically dominant.[15]

Yet they were sufficiently influential to ensure the establishment of the system. The planters ensured public subsidization of the scheme until 1894, but the colonial legislature continued to grant loans to the Immigration Trust Board (f. 1874) to keep the importation of indentured labor going until 1911. Other sectors, such as the coal industry, railway construction, municipal public service, and so on, made use of indentured workers. White settler hostility to the presence of Indians grew, especially as many ex-indentured immigrants opted to stay after the expiry of their contracts. Under pressure from these elements, the colonial legislature passed a £3 tax law in 1895 to force the Indian laborers to reindenture, or to return to India. The law linked reindenture with repatriation.[16]

Of the 95,382 indentured Indians being analyzed here, two-thirds came from the Tamil- and Telugu-speaking districts of the Madras Presidency and one-third from the Bhojpuri-speaking districts in the United Provinces and Bihar.[17] Over 94 percent of the individuals were Hindus, the balance being made up mainly by Muslims and partly by Christians. The law required a ratio of sixty men to forty females. In practice this was never maintained. In Natal's case, the figures were 64 percent to 28 percent with 8 percent unknown. Employers preferred mainly able-bodied young males, and indeed the sample shows the age distribution to be concentrated between the ages of eighteen and thirty, with the curve reaching a peak at twenty-five. The deliberately contrived shortage of Indian women was a source of many personal and social problems for Indian men, and employers were not above using the scarcity to enhance control over the men. Family migration was discouraged because Natal's white colonists did not want to see the Indians as permanent settlers. Yet our sample shows that over 16 percent were children accompanying one or both parents.

Of great significance are the socioeconomic backgrounds of the indentured Indians. The caste backgrounds in many though not all instances indicate also the socioeconomic status.[18] The indentured immigrants were overwhelmingly related to agriculture. The two largest castes from the Madras Presidency were *Pariah* (14.6 percent) and *Vanniah* (14.3 percent). The first were agricultural laborers or otherwise engaged in menial work; the second were probably peasant farmers. There were market gardeners, goatherds, boatmen, and fishermen. *Madigas* (leather workers) and *Baljas* (probably traders) were also in the sample. In the Madras Presidency sample, there was a fair sprinkling of high castes like *Reddis* (reputedly good farmers) and *Chettis* (traders and moneylenders).

The leading groups from the United Provinces and Bihar were *Chamars* (leather workers, 15.8 percent) and *Ahirs* (cowherds, 12.2 percent). There were high castes like *Brahmins* (priests), *Thakoors* (agriculturists), and *Rajputs* (farmers), but as in the case of the immigrants from the Madras Presidency, the castes related to agricultural labor (*Koiree, Koormi*) or service (*Dosadh,* watchmen, and *Goala,* shepherds) predominated. Both sets of immigrants had people with artisan and agricultural skills. The overall range suggests people from lower to middle socioeconomic status; yet the poorer classes of landless people predominated, the individuals who were most likely to be marginalized by the socioeconomic upheavals in India.

The predominantly agricultural background of the indentured immigrants suited the employers since it was sugar cultivation that first brought them to Natal. Indeed, the sugar industry remained the employer of 65 to 70 percent throughout the period under discussion. In the 1870s, the cultivators of other commercial crops like tea, maize, tobacco, beans, and wattle utilized indentured labor. But in the 1880s and thereafter, nonagricultural sectors like railway construction, coal mining, municipalities, and port authorities increasingly engaged indentured workers. A small category of indentured workers known as Special Servants was recruited for their skills and worked in hospitals, restaurants, private clubs, and so on.[19]

Except for the Special Servants, who were always treated with a great deal of circumspection by their employers, the indentured Indians were treated as a captive labor force. They had no choice of employers and no right to negotiated wages for the duration of their contracts. The workers could not terminate their contracts before five years of industrial residence, and they had no right to transfer from one employer to another. The long hours, often far in excess of the regulated nine hours a day, six days a week, deprived them of private and personal lives. The living conditions were abominable in most cases. Formal and informal controls, operating more strongly in agriculture than industry, were used to ensure compliance. The caste and language differences among the workers were often used by employers to create divisions among them and to impose a hierarchical order toward that end.

These punitive and collaborative structures manipulated the workers to the point where the protection they enjoyed in theory was meaningless. The Protector of Indian Immigrants, appointed in 1874 to safeguard the interest of the indentured workers, was powerless to exercise his authority in the face of planter political power. He was required to report annually on how the system worked. The reports tended to be bland and uncritical especially after 1890. The concealment of actual conditions on the estates testified to the collusion between the colonial authorities and the sugar planters. Even though the suicide rate among Natal's indentured Indians was unusually high, second only to that of Fiji among colonies using indentured labor, no official inquiry was ever held.[20] Pass and vagrancy laws further restricted the freedom of indentured workers. An indentured laborer who might flee to press charges against the employer was usually prosecuted for absconding. Women workers, whose worth in capital accumulation was belatedly recognized by agricultural planters, were particularly vulnerable to sexual harassment and other forms of exploitation. They were gradually phased out after 1900, and sadly had few skills to enter the free labor market.[21]

As captive laborers, the indentured Indians had few avenues of redress. Strikes and protests, of which there were a few before 1913, were dealt with quickly. There were likely to have been individualistic types of passive resistance that did not threaten to undermine the system. Under normal circumstances, the freed Indians might agitate for changes within the system. But the colonial legislature moved increasingly to deprive the Indians of their political rights. The £3 tax referred to earlier and the £1 poll tax made it clear that they were welcome only as indentured Indians, and not as free Indians competing on the open job market. Their disfranchisement in the mid–1890s was the first step toward excluding the Indians from the colony's political processes. This had grave implications for the socioeconomic opportunities available to an immigrant community, indentured or otherwise. The opportunities for integrating themselves into Natal's institutions shrank; and henceforth, the only option open to them was either to return to India or to stand up for their rights.

In the 1890s, and even earlier, the indentured Indians probably lacked the kind of sociopolitical awareness that would galvanize them into action.   Leadership was difficult to sustain in the controlled environment of the plantation and other workplace environments. Besides, there was a rapid turnover as workers completed their indentures to move into the free labor market or return home, thus making organization difficult.   And an organization such as M. K. Gandhi's Natal Indian Congress (f. 1894) concerned itself with the interests of Indian merchants who had come independently from western parts of India.   The NIC rarely took an active interest in the conditions of indentured laborers.   Its annual membership fee prohibited most indentured Indians from considering joining the organization even if their affiliation was solicited.   It was only in the 1900s that circumstances emerged to encourage among the indentured Indians a kind of consciousness that was to culminate in the massive strike of 1913–14 that finally gave Gandhi the mass support that had eluded him up to that point.   The indentured workers had finally rebelled against the coercive nature of the labor system.[22]

Indentured emigration to Natal, then, was not the product of rational choice.   State instrumentality and coercion were significant features of this form of emigration from the beginning to the end. Circumstances in nineteenth-century India created forces by which the emigration was channeled through colonially established structures. Whitehall worked closely with the government of India and established the system to serve larger imperial interests.   In Natal, the beneficiaries of this system were the planters and other employers who received support from the colonial legislature.   If the employers of indentured laborers lost the state subsidy in the 1890s it was because newer elements among the white settlers gained access to political power and determined to see the system end and the Indians returned to India. With time the Natal African population would be drawn into a capitalist relationship; and by 1911, when indentured immigration ended, the machinery for replacing indentured with African labor was already in place with similar elements of coercion built into it.   Free Indians who remained in South Africa would drift to urban centers in the decades ahead for employment there.

The coercive nature of indentured emigration is apparent from the beginning through its operation in the recipient colonies.   Indentured workers constituted a captive labor force and were not free during the terms of their industrial residence to compete on the open labor market.   The option presented to them after the 1890s was to remain in it or return home.   Indeed, every effort was made to keep them locked within the system.   Those who stood outside the system also faced increasing restrictions.   All of this increased conflict and competition in which race and class were prominent.   They are all part of the circumstances that surround indentured migration, which, as was pointed out at the beginning, cannot be explained by a mere recounting of demographic, ethnic, and economic factors.

Notes

1. Eric R. Wolf, *Europe and the People without History* (Berkeley, 1982), 355, 362-63.

2. A variety of works have highlighted this approach in recent years, the most notable of which are Alan Adamson, *Sugar without Slaves: The Political Economy of British Guiana 1838-1904* (New Haven, 1973); L. Cheng and E. Bonacich, eds., *Labor Immigration under Capitalism: Asian Workers in the United States before World War II* (Berkeley, 1984); S. Marks and P. Richardson, eds., *International Labour Migration: Historical Perspectives* (London, 1984); Colin Newbury, "Labour Migration in the Imperial Phase: An Essay in Interpretation," *Journal of Imperial and Commonwealth History* 3 (1975): 234-56; D. G. Papademetriou, "Rethinking International Migration: A Review and Critique," *Comparative Political Studies* (January 1983):469-98; D. Peek and Guy Standing, eds., *State Policies and Migration Studies in Latin America and the Caribbean* (London, 1982); P. Saha, *Emigration of Indentured Indian Labour, 1834-1900* (Delhi, 1970); and K. Saunders, ed., *Indentured Labor in the British Empire, 1834-1920* (London, 1984).

3. Hugh Tinker, *A New System of Slavery: The Export of Indian Labour Overseas, 1830-1920* (London, 1974), 16-17; K. O. Laurence, *Immigration into the West Indies in the 19th Century* (Mona, 1971).

4. The statistics are drawn from a variety of sources. In Mauritius's case, the 25,000 (approximately) who came before the system was introduced have also been added. The sources are Laurence, 26, 27; *Geoghegan Report on Coolie Emigration from India*, July 1, 1874, Parliamentary Papers, vol. 47, Paper 314; J. Manrakhan, "Examination of Certain Aspects of Slavery-Indenture Continuum of Mauritius Including a Scenario That Never Was," in *Indian Labour Immigration*, ed. U. Bissoondoyal and S. B. C. Servansing (Moka, 1986), 40; Tinker, 371; Singaravelou, "Indians in French Overseas Departments (Guadeloupe, Martinique, Reunion)," Paper, Conference on South Asian Communities Abroad, Oxford University, March 1987; K. L. Gillion, *Fiji's Indian Migrants: A History to the End of Indenture in 1920* (Melbourne, 1962), 59; and ships' registers for Natal's indentured Indians, 1860-1911, Department of Interior, Durban.

5. Figures are cited in Brij V. Lal, *Girmitiyas: The Origins of Fiji Indians* (Canberra, 1983), 44. See also S. Arasaratnam, *Indians in Malaysia and Singapore* (Kuala Lumpur, 1962), 16, 32. The figure of 4.25 million is made up as follows: to Burma between 1852 and 1937, 2.5 million, to Ceylon between 1834 and 1938, 1.5 million, and to Malaysia between 1860 and 1938, 0.25 million.

6. The description of the system is to be found in a variety of sources. Two useful accounts are Tinker's *New System of Slavery* and Basdeo Mangru's *Benevolent Neutrality: Indian Government Policy and Labour Migration to British Guiana, 1854-1884* (London, 1987).

7. Quoted in Thomas R. Metcalf, "Indian Migration in South Africa," in *Studies in Migration: Internal and International Migrations in India*, ed. M. S. A. Rao (New Delhi, 1986), 350.

8. The broad outlines of this debate are to be found in volume 5, 1986, of *Indian Economic and Social History Review (IESHR)*. An article by Morris D.

Morris drew responses from Toru Matsui, Bipin Chandra, and T. Raychaudhuri. Some other pertinent articles in the *IESHR* are S. Bhattacharya, "Laissez faire in India," *IESHR* 2 (1965):1-22; Bipin Chandra, "Two Notes on the Agrarian Policy of Indian Nationalists, 1880-1905," *IESHR* 1 (1964):143-74, and "Indian Nationalists and the Drain," *IESHR* 2 (1965):104-44; Dharma Kumar, "Landownership and Inequality in Madras Presidency: 1853-54 to 1946-47," 12 (1975): 229-61; Eric Stokes, "The Structure of Landholding in Uttar Pradesh, 1860-1948," *IESHR* 12 (1975):113-32; B. R. Tomlinson, "India and the British Empire, 1880-1935," *IESHR* 12 (1975): 337-81. Some monographic and edited works are *The Cambridge Economic History of India*, vol. 2, *c. 1757-c. 1970* (Cambridge, 1983); Robert E. Frykenberg, ed., *Land Control and Social Structure in Indian Society* (New Delhi, 1979); Dharma Kumar, *Land and Caste in South India: Agricultural Labour in the Madras Presidency during the Nineteenth Century* (Cambridge, 1965); Thomas R. Metcalf, *Land, Landlords and the British Raj: Northern India in the Nineteenth Century* (Berkeley, 1979); M. S. A. Rao, ed., *Studies in Migration: Internal and International Migrations in India* (New Delhi, 1986); and Saha, *Emigration*, (see n. 2).

9. Neil Charlesworth's *British Rule and the Indian Economy, 1800-1914* in the series *Studies in Economic and Social History* (London, 1982), 33.

10. See Saha, *Emigration*, 59-60, 63-68; B. M. Bhatia, *Famines in India: A Study in Some Aspects of the Economic History of India, 1860-1965* (Bombay, 1963), 232; and *The Imperial Gazetteer of India: The Indian Empire*, 1908, vol. 3, 1-2, 248, 250.

11. *The Imperial Gazetteer of India*, vol. 3, 89, 90-91; vol. 4, 207, 214, 236, 239. See also B. Chaudhuri, "Agrarian Relations in Eastern India," *The Cambridge Economic History of India*, vol. 2, *c. 1757-c. 1970*, 86-77.

12. Bhatia, *Famines in India*, 15, 23, 134-60. All the major famines are reported in *The Imperial Gazetteer of India*, vol. 3, 476-92.

13. Lal, *Girmitiyas*, 63-64.

14. Patrick Harries, "Plantations, Passes and Proletarians: Labour and the Colonial State in Nineteenth Century Natal," *Journal of Southern African Studies* 13, 3 (April 1987): 372-99.

15. D. M. North-Coombes, "Indentured Labour in the Sugar Industries of Natal and Mauritius, 1834-1910," in *Essays on Indentured Indians in Natal*, ed. S. Bhana (Yorkshire, 1990).

16. L. M. Thompson, *Indian Immigration into Natal, 1860-1872* in *Archives Year Book for South African History*, vol. II (Pretoria, 1952).

17. The brief examination of the sample is based upon a study completed by the author. The revised and expanded version of that study is *Indentured Indian Emigrants to Natal, 1860-1902: A Study Based on Ships' Lists* (New Delhi, 1991). The word *presidency* refers to a large administrative unit created by the British.

18. See *The Imperial Gazetteer of India*, 1: 314-20, 329-30, 347, 498, for details about the caste system in nineteenth-century India.

19. See Bill Guest and J. M. Sellers, eds., *Enterprise and Exploitation in a Victorian Colony: Aspects of Economic and Social History of Colonial Natal* (Pietermaritsburg, 1985), 181-97, 214-17, 327-28.

20. M. Tayal, "Indian Indentured Labour in Natal, 1890-1911," *Indian Economic and Social Review* 14, 4 (1978): 519-46; R. Warhurst, "Obstructing the Protector," *Journal of Natal and Zulu History* 7 (1984): 31-40; North-Coombes, (see n. 15); S. Bhana and A. Bhana, "An Exploration of the Psycho-Historical Circumstances Surrounding Suicide among Indentured Indians, 1875-1911," in Bhana, *Essays*.

21. J. D. Beall, "Women under Indenture in Natal," in Bhana, ed., *Essays*.

22. The sources of the militancy among the indentured workers are debated in the following works: Frene N. Ginwala, "Class, Consciousness and Control—Indian South Africans, 1860-1946" (Ph.D. diss., Oxford University, 1976); M. Swan, *Gandhi: The South African Experience* (Johannesburg, 1985), and "Indentured Indian's Accommodation and Resistance, 1890-1913," in Bhana, ed., *Essays*; M. Tayal, "The 1913 Natal Indian Strike," *Journal of Southern African Studies* 10, 2 (April 1984): 239-58; J. D. Beall and D. M. North-Coombes, "The Disturbances in Natal: The Social and Economic Background to 'Passive Resistance,'" *Journal of Natal and Zulu History* 6 (1983): 48-81.

9

Popular Sources of Chinese Labor Militancy in Colonial Malaya, 1900–1941

Donald M. Nonini

Introduction

During the years 1936 to 1941, migrant Chinese workers in Malaya displayed an unprecedented militancy against employers and the British colonial state—strikes, demonstrations, informal work stoppages, organization of labor unions, violent clashes with the police, and forcible occupations of the workplace, involving tens of thousands of Chinese rubber tappers, tin miners, factory operatives, and government workers.[1] This activism, moreover, was marked by interethnic cooperation between immigrant Chinese and Indian laborers in strikes on several occasions. The militancy of the years 1936 to 1941 was but a prelude to the mass organization and widespread labor actions of the immediate postwar years 1945 to 1947 by Chinese and Indian laborers unified under the Pan-Malayan General Labour Union, and directed against colonial employers and the state.[2] It has been argued by scholars such as M. R. Stenson that the General Labour Union, led and to some extent controlled by the Malayan Communist party (MCP), was nonetheless a "genuinely popular movement" whose strikes led to a "major improvement in wages, conditions and benefits" for Chinese and Indian immigrant workers.[3] These successes in turn brought on a massive assault by the British colonial state—its repression of the Malayan labor movement and of Malayan Communists who led it—which initiated the insurgency of the Malayan Communist party and the "police action" memorialized as the "Emergency" of 1948 to 1960 in the annals of the Cold War.

I accept the argument of Stenson and others that the Malayan labor movement under the postwar General Labour Union was at the very least a "genuinely popular movement," although it was also more than that. In this essay, I propose that the sources of its popularity are largely to be found in changes in the political economy of Malaya and in the emergence of discontent among working-class Chinese during the interwar period from 1920 to 1941. Developments during the Japanese occupation of Malaya and the immediate postwar years to 1948, I would argue, only accelerated and intensified these trends. Already by the mid-1930s, these trends had resulted in the appearance of spontaneous, largely unorganized labor actions by thousands of migrant Chinese workers, which the Malayan Communist party thereafter sought to direct.[4] The objectives of this essay, then, are to identify these changes in political economy and in Chinese attitudes and to explain the sources of this protest from below during the prewar years.

The approach to Malayan Chinese labor militancy and its cause, adopted in this essay centers on the changing interaction between the political economy of a colonial society and the culturally based perspectives of a "moral economy" among laborers—an interaction that, over time, led to the emergence of popular discontent. This approach serves to correct several competing accounts of the activities of Malayan Chinese laborers that either reject the idea that their militancy arose from genuine grievances, are simplistic as to the causes involved, or simply ignore the phenomenon of militancy altogether. Four such alternatives come to mind—what can be called "conservative," "liberal," and "[bio]-culturalist" explanations, and the account, such as it is, provided by certain studies in the social anthropology of urban Chinese in Southeast Asia.

The "conservative" account holds that the "disorder" and "unrest" created by Chinese labor's militancy from 1930 to 1950 came from an exogenous cause, the "outside agitation," manipulation, and coercion of laborers by Malayan Communist party infiltrators and thugs, directed by the Communist International. This account comes very close to the views of colonial employers of the period, and of the police and some government officials.[5]

The "liberal" account states that during the two periods from 1936 to 1941 and from 1945 to 1947, militancy arose from "economic" causes. Two such causes have been invoked: wage increases failed to keep pace with the rise in the cost of living, and in the postwar years, supplies of foodstuffs, particularly rice, were inadequate.[6] Both factors caused general dissatisfaction, which led to strikes and other militant action by Chinese laborers. This was the view held by certain British officials sympathetic to Chinese labor and by some scholars.[7] The "culturalist" or "bioculturalist" (i.e., Lamarckian) account in contrast holds that certain Chinese "races" residing in Malaya—Hailams (Hainanese) and Hakka—were particularly prone to leftist politics owing to cultural or biological factors, or both. Where Chinese labor militancy occurred, this is said to have taken place because of the activities of Hailams or Hakka or both. Hailam and Hakka cultural or "racial" characteristics, such as clannishness, secretiveness, a desire for prestige, and resentment of other Chinese, have thus been invoked. (These "races" are what are referred to in this essay as "speech groups.") This culturalist or bioculturalist account was advocated by some scholars and journalists.[8]

Anthropological studies of the social organization of urban "overseas Chinese" communities have also made claims, both implicit and explicit, about Chinese laborers and their relationship to nonlaborers among Chinese. It was argued that vertical ties based on China native-place, "speech group,"[9] and extended kinship ties among Chinese migrants of varying social strata cross-cut potential class differences and allowed wealthy Chinese merchants referred to as *towkays* to serve by value consensus as the leaders of this community's associational structure.[10] The prevailing assumption was that Chinese laborers in urban areas were, in particular, incorporated into and normatively regulated by this structure through their membership in native-place-based trade guilds. However, the fact that immigrant Chinese laborers *were* at times publicly militant against other Chinese then becomes difficult to explain in terms of the timeless functionalist propositions of these studies, which allow little role for either economic compulsion or coercion in the "integration" of urban "overseas Chinese society"—or for resistance by workers to such "integration."

Against these accounts, the argument of this essay is the following. I argue that Chinese labor militancy in Malaya in the late 1930s only became *possible* when changes in the colonial economy and in the capitalist labor process weakened the control of Chinese contractors over their laborers, and lessened the influence of traditional urban guilds of "masters and men" over Chinese labor. As a result of the freeing of Chinese workers from these constraints, they were able to develop new sources of power in their struggles with employers and the colonial state. Here the focal concern is "control of labor" and its relationship to social and political changes.

However, these changes did not, by themselves, lead to Chinese labor militancy in the years from 1936 to 1941. This was brought about because a class-based "moral economy"—a set of cultural notions about social justice and the past held by Chinese immigrant laborers—was consistently being violated by capitalist employers and Chinese contractors during these years. The imperatives of capital accumulation spurred them to take actions that violated this moral economy; Chinese migrant laborers resisted these actions by their militancy.

The notion of "moral economy" is, of course, not my own but comes from the British Marxist historian E. P. Thompson, who writes that for the eighteenth-century English crowd, there was "a consistent traditional view of social norms and obligations, of the proper economic functions of several parties within the community, which, taken together, can be said to constitute the moral economy of the poor. An outrage to these moral assumptions, quite as much as actual deprivation, was the usual occasion for direct action."[11] I do differ from Thompson in that I believe that the view of social norms and obligations held by Chinese immigrant laborers in the period from 1920 to 1941 was by no means "traditional," for, as James C. Scott has pointed out, members of a social class often refashion what is in fact an idealized vision of the recent past into "the way things always have been" in the face of their ideological struggles with opposed classes during periods of rapid social change. This does not mean that their vision is, by any means, ungrounded in reality.[12]

I first turn to a brief description of the colonial society of British Malaya, and of the place of Chinese migrant laborers within it.

Colonial Society and Chinese Immigrant Labor in British Malaya, 1900–1941

The colonial economy was dominated by British capitalist enterprise committed to the profitable "development" of the Malayan peninsula's natural resources—particularly its natural rubber and tin—through the extraction, processing, and exportation of these materials by "native" laborers, under the overall direction of British managers. The generation of wealth by private enterprise within colonial Malaya and its appropriation by British capitalists during this period were manifested largely by the successful commercial development of natural rubber cultivation and the sustained mining of tin ore. Natural rubber provided the raw materials for the rubber tires of the expanding automobile industries of North America, Britain, and Europe. Tin was an essential input into production in the tin-container and metal-plating industries of these countries.

By 1941, as a consequence, the core of the West Coast region of the Malayan peninsula was what was called the "tin and rubber belt"—a more or less continuous ribbon-shaped inland landscape of tin fields and rubber plantations and small holdings, extending from the state of Kedah in the north to Singapore, several hundred miles to the south. Within or close to this belt were located Malaya's major urban commercial and political centers, the vast majority of the colony's population, the peninsula's most advanced railway and paved road networks, and the most economically valuable enterprises of British colonialism in Southeast Asia.

Tin deposits in Malayan alluvial soils and the untapped latex of the rubber tree *Hevea brazilensis* were by themselves only potential resources, of no value in their "natural" state. For rubber and tin to be extracted, collected, processed in Malaya, and exported overseas, much labor had to be expended. The reality of British racism dictated that the labor so required was not that of white Europeans but instead that of so-called native subject peoples—in the case of Malaya, the majority of these were to be Chinese immigrating from southern China and Indian Tamils from southern India. An immigrant proletariat proved essential to the development of capitalist enterprise, since the indigenous Malay peasantry almost completely resisted the attractions of mining and plantation manual labor, with most peasants instead remaining partly self-sufficient padi cultivators or becoming successful rubber small holders.[13] A general sense of the demographic and economic importance of the immigrants can be obtained from the census of 1931: in that year no less than 34 percent of the total population of British Malaya were listed as "Chinese," and 15 percent as "Indian"—the vast majority of both groups being first-generation immigrants originally brought over as indentured or wage laborers, or their sons and daughters.[14] The exploitation of "native" (that is, non-European immigrant) labor was thus the linchpin of the colonial economy.

This process was organized in such a way that Asian laborers were allocated to different sectors of the economy and to different occupations within these sectors in accordance with their "race," in what had become, by the advent of World War II, a highly refined ethnic division of labor. Immigrant Chinese laborers in particular moved in great numbers into tin mining, skilled urban crafts, and artisanry and became the majority of workers in these sectors, and also entered the rubber plantation sector in substantial numbers. In 1938, for instance, in the tin-mining sector, there were fifty-two thousand Chinese laborers, making up 78 percent of the mining labor force; on rubber plantations, there were seventy-six thousand, constituting 21 percent of all plantation workers; there were forty-five thousand Chinese laborers in factories, composing 79 percent of industrial workers; and about six thousand Chinese worked in government departments.[15]

Dominant Economic and Political Groups

The theoretical perspective assumed in this essay suggests that Chinese laborers' activism must be viewed in the context of the political economy of colonial Malaya—that is, in terms of the class relations characterizing its mode of production and the political manifestations of these relations. The colonial ethnic division of labor, then, expressed—though it was not reducible to—these class relations. These relations can most concisely be summarized by describing the positions of the dominant classes that controlled the wealth of the Malayan economy and exercised greatest political power.

How was the colonial capitalist economy organized? At its highest level, the economy was shaped by the colonial state itself. British officials, the possessors of paramount political authority, sought continually throughout this period to provide the social and political conditions necessary to promote the capitalist accumulation process, particularly for large-scale European enterprise. Of all the government actions that promoted capitalist enterprise, those most relevant here were the supervision of the conditions of immigration and employment of laborers from southern China and the imprisonment, banishment, and harassment of "subversive" Chinese labor leaders, for these actions had direct consequences for the bargaining power of Chinese labor vis-à-vis colonial employers.

The colonial state was also itself the largest proprietor of economically useful property and the largest employer of immigrant labor in the peninsula. Railways, ports, harbors, roads, market facilities, irrigation and drainage projects, land clearance schemes, and similar ventures were established and carried forward under the direction of British officials and Chinese contractors and constructed through the exertions of immigrant Chinese and Indian laborers over this period. Not only were immigrant laborers employed for the construction of these projects. Once in operation, a large complement of government-employed laborers, mostly semiskilled and unskilled, were required for their maintenance. Thus both Chinese and Indians became stevedores, bus drivers, rail-engine maintenance workers, night soil collectors, lightermen, and so on. Much of the antagonism by British officials toward the demands made by Chinese laborers to private enterprise during this period must be seen in light of the state's role as a direct employer of immigrant labor.

In addition to the state, the colonial economy was dominated by a complex of several groups of British-owned "agency houses" and "mining agencies," which among them controlled and managed the largest and most productive rubber plantations, tin mines and tin smelters, shipping lines, and insurance companies, and possessed exclusive rights to import and sell specific European manufactured goods. These agency houses and mining agencies organized themselves into groups of associated enterprises through extensive interlocking directorates.[16] By the early twentieth century, the British directors of these enterprises came to exercise both formal and informal political power by participating as "unofficials" in federal and state councils, by lobbying colonial officials through their employers' associations in London and in Malaya, by being members of the exclusive social clubs patronized by British officials, and by their influence over the English-language press and "public opinion" in Malaya.[17] In addition to the British-owned agency-house/mining agency complex, a relatively small number of Chinese capitalists, the *towkays* referred to above, owned and operated medium- and small-scale rubber plantation and tin-mining enterprises, rice mills, consumer goods factories, and businesses at intermediate levels of the import and export hierarchies. These wealthy Chinese occupied dual roles as "unofficials" in federal and state councils and as the highest officeholders in Chinese community associations (chambers of commerce, native-place organizations, etc.). The economic interests of this group, at least with respect to Chinese labor, largely converged with those of the British agency-house/mining agency complex.

In order to understand how Chinese migrant laborers in Malaya came to be able to challenge the terms of their exploitation by employers and contractors by the late 1930s, it is necessary to discuss the process of Chinese labor immigration and recruitment and the operation of the contractor system through which this process, as well as the process of production itself, were organized.

Mechanisms of Chinese Immigration and Labor Control: The "Pig Trade" and the Contractor System

For European and Chinese capitalists in Malaya, what developed as the Chinese contractor system was an indirect form of labor control that minimized both their active supervision of Chinese laborers and their wage bills, while providing the sweet compulsion to protracted physical labor that only coercion and virtual debt bondage could give. For European employers, the contractor system was an inexpensive form of labor control compatible with the stress on racial difference between Europeans and Chinese—Europeans were ignorant of Chinese languages and customs and wished to remain so—and this system placed few responsibilities for the management of labor upon them. Moreover, the Labour Code of the state regarded the Chinese contractor as the "employer" legally responsible for meeting code requirements regulating the conditions of employment, not the capitalist with whom he contracted. For Chinese contractors, the system provided numerous opportunities for the enhanced exploitation of laborers through extraeconomic means. In this section, I describe the process of Chinese labor immigration up through the 1920s organized by the contractor system, the working conditions of contract laborers, and the mechanisms by which exploitation took place.

From the early nineteenth century up through the 1920s, Chinese migration to Malaya was organized by a system of labor recruitment and control spanning the treaty ports of the southern coast of China—Amoy, Hong Kong, Macau and Swatow (Shantou)—and the major ports of influx in Malaya—Singapore and Penang.[18] *Kheh-thau*, Chinese labor recruiters or brokers who had previously lived and worked in Malaya, traveled into the rural commercial hinterlands of Canton, Amoy, and Swatow to entice peasants from their own native villages or counties (*xian*) to follow them to the "South Seas" to gain the riches to be found there. Those so recruited were expected to reimburse the contractor for whom they worked for the cost of their passage once they were in Malaya. The young men recruited—most of them from economically pressed families with too little land and too many family members[19]— were then taken by the *kheh-thau* or his assistant to a Chinese port and housed, often under guard, in hostels or "lodging houses" owned by labor agents until their embarkation for Malaya. These agents also owned lodging houses in Singapore or Penang and were thus, along with *kheh-thau*, the principal intermediaries in what came to be called the "pig trade."

The Chinese laborers so recruited were termed politely "newcomers," *sin-kheh*, or colloquially "little pigs." When steamer transport became available, they boarded for passage to Malaya, accompanied by their *kheh-thau*. Once they arrived in Singapore or Penang, the "little pigs" were taken to the corresponding lodging houses in these cities where they remained, again often under guard, until the *kheh-thau* found a rubber plantation, tin mine, or other employer "up-country" in need of their labor, if he had not done so already. At this point, if the *kheh-thau* had been acting merely as a broker, he consigned them to a contractor in return for reimbursement for their cost of passage plus a profit. They were then taken by the contractor or *kheh-thau* to the site of employment.

Having arrived at the plantation, mine, or other work site, the laborers were organized into work gangs called *kongsi*, under the control either of the contractor, who frequently had been their *kheh-thau* as well, or of the contractor's overseer. The *kongsi* was the basic unit of social organization for Chinese immigrant labor up to the 1930s, and in some areas until the Japanese occupation in 1941. The *kongsi* was structured as a contracted work unit, directed by the contractor or his overseer, detailed to perform a certain task for an employer—for instance, clearing land for rubber trees—for a certain period of time. Up through the 1920s, it appears that the European or Chinese employer paid the contractor a flat lump sum for each *sin-kheh* in the *kongsi* at the beginning of the period of employment. From this amount, the contractor paid wages, retrieved his outlay of expenses for recruitment, and made a profit.

There were various arrangements by which contractors took advantage of laborers and appropriated surplus value from them. Laborers in the *kongsi* were required to purchase foodstuffs, opium, and other commodities needed from the contractor or his clerk through a "truck system" by which the cost of these commodities was debited from their wages when they were paid. These goods were usually sold to *sin-kheh* for far above their free market prices. Laborers shopped at the contractor's store not so much out of convenience but out of fear that if they did not, the contractor would require more onerous tasks from them at work.[20] As mentioned above, *sin-kheh* were expected to repay the contractor for the cost of their passage, and this was invariably at high rates of interest. Until 1914 when Chinese indentures were outlawed in Malaya, *kheh-thau* were allowed to indenture *sin-kheh* for a year's labor or even longer, in repayment for their passage; prohibition after that year appears to have made little difference to the "on-the-ground" arrangements binding indebted laborers to their contractors.[21] Wages were therefore extremely low, and even given the invidious wage bargain struck between contractors and *sin-kheh*, the former were often unscrupulous in their accounting of wages and cheated *sin-kheh* of what they were due. Paydays were irregular, contractors were known to abscond with the wages of the members of their *kongsi*, and these problems were compounded by a system of subcontracting—at times to the depth of two or even three levels of subcontractors—which made it impossible for *sin-kheh* to hold contractors to account.

While engaging in these arrangements of exploitation, contractors had several means of enforcing their control over *kongsi* members. Some contractors relied on moral suasion deriving from their common native-place ties with *sin-kheh* in China. There was the indirect compulsion of de facto debt bondage created by the *sin-kheh* having to pay for the cost of their passage and for commodities purchased without alternative from the contractor under the truck system. In many *kongsi*, contractors sold laborers the opium to which they had become addicted once in Malaya. This daily, renewed chemical bondage encouraged the laborers' continued docility.[22] The compliance of *sin-kheh* with the contractors' or overseer's orders was also ensured, in many cases, by coercion—by the threat of whip and gun or by their actual application to the bodies of laborers. *Sin-kheh* appear to have had recourse, under these oppressive conditions, to but one form of resistance—absconding from the workplace.

A retired British rubber planter described the violent conditions of work for Chinese plantation laborers in northern rural Malaya, in what must have been a typical rural scene in the first two decades of the twentieth century:

> After breakfast was over we walked to a distant part of the estate, which was being reclaimed from a heavy growth of "Lallang" grass . . . by a gang of about forty Chinamen, who were being watched over by a Chinese foreman and a half-

caste supervisor, the latter being armed with a gun, which he carried in the same way that a City man carries an umbrella, whilst the former had a heavy stock-whip. Whenever a coolie stopped working the foreman would shout at him to go on; if this order was not obeyed quickly he got a blow on the legs with the whip. If he showed any signs of turning on the foreman in retaliation for such punishment, he found himself shouted at by the supervisor and threatened by my colleague.

Such methods of handling these Chinamen rather astonished me, and I demanded enlightenment from my friend, who told me that they were known as "Kongsi" men, and were indentured on a three years' contract. The man who supplied them had charged the Company about £10 a coolie, and brought them over from China under contract to the estate to work for three years, and during that time they were supposed to be paying off the £10 that had been expended on them; they themselves received a very small sum each day, amounting to something like ten cents.

When they had ceased their digging operations at midday they were all herded back to their "Kongsi" house for their meal of rice which the estate supplied, and while there they were guarded by two Sikh watchmen with loaded rifles, in case they decided to revolt or endeavoured to escape.[23]

The contractor system that organized the recruitment and immigration of Chinese laborers and supervised their labor once in Malaya thus depended on unfree labor, bound by coercion, debt peonage, and inexperience to the capitalist production site. The laissez-faire policies of the colonial state did little more than monitor and reform the most egregious abuses of this nearly autonomous system, as when outraged public opinion in Great Britain and Malaya led to the abolition of legal Chinese indentures in 1914. Colonial capitalist enterprise remained the prime beneficiary of the accelerated exploitation this system represented up through the 1920s.

The Interwar Years 1920–1941: Emergence of Chinese Labor Militancy

During this period, changes occurred in the capitalist labor process and in social and political conditions that weakened the contractor system as a mode of labor control, with the result that large numbers of Chinese immigrant laborers were provided with the strategic space for challenging the terms of exploitation. These changes coincided in time with a weakening of *towkay* power over Chinese laborers as guilds went into decline. It thus became possible for Chinese laborers in a variety of sectors to organize themselves in new forms of association and by the late 1930s for them to display a "spontaneous," coordinated militancy for the first time in the colonial economy.

Although changes affecting the contractor system and Chinese guilds made labor militancy feasible—that is, allowed Chinese workers to engage in aggressive labor actions despite the opposition of employers and the colonial state—these changes did not, per se, determine this militancy. The immediate causes lay elsewhere. The shifting imperatives of capitalist accumulation during the Depression years of the 1930s led British and Chinese employers to violate their explicit and implicit agreements with Chinese immigrant laborers, agreements that were central to the "moral economy" of the latter under the contractor system. It was against these violations that Chinese labor militancy—strikes, demonstrations, violent clashes with police—was directed.

Immigration, Changes in the Labor Process, and the New Power of Chinese Labor

By the mid–1930s, three changes combined to improve the economic position of Chinese immigrant laborers and to make their militancy possible. This allowed an extraordinary lifting of the preexisting conditions of "dull economic compulsion" and coercion by contractors and the state, a lifting of control that allowed Chinese workers in large numbers to manifest publicly their resistance to exploitation for the first time.[24] One change was the imposition of restrictions on Chinese immigration in 1930, which led thereafter to a serious labor scarcity. Another change consisted of several related transformations in the internal and external conditions under which the contractor system operated, which began to take effect during the same period. Yet a third change was the adoption by Chinese laborers of family farming based on "squatting" on employers' land and state land (e.g., Forest Reserves), which provided a viable alternative to employment within the capitalist sector.

Up to 1930, Chinese immigration into Malaya had been unrestricted by the colonial state. But in 1930, at the nadir of the Depression, with Western enterprise in distress and unemployment at its highest ever, the government began to repatriate laborers to China in great numbers at its own expense, and officials set immigration quotas for the first time for Chinese males. The informal imposition of immigration quotas in 1930 was ratified officially with the Aliens Ordinance of 1933.

These quotas deprived employers and contractors of a major weapon used in the past to guarantee the compliance, if not docility, of immigrant Chinese laborers: increasing the local labor supply by increasing the immigration of laborers.[25] At the time they were imposed, these quotas were viewed by most officials as only a temporary measure. Nonetheless, quotas for males remained in effect from 1930 to 1941,[26] although Chinese female immigration continued to be unrestricted until 1938. Two ideological factors influenced state officials to ensure that Chinese immigration after 1930 was restricted to low levels. One factor was the Sinophobia both of a large proportion of British officials and of a conservative Malay precolonial aristocracy just then being co-opted into the lower levels of colonial governance. Both groups feared that Malaya would come to be swamped by "alien" Chinese. The other factor consisted of British officials' fears that recent Chinese immigrants influenced by the Chinese Communist party and international communism would "subvert" British rule in Malaya. Although both factors sufficed to prevent the return of unrestricted immigration, after 1938 they were reinforced by political unrest in southern China, which made migration to Malaya difficult in any event. (Immigration from China ceased altogether, never to resume, when the Japanese armies occupied Malaya in late 1941.) Moreover, the unforeseen development of strong opposition by the Indian government by 1935 to the continued importation of southern Indian labor made it impossible for employers to substitute Indian for Chinese labor.[27] As colonial capitalism by the mid–1930s began to recover from the worst effects of the Depression, and plantation and mining production resumed, these restrictions on labor immigration led to a severe shortage of Chinese labor and thus increased its leverage on the labor market.

A set of related changes in the conditions under which the *keh-thau*/contractor system operated also promoted the militancy of Chinese immigrant labor by the 1930s. One change internal to the operation of this system reflected the new freedom of labor, but also, I would argue, reinforced its potential for discontent. By the 1930s, the basis for calculating the wages of contract laborers had changed from the flat wages paid to (legally, then de facto) indentured Chinese laborers through the 1920s to one grounded in performance incentives. According to Yeo, "generally [the contractor] received a lump-sum payment once or twice a month from the management *based on the output of the workers under his charge.* After deducting a certain percentage from the payment [for expenses], he remunerated his men accordingly" (emphasis added).[28] I would argue—on the basis of ethnographic research among Chinese Malaysian laborers—that the new incentive wage system, much like piece-rate wages, promoted an ideological struggle between laborers and contractors over the particularities of what constituted a just wage.[29] The "effort bargain" struck over how much wage should rightly be paid for a certain level of effort and output came to be challenged time and again in the late 1930s, as capitalist employers and contractors sought to alter it by reducing wages, and while laborers sought to uphold it by maintaining wage levels or restoring them.

Changes external to the contractor system derived from the emergence of a more skilled, settled, and sophisticated Chinese migrant labor force, which became increasingly able to challenge the anachronistic forms of labor control represented by the contractor system. First, as a result of the quotas imposed on Chinese males, the cost of a ticket for passage from China for a Chinese male laborer rose steeply, and this added greatly to the outlay of expenses by the *kheh-thau* and labor contractor. This in turn meant that few *kheh-thau* could afford to subsidize the cost of immigration of *sin-kheh*. Given the high demand for Chinese labor by the mid–1930s, a substitute for *kheh-thau* recruiting of labor in China emerged. The lodging houses of Singapore and Penang became informal labor exchanges where both *lau-kheh*, "old guests," and contractors met to form new contract labor groups. *Lau-kheh* were experienced migrants who had resided in Malaya for at least one year and had previously been employed as *sin-kheh*, but were now free of their initial contracts and indebtedness.

Second, as the proportion of *lau-kheh* in the Chinese laboring population increased, so too did their level of sophistication about the colonial economy and the possibilities for better employment, leaving laborers less reconciled to the contractor system and the various ways in which it took advantage of laborers. Moreover, as Yeo has pointed out, by the mid–1930s, employers and contractors had to deal with the fact that the spread of Chinese-language education in Malaya "had produced a sizeable pool of educated Chinese workers with a deeper knowledge of Malayan and world conditions."[30] As laborers became more intensively literate, they were able to read the works of the leftist writers of the "Proletarian Literature Movement" in China, and to keep abreast of current economic and political conditions in Malaya and China alike by reading the Chinese-language press.[31]

Third, *lau-kheh*, being freer of the indebtedness created by the contractor system, were more mobile than a prior generation of migrant laborers, and thus more able to take advantage of better-paid wage labor throughout the peninsula. Internal demographic growth from the early 1900s onward meant that increasingly Chinese laborers were Malayan-born and were far more acquainted than *sin-kheh* with local conditions of employment—however straitened these might at certain times be.

Finally, employers in the 1930s persisted in relying on the contractor system at a time when the reorganization of the capitalist labor process, coinciding with advances in technology occurring with industrialization of the colonial economy, required that laborers possess increased levels of skills and autonomy from contractor supervision. This new requirement contradicted the modes of labor control that up to that time had been part of the contractor system, such as coercion, forced indebtedness, and opium addiction. What is significant is that none of these modes of control could instill industrial discipline in or be efficiently employed against a better-educated and increasingly skilled Chinese labor force organized cooperatively in the new technical divisions of labor found in factories and other industrial work sites. Nor were they compatible with the development of a flexible, geographically wide-ranging and competitive market for free laborers, in particular Chinese, whom the ethnic division of labor allowed to enter the new technically advanced occupations.[32] The one exception to this generalization was the rubber plantation sector, in which Chinese contract laborers were still employed; moreover, wage levels in the rubber industry set the scale for other kinds of labor by Chinese.[33] Elsewhere, however, new technical skills and freedom from direct contractor control were required of Chinese laborers producing for the new, relatively large-scale sawmills, rubber and pineapple factories, tin smelters, railways, and engineering shops founded during this period.[34] Stenson summarizes these several developments in stating that the control of the contractor over Chinese laborers "probably suffered a steady decline in the late twenties."[35] Nonetheless, estate, mining, government, and other industrial employers persisted in using the contractor system, with its attendant abuses. This appears to have been due to its perceived economic advantages for employers, within the colonial ethnic division of labor referred to above.

A third change that conferred strategic space on Chinese laborers vis-à-vis colonial employers was the adoption by many laborers of family-based farming, made possible by "squatting" on state and employers' lands, as a viable alternative to employment in the capitalist sector. Chinese laborers were able to do this by taking advantage of several developments after 1920. As noted above, from 1930 onward, Chinese women were allowed to immigrate without restriction. They began to enter Malaya in greater numbers than previously, owing to the Japanese invasion and to internal political unrest in China, and to the lowered cost of passage for women. One consequence was that it was not only risky for Chinese male laborers to return to China for their brides (as had long been the practice) since there were no assurances then that they could ever come back to Malaya; it was also possible for the first time for large numbers of Chinese men to marry Chinese women, as the sex ratio tended toward parity in the mid- to late-1930s.[36]

One result of this was to accelerate a trend already under way by the end of World War I, in which periodically unemployed and under-employed Chinese laborers sought out new means of subsistence external to capitalist production, particularly vegetable gardening, padi cultivation, and fruit growing based on their own and family labor.[37] *Lau-kheh* began to live during part or all of the year outside the all-male labor *kongsi* in separate households with their wives and children. Vegetable gardening based on "squatting" on government land, especially, proved to be economically successful, as the demand for fresh vegetables increased with the growth of the urban population during the interwar period, while costs for the Chinese farmer remained low, given the use of family labor with labor-intensive cultivation methods. At the same time the economic dislocation of the Depression years (e.g., the diminished purchasing capacity of laborers) prompted the colonial state to encourage food-crop production. Unemployed Chinese in many settings, moreover, found themselves with little choice—either grow food or starve—while government officials regarded vegetable cultivation as a safety valve for labor discontent.

Lau-kheh in the central states of Perak, Selangor, Negri Sembilan, and elsewhere on the West Coast thus lived in increasing numbers with their wives and children in family-based households,[38] intensively cultivated their vegetable gardens and fruit orchards, and raised livestock and fish for a living.[39] Although no census of "squatters" during these years was ever taken (nor was it likely to be accurate if it had been), it is evident that several thousand Chinese workers had turned to this new subsistence base by the Depression years of the 1930s. As long as they were able to "squat" without interference on government lands, they only were drawn into employment as tin miners, rubber tappers, or other industrial laborers when labor was in short supply and wages were exceptionally high. In having access to this alternative mode of livelihood, Chinese laborers came to acquire substantial bargaining leverage vis-à-vis colonial capitalists over the conditions under which they entered the labor market. As Francis Loh has argued, vegetable growing, which unemployed Chinese tin laborers in the Kinta Valley of Perak and elsewhere had been initially resorted to out of desperation, developed into a weapon of resistance by Chinese laborers against capitalist exploitation.[40]

Decline of the Trade Guilds
The urban trade guilds represented, in the case of certain occupations, a form of labor control outside the contractor system. But by the 1920s, guilds too had begun to decline in importance—and so also did *towkay* capacity to control working conditions for urban Chinese workers. From the mid-nineteenth century through the early 1900s, guilds had been common for skilled artisans such as cobblers, goldsmiths, tailors, and carpenters. Masters, journeymen, and apprentices were all members, and wage rates, working hours, and production standards were all set, competition restricted, and welfare "functions" performed, within them.[41]

An uncritical use of the "ethnographic present" tense even as late as the 1960s by Freedman, Crissman, and other anthropologists makes it appear that Chinese laborers were indefinitely subordinated to their employers in guilds within the hierarchical segmented structures of "overseas Chinese communities." It is clear from evidence of the period, however, that by no later than the 1920s the native-place-based guilds of "masters and men" were in serious decline. By that time, very large numbers of urban Chinese workers had abandoned them for new forms of association, and trade guilds had become largely irrelevant to the working lives of Chinese employed by the new large-scale industrial work sites then coming into existence in both urban and rural settings.[42]

The causes of guild decline were several. First, guild organization had long been strongest for certain skilled occupations that required an extended apprenticeship—tailoring, shoemaking, carpentering, goldsmithing, and the like. These occupations were generally not in the rapidly expanding sectors of the economy, and some became obsolete during this period.[43] Second, insofar as *towkay* control of workers in the guilds depended on secret society coercion, the prohibition against and continued repression directed at the "Triad societies" from the 1890s onward by the colonial state had the cumulative effect of removing this buttress of *towkay* dominance, except in a few areas.[44]

Third, as Gamba suggests in his study of the origins of trade unionism in Malaya, the emergence of the new factories and workshops owned by European and Chinese employers, including the colonial state, threw together side by side Chinese laborers from different native places in China. Recruitment to this employment depended not on native-place ties but, as pointed out above, their possession of new differentiated technical skills and was based on the existence of a national labor market of "free" (i.e., geographically mobile and legally unencumbered) workers, the *lau-kheh*. Younger workers refused to enter the native-place-based guilds when they found that the expansion of the colonial economy and the demand for Chinese labor ensured that the going wage rate could be obtained without guild intervention.[45]

Chinese Labor Militancy, 1936–1941

It was under these conditions of decline for both the contractor system and trade guilds that, commencing in 1936, Chinese laborers engaged in extensive mass strikes, demonstrations, and violence against managers, overseers, officials, and police, for the first time in colonial Malaya's history. The months between September 1936 and April 1937 were marked both by economic recovery of capitalist enterprise from the depths of the Depression and by an unprecedented wave of strikes by Chinese laborers. After a short period of "normalcy,"

Chinese labor militancy reappeared in the months from late 1937 through September 1940.[46]

In September 1936, Chinese cutters at a pineapple factory in Singapore went on strike; the strike spread to other pineapple factories in the city and adjacent southern Johore State, involved some fifteen hundred workers, and continued for three weeks. Strikers also demonstrated outside the Chinese Protectorate office in Singapore, until dispersed by the arrival of police. During this same interval, between four thousand and five thousand Chinese construction workers in Singapore and southern Johore also struck, and stopped work from one to two weeks. Again, there was a demonstration by strikers who surrounded the office of the protectorate; it ceased when police arrested several demonstrators. In October both Chinese and Indian employees of the Singapore Traction Company struck, while thirteen thousand Singapore Sanitation Department night-soil "coolies" and other municipal laborers—some Chinese, some southern Indian—also stopped work. Both strikes were brought to an end after several days, when employers offered wage and other concessions.

In November the location of the most serious strikes and other militant action by Chinese laborers shifted from Singapore in the south to the central Malayan States. In the Malayan Collieries at Batu Arang in Selangor State, four thousand Chinese miners put down their tools for several days. This was by far the most significant strike action to date, for this mine provided the major supplies of coal for the government's rail system and electric power plants. In December, tin-mining workers went on strike at three other mines in Selangor; the strike continued for several days before settlements were reached.

In the city of Ipoh in Perak State during late 1936, Chinese fitters employed in foundries servicing the tin-mining industry organized themselves into a "Fitters' Guild," in actuality a union, and successfully demanded a wage hike. Tin-mining workers in Perak received large wage increases merely by threatening to strike. In early 1937, three thousand engine drivers in the Perak mines received higher wages when they too threatened to strike. Skilled Chinese workers in Perak associated with the tin mines, and other workers as well, demanded and received higher wages: tailors, tinsmiths, carpenters, masons, painters, shoemakers, goldsmiths.[47] As Francis Loh has pointed out, it was precisely the well-established alternative to capitalist employment of family vegetable gardening in this area that allowed Chinese workers to both demand *and* receive higher wages without actually having to resort in most instances to strikes.[48] What was characterized at the time as a "strike wave" spread to other sectors in central Malaya in early 1937. Between January and March, there were altogether eleven strikes in Selangor among Chinese engine drivers, foundry workers, pineapple cutters, sawmill workers, match makers, shoemakers, and rubber factory laborers. In March, Chinese rubber tappers struck on European estates in southern Selangor, in Negri Sembilan, Malacca, northern Johore and Pahang; the strikes involved between ten thousand and twenty thousand tappers at their peak, and lasted for about three weeks. Efforts by the colonial state to reimpose labor discipline took on a political dimension, as officials and police sought to destroy the power of unions they regarded as led or influenced by the MCP. In the course of the tappers' strikes, police arrested those they regarded as Communist strike leaders; tappers held several large and small demonstrations against the Chinese Protectorate, European estates, and the police; and there was at least one violent clash between demonstrators and police, leading to the killing or wounding of three strikers and the detention of more than one hundred demonstrators. At the coal mines of the Malayan Collieries, a general sympathy strike was declared in late March, and five thousand Chinese and Indian miners stopped work; for several days strikers forcibly occupied the mine until driven out by a police charge, followed by more than one hundred arrests and the resumption of mining operations.

Minor concessions by employers to strikers' demands combined with large-scale arrests by police over several months of those whom they saw as "Communist agitators" led by May 1937 to the return of "normalcy" to the areas of strike activity. But not for long. From late 1937 through late 1940, there occurred a recession that led to lowered rubber and tin prices, and employers reacted by instituting wage cuts for Chinese and Indian labor. While Chinese rubber tappers remained superficially quiescent, during July and August of 1937 there was resistance elsewhere. Chinese mining workers at the Hong Fatt mines in central Malaya responded to wage cuts by "rioting," which was quelled by the police, but the employer, fearing flooding of the mines, quickly capitulated by restoring higher wages. In Singapore, a strike by employees of the Singapore Traction Company, most of whom were Indian, was initiated by the multiethnic Traction Company Employees' Association, and lasted for six weeks until settled by arbitration. From September 1938 through September 1940, Chinese ricksha pullers, sawmill laborers, tailors, rubber factory workers, stevedores, and construction "coolies" in Singapore all struck. So too did tin miners in Selangor, and rubber tappers in Negri Sembilan, among other groups. More than eighty strikes occurred during 1939, and even more during the early months of 1940. Most strikes during these months led to the granting of concessions and were rapidly concluded.

A Moral Economy of the Just Wage and a Vision of the Past

What were the determinants of the labor militancy just described? To some extent, particularly by 1939, the Malayan Communist party played some role through two organizations it controlled—the Malayan General Labour Union and the Anti-Enemy Backing-Up Society (AEBUS). Beginning in 1937, with the party's joining the broad-based Malayan Chinese National Salvation Movement against Japanese aggression in China, it began to rebuild its organizational base, which had been rendered ineffective by police arrests, detentions, and banishings of its labor organizers during the early 1937 strike wave.[49] As Stenson observes, "the MCP lost no opportunity to strengthen and deepen its own organizational influence over the Chinese community."[50] The party's new organizers began to employ the pretext of calling on Chinese laborers to form "relief committees" to collect relief funds for Chinese in southern China, but these committees rapidly took on the activities of de facto labor unions, and by 1939 successful strikes and other militant action commenced in many areas.[51] Opposition by the colonial state was at first mild, given pressure from the Colonial Office in London to promote local registered trade unionism within an empire preparing for war. However, by late 1939 alarm by employers and officials about AEBUS success in organizing strikes led to another series of police raids, arrests, and banishments of Communist trade unionists.[52]

Nonetheless, MCP organizational influence took advantage of preexisting genuine grievances. It was important only in channeling the discontent of Chinese labor during the last three years between 1936 and 1941, and even then such discontent existed already, and at times manifested itself independently. From 1936 through 1937, according to Stenson, "the most marked characteristic of the strikes as a whole was their spontaneity and the absence of disciplined, coordinated direction."[53] One has the distinct sense of Malayan Communist party cadres during these two years seeking to ride the crest of labor's discontent and militancy, while claiming premature responsibility for its relatively unorganized successes.[54]

What then were the Chinese laborers' grievances on which they acted with such determination? Recurrently, from 1936 to 1937, and again from 1938 to 1940, Chinese laborers' protests were aimed against a variety of new initiatives by employers who either failed to restore preexisting levels of wages and other benefits, which had been reduced during the Depression, when prosperity returned, or sought to rescind wage and other gains previously granted. According to Yeo, in the years before 1936,

> the depression had forced wages down to the bare subsistence
> level in the rubber, mining and other industries. . . . Drastic
> wage cuts and other difficulties were, however, accepted by
> Chinese workers as inevitable exigencies of the time.
> *Commensurate wage increases were expected to follow the*
> *return of prosperity to the country.* The economic gloom
> started to lift in 1934. The prices of Malayan exports such as
> tin and rubber rose sharply [emphasis added].

He concludes by stating that by 1936, "while the cost of living had also
risen, the expected wage bonanza was nowhere to be seen."[55]

One notable example, up close, reveals the thinking of Chinese
strikers during the March 1937 rubber tappers' strikes in Selangor:

> The *Straits Times*, the leading English-language daily
> newspaper, sent a correspondent to ascertain the views of the
> strikers. The chief complaint of the workers was said to be
> the failure of the employers to raise wages. They had read in
> the Chinese press of rising rubber prices. Calculating the
> employers' costs of production, they were of the opinion that
> their wages could easily be increased. They refused to accept
> the employers' argument that prices were only temporarily
> high and that if wages were raised now they would be
> difficult to reduce later. *They preferred to be paid by results*
> [emphasis added].[56]

What can be seen at work is a moral economy of expectation and
social norms held to by Chinese laborers: one that insisted that
reciprocity between employer and laborers depended on mutual
sacrifice and mutual reward—that a just wage reflected a sharing of the
wealth when prosperity returned as well as a sharing of deprivation in
times of depression. For most Chinese laborers, this moral economy of
"just deserts" was reinforced by the operation of the incentive wage
arrangement between laborers and contractors referred to above.

The demands made by Chinese rubber tappers during this strike,
when compared to prevailing conditions on European plantations,
suggest the struggle between laborers and management to define the
"effort bargain" in line with the notion of a just wage. Repeatedly the
issues seem to be: How much effort should be expended for a certain
wage? How are the "tasks" paid at a going daily rate to be defined?
What kinds of work are to go unpaid, as just part of the job? Thus, for
example, Chinese rubber tappers demanded that the daily "standard
task" of trees to tap be 250, while the prevailing number set by
managers was 300 to 390; they demanded that they be paid three cents
per pound for "scrap rubber," while employers' practice was to consider
its collection a normal part of the "standard task"; tappers asked that
they be paid fifty cents per month for their tapping knives, while the

employers insisted they provide their own—even though previously (before the Depression) these had been provided by the plantation.[57]

In these and other instances of demands by Chinese laborers prior to or during strike actions, what can be inferred is the existence of a vision of labor's recent Golden Age—the years before the Depression—in which a just wage and fair working conditions prevailed. This vision provided a reference point against which, recurrently, current wages and benefits were measured—and found wanting. As Scott has pointed out, the conditions of the past that are being invoked in this way may "objectively" have been extremely exploitative; nonetheless a disadvantaged group, in its ideological contest with an opposed group, may invoke them as being ideal when compared to the even more flawed conditions of the present.[58]

It remains to point out that the belief held by Chinese laborers that European and Chinese employers had reneged on explicit or implicit promises to improve wages and working conditions when prosperity returned appears to have some factual basis. Yeo notes that in 1936 "employers were enjoying attractive profits for the first time in years and were preoccupied with issues other than wage increase."[59] In the case of the 1937 rubber tappers' strike, Virginia Thompson states that their strike

> reflected their dissatisfaction over not sharing in the rubber industry's returning prosperity by a restoration of depression wage cuts. In this case London had a share in the responsibility: while the government in Malaya and some of the planting community approved the laborers' demands, the directors of British registered companies were loath to sacrifice the first dividends they were enjoying for some time.[60]

Thus what were viewed as imperatives of capitalist accumulation violated the moral economy that—however uneasily, framed normatively the relationship between Chinese workers and local employers. Chinese strikers' demands for improvements or restorations in benefits also focused on the contractor system, whose abuses during the Depression years made these demands even more urgent. Stenson observes that during this period, "the contract system, under which most Chinese were employed, was associated with a marked deterioration in conditions of labour, being characterized by out-working, excessive employment of apprentices, employee indebtedness, false assessment of wages and absconding by bankrupt contractors."[61] It appears that the Depression cost-cutting measures of capitalists were passed down to contractors, and from contractors to their laborers, while the labor redundancies of the early Depression years allowed these abuses to continue without effective worker resistance for several years, until the changed conditions of the late 1930s. When at this time the bargaining power of Chinese laborers shifted in their favor, their strikes and other forms of militancy were directed toward the abolition or reform of the contractor system and the great and petty indignities it inflicted on them.

When the lack of reciprocity by employers—and the colonial state—threatened the survival of Chinese laborers, their militancy was at its most extreme. As Yeo states above, wages during Depression years for Chinese were at a "bare subsistence level." Similarly, Chinese "squatters" were most resistant when threatened with arrest and eviction by police and colonial bureaucrats, for here not only were indignities inflicted, but their and their families' livelihoods were also jeopardized.

In Jelebu, Negri Sembilan, during the 1930s, "the police were often called upon to arrest illegal occupiers. . . . Elderly residents in the district remember with fear the intimidation and beatings they and their friends were given by the Police, which sometimes involved European officers. As a result, the authorities were shunned by the Chinese, and antagonism grew to such an extent that policemen and some officials were occasionally attacked."[62]

Yet, to conclude, it is important to see that the moral economy of Chinese laborers was, above all, a cultural creation: central to it were culturally based norms of the just treatment due workers, grounded in assumptions of an idealized past. Such a moral economy may have been, I propose as a question for future research, supported by the existence of an emergent proletarian "public sphere"[63] composed of Chinese working-class institutions about which as yet we know little. Labor unions (even if unregistered), social clubs, sporting teams, and night schools, for example, would have constituted some of these institutions in the 1920s and 1930s. Certainly the intensification of literacy among Chinese laborers, their increased opportunities for communication among one another, and their permanent settlement in family-based households from the 1920s onward would all have contributed to the emergence of such a public sphere. If I am correct about its existence, it was this proletarian public sphere that Malayan Communist cadres were able to penetrate by the late 1930s and came to dominate after the war, from 1945 to 1947, when the Malayan labor movement was at its strongest and most militant.

Conclusion

The central contention of this essay has been that Chinese immigrant labor militancy of the late 1930s derived from popular sources of grievance grounded in a moral economy of a just wage and fair work, which was recurrently violated by the actions of European and

Chinese employers and contractors. Militancy was made possible, to begin with, by the weakening of "traditional" forms of labor control by Chinese contractors and by Chinese *towkays* through the trade guilds. This provided the strategic space allowing Chinese laborers to respond aggressively with strikes and demonstrations to employers' and contractors' failure to reinstitute the wage and other benefits of the pre-Depression years when relative prosperity returned in the late 1930s.

As to the competing accounts of Chinese labor militancy during these years, the conservative explanation emphasizes the manipulations of Chinese laborers by Malayan Communist party cadres "from the top down," assuming that they were merely the passive objects of Communist control. This invocation of the Communist International deus ex machina simply denies flatly that there were ever any popular sources of Chinese labor militancy, and overestimates the power of the MCP at this time. Such an explanation is refuted by the entire argument of this essay, which holds that MCP labor organizers took advantage of spontaneous labor actions already under way by 1936–37, and seized on widespread grievances among workers to further their own political objectives. Nonetheless, questions concerning the dialectic between Chinese popular discontent and protest, on one hand, and the organizational efforts of Malayan Communist party cadres in the late 1930s and from 1945 to 1947, on the other, are crucial ones for the study of Malayan labor history, and deserve further inquiry. The liberal account, which focuses on the economic determinants of militancy, can be seen as flawed because of its economism. Much as for the historiography of eighteenth-century England criticized by E. P. Thompson, the notion that protest occurs because of "economic" determinants ignores the most interesting sociological questions, that is, "being hungry [or denied higher wages] . . . what do people do? How is their behavior modified by custom, culture, and reason?"[64] The thrust of the argument of this essay is that we must go beyond such simplistic stimulus-response explanations. As to the [bio]-culturalist explanation of Chinese labor militancy, the more Lamarckian version of this account, which connects the "race" (and "blood," etc.) of Hailams and Hakkas with predispositions toward political radicalism, has long since been discredited. A more strictly culturalist version must be seriously considered; however, as a general explanation for Chinese labor militancy, it too cannot be sustained, since the labor actions of the late 1930s extended far beyond Hailams and Hakkas to include the members of other speech groups, such as Cantonese, Teochew, Hokchiu, and Henghwa. Still, the issue of what cultural traits among Hailams and Hakkas might have promoted leftist values is worth further study. Turning finally to certain anthropological studies of urban "overseas Chinese" communities in Southeast Asia, the labor militancy exhibited by Chinese workers from the 1930s onward through the postwar years refutes the timeless functionalist portrayal of a coordination of interests between lower-class Chinese and Chinese *towkays* through trade guilds within the associational structure of these communities, which is presented in these studies. The theoretical implications of the failure of these studies to adequately acknowledge the existence of, much less explain, this militancy need to be investigated, but surely the emphasis on value consensus and vertical ties among urban Chinese needs to be complemented by serious attention to the political economy of the Southeast Asian colonial societies, such as Malaya, in which urban Chinese lived.

Despite the many obstacles posed by the opposition of employers and the colonial state—which often entailed great economic risks and even physical danger for both labor organizers and the militant rank and file—Chinese workers during the mid- to late-1930s were able to achieve major improvements in their wages and working conditions through strikes, work-site occupations, demonstrations, and other actions. Although these victories proved to be temporary, having been reversed by 1941 by employers in combination with the state, they nonetheless prepared Chinese—and also Indian—workers of the postwar years 1945 to 1947 to undertake the large-scale militant labor actions for which those years are well known. I propose as a hypothesis for further inquiry that during this brief postwar period, it was again the moral economy of laborers, in the face of capitalist initiatives to reinstitute labor discipline and the older harsh terms of exploitation, which goes far to explain "industrial unrest." This moral economy, still centered on the notion of a right to economic survival and to a just wage, was bolstered by new "subversive" ideas of self-determination and equality with Europeans. It was just such a moral economy in its new form that represented the cultural basis of popular support for the General Labour Union, the core of the postwar Malayan labor movement. Above all else, the reconstruction of Chinese migrant labor militancy attempted in this essay should be seen as part of a larger movement of historical recovery—to alert us to the voices and actions of lower-class Chinese in Malaya, which have been silenced and occluded in the annals of the victors of the Cold War, and to restore them to their proper place in the active making of the history of contemporary Malaysian society.

Notes

1. Research for this essay was supported by a grant from the Joint Committee on Chinese Studies of the American Council of Learned Societies and

the Social Science Research Council, with funds provided by the Andrew W. Mellon Foundation. This support is gratefully acknowledged. Transliterations of Chinese terms in Malaya are given according to prevailing Malayan orthography, and in China according to the Pinyin system. In the period from 1920 to 1941, British Malaya consisted of three administratively integrated but legally separate territories: the Straits Settlements of Singapore, Penang, and Malacca; the Federated Malay States of Perak, Selangor, Pahang, and Negri Sembilan; and the Unfederated Malay States of Kelantan, Trengganu, Johore, and Kedah. Overall direction came to be in the hands of the high commissioner in Singapore during this period.

2. Michael Morgan, "The Rise and Fall of Malayan Trade Unionism, 1945-50," *Malaya: The Making of a Neocolony*, ed. Mohamed Amin and Malcolm Caldwell (Nottingham, 1977). Charles Gamba, *The Origins of Trade Unionism in Malaya: A Study in Colonial Labour Unrest* (Singapore, 1962); M. R. Stenson, *Industrial Conflict in Malaya: Prelude to the Communist Revolt of 1948* (Kuala Lumpur, 1971).

3. Stenson, 108, 114.

4. On the Malayan Communist party during the interwar years from 1920 to 1941, see Gene Z. Hanrahan, *The Communist Struggle in Malaya* (New York, 1954), 1-27; Stenson, 1-37; Stephen M. Y. Leong, "Sources, Agencies and Manifestations of Overseas Chinese Nationalism in Malaya, 1937-1941," (Ph.D. diss., University of California at Los Angeles, 1976), 222-42.

5. Thus, for example, a major work on the Chinese in Malaya by Victor Purcell, himself a retired government official, stated that Chinese laborers were forced to participate in trade unions in the immediate postwar years (1945-46) by communist "bullies and rascals," "by a small group of extortioners and intimidators." Victor Purcell, *The Chinese in Malaya* (Kuala Lumpur, 1967), 275.

6. For instance, in the case of strikes by construction and pineapple-factory workers in 1936 in Singapore and Johore, Yeo writes that "economic causes alone would have brought about these strikes." Yeo Kim Wah, "The Communist Challenge in the Malayan Labour Scene, September 1936-March 1937," *Journal of the Malaysian Branch, Royal Asiatic Society* 49, 2(1976): 46. Similarly, Gamba writes of the years 1945-47 that "many strikes were called by unions which were little concerned with the political situation in the country, and which were seeking economic improvements. . . . The inadequate rice rations and the shortage of other essential commodities led to a steep rise in the cost of living. Thus, labour, to compensate itself for the fall in real wages, demanded cash wage increases." Gamba, 38-41.

7. See Yeo, 46, 48-49.

8. An example of a biocultural account—note the suggestion of association between "blood" and "politics"—is that of Victor Purcell, who writes that "the Hailams . . . are a race somewhat different from the mainland Chinese and are said to have a good deal of aboriginal blood in their veins. They were the first to take a left line in politics, partly, perhaps, to increase their prestige with the other Chinese by drawing attention to themselves. Later the Khehs (Hakkas) also showed a disposition to leftist politics. They, too, are a type of Chinese distinctly apart from the remainder." Purcell, 214. See also Hanrahan, 7; Harry Miller, *The Communist Menace in Malaya* (New York, 1954), 20-21.

9. "Speech groups" were groups of Chinese immigrants who spoke the same language in the Southeast Coast or Lingnan regions of China. Because in most instances, speech-group ties were identical to or largely overlapped with China native-place ties, those who spoke the same Chinese language saw themselves as sharing a common identity. Of the members of the most common speech groups represented in Malaya, those of the Hokkien speech group came

from the hinterlands of the cities of Amoy and Quanzhou in Fujian; Teochew speakers came from the prefecture of Chaozhoufu in eastern Guangdong province; Hailam or Hainanese speakers from the island of Hainan; Cantonese from the hinterland of Canton in southern Guangdong province; Hakka speakers from the highland parts of the catchment area of the Han River and its tributaries in eastern Guangdong, and from upland areas of the commercial hinterland of Canton. The term *speech group* is more accurate than earlier usages such as *tribe* or *dialect group*." See G. William Skinner, *Chinese Society in Thailand: An Analytical History* (Ithaca, 1957), 35-40.

10. See Maurice Freedman, "The Growth of a Plural Society in Malaya," in *The Study of Chinese Society: Essays by Maurice Freedman*, ed. G. William Skinner (Stanford, 1979), 27-38; Lawrence W. Crissman, "The Segmentary Structure of Urban Overseas Chinese Communities," *Man* 2, 2(1967): 185-204. Typical of this approach was Freedman, who wrote, "The Chinese evolved no class system comparable to that of the Malays. They were both physically and economically mobile. In any one area of the country they grouped themselves on the basis of interlocking associations which gave them the means of exercising control within their own ranks and of dealing with the outside world represented by Malay and British officials. . . . [In the twentieth century] the associations giving Chinese society its form and chains of command have been more various; among them, Chambers of Commerce, trade associations, and organizations recruiting on the basis of like territorial origin in China (a species of *Landsmannschaften*) have been the most important." Freedman, 33.

11. E. P. Thompson, "The Moral Economy of the English Crowd in the Eighteenth Century," *Past and Present* 50 (1971): 79.

12. James C. Scott, *Weapons of the Weak* (New Haven, 1985), 178-83.

13. Donald M. Nonini, *British Colonial Rule and the Resistance of the Malay Peasantry 1900-1957* (New Haven, forthcoming), chaps. 3-4.

14. Figures cited in Lim Chong-Yah, *Economic Development of Modern Malaya* (Kuala Lumpur, 1967), 192, 344.

15. Virginia Thompson, *Labor Problems in Southeast Asia* (New Haven, 1947), 77.

16. James Puthucheary, *Ownership and Control in the Malayan Economy* (Singapore, 1960); G. C. Allen and A. G. Donnithorne, *Western Enterprise in Indonesia and Malaya* (London, 1957).

17. J. N. Parmer, *Colonial Labor Policy and Administration: A History of Labor in the Rubber Plantation Industry in Malaya, c. 1910-1941* (Locust Valley, N.Y., 1960); John G. Butcher, *The British in Malaya 1880-1941: The Social History of a European Community in Colonial South-East Asia* (Kuala Lumpur, 1979).

18. The description of the immigration and labor-recruiting process given in this section represents its mature form as of the 1920s, unless otherwise noted. It is based on W. L. Blythe, "Historical Sketch of Chinese Labour in Malaya," 1953 reprint of *Journal of the Malayan Branch, Royal Asiatic Society* 21, 1(1947): 26-28; J. N. Parmer, *Colonial Labor Policy*, 28-29, 99-103; and G. W. Skinner, *Chinese Society*, 52-58. For the years before 1920, see the works by Skinner and Blythe cited above and Persia Crawford Campbell, *Chinese Coolie Emigration to Countries within the British Empire* (London, 1923).

19. Chen Ta, *Emigrant Communities in South China* (New York, 1940), 259-60.

20. Yeo, "Communist Challenge," 43.

21. Blythe, 20-25. Parmer, *Colonial Labor Policy*, 99-101.

22. Chinese contractors were no doubt well aware of this fact. As one *towkay* put it before the Opium Commission of 1924, "'the opium smoker is

steady. He thinks carefully before he acts. . . . The opium smoker is more law-abiding because he fears he will get no opium in the prison.'" Cited in R. N. Jackson, *Immigrant Labour and the Development of Malaya 1786-1920* (Kuala Lumpur, 1961), 56.

23. Leopold Ainsworth, *The Confessions of a Planter in Malaya: A Chronicle of Life and Adventure in the Jungle* (London, 1933), 46-47.

24. This is not to imply that strikes were completely unheard of before the 1930s but only that they were extremely uncommon. A reference to the earliest public Chinese labor action of which I have knowledge mentions strikes by laborers occurring in Kuala Lumpur and elsewhere in 1912. Blythe, 25-26. Nonetheless, resistance, if it was expressed at all, generally took covert forms such as absconding from the work site.

25. The efforts of British planters and tin miners for the two decades from 1910 to 1930 to ensure a level of influx of Chinese laborers from China sufficient to maintain low wages are described by Parmer, *Colonial Labor Policy*, 79-92.

26. The quota varied between 500 and 6,000 Chinese male laborers per month, "fluctuating with the labour needs of Malaya in so far as these could be judged." Blythe, 29.

27. Parmer, *Colonial Labor Policy*, 70-78.

28. Yeo, "Communist Challenge," 41.

29. Donald M. Nonini, "The Chinese Community of a West Malaysian Market Town: A Study in Political Economy" (Ph.D. diss., Stanford University, 1983), chap. 5.

30. Yeo, "Communist Challenge," 44.

31. Ibid.

32. It was probably for this reason that by 1930 Chinese contract labor had all but disappeared from the (by this time) dominant, mechanized European tin-mining sector: what Chinese laborers there were, were directly employed and paid a daily wage. Jackson, 145.

33. Virginia Thompson, 93.

34. Stenson, 7.

35. Ibid.

36. M. V. Del Tufo, *A Report on the 1947 Census of Population* (London, 1949).

37. The description of Chinese "squatters" in vegetable gardening in the passage that follows comes from Francis Kok-Wah Loh, "Beyond the Tin Mines: The Political Economy of Chinese Squatter Farmers in the Kinta New Villages, Malaysia" (Ph.D. diss., Cornell University, 1980), 34-54; Lawrence R. L. Siaw, *Chinese Society in Rural Malaysia: A Local History of the Chinese in Titi, Jelebu* (Kuala Lumpur, 1983), 30-49.

38. "One important change which resulted from the improvement in the sex ratio was a drift of Chinese labourers from the old single-sex communal mess or *kongsi* house to family establishments of their own on the outskirts of rubber estates or near tin mines." Stenson, 12.

39. Loh, Siaw, 35-40.

40. Loh, 55-63.

41. Stenson, 4; Gamba, 2.

42. Gamba, 2-5; Stenson, 4-5.

43. Gamba, 2-3.

44. Yeo, "Communist Challenge," 37.

45. Gamba, 25-26.

46. The following reconstruction is based on Virginia Thompson, 62-116; Yeo, "Communist Challenge"; Stenson, 11-53; Loh, 56-58; Khoo Kay Kim, "A Brief History of Chinese Labour Unrest before 1941," *Malaysia in History* 25

(1982): 59-64; Blythe, 32-35;   P. P. Pillai, "Labour in Malaya," *Labour in Southeast Asia: A Symposium,* ed. P. P. Pillai (New Delhi, 1947), 147-56; Leong, 222-42, 407-608.

    47. Loh, 56-57.

    48. Ibid., 55-59.

    49. Leong, 414, 481-95.

    50. Stenson, 20.

    51. Stenson, 19-24; Leong, 481-95.

    52. Leong, 496-99.

    53. Stenson, 15.

    54. See, for example, MCP attempts in the November 1936 Malayan collieries strike to organize miners. Yeo, "Communist Challenge," 47-48.

    55. Ibid., 44-45.

    56. J. N. Parmer, "Chinese Estate Workers' Strikes in Malaya in March 1937," *The Economic Development of South-East Asia,* ed. C. D. Cowan (London, 1964), 158.

    57. Parmer, "Chinese Estate Workers' Strikes," 170.

    58. Scott, 178-83.

    59. Yeo, "Communist Challenge," 45.

    60. Virginia Thompson, 105.

    61. Stenson, 16.

    62. Siaw, 40.

    63. On the notion of "public sphere," see Jurgen Habermas, *The Structural Transformation of the Public Sphere* (Cambridge, Mass., 1989).

    64. E. P. Thompson, "Moral Economy," 77-78.

MIGRATION IN
TWENTIETH-CENTURY
EUROPE

10

The Politics of
Immigrant Workers in
Twentieth-Century France

Donald Reid

Immigrant workers respond in a variety of ways to the separation from their homelands and to the mechanisms of differentiation and integration operating in the countries in which they work.[1] To what extent do they develop political responses to their situation? Study of immigrant workers employed in French industry since World War I offers an excellent opportunity to answer this question. Low birthrates and widespread peasant resistance to leaving the land shaped French industrialization during the second half of the nineteenth century and spurred the organized recruitment of foreign labor before World War I.[2] In the 1920s, massive recourse to immigrant labor helped French industry compensate for the wartime hecatomb.[3] The French imported new populations of foreign labor after World War II. Between 1962 and 1974, foreigners accounted for four-fifths of the increase in the number of male wage earners in France.[4] On the eve of the Great Depression and again at the end of the postwar economic growth in 1973, 6–8 percent of the labor force in France was foreign.

The influx of immigrant labor has contributed to a continual making and remaking of the French working population. France is the industrial nation with the third highest percentage of first-, second-, and third-generation immigrants in its population (after the United States and Canada).[5] Immigrant workers—both those who stayed and those who returned home—have profoundly marked French economic, social, and political development. This essay analyzes and compares

the political worlds of selected interwar European immigrant groups
and those of post–1945 non-European immigrant populations.

The Immigrant Experience

Strictly economic interpretations of labor migration consider
workers as displaced units of labor power.[6] Yet immigrant workers are
not passive wanderers buffeted about by political and economic forces.
Despite its temptations, *"misérabilisme"* reveals little. Recognition that
immigrant workers help make their history in a variety of ways, some
political and some not, is much more fruitful. And for the very reasons
that immigrant workers' politics are often ignored, the subject is a
privileged one for exploring the ambiguities of categories like
nationality and class.

The lives of individuals in contemporary liberal democracies are
structured in myriad ways by the interplay of state tolerance and
control. Most citizens, however, are too enmeshed in their own
seemingly natural social and economic relations to recognize this.[7] The
"difference" that the immigrant worker lives with respect to the citizen
of the receiving nation unmasks the politicization of everyday life.
Observers have noted immigrant workers' "politicizing of the ordinarily
nonpolitical" as a result of the limitations inherent in their legal status:
"the proclivity of foreign workers to attach political salience to aspects of
daily life that most citizens would regard as less politically significant."[8]
And immigrant workers' knowledge that they can be expelled for failure
to maintain political "neutrality" while in France forces them to consider
the potentially political nature of many forms of personal expression
that French citizens take for granted.[9] While accounts of native
workers' politics often exclude discussion of struggles for better housing,
for instance, these are deeply political activities for immigrant workers.

Along with limitations on civil rights, has come under representation or distorted representation in the institutions of the workplace and
the polity. Immigrant workers have been deprived of representation at
both the workplace and the polling place. The 1884 legislation
governing unions barred foreigners from serving as union leaders.
Because only French citizens were eligible to vote and stand for mine-
safety delegate in the 1920s, this official was necessarily French, even at
the Briey iron-ore mines, where only 5 percent of the labor force was
French.[10] The recent extension of workplace rights has not done away
with such "representation." "Even in the most engaged unions," writes
Mohand Khellil, "migrant workers are seen as social cases. They are
thought of as foundlings: they do not express themselves directly, but
'we speak for them,' because 'we know their problems better than
they.'"[11] A similar displacement may occur when foreign governments
speak for their citizens working in France.

Despite limitations on individual and group rights, immigrant workers have often developed political responses to their situation. To understand these phenomena, we must recognize that individuals' political choices cannot be interpreted solely in terms of attributes like country of origin, place in the social structure, or position in the employment hierarchy. Individuals' experiences and aspirations—and their continual reinterpretation of each in terms of the other—are crucial.[12] This process may generate conflicting class as well as national identities: Algerians working in France are generally considered "privileged" in Algeria but a subproletariat in France.[13]

Immigrant workers are not ciphers when they arrive in the host country. They bring with them a wealth of experiences and expectations that they use to isolate themselves from, interact with, and interpret their new environment. In turn, through living and working in a new land, immigrants may develop aspirations to change the relations of power in the family, the community, the factory, and/or the national polity. For many immigrant women, especially those from rural areas in the Iberian peninsula and from North Africa, life in France can be a transformative experience. Having discovered a new degree of freedom, they may refuse to return to the restrictive social environment of their native land.[14] Immigration encourages all involved, from immigrants to nation-states, to endorse new forms of identification, differentiation, and incorporation, but these acts may and do have unexpected, destabilizing consequences.

European Immigration, 1920–1950: Background

The clear differentiation between French and non-French workers so deeply ingrained in the legal and social practices of contemporary France did not take shape until the end of the nineteenth century and the beginning of the twentieth century,[15] when new forms of labor migration joined the long-standing *va-et-vient* of Belgians, Spaniards, and Germans.[16] At a time when native French labor gained a number of rights—the official end of labor passports (*livrets*), access to job placement services, and the expansion of social welfare programs— immigrant labor became subject to conditions like those from which French labor was escaping. Residence permits and expulsion regulations restricted immigrant workers' mobility; exclusionary provisions in labor legislation limited their access to the benefits offered French workers.[17] The importation of large numbers of foreign workers during World War I led to the introduction in 1917 of a mandatory *carte d'identité* for foreigners that allowed the state to monitor individual migrants and their movements in France.[18]

After World War I, the French state signed accords with major labor–exporting nations that guaranteed foreign workers the same wages and benefits as French workers received. (As a result, immigrant workers had to rely on their home governments for enforcement of these provisions. This reinforced immigrant workers' dependence on their home governments and complicated efforts to make common cause with French workers.)[19] While the French government relinquished control of hiring foreign labor in the interwar years, it continued to assist in the enforcement of labor contracts and the repression of political dissidents among immigrant workers. In 1924, employers' associations formed the Société générale d'immigration (SGI), which recruited labor in Poland and elsewhere, eliminated the unfit and undesirable, and supervised the transport of workers to France and their distribution to employers throughout the country.[20] In the 1930s, the French state abandoned the relatively lax supervision it had exercised in the 1920s and responded to the xenophobic pressures created by the Depression with restrictive policies on the entry of foreign labor.[21]

The divided interwar labor movement pursued two courses with respect to immigrant labor. The "reformist" Confédération générale du travail (CGT) sought to protect the interests of native labor. It favored close regulation of the importation of foreign labor by a tripartite commission composed of representatives of organized labor, employers, and the state. In contrast, the Communist-affiliated Confédération générale du travail unitaire (CGTU) opposed all limits on labor migration in the interests of proletarian internationalism. Following the policy of the Third International, the Parti communiste (later français) (PCF) welcomed foreign Communists but demanded that they work within the party of the country in which they currently resided, in this case the PCF. The CGTU and the PCF devoted more effort to the recruitment of immigrant workers than the CGT or the Parti socialiste but were stymied by a combination of the anticommunism many immigrants brought with them and the constant threat of state repression.[22] In just five months in 1925, for instance, France expelled ninety-five Italian and Polish CGTU militants operating in the Moselle.[23] Yet despite these inauspicious beginnings, the development of a shared European political universe during the 1930s and 1940s created the basis for French and foreign workers to cooperate in political action and later for the assimilation of second-generation immigrants into the French polity.

Italians in the Lorraine between the Wars

Metallurgical firms in the Lorraine began importing Italians to work in iron ore mines at the turn of the century. Until the Depression, Italian workers in the Lorraine were primarily single males without firm roots in France. This changed in the 1920s when employers, desirous of creating a more stable labor force to replace French wartime losses, constructed housing and encouraged family immigration. Some Italians took advantage of the possibilities for on-the-job promotion in the mines to head crews composed of newer arrivals from Italy and Poland.[24] Others were able to move from work in the mines to the factory. By 1930 a stable Italian community whose members shared workplace grievances with the French was clearly taking shape.[25]

From an early period, Lorraine firms had investigated the politics of the Italians they imported.[26] However, studies of the origins of Italian workers reveal that individual villages in which economic hardship had converted the inhabitants to socialism provided large numbers of immigrants to the Lorraine. There they reconstituted old community ties. Many Italian immigrant workers, therefore, had both an oppositional ideology and the social network necessary to sustain it. As foreigners and unskilled laborers, they were less easily influenced by the paternalist management of Lorraine employers than skilled French workers. Despite their transience, Italians provided the backbone of major prewar strike movements in the mines.[27] Lacking the right to vote, however, they could not challenge company hegemony in the mining community. Writing in 1930, Axel Sömme described a mining community with a labor force that was one-quarter French and three-quarters foreign. The votes of company supervisors combined with those of small businessmen and farmers to outweigh those of French workers.[28]

Fascists and antifascists competed for the allegiance of the Italian community in interwar France.[29] To secure the support of Italians in France, Mussolini's regime created a wide variety of social and cultural services for them; the Italian government even paid for pregnant women to return to Italy to give birth.[30] However, the majority of workers in the Lorraine were hostile to Mussolini. As the French Left became preoccupied with fascism in the 1930s, this shared concern brought the new generation of settled Italian workers into the French labor movement. Exiled Italian Socialists and Communists believed that if the Left came to power in France it would lead the fight against fascism in Europe.[31] Italian workers joined with their French counterparts to fight both for better pay and working conditions and against fascism.

Polish Immigration to France between the Wars

Using the SGI and other sources, French mining firms imported several hundred thousand Poles from the mines of the Ruhr and the farms of Poland in the 1920s. More vigorously than their counterparts in the Lorraine, large mining companies in the Nord/Pas-de-Calais set out to create a self-enclosed foreign mining community. Firms encouraged

Poles to bring their families; they built "little Polands" in mining towns and sponsored Polish-language schools, Polish cultural associations, and Polish churches. Polish priests assumed the role of national spokesmen, especially during the early years of migration. Company schools acquired special exemption from French law to permit up to half of the school day to be devoted to instruction in Polish. These arrangements suited both the companies and the Polish state. Employers hoped to insulate Polish miners from French unions; like Italy, the new Polish state wanted to maintain the allegiance of its citizens working in France.[32] As did Italians in the Lorraine, Polish miners took advantage of the limited possibilities for on-the-job advancement from laborer to hewer, and in some cases foreman. At Ostricourt in 1930, 27 percent of the French and 60 percent of the Poles were hewers, while 58 percent of the French and only 40 percent of the Poles were laborers. Twenty percent of the foremen were Polish.[33]

The Depression accentuated differences between French and Polish miners, but the Popular Front provided a political counterbalance a few years later. In the early 1930s, companies reduced their contingent of foreign miners. Polish miners living in France long retained vivid memories of the expulsion of Poles involved in a sit-down strike over forced repatriations and working conditions at LeForest in 1934. What has stuck in their minds is the sight of Poles forced to sell off their furniture—symbol of their rootedness in France—at a fraction of its value.[34]

Polish miners were not very active in French syndical and political activity in the 1920s. Not surprisingly, the French Left in the 1930s was more attuned to Italians, whom it could interpret in its own fascist/antifascist problematic, than to the relatively apolitical Poles, who could not be easily assimilated into contemporary Left discourse.[35] However, the expulsions and the rampant xenophobia of the 1930s gave Poles new reasons to take an interest in French politics. One Polish miner remembered the expulsions as having created "a more pronounced solidarity between French and Polish workers" against Colonel De La Rocque's quasi-fascist, antiimmigrant league, the Croix de Feu. He recalled the temporary breakdown of national barriers in the 1936 strikes and demonstrations: "There were no more Poles, there were no more French. There was great camaraderie. It was euphoria."[36] Although culturally isolated, Poles and French held the same jobs in the mines and could cooperate in workplace struggles. After the 1936 strikes, Polish miners rallied en masse to the CGT and in 1937 the formerly anti-CGT Société des ouvriers polonais en France recommended that its twenty thousand members join the CGT-sponsored Fédération des émigrés polonais en France.[37]

Immigrant Labor in the Resistance and after the War

During the Vichy regime, the legitimacy of the French state and the meaning of the French nation were put in question. With the democratic channels of political expression closed off to all Frenchmen, foreign workers assumed a political role denied them in the Third Republic. Italians, Poles, and other foreigners made vital contributions to the Resistance. Italians in the Lorraine interpreted their participation in the Resistance as a sign of their commitment to France.

> "Nothing anyone does will be able to erase what we have done for France," [one Résistant of Italian origins] is supposed to have cried just before being shot. For those who had often been reproached for not having "French blood" in their veins, this sacrifice was like a means of erasing the ultimate stigma of their origins. . . .[38]

One northern French miner told interviewers that the slogan "No coal for the Germans" "touched the patriotic sentiments of both the French and the Polish and other immigrants.[39] The famous spring 1941 coal miners' strike was "a crucial moment for the Polish community: the beginning of a real fraternity with native miners."[40] Foreign workers fought for the liberation of France and for the liberation of their homelands from dictatorship, fascism, and foreign occupation.[41]

Writing about the Lorraine in 1930, Sömme had predicted that "foreign workers will not forget their origins right away and what will remain of their former nationality will reinforce their socialist spirit."[42] After the war, both Italians in the Lorraine who remained Italian citizens and their descendants who took French citizenship became integrated into Lorraine society through occupational mobility in the steel industry and active participation in the PCF. In contrast to the Mussolini era, postwar Italy's efforts to maintain the allegiance of its citizens working in France bolstered the PCF. The Italian government made special provisions for them to return to Italy to vote. As in the past, Italian Communists living in France were expected to join the PCF; in turn, the PCF gave full support to Italian Communists in Italian elections.[43] Change in nationality did not affect this political commitment. The children and grandchildren of Italian immigrants to the Lorraine became French citizens and served as the mainstay of the CGT and the PCF; they reversed the electoral mathematics of Sömme's interwar mining community. This allegiance to the PCF, Louis Köll concludes, was born of an Italian heritage and experiences in France: "The revolutionary socialist tradition brought from Romagne or the Marches and kept up within many immigrants' families was revivified before the war by anti-fascism and during the war of 1939–1945 by the Resistance in which the PCF played a predominant role in the area."[44]

The PCF did not provide such an integrative force among Poles in France. While united in their desire to see Poland freed from German occupation, they split over support of the postwar regime.[45] Large numbers of Poles answered the call to rebuild their native land, but news of the consolidation of the Communist government dampened Poles' ardor to leave France. For many Poles and other East Europeans who remained in France, what had begun as economic migration became a form of political exile. The most resolutely anti-Communist among them pursued their Catholic nationalism in the Confédération française des travailleurs chrétiens (CFTC). In 1951 Eastern European national sections in the CFTC formed the Fédération internationale des travailleurs chrétiens réfugiés et émigrés (FITCRE) to prepare for the eventual overthrow of Communist regimes in their homelands.[46] Such movements were never large, however, and gradually lost favor. Poles in northern mining communities maintained a distinct national identity until 1945. At that point those who stayed in France saw the myth of a "return" to Poland dissolve. Their descendants integrated into French society through school, army, job, and marriage.[47]

Immigrant workers' concern for the political future of their native lands could serve both to integrate and to differentiate them from the French. During the interwar years, Italians in the Lorraine and Poles in northern mining communities created self-reproducing communities in France; limited on-the-job mobility gave them a stake in French economic life. In the 1950s their children benefited from a labor market that offered greater possibilities for social promotion.[48] Participation in the Popular Front and the Resistance permitted many immigrants to further a political agenda for their native land, while integrating into French life. The PCF's status as a "countersociety" made it especially suited for this role. For many Poles, however, the actions of the Communist regime in their homeland confirmed their nationalist and religious opposition to the PCF. In the long run, however, Italians in the Lorraine, Poles in the northern mining communities, and their descendants have come to identify strongly with France. Faced with factory and mine closings in the 1970s, they argued that their widespread participation in the Resistance and in the rebuilding of France after the war established their right to special consideration from the national polity.[49]

The Growing Reliance on Non-European Immigrants

After an initial period of state-controlled immigration, French postwar policies on immigration from the 1950s to the 1980s replicated the interwar experience of the massive immigration of the 1920s followed by the restrictive policies of the 1930s. Following the merger of the CGT and the CGTU in 1935, the unified CGT rejected the CGTU's internationalism in favor of participation in a state administrative apparatus to control immigration. When the Left came to power after the Liberation, the CGT got the opportunity to put this program into action. The Provisional Government terminated the SGI in 1945 and gave the legal monopoly over recruitment to the Office national d'immigration (ONI), governed by a tripartite board of union, employer, and state representatives. (Exception was made for workers from Algeria and from French colonies.) Employers who could not find suitable French workers and wanted to hire foreign labor had to present a proposed contract to the ONI. The ONI verified that the wages and working and housing conditions offered were up to the standards for French workers and then passed on the demand to its representatives in sending nations. The ONI, in cooperation with the governments of these countries, received demands for employment from prospective immigrant workers, organized the necessary medical exams, and arranged for the trip to France.[50] This system worked to prevent the formation of a "reserve army" of unemployed foreign workers who could compete with native labor in France. The ONI was fairly successful: only 26 percent of immigrant workers entered the country as "clandestines" (on tourist visas or without passports) in 1948.[51]

Indeed, employers complained that the ONI control was too restrictive.[52] Like much postwar social policy, ONI control of labor immigration broke down after 1948. France relaxed its policy on labor migration, tacitly allowing foreign workers to enter the country without work permits and then to "regularize" their situation once they had found employment. (The ONI was financed in part by collection of "regularization" fees.)[53] By 1968, the percentage of immigrant workers who regularized their situation after entry into France reached 82 percent. The CGT responded by opposing all new labor immigration until postwar ONI controls were reintroduced. The new laissez-faire policy suited employers since they did not have to promise employment or find housing for unseen workers, and because until "clandestine" workers regularized their situation, they were particularly pliant. From the foreign workers' point of view, this unregulated immigration allowed them to look for work in areas where members of their community, ethnic, or national group already lived.[54] While the working and living conditions of immigrant workers worsened, chain migration increased their resources to resist.

As the economies of prewar laborexporting nations picked up in the 1950s, the supply of European workers began to dry up. An increasingly non-European labor force from countries experiencing decolonization and the establishment of neocolonialist regimes took its place. The absence of an immigration policy encouraged growing reliance on immigrant workers who came for brief stays to do low-status,

low-paying work that lacked job security and offered little chance for
social promotion or cultural integration. The jobs in mining and
metallurgy Poles and Italians had taken between the wars had provided
a degree of access to a vibrant workplace culture. Changes in the
organization of work weakened both these modes of incorporation into
French society.

Since 1945, French workers have secured social benefits that
account for an increasingly large percentage of the total wage bill for
employers and the state. To the extent that employment of short-term
immigrant workers unaccompanied by families allowed for a reduction
in these costs, it permitted employers and the state to avoid the full cost
of the "social capital" accrued by French workers in the past.[55] The
higher turnover of non-European immigrants in the 1950s and 1960s
also freed employers from the need to promote them or to give them
seniority pay.[56] And during the technological transformations that
accompanied the economic growth of the 1950s and 1960s, and the
industrial "restructuring" of the 1970s, immigrant workers' mobility—
"natural" or coerced—was a boon to employers.

Very diverse labor forces emerged from the breakdown of
organized migration; in 1964, Citroën employed seventeen thousand
workers from twenty-seven national groups.[57] Many firms encouraged
such heterogeneity to limit opportunities for immigrant workers to
organize. Interpreters had always been used to control foreign labor;
such a strategy was most effective when workers from many different
linguistic groups worked together.[58] This reinforced divisions created
by the state's negotiation of individual bilateral agreements governing
the allocation of social welfare benefits and other matters with nations
supplying migrant labor.[59]

Labor from Algeria

French experience with Maghrébin (North African) labor before
the 1950s provided a model for later non-European labor immigration.
(See Figure 1). Through its quasi-colonial administration of Algeria,
France generated "push" and "pull" elements in the movements of
Algerian labor to France. Economic and demographic conditions in the
countryside, for which the French were in part responsible, "pushed"
Algerians to migrate;[60] the French economy's need for unskilled labor
"pulled" them across the Mediterranean. These processes created the
conditions for politicization of Algerian workers in France. Unlike most
interwar immigrant workers, however, the Algerians had political
aspirations for their homeland that ran counter to the policies of the
French government.

The history of Algerian emigration to France since World War I
can be divided into three periods. Between the wars, the short-term

millions

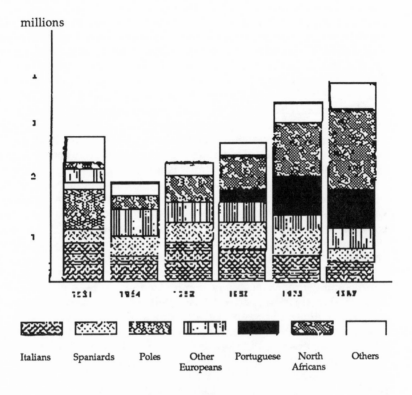

Figure 1. Foreigners in France by nationality,
in 1931, 1954, 1962, 1968, 1975, and 1982.

Source: Pierre George, *L'immigration en France* (Paris: Armand Colin, 1986), p. 19.

migration of married peasants was an integral part of the rural society's struggle for survival. Algerians who went to France in the 1950s and 1960s were rural proletarians, younger and often unmarried, who saw themselves losing this battle. Their ties to the rural village were weaker; they stayed longer in France and often founded families there. In the 1970s emigration tapered off, leaving a large Algerian community in France.[61]

Algerians who went to work in France between the wars stayed only a short time and rarely brought their families: in 1938, 92 percent of North Africans in France worked, compared to 57 percent of Italians and 54 percent of Poles. Families in Algeria dispatched a young man to

France to earn a lump sum that was used to pay off farm debts or to
purchase land. To assure a continuous income, Algerians practiced
"*noria*," a form of chain migration in which one family member replaced
another at a job in France. Employers often recruited workers from the
same village in order to reduce the effects of frequent labor turnover.
Patriarchal family heads recognized that time in France was a threat to
social stability and limited stays abroad; when the emigrant returned,
the village made efforts to "exorcise" the effects of his stay in France.[62]

Emigration practices began to change after World War II. In 1947,
the Algerian Statute granted Algerians complete freedom to travel in
France. This extended to Algerians a basic right of all Frenchmen in a
period when Algerian nationalism was displaying new vigor. It also
served as a palliative for a rapidly growing Algerian population whose
opportunities were limited by European control of Algerian resources.
And it facilitated the supply of cheap labor for French industry at a time
when the ONI was restricting European labor immigration.[63] Between
1946 and 1954, the number of Algerians in mainland France increased
tenfold to between two hundred thousand and two hundred fifty
thousand. By 1954, one in seven Algerian adult males was in France.
The booming French economy continued to require Algerian labor
through the Algerian war, especially with many young Frenchmen
serving in Algeria.[64] Familial allocations and the hope of getting
government-subsidized housing encouraged a small but growing
number of Algerians to bring their families and to stay longer in France
than they had in the past.[65]

Most Algerian workers came to France from rural areas where
familial, communal, and ethnic loyalties outweighed national
consciousness. A sociologist writing in 1954 about Algerian workers in
France commented on the complete absence of the kind of national
organizations that thrived among Poles and Italians in France.[66] Unlike
European immigrants, many Algerian workers in France developed a
national consciousness only through the experience of leaving Algeria
for France. Accounts of interwar Algerian emigration to France reveal
the shame emigrants experienced.[67] This shame gave way to guilt
among the rural proletarians who sought to escape a patriarchal
authority rooted in a rural economy unable to provide opportunities for
all its "sons." Charles-Robert Agéron suggests that going to work in
France to support the family provided the perfect alibi for young men
who wished to break free of the father's authority.[68] As the world of the
village began to recede, Algerians working in France turned to the
community formed by other Algerians in France and extended affective
sentiments for the village to the idea of the nation.

Kabyles, whose culture and traditions differed from those of the
Arab majority in Algeria, made up the majority of Algerian workers in

France. While ethnic frictions persisted after independence, Algerian workers in France (perhaps influenced by nationalist propaganda) told one researcher during the Algerian war that they now saw that the French had artificially maintained ethnic and tribal divisions in Algeria; however, the undifferentiated discrimination they experienced at the hands of the French helped to eradicate these splits and to create national consciousness.[69]

Algerian Worker Politics in France before 1954

Important strands of Algerian nationalism developed first among Algerians working in France. During the 1920s, the Communists played a crucial role in organizing these workers. The PCF felt that workers from the colonies would be particularly receptive to their message since they would presumably be uncontaminated by other ideologies. According to one party tract, colonial workers in France had "a spirit untainted with democratic and anarcho-reformist ideology."[70] North African workers cooperated closely with French Communists in the 1920s but soon developed a nationalism at odds with PCF policy. The first Algerian nationalist party, the Etoile Nord-Africaine (ENA), emerged from the Communist Union intercoloniale in 1926; as late as 1928, sixteen of the twenty-eight directors of the ENA were Communists. The ENA recruited from the some eight thousand Maghrébin members of the CGTU, most of whom lived in the Paris area.[71]

In 1927 the charismatic Messali Hadj, ex-soldier and laborer, became leader of the ENA. At the time Messali was a Communist and had attended the party's school for cadres at Bobigny.[72] After the 1927 Chinese Revolution, however, the Third International directed Communist parties to adopt a "class-against-class" strategy at the expense of nationalist revolutionary struggles. The PCF reduced its support for the ENA. The French government dissolved the ENA in 1929; when the ENA was reconstituted in 1933 it forbade dual membership in the PCF. Messali rejected "Communist tutelage" and promoted a pan-Maghrébin Islamic ideology. The ENA had some five thousand members when the government dissolved it again in 1937. That year Messali founded the Parti du peuple algérien (PPA); after the war it was reconstituted as the PPA-Mouvement pour le triomphe des libertés démocratiques (PPA-MTLD), which grafted a puritanical religious discourse to nationalism. The dues of the more than nine thousand members working in France in 1954 helped keep the party solvent.[73] That year the PPA-MTLD splintered, giving birth to Messali's Mouvement national algérien (MNA) and to the rival Front de libération nationale (FLN).

Longer stays in France provided Algerian workers new impetus to cooperate with French labor. One proud Maghrébin reported on the seventy thousand North Africans who participated in a 1951 CGT demonstration, a *"manifestation-choc,"* in Paris: PCF and CGT leaders "stand as one to salute the effervescent, bubbling, virile, warmly applauded force before which the French mass seems old."[74] Yet, if Algerian workers suppled an *élan* that construction workers and *métallos* had once given CGTU demonstrations, this only made it more difficult for the PCF to resolve the vexed relationship of class to nation among the French and the Algerian workers.

The Algerian War (1954–1962)

Traveling to and from France, migrant workers disseminated nationalist and socialist ideas in rural Algeria. Although short-term migrants remained well integrated in the familial and rural structures from which they came, their sojourns in France were not without effect. Observers noted that Algerians who had worked in France were more demanding and were frequently chosen to present village demands to the administration. Not surprisingly, one reason *colons* opposed the migration of Algerians to work in France was the fear that the native population would become more demanding.[75] The FLN launched the war of independence in a Kabyle area in 1954; Khellil argues that the massive participation of Kabyles in the French labor market created conditions that "greatly furthered" the war for independence.[76]

The war galvanized Algerian workers in France. Shortly after the FLN took up arms, Simone de Beauvoir saw a change among the Algerians living in her neighborhood in Paris: "Leather-jacketed North Africans, looking very well-groomed, began to frequent the Café des Amis; all alcohol was forbidden; through the windows I could see the customers sitting down in front of glasses of milk. No more brawls at night. This discipline had been imposed by the FLN militants."[77] Throughout France, Algerian workers established their cultural difference from the French. The head of a large factory in the Moselle reported that 70 percent of his fourteen hundred Algerian employees observed the Moslem holy month of Ramadan in 1955, compared to 20 percent the previous year. Algerian workers' attendance at night language classes declined as French was targeted as the language of the oppressor.[78]

This break with all things French made it increasingly difficult for the PCF to maintain the fiction of Algerian and French working-class unity. Algerian nationalists criticized the PCF for giving incorporation of the party into the French political system priority over active support for the independence struggle.[79] Algerian workers' allegiance to the CGT wavered when French workers did not go into the streets to support Algerian independence; both the Messalistes and the FLN created their own unions during the war.[80] By the final years of the conflict, the

FLN had gone outside the PCF organization to work with the *proto-gauchiste* Francis Jeanson.[81]

Yet the war created a break not only between French and Algerians but among Algerian nationalists in France as well. Although the ideology of national liberation was born of the immigration experience, Algerian workers in France lost their political leadership during the war (a process that had begun at the time of the Popular Front). As long as Algeria was French territory, the nationalist project masked the break between Algerians in France and in Algeria. Once the FLN, with its power base in Algeria, launched the insurrection, however, workers in France became supporting actors. The more secular FLN wiped out the Messaliste MNA, which had originally commanded the allegiance of politicized Algerian workers in France.[82] Alistair Horne estimates that by May 1958, 90 percent of the Algerians in France were loyal to the FLN.[83] The FLN turned colonialism on its head by financing the anticolonial struggle with moneys from Algerians in France. Each month FLN militants collected a stiff tax, using coercion if necessary: 10 percent for most workers. At its peak, the FLN may have collected more than three hundred thousand subscriptions and brought in one billion francs per month.[84] The FLN led Algerian workers in France in a number of strikes and demonstrations.[85] Many Algerian workers were arrested for these activities, or just for appearing on FLN tax collectors' lists. In jail, the FLN continued its political work. One Algerian worker who spent thirty-two months at Larzac entered "neutral and ignorant" but left thoroughly politicized: "They made us recite our lessons like children at school."[86]

Algerian Labor in France since Independence

Independence was the prelude to creation of a permanent Algerian community in France. The war had been a period of enforced settlement for Algerians in France. The French wartime policy of restricting Algerians' right to return home probably contributed to the breakdown of *"noria."*[87] But many Algerians living in France went back to Algeria in 1962–63, in the hope that once independent, their nation would be able to transform the economy that had forced them to expatriate. They soon discovered otherwise, however, and most returned to France to work. The Evian Accords, which ended the war, allowed for the continued unrestricted admission of Algerians into France (although the French later set ceilings). The number of long-term Algerian immigrants in France rose dramatically during and after the 1960s. By 1968, 30 percent of Algerians in France had spent between eight and seventeen years there; in the early 1980s the average Maghrébin stayed fifteen years in France.[88] Growing numbers of Algerian workers brought their families to France. These developments revealed the breakdown of the model of short stays and constant turnover of non-European labor that French authorities had envisaged (with the Algerian example in mind) since the 1950s.

The new regime in Algiers recognized the problems that a large expatriate population could create: Ben Bella, the first leader of independent Algeria, spoke of preventing a "Miami" from developing in France. Having fought the MNA in France during the war, the FLN was determined to maintain its hegemony over the immigrant worker population after 1962.[89] The FLN took advantage of its experience organizing Algerians in France during the war to transform the FLN in France into the Amicale des Algériens en Europe (AAE). The AAE and affiliated associations for workers, women, and youths fund programs to maintain the cultural and religious identity of Algerian residents in France; the AAE still acts as a representative and mediator for Algerians living in France in their dealings with the French state, social service organizations, and employers. In the late 1970s, the AAE had approximately one hundred thousand members in France. "If one were to consider the AAE as a political party," writes Mark Miller, "it would rank as one of the largest and most active political organizations on French soil."[90]

The fundamental issue facing the AAE is the relationship of the Algerian state to the Algerian community in France. For the first decade after independence, the Algerian government had accepted emigration to France as a safety valve for the unemployed and a source of income through wages sent home. This changed when Algeria embarked on a new economic policy that involved nationalization of the oil and natural gas industry in 1971 with agrarian reform to follow. The nationalization unleashed hostility toward Algerians in France, especially among the *pieds noirs* (Algerians of European origin who had emigrated to France after independence). This culminated in a series of racist attacks in 1973 in which thirty-two Maghrébins died. Algerian workers in France responded with the largest immigrant worker protests since the Algerian war. These demonstrations underscored the development of an independent identity and organizational capacity in the Algerian community in France. They were not sponsored by the AAE (which, in fact, originally opposed the movement).[91] After some hesitation, the Algerian government responded in September 1973 by halting any further migration of workers to France. The gesture revealed a new form of economic independence from the former ruling power. Yet the public rupture with France marked a parallel break with the Algerian community in France. The move left Algerians in France increasingly on their own while cutting off the possibility for Algerian peasants to escape the unpopular agrarian reform plan by going to France.[92]

Discussion of the National Charter for Algeria among Algerians in France in 1976 demonstrated their increasingly ambiguous relationship to Algeria. In the Paris region, sixty thousand Algerians debated the charter in an AAE-sponsored meeting.[93] Algerians in France who had lived through the war for independence had a clear sense of national identity, but their connection to Algerian society was increasingly tenuous. In response to their demands, the government amended the charter to include the need to make the "return and progressive reinsertion" of immigrants "one of the major objectives of the socialist revolution."[94] But talk of creating the conditions for the reinsertion of Algerians in France into Algeria has led to relatively few returns;[95] a poorer and less secular Algeria has increasingly become a foreign land to the Algerian community in France. Algerians in France who keep alive the myth of returning to Algeria recognize that their long stays in France would make them "immigrants" in Algeria (like the French *pieds noirs* who "returned" to France after 1962). The situation is particularly difficult for the children of Algerians in France, who may have been to Algeria for only short periods of time, if at all.

The real significance of periodic pronouncements about a "return" is their role in maintaining the politically important pretense for Algeria, France, and Algerians in France that the Algerian diaspora will one day end up in Algeria. The language of "return" has also allowed the AAE to develop a close working relationship with the PCF and the CGT.[96] With independence won, the conflict between French and Algerian nationalisms that divided the PCF and the FLN has disappeared. The Communists' view that even long-time immigrant workers should consider themselves citizens of their native lands (rather than work out a separate identity commensurate with their quasi-permanent residence in France) complements AAE policy in France.

Algerians in France had second-class citizenship before independence; the immigration experience since 1962 has perpetuated this condition. After independence, France and Algeria continued to speak of an eventual "return" of Algerians in France to Algeria. The unwillingness and inability of both nations (and of many Algerians in France as well) to recognize the permanence of the Algerian presence in France has stymied efforts by Algerians in France to formulate an identity and to articulate their own political voice.[97]

Immigrant Labor in the 1960s and 1970s: The Housing Crisis

Although most interwar immigrant workers had to find their own housing, coal and steel companies had provided housing and social services for many of the immigrant workers they employed. The 1950s and 1960s saw the decline of such industries, which required fixed labor forces far from urban centers. As employers came to see foreign workers as unstable, interchangeable units of labor power, fewer were willing to invest in their welfare. Employers who went through the ONI to obtain workers had to show that housing would be available; the breakdown of ONI controls coupled with the influx of workers not covered by ONI (including Algerians) raised the real specter of an alien subproletariat living in suburban shantytowns (*bidonvilles*).

During the Algerian war, the French government responded by setting up the Fonds d'action sociale (FAS), originally funded with moneys saved from the family benefits paid by Algerians who worked in France, but never ultimately brought families there. In 1964, the FAS was extended to all immigrant workers. The FAS is a quasi-public agency that supports cultural activities and social welfare projects.[98] The government originally intended the FAS to improve conditions for Algerians working in France (and hoped it would provide a defense against FLN propaganda and tax collecting). The main activity of the FAS has been financing housing for immigrant workers through organizations like Sonacotra (Société nationale de construction pour les travailleurs).[99] During the Algerian war, the authorities used the "*foyer-hôtels*" to keep an eye on Algerian workers; after the war, many directors continued to be former French military officers who had served in Indochina or Algeria.[100] While relaxation of ONI controls reduced the state's role in the recruitment and allocation of labor, the FAS brought the state indirectly into the provision of housing for immigrant workers, an area in which employers had previously played a large role.

After 1968

During the 1960s and 1970s French Communists were unable to repeat their earlier success organizing Italians in France; most Europeans working in France came from Spain and Portugal, nations in which the Left had been repressed for decades. Spaniards who went to work in France in the 1960s shared little with the Spanish Republican refugees who had flooded across French borders in 1939.[101] The PCF and the CGT also proved less flexible than new forces on the Left in accommodating to the special situation of many non-European workers in the years after May 1968.

There is no consensus about immigrant workers' participation in the massive wave of strikes and demonstrations of May 1968. The expulsion of a number of immigrant workers for failure to remain "neutral" during the *événements* seems to have been a Gaullist effort to blame the strikes on immigrant workers, not a real indication of their role.[102] Yet May 1968 marked a turning point not just in the French Left, but in the French Left's relation to immigrant workers, in immigrant workers' activism, and in state policy on immigration. Before 1968, elements of the non-Communist Left, including the Association de solidarité avec les travailleurs immigrés (ASTI) and civil rights groups, had established contact with immigrants in *bidonvilles*, most often through literacy programs. Such associations were for some time the only groups to show interest in the particular problems of non-European immigrant workers.[103] The Nanterre campus, catalyst of the May *événements*, was ensconced between two large *bidonvilles* (which had been considered the *"point d'encrage"* of the FLN in France during the Algerian war).[104] Many students were active in the Nanterre ASTI and must have been struck by the disparity between the campus and immigrants' living conditions.[105]

In the years after May 1968, *gauchistes* added their forces to groups in the non-Communist Left like ASTI that were reaching out to immigrant workers. They played a role disproportionate to their small numbers by amplifying submerged traditions of the PCF: the internationalism of the CGTU and the Third Worldism of the Jeanson network. Contact and cooperation with immigrant workers in turn radicalized French militants.[106] *Gauchistes* shunned electoralism and therefore did not necessarily see immigrant workers' lack of citizenship as a problem. They celebrated immigrant workers' marginality as a reflection of their own. The "Third Worldism" of many immigrant worker militants acted as antifascism had in the 1930s to bring together immigrant workers and sympathetic French leftists. *Gauchistes* touted immigrant worker combativity as an alternative to the apparent conservatism of French workers and their PCF and CGT representatives. Once engaged in a conflict, Third World workers—denied the same rights as French workers—developed methods of protest that were radical by French standards. "It is as if the struggles they undertook were inspired more by national liberation struggles than normal social conflicts."[107] As non-European immigrant workers stayed longer in France, they became more active in housing and workplace struggles where they lived as well as more critical of regimes at home.

FAS funds proved quite inadequate to provide decent housing for the large immigrant worker population. As appalling as conditions were in the *bidonvilles*, immigrant workers fought the razing of these slums when, as often happened, the government had failed to provide adequate replacement housing. In contrast to the mixture of nationalities in many workplaces, immigrant workers frequently lived in village or ethnic groups in France.[108] These often proved more cohesive and militant than workplace organizations. In a widely publicized conflict, Malians residing in a run-down former chocolate factory in Ivry drew on their native village organizational structure to conduct a five-year fight for better housing in the early 1970s. While the Communist municipality at Ivry proved lukewarm to the plight of the nonvoting Malians, *gauchistes* provided support and lauded the Malians' use of African communal strategies in waging their struggle.[109]

Segmentation of French and foreign labor created the conditions for strikes composed solely of immigrant workers. The 1972 Penarroya strike, in which one hundred Maghrébins went out over demands largely specific to their needs as immigrant workers, was widely publicized. With the aid of *gauchistes*, the strikers won the support of the largely immigrant labor force in other Penarroya factories in France. Such strikes of immigrant workers were carried out at first outside or in opposition to French unions, although the Confédération française démocratique du travail (CFDT) soon came to play an active, supportive role in these movements.[110] A desire to defuse these conflicts by integrating immigrant workers into the existing mechanisms for conflict resolution led the government to extend various forms of workplace representation to them in 1972–75.

The failure of homeland associations to look after immigrant workers' interests in France underscored for many the repression and corruption of regimes in their native lands.[111] The early 1970s saw the florescence of movements among the most politicized Maghrébin and African workers directed at the radical transformation of their homelands. These groups were often in close touch with *gauchistes* who argued that governments in newly independent nations tended to degenerate into neocolonial bureaucracies. The new proletariat forged in France could, under proper leadership, become the vanguard of a movement to overthrow reactionary homeland regimes. For Sally N'Dongo, a leader of Senegalese workers in France and opponent of the Senagalese government, "An African worker who attains consciousness that he belongs to a class will not revert to being a fatalistic peasant on his return home. . . . [B]ehind his plow, he will continue to ask questions. . . . [S]uch an act of awakening which we take for granted here, we would not be able to lead in our own country."[112]

Government Action and Immigrant Reaction

Immigrant worker activism, fear that easy access to immigrant labor discouraged modernization, and the *crise* of 1973-74 led the French state to reconsider its policy on labor immigration. After 1968 workers from European Economic Community (EEC) nations were guaranteed the right to come and work freely within member states. While France encouraged immigration from European countries in and out of the EEC, it now limited the entry of Algerians into France. In the decade after 1964, the number of Algerians rose 71 percent to 871,223, while the number of Portuguese shot up 434 percent to 849,468, due to significantly higher quotas set for the admission of Portuguese. The state abandoned its laissez-faire policy toward immigration and reactivated the ONI. The percentage of immigrants who regularized their situation after entry into France fell from 82 percent in 1968 to 44.3 percent in 1972.[113]

In 1972, ostensibly in response to immigrant workers' grievances about uncontrolled entry and inadequate housing, the ministers of the interior and of labor, Marcellin and Fontanet, issued sweeping decrees governing immigrant labor (other than from Algeria and Francophone Africa). In making the work permit and the availability of housing conditions for receiving the residence permit, the decrees sought to end the *immigration sauvage* of the previous decades. While long-term immigrant workers who continued to work could eventually qualify as permanent resident aliens, the decrees made recent arrivals afraid to change jobs or housing, or to participate in strikes. This restriction particularly affected immigrant workers who were accustomed to following the peasant-turned-worker strategy of quitting rather than pursuing legal or syndical routes for the resolution of grievances (as their French counterparts might). The decrees were designed to provide the state significant control over the labor market by trade and region, while putting militants and temporarily unemployed workers at risk of expulsion.[114]

Immigrant workers and their supporters argued that the Marcellin/ Fontanet decrees made immigrant workers more subservient to employers, while forcing them to bear the burden of the inadequate supply of affordable housing. Immigrant workers threatened with expulsion launched hunger strikes to dramatize their plight. A coalition opposed to the decrees even put up a fictional candidate in the 1974 presidential elections, Djellali Kamal.[115] These protests won concessions, culminating in abrogation of the decrees in 1975. In any case, the decrees had lost some of their *raison d'être* the year before, when France responded to the *crise* by joining other European countries in ending non-EEC labor immigration. A new wave of protests forced the government to modify its stance in order to allow immigration for family reunification. In the late 1970s France stepped up deportations of delinquent second-generation youths, while offering financial incentives for foreign workers to depart.[116]

Here to Stay: A New Generation of Housing and Workplace Conflicts

In 1976, one-fifth of the four million foreigners in France were "isolated" male workers (either unmarried or unaccompanied by their families).[117] As these workers extended their stays in France, they found living conditions in the *foyer-hôtels*, established with a transient labor force in mind, intolerable. Residents also condemned the authoritarian surveillance that had characterized these dormitories since their inception during the Algerian war.[118] The refusal of residents in the Sonacotra Foyer Romain Rolland in Saint-Denis to pay a rent increase in January 1975 sparked a nationwide movement. N'Dongo described the rent strike as "often the spark, the first *déclic* which makes African workers understand that combat pays and that to be successful at it they have to organize themselves."[119] By 1978 the movement had spread to twenty thousand inhabitants of 120 dormitories run by Sonacotra and similar outfits. The strikers' Comité de coordination des foyers en lutte cooperated with *gauchiste* groups, but spurned attempts by French unions and the AAE to negotiate separate settlements for individual *foyers*. The strikers wrested concessions on living conditions and tenant rights from Sonacotra, but in 1980 the movement finally collapsed as the government expelled some strikers and withheld rent from others' wages.[120] Yet, "For the first time, a widespread, long-term collective action was led by immigrant workers, all nationalities united."[121] The refusal of the Comité to allow its struggle to be coopted by either French unions or the AAE was evidence of a movement of immigrant workers independent of both French groups and national homeland associations.

The militance immigrant workers showed in the Sonacotra rent strike extended to the workplace. When immigrant workers had worked for short periods and left, the impossibility of escaping the lowest jobs on the rung may have seemed tolerable. By the late 1970s, however, the large population of long-term immigrant workers saw things differently and launched strikes against their status as unskilled workers "for life."[122] Firms resisted this effort to break down labor segmentation by foreign origin, for fear that if they could no longer keep immigrant workers in these jobs, they would have to upgrade the positions to attract French labor. In 1982 large strikes of immigrant workers in major automobile factories focused on this issue. Faced with plans to replace their assembly-line jobs with robotics, immigrant workers demanded access to the training necessary for promotion within the firm.[123] While the sight of striking Maghrébins on the news alienated many Frenchmen, the strike reflected efforts by workers of non-European origin to secure living and working conditions commensurate with long-term residency. As Nancy Green has commented, "Formulating such demands and feeling that they can be brought to public attention via the extreme visibility of a strike" may themselves be crucial elements in the adaptation/integration process into the host society.[124]

Immigrant Workers Today

After 1974, the arrival of new adult male labor declined, but illegal immigration, family unifications, and births largely compensated for deaths, returns, and naturalizations among the population of foreigners in France. For immigrant workers fearful of losing the opportunity to work in France should they go back to their native land, 1974 threw into question the idea of the "return" (as the establishment of a Communist Poland did for many Poles after 1945). By the early 1980s, 70 percent of the foreigners residing in France had lived there more than ten years.[125] "Return" has become a politically convenient metaphor to threaten second-generation Maghrébins born in France. Their counterparts among the children of interwar European immigrants integrated into French society through marriage, job advancement, and shared political commitments with the French. Second-generation descendants of immigrant workers from Third World countries have not had these experiences to nearly the same degree.[126] They have faced a racism redolent of the colonial period, reduced chances to escape their fathers' dead-end jobs due to technological change and the end of rapid economic growth after 1973, and a crisis in the labor movement, which had played an important role in integrating earlier groups of immigrant workers.

While many French have refused to recognize the permanence of a large community of Third World origin in their country, the governments of immigrants' native countries have been loath to see the growing indifference of second- and third-generation "immigrants" to their putative homelands. These youths live in a political no-man's-land: second-generation Algerians in France reject French citizenship (still associated with the Algerians who fought with the French against the FLN), but feel little desire to fulfill the responsibilities of Algerian citizenship. For some African and Maghrébin workers, Islam has provided a cohesive pan-national identity opposed to both communism and French culture, much as the Catholic church did for Poles between the wars.[127] Although the spread of Muslim fundamentalism among Maghrébins in France has been exaggerated for political purposes, it appeals to some members of the second generation as an alternative to the choice of nationality.[128]

Antoine Prost speaks of the "pause" in migration between 1930 and 1950 that allowed for assimilation of the immigrants who had come in the 1920s.[129] Have the years since 1974 seen a similar development? Around 1980, the PCF came out against further immigration and the "dumping" of immigrants in the towns they controlled (a period marked by the Communist Vitry municipality's bulldozing of a Malian *foyer*). In succeeding years, however, the PCF reverted to a much more tolerant, conciliatory stance on immigrants. Some Communist voters then

switched their allegiance to Jean-Marie Le Pen's xenophobic Front
National. In the 1988 presidential elections Le Pen rallied an important
element of the French electorate (14.4 percent in the first round) around
a program of expelling Third World immigrants. While Le Pen claims
that non-Europeans could never integrate into French society, much of
his appeal was to workers and members of the lower middle class who
feared that immigrants would break out of their segmented place in the
French economy.[130] Le Pen's showing is a reminder that the period
which Prost identifies as one of assimilation included the Vichy years,
when accusations now leveled against non-Europeans in France formed
the basis of Vichy policy toward nonnative Jews.

In contrast to Le Pen, Socialists embraced elements of the 1960s–
1970s collaboration between immigrant workers and the non-
Communist Left. Second-generation immigrants greeted the Socialist
victory in 1981 with particular enthusiasm. The Socialist administration
reversed many anti-immigrant policies instituted in the late 1970s.[131]
While the 1982 "retreat" by the Socialists limited further action, support
among some Socialists for giving long-term immigrant workers the vote
in municipal elections revealed a will to counteract xenophobia by
integrating immigrant workers into the political system.[132] Such a
proposal suggested a receptivity to radical ideas like the dissociation of
citizenship and the right to vote in an effort to open up French society to
non-Europeans living in France.

Yet the Socialist' loss of interest in this measure raises fundamental
questions about the place of immigrant labor in French society. In the
past, foreign workers have lived and labored in France without the same
rights as native French workers. These have been reserved for
foreigners who abandoned citizenship in their native lands to become
French citizens. This procedure worked for the descendants of interwar
European immigrants. However, the situation has changed in the
postwar period. Mutual reluctance on the part of the French and Third
World peoples to engage in large-scale naturalization of non-European
populations raises questions about the relationship of nationality and
the full extension of the rights of the citizen. Such debates ironically
echo earlier ones about the rights to be granted native peoples in
colonial regimes.

Conclusion

Contemporary political discussion of immigrant workers in France
generally relies upon the acceptance of a radical break between
interwar European immigrants and post–1945 Third World immigrants.
Decades of rejection of European immigrant groups are effaced and
their entry into French society used to "prove" the putative
"unassimilability" of Third World peoples.[133] While not denying the

important cultural differences between pre- and post- 1945 immigrants (and within these groups), this essay has argued that reification of these differences does little to explain the experiences of various immigrant groups. Instead, one needs to analyze the political and economic situations in which immigration has taken place and the responses to it of both the French and the immigrants.

This leads to examination not just of changes in geographic origins but of developments in the French polity as well. For significant segments of the interwar immigrant labor force, antifascism and participation in the Resistance brought together allegiance to the homeland and integration into the French polity. For Algerians—the most important group of post-1945 non-European immigrant workers— the parallel experience was the struggle for independence from France culminating in a long war of national liberation. In this instance, home-country nationalism divided French and foreigner. Not surprisingly, Algerian workers and their descendants in post-1962 France have found it more difficult than their European predecessors to develop a political identity that expressed the particularities of their situation.

In the interwar years important elements of the immigrant labor force came to work in heavy industries, which provided greater opportunities for intergenerational promotion and integration into working-class culture and politics than has much of the employment offered since 1945 to immigrant workers from North Africa and Africa. In more general terms, current debates over France's ability to repeat its earlier incorporations of waves of immigrants may reveal more about a crisis in French society and its integrative mechanisms of education, religion, and politics than about a putative unassimilability of alien peoples.[134]

Nowhere has this been clearer than on the French Left. Through the 1950s a still vibrant workers' culture was a crucial agent in the integration of many immigrant workers into French society. More recently, however, erosion of this workers' culture and the PCF's defensive, inward-turning response have weakened this once central element in the integrative process.[135] While *gauchisme* seemed to offer an alternative in the early 1970s, some now accuse the *gauchiste* displacement of earlier forms of French/immigrant solidarity of contributing to the isolation of immigrant workers.[136] In the early 1980s, immigrant workers were the subject of ironically mutually reinforcing radical political discourses in which the foreigners' right to "difference," a legacy of 1968, was paired with Le Pen's claims that certain ethnic and national groups would be forever beyond the pale of French society. Most recently, groups like SOS-Racisme have responded by moving away from an emphasis on the "right to difference" and toward an integrationist line.

Recognition that some immigrant groups espouse political positions in response to their particular situation brings out both the the active role of immigrants in forging their destiny and the importance of the political environments in the sending and receiving nations in shaping the immigration experience. In the uprooting and disruption that characterize migration and the shift from agricultural to industrial labor, the development of political consciousness is a primary way immigrant workers rethink their relationship to their homeland, the country in which they have come to work, and their social class. And through political action in the neighborhood, the workplace, and the polity, immigrant workers and their descendants grapple with the fundamental ambiguities of their political, social, and cultural position.

Notes

I should like to thank the National Humanities Center for providing a stimulating environment in which to write this essay and Gary Cross, Nancy Green, Lloyd Kramer, and Carl Strikwerda for their comments on earlier drafts of it.

1. The most common terms in France for nonnative worker—"immigrant worker" and "foreign worker"—carry dual meanings. "Immigrant worker" (*"travailleur immigré"*) presents the ethnocentric perspective of the receiving country; every immigrant is also an emigrant. (To escape this dilemma, "migrant" is sometimes used.) "Foreign worker" ("travailleur étranger") carries two connotations: either the nonnative worker is excluded from French society or the cultural difference of this worker must be respected. See R. D. Grillo, *Ideologies and Institutions in Urban France: The Representation of Immigrants* (Cambridge, 1985), 63-83. Françoise Gaspard and Claude Servan-Schreiber suggest that *"travailleur immigré"* should give way to the *"immigrant"* in recognition that Third World workers and their families who are in France today are not going to return to their putative homelands, *La Fin des immigrés* (Paris, 1984). The focus in this paper is on male immigrants working in industry and living in urban areas. Foreigners working alone or in families in agriculture had less chance to participate in an immigrant community or in politics.

2. Albano Cordeiro, *L'Immigration* (Paris, 1983), 8-26. Gérard Noiriel, "L'Immigration en France, une histoire en friche," *Annales E.S.C.* 41 (1986):751-69. Noiriel develops these ideas in his stimulating book *Le Creuset français: Histoire de l'Immigration XIXe-XXe siècles* (Paris, 1988). See also Catherine Wihtol de Wenden's fine study *Les Immigrés et la politique* (Paris, 1988).

3. See Gary Cross's excellent *Immigrant Workers in Industrial France* (Philadelphia, 1983); also, J.-C. Bonnet, *Les Pouvoirs politiques français et l'immigration dans l'entre-deux-guerres* (Lyon, 1976). Noiriel, "L'Immigration," 736 n. 36, points out the failure of Charles Tilly and Edward Shorter in *Strikes in France 1830-1968*, to take into account the influx of immigrant labor in explaining changes in strike activity between the wars.

4. Françoise Briot and Gilles Verbunt, *Immigrés dans la crise* (Paris, 1981), 20.

5. Germain Lemarquis, "Mouvement ouvrier français et immigration," *Politique aujourd'hui* (March-April 1975): 50-75.

6. Michael Piore, *Birds of Passage and Promised Lands: Long-Distance Migrants and Industrial Societies* (Cambridge, 1979), offers a good critique of this approach.

7. Many studies point out the advantage to the receiving nation of obtaining adult labor without paying the social costs of producing it. However, receiving nations do not have the opportunity to instill their normative values into the children who will become immigrant workers.

8. Mark J. Miller, *Foreign Workers in Western Europe* (New York, 1981), 22.

9. Gilles Verbunt, *L'Intégration par l'autonomie* (Paris, CIEMM), 64 n. 4. Cordeiro, *L'Immigration*, 38.

10. Georges Mauco, *Les Etrangers en France* (Paris, 1932), 280 n. l, 476.

11. Mohand Khellil, *L'Exil Kabyle: Essai d'analyse de vécu des migrants* (Paris, 1979), 144. Grillo, *Ideologies and Institutions*, treats this issue very well.

12. Charles Sabel, *Work and Politics* (Cambridge, 1982).

13. Huseyin Çélik, "Les Travailleurs immigrés parlent," *Les Cahiers du Centre d'Etudes Socialistes* 94-98 (1969):13. Khellil, *L'Exil Kabyle*, 143.

14. Gaspard and Servan-Schreiber, *La Fin des immigrés*, 42-44. The history of women immigrants and politics raises important questions beyond the scope of this essay.

15. See Nancy Green, " 'Filling the Void': Immigration to France before World War I," in *Labor Migration in the Atlantic Economies*, ed. Dirk Hoerder (Westport, Conn., 1985), 143-61. Particularly relevant for this essay is Green's discussion of the politics of East European Jewish immigrants to Paris in *The Pletzl of Paris: Jewish Immigrant Workers in the Belle Epoque* (New York, 1985).

16. See Donald Reid, "The Limits of Paternalism: Immigrant Coal Miners' Communities in France, 1919-1945," *European History Quar-terly* 15 (1985): 99-118.

17. Gary Cross to author, 8 June 1988. Noiriel, *Le Creuset français*, 69-124.

18. Mauco, *Les Etrangers en France*, 132, in Gérard Noiriel, "Les Immigrés italiens en Lorraine pendant l'entre-deux-guerres: du rejet xénophobe aux stratégies d'intégration" in *Les Italiens en France de 1914 à 1940*, ed. Pierre Milza (Rome, 1986), 618.

19. Lemarquis, "Mouvement ouvrier," 52-53. Noiriel, *Le Creuset français*, 116.

20. See Cross, *Immigrant Workers*. During these years, Antoine Prost reports that the SGI brought one-third of the foreign workers who came to France, one-third entered legally with contracts at border checkpoints where they were given medical exams, and one-third entered under other pretexts and sought to find a job and then regularize their situation. "L'Immigration en France depuis cent ans," *Esprit* 34 (April 1966): 539.

21. Cross, *Immigrant Workers*, 186-212. Pierre Guillaume, "Du bon usage des immigrés en temps de crise et de guerre," *Vingtième siècle* 7 (July-September 1985): 117-25.

22. Ralph Schor, *L'Opinion française et les étrangers 1919-1939* (Paris, 1985), 246-52, 260-74. If shared left-wing sentiments could form bonds between native and immigrant workers, the reverse could be true as well. White Russians who worked in French factories found themselves ostracized. One reported that wherever he went to work, he was never called by his name, but always Rasputin, Kornilov, or Wrangel. He eventually quit factory work and became a taxi driver. Jean Anglade, *La Vie quotidienne des immigrés en France de 1919 à nos jours* (Paris, 1976), 20.

23. Léon Gani, *Syndicats et travailleurs immigrés* (Paris, 1972), 118.

24. Mauco, *Les Etrangers en France*, 220-21.

25. I draw extensively on Gérard Noiriel's superb *Longwy: Immigres et prolétaires 1880-1980* (Paris, 1984) for my interpretation of events in the Lorraine.

26. Jacques Jeandin, *Trieux. 79 jours au fond pour la Lorraine* (Paris, 1977), 12.

27. Serge Bonnet and Roger Humbert, *La Ligne rouge des hauts fourneaux* (Paris, 1982), and Noiriel, *Longwy*, 64-95.

28. Axel Sömme, *La Lorraine métallurgique* (Paris, 1930), 183.

29. Rudy Damiani, "Les Italiens dans le Nord et le Pas-de-Calais entre 1919 et 1939," in *Les Italiens en France*, 633-59.

30. Caroline Wiegandt-Sakouin, "Le Fascisme italien en France," in *Les Italiens en France*, 431-69.

31. Pierre Guillen, "Le Rôle politique de l'immigration italienne en France dans l'entre-deux-guerres," in *Les Italiens en France*, 338.

32. Schor, *L'Opinion française*, 236-37, 245. Alain Girard and Jean Stoetzel, *Français et immigrés*, 2 vols. (Paris, 1953), 2:198-204.

33. Mauco, *Les Etrangers en France*, 212, 215.

34. For vivid recollections of the Le Forest strike and expulsions, see Jacques Renard and Sophie Goupil, eds., *Paroles et mémoires du bassin houiller du Nord-Pas de Calais* (Lille, 1981), 59-61, 67-69. See also Janine Ponty's excellent *Polonais méconnus* (Paris, 1988), esp. 304-9.

35. Olivier Milza, "La Gauche, la crise et l'immigration (Années 1930-Années 1980)," *Vingtième siècle* 7 (1985): 127-40.

36. Renard and Goupil, *Paroles et mémoires*, 81-82.

37. Girard and Stoetzel, *Français et immigrés*, 2:202-3.

38. Noiriel, "Les Immigrés italiens," 628.

39. Renard and Goupil, *Paroles et mémoires*, 125.

40. Janine Ponty, "Une Intégration difficile: Les Polonais en France dans le premier vingtième siecle," *Vingtième siècle* 7 (1985): 57.

41. For Missak Manouchian, Armenian Communist Resistance leader in France, "The policies of imperialist Germany in the past and of Hitler's Germany today are at the origin of the massacres in 1914-18 and of the endless tribulations of the European poeoples now enslaved." Gaston Laroche, *On les nommait des étrangers* (Paris, 1965), 29-124 (quote on 52-53). For the controversy involving the PCF and Manouchian's arrest, see Maurice Rajsfus, *L'An prochain, la révolution* (Paris, 1985), chap. 4.

42. Sömme, *La Lorraine métallurgique*, 186-87.

43. Miller, *Foreign Workers*, 45-48.

44. Louis Köll, "Immigration italienne et intégration française à Auboué (M.-et-M.) (1901-1939)," *Annales de l'Est* 5e série, 30 (1978): 264-65. See also Serge Bonnet, "Political Alignments and Religious Attitudes within the Italian Immigration to the Metallurgical Districts of Lorraine," *Journal of Social History* 2 (1968):123-55. Second-generation Belgian immigrants had played a crucial role in establishing the *Guesdiste* stronghold in Roubaix before World War I, Noiriel, *Le Creuset*, 230-31. Michael Hastings, "Communisme et folklore. Etude d'un Carnaval rouge Halluin 1924," *Ethnologie française* 16 (1986): 137-50, analyzes the way Communist children and grandchildren of Belgian immigrants used Flemish folklore to celebrate a triumph over the local *patronat*. The Spanish Civil War refugees who crossed into France in 1939 fought in the Resistance, seeing it as a continuation of the war to liberate their country. When the Allies refused to unseat Franco at the end of the war, many Spanish Communists became active in the PCF and the CGT. For a local example, see François Koerner, "L'immigration et l'intégration des populations étrangères dans le Puy-de-Dôme," *Cahiers d'histoire* 32 (1987): 56. While pursuing the "liberation" of their homeland, they began integration into French social and political life.

45. Mining firms' policy of encouraging the cultural isolation of Poles from French labor had unexpected consequences after 1945. Companies had supported schools in which Polish teachers taught the children of Polish miners. When the nationalized coal industry abandoned the system, it was chagrined to find the new pro-Communist Polish regime introducing Polish-language teachers favorable to its point of view into northern mining communities. Girard and Stoetzel, *Français et immigrés*, 2:200.

46. Gani, *Syndicats et travailleurs immigrés*, 124-25.

47. Ponty, "Une Intégration difficile," 58.

48. Verbunt, *L'Intégration*, 8.

49. Noiriel makes this point in *Longwy*.

50. Briot and Verbunt, *Immigrés*, 16-17. The SGI had eliminated "radicals"; the CFTC accused CGT representatives on ONI missions to Italy of cooperating with their counterparts in the Italian CGT in selecting them. Gani, *Syndicats et travailleurs immigrés*, 33. While the CFTC opposed recruitment primarily of "red" northern Italians, it supported admission of "displaced persons" from Eastern Europe into France. The CGT fought this policy, believing that most "DPs" were anti-Communists and perhaps ex-collaborators. Stephen Castles and Godula Kosack, *Immigrant Workers and Class Structure in Western Europe* (London, 1973), 133.

51. Stephen Castles with Heather Booth and Tina Wallace, *Here for Good: Western Europe's New Ethnic Minorities* (London, 1985), 51.

52. Xavier Lannes, *L'Immigration en France depuis 1945* (La Haye, 1953).

53. Cordeiro, *L'Immigration*, 38.

54. Briot and Verbunt, *Immigrés*, 17.

55. Cordeiro, *L'Immigration*, 38.

56. Maryse Tripier, "Concurrence et différence: les problèmes posés au syndicalisme ouvrier par les travailleurs immigrés," *Sociologie du travail* 14 (1972): 333.

57. Gani, *Syndicats et travailleurs immigrés*, 137.

58. See Robert Linhart, *The Assembly Line*, trans. Margaret Crosland (Amherst, 1981).

59. "Since each nationality group is in France under separate agreements, conditions, and regulations, it is difficult for those trying to organize them to create a coherent and unified program. The general confusion over exactly which groups enjoy which rights simply contributes to the insecurity and precariousness of the migrant's status." Gary Freeman, *Immigrant Labor and Racial Conflict in Indus-trial Societies: The French and British Experience, 1945-1975* (Princeton, N.J., 1979), 234.

60. Belkacem Hifi, *L'Immigration algérienne en France* (Paris, 1985), 27-53.

61. Abdelmalek Sayad, "Les Trois 'âges' de l'émigration algérienne en France," *Actes de la recherche en sciences sociales* 15 (June 1977): 59-79.

62. Ibid., 63-65. Malek Ath-Messaoud and Alain Gillette, *L'Immigration algérienne en France* (Paris, 1976), 37-38, 55-59. Kamal Bouguessa, "Mode de vie et reproduction: La Communauté algérienne en France pendant la colonisation," in *Maghrébins en France. Emigrés ou immigrés?* (Paris, 1983), 51-69.

63. The decision was also a victory of French industrialists over Algerian *colons*, who feared that their labor costs would go up if Algerians had unrestricted access to the mainland. Cordeiro, *L'Immigration*, 29.

64. Anglade, *La Vie quotidienne*, 126. Bernard Granotier reports that an effort was made to use psychological testing of Algerian workers to determine those most likely to become radical leaders in France; these were sent back to Algeria. *Les Travailleurs immigrés en France*, 3rd ed. (Paris, 1976), 101.

65. Charles-Robert Agéron, "L'Immigration maghrébine en France. Un Survol historique," *Vingtième siècle* 7 (1985): 66.

66. Léo Bogart, "Les Algériens en France. Adaptation réussie et non réussie" in Girard and Stoetzel, *Français et immigrés*, 2:19, 70.

67. Sadek, "Les Trois 'âges'."

68. Agéron, "L'Immigration," 64.

69. Andrée Michel, *Les Travailleurs algériens en France* (Paris, 1956), 210, 213-17. Henri Krasucki, "La C.G.T. et les travailleurs algériens," *La Pensée* 90 (March-April 1960): 82.

70. Schor, *L'Opinion française*, 288.

71. Charles-Robert Agéron, *Histoire de l'Algerie contemporaine* (Paris, 1979), 2:349-61. Agéron, "L'Etoile Nord-Africaine et le modèle communiste. Eléments d'une enquête comparative," *Cahiers de Tunisie* 117-18 (April 1981): 199-236. Agéron, "Emigration et politique: L'Etoile Nord-Africaine et le Parti du Peuple Algérien" in *Les Mémoires de Messali Hadj 1898-1939* (Paris, 1982), 273-96. Benjamin Stora, "Avant la deuxième génération: Le Militantisme algérien en France (1926-1954)," *Revue européenne des migrations internationales* 1 (1985): 69-91. For Messali's account of these years, see *Les Mémoires*, 91-201. On strikes by North African workers in France, see Odile Jusserand, "Formation de la classe ouvrière maghrébine dans l'immigration: Grèves et grévistes en France (1919-1935)," in *Approaches de mutations sociales et de la politisation au Maghreb* (Nice, 1981), 33-49. For the split between the major parties of the French Left and Algerian nationalists at the time of the Popular Front, see Benjamin Stora, *Nationalistes algériens et révolutionnaires françaises au temps du front populaire* (Paris, 1987). Stora's discussion of the revolutionary non-Communist Left's support for Algerian nationalists is particularly interesting in light of *gauchiste* backing of immigrants' movements for revolution in their homelands in the early 1970s (47-83). For the much smaller movements of Africans in France during the interwar years, see Phillipe Dewitte, *Les Mouvements nègres en France 1919-1939* (Paris, 1985).

72. Mohammed Harbi, *Aux origines du FLN: Le Populisme révolutionnaire en Algérie* (Paris, 1975), 312. Henri Alleg, "Le Torrent souterrain" in *La Guerre d' Algérie*, ed. Henri Alleg, 3 vols. (Paris, 1981), 1:212.

73. Agéron, *Histoire*, 2:591.

74. M'hamed Ferid Ghazi, "Doublement prolétaires," *Esprit* (February 1952): 229-30.

75. Ath-Messaoud and Gillette, *L'Immigration algérienne*, 30-33, 44. J. J. Rager, *Les Muselmans algériens en France et dans les pays islamiques* (Paris, 1950), 165.

76. Khellil, *L'Exil Kabyle*, 173. Stephen Adler, "Emigration and Development in Algeria," in *Guests Come to Stay*, ed. Rosemarie Rogers (Boulder, Colo., 1985), 273.

77. Alistair Horne, *A Savage War of Peace: Algeria 1954-1962* (New York, 1979), 236.

78. Michel, *Les Travailleurs algériens*, 211 n. 2.

79. Irwin M. Wall, "The French Communists and the Algerian War," *Journal of Contemporary History* 12 (1977): 521-43. See also Claude Poperon, *Renault, regards de l'intérieur* (Paris, 1983), 150-56.

80. Lemarquis, "Mouvement ouvrier," 66-69.

81. See Hervé Hamon and Patrick Rotman, *Les Porteurs de valises. La Résistance française à la guerre d'Algérie* (Paris, 1981).

82. Messali's "workerist" attacks on the utative bourgeois character of the FLN won support from Algerian workers in France and may have influenced the

FLN to aopt a specifically socialist program. CEDETIM, *Les Immigrés* (Paris, 1975), 101-2.

83. Horne, *A Savage War*, 409. William B. Quandt, *Revolution and Political Leadership: Algeria, 1954-1968* (Cambridge, 1969), 121-22. Patrick Kessel and Giovanni Pirelli provide an account of an Algerian worker in France who was converted to the FLN during the revolution. *Le Peuple algérien et la guerre. Lettres et témoignages 1954-1962* (Paris, 1963), 345-47. One might balance this with the story of an Algerian worker who paid his monthly dues to the FLN, but refused to participate in the eight-day general strike in 1957. Threatened by the FLN, he returned to Algeria only to find that his wife had become an FLN women's leader. Mohamed, *Journal de Mohamed* (Paris, 1973), 41-45, 51-55.

84. Anglade, *La Vie quotidienne*, 126. Horne, *A Savage War*, 237. Mahamed Lebjaoui, *Vérités sur la Révolution algérienne* (Paris, 1970), 176.

85. Michel, *Les Travailleurs algériens*, 209 n. 1, 211 n. 1, 212. Tayeb Belloula, *Les Algériens en France* (Algiers, 1965), 89-102; Jean Freire, "Un Etat vient au monde," in *La Guerre d'Algérie*, 3:366-71.

86. Anglade, *La Vie quotidienne*, 126.

87. Khellil, *L'Exil Kabyle*, 164-65.

88. Ath-Messaoud and Gillette, *L'Immigration algérienne*, 42. Michel Tibon-Cornillot, "Le Défi de l'immigration maghrébine," *Politique aujourd'hui* (February-March 1984): 43.

89. The new state's initial fear was that Kabyle workers might oppose the predominantly Arab government in Algeria. Adler suggests that this is one reason why the Algerian government was willing to accept French limitations on the number of Algerians it would admit. Over time, however, the threat of Kabyle separatism faded, in part because the remittances sent home to Kabylie sustained the traditional social structure during the transitional years of independence. "Emigration and Development," 271-73.

90. Miller, *Foreign Workers*, 37-37 (quoted) Belloula, *Les Algériens*, 127-201.

91. Miller, *Foreign Workers*, 97-100.

92. Hifi, *L'Immigration*, 24 n. 3.

93. Miller, *Foreign Workers*, 52. See also Adler, "Emigration and Development," 272.

94. Jacqueline Costa-Lascoux, "L'Immigration algérienne en France et la nationalité des enfants d'Algériens," in *Maghrébins en France*, 312 n. 49. Adler, "Emigration and Development," 272.

95. Adler, "Emigration and Development," 276-79.

96. Opponents of the regime refuse to join the CGT because of its close ties with the Amicale. Gérard Noiriel, *Vivre et lutter à Longwy* (Paris, 1980), 200.

97. René Gallissot, "Le Mixte franco-algérien," *Les Temps modernes* 40 (March-May 1984): 1707-25.

98. Cordeiro, *L'Immigration*, 43-44.

99. Marie-France Moulin, *Machines à dormir* (Paris, 1976), 29-41.

100. Verbunt, *L'Intégration*, 320-21. Personnel managers at firms like Citroën were also often former colonial officers. Linhart, *The Assembly Line*, 64.

101. Guy Hermet, *Les Espagnols en France: Immigration et culture* (Paris, 1967). Observers noted that during the 1960s, "in Italy, Spain, and Portugal external migration [i.e., to France] frequently presented less of a break with the community of origin than did internal migration—that many external migrants were rather traditional in their outlook, whereas it was often the most enterprising and those most ready to make a basic change in their life situations who migrated internally." Rosemarie Rogers, "Post World War II European Labor Migration: An Introduction to the Issues," in *Guests Come to Stay*, 20.

Experience with state-run unions in Spain and Portugal made immigrants from these countries mistrustful of French unions. Tripier, "Concurrence et différence," 333.

102. Granotier, *Les Travailleurs immigrés*, 155. Gilles Verbunt, "Esclaves de notre temps," *Etudes* (March 1969), 337. As far as the Portuguese government was concerned, the danger was that French agitators would infect its workers, not the inverse: it hired buses and persuaded a number of Portuguese workers to return home until the disorders ended. Castles and Kosack, *Immigrant Workers*, 173.

103. Briot and Verbunt, *Immigrés*, 122-23. Gilles Verbunt, "Les Associations," *Les Temps modernes* 40 (March-May 1984): 2053.

104. Mirielle Ginesy-Galano, *Les Immigrés hors la cité. Le Système d'encadrement dans les foyers (1973-1982)* (Paris, 1984), 29.

105. Verbunt, *L'Intégration*, 299 n.12.

106. Tewfik Allal, Jean Pierre Buffard, Michel Marie and Tomaso Regazzala, *Situations migratoires* (Paris, 1977), 153-57.

107. Fouad Lamine and Bernard Navacelles, "De l'isolement vers l'unité," *Politique aujourd'hui* (March-April 1975): 76. For their study of the Ladrecht coal strike, Françoise Gardes-Madray and Jacques Brès interviewed an Algerian miner who had begun work in French mines in 1947, left to join the FLN in 1954, and returned to the mines in 1964. The authors emphasize the connections that the Algerians made between the strike and the Algerian war. *Parole ouvrière: Autour de Ladrecht* (Paris, 1986), 144, 191.

108. Michel Samuel, *Le Prolétariat africain noir en France* (Paris, 1978), 109-50.

109. André Gorz and Philippe Gavi, "La Bataille d'Ivry," *Les Temps modernes* 26 (March 1970): 1398-1414.

110. Daniel Anselme, "Penarroya" in *4 Grèves significatives* (Paris, 1972), 141-73. Miller, *Foreign Workers*, 91-97. Manuel Castells, "Immigrant Workers and Class Struggles in Advanced Capitalism: The Western European Experience," *Politics and Society* 5 (1975): 64.

111. Sally N'Dongo, *Voyage forcé. Itinéraire d'un militant* (Paris, 1975), 75-101. While the AAE established close links with the CGT and the PCF, other national associations developed relationships with French authorities. "The French government especially has acted to strengthen homeland regimes, usually in former colonies, through cooperation or collusion with homeland fraternal organizations that in effect police foreign workers on French soil." Miller, *Foreign Workers*, 39. Immigrant workers who wanted to protest their native regimes often arranged with a French union to sponsor the demonstration in order to evade charges of breaking political neutrality; for the French union this could be a means of gaining new recruits. Ibid., 63.

112. Sally N'Dongo, *Exil, connais pas . . .* (Paris, 1976), 87. See Adrian Adams, "Prisoners in Exile: Senegalese Workers in France," *Race and Class* 16 (1974): 157-79.

113. Freeman, *Immigrant Labor*, 85-98. Anglade, *La Vie quotidienne*, 84. Pierre Lanier, *Travailleurs étrangers et responsabilités collectives* (Lyon, 1974), 15. Decolonization played a secondary role in Portuguese migration to France. Large numbers of young Portuguese males went to work in France to escape four-year service in their nation's ill-fated colonial wars. Jean Benoit, *E . . . comme esclaves* (Paris, 1980), 115. The money which Portuguese workers sent home helped support Portugal's military presence in Africa. Françoise Pinot, *Les Travailleurs immigrés dans la lutte de classes* (Paris, 1973), 10.

114. Freeman, *Immigrant Labor*, 93 (quote). Lamine and Navacelles, "De l'isolement," 79-80. Briot and Verbunt, *Immigrés*, 51. Miller, *Foreign Workers*, 16.

115. Miller, *Foreign Workers*, 100-104.

116. Lamine and Navacelles, "De l'isolement," 81-82. Miller, *Foreign Workers*, 102. Castles, *Here for Good*, 52-55.

117. Gilles Verbunt, "Travailleurs immigrés: grève des foyers," *Projet* 109 (1976): 981.

118. Moulin, *Machines à dormir.*

119. N'Dongo, *Exil*, 86-87.

120. Antonio Perotti, "Le conflit des foyers Sonacotra," *Projet* 139 (1979): 1149. Verbunt, "Travailleurs immigrés," 981-85. Verbunt, *L'Intégration*, 319-35. Ginesy-Galano, *Les Immigrés.*

121. Verbunt, "Intégration," 981.

122. Briot and Verbunt, *Immigrés*, 126. Verbunt, *L'Intégration*, 57.

123. Gaspard and Servan-Schreiber, *La Fin des immigres*, 87-88. Floriane Benoît, *Citroën. Le Printemps de la dignité* (Paris, 1982).

124. Nancy Green to author, 2 November 1988.

125. Gaspard and Servan-Schreiber, *La Fin des immigrés*, 16.

126. Briot and Verbunt, *Immigrés*, 170. Costa-Lascoux, "L'Immigration," 299-320.

127. Juliette Minces, *Les Travailleurs étrangers en France* (Paris, 1973), 439. One could fruitfully compare the roles of religion and politics in the differentiation and integration of immigrant workers. See Ralph Schor, "Le Facteur religieux et l'intégration des étrangers en France (1919-1939)," *Vingtième siècle* 7 (1985); 103-15.

128. See "Interview de M. Gaston Defferre, ministre de l'Intérieur, Maire de Marseille," *Les Temps modernes* 40 (1984): 1575.

129. Prost, "L'Immigration," 541.

130. Isabelle Taboada-Leonetti, "Les Elites étrangères," *Les Temps modernes* 40 (March-May 1984): 2072-73.

131. Briot and Verbunt, *Immigrés*, 131-32. Gaspard and Servan-Schreiber, *La Fin des immigrés*, 89 n.1. Milza, "La Gauche," 131-40.

132. For the argument in favor of extending political rights to immigrant workers, see Etienne Balibar, "Sujets ou citoyens?" *Les Temps modernes* 40 (1984): 1726-53. Rémy Leveau and Catherine Wihtol de Wenden, "Evolution des attitudes politiques des immigrés maghrébins," *Vingtième siècle* 7 (1985): 82-83.

133. Pierre Milza, "Y a-t-il un 'melting pot' français?" *Revue des sciences morales et politiques* (1986): 235-54. Gérard Noiriel, "Le Fin mot de l'histoire," *Vingtième siècle* 7 (1985): 141-50.

134. Milza, "Y a-t-il un 'melting pot' français?"; note the hostile response to Milza in the appended comments.

135. Ibid., 248.

136. Olivier Brachet, "Pourquoi Lyon fait-il parler de ses immigrés," *Les Temps modernes* 40 (1984): 1687-88.

11

Foreigners in the Fatherland: Turkish Immigrant Workers in Germany

Ruth Mandel

It is now three decades since the first Turkish workers were recruited and brought to the Federal Republic of Germany in 1961. During the early years of the recruitment no one foresaw the major ramifications to which this migration would lead, but its sociocultural, economic, political, and demographic effects have irrevocably altered not only the face but the very essence of postwar Germany. The agreement set forth in the bilateral treaty entered into by the Federal Republic of Germany and Turkey was similar in kind and intent to other treaties drawn up in the same period between the Federal Republic and Italy, Yugoslavia, Greece, Spain, and Portugal. The small trickle of southern Europeans and Asians into northern Europe soon grew into a wave, perceived by some as one of tidal proportions. It was intended that the imported workers would fill the lacuna created by the freezing of East-West relations as a result of the Cold War. In addition, the subsequent erection of the Berlin Wall effectively halted the East German labor pool upon which the postwar West German economy had become dependent.

If we employ the unfair advantage of hindsight, it would appear that the framers of what was to be known as the Guest Worker Program were lacking in foresight. The utilitarian assumptions, devoid of social and cultural considerations and motivated by an implicit faith in a policy of *Konjunktur* (economic conjuncture), helped to set the scene for the drama known as the *Ausländerproblematik/Frage* (foreigner problem or question) that was to unfold and that would critically and irrevocably alter the course of contemporary Germany.

The initial work contracts, drafted to be terminated or renewed annually, reflected the intentions of the designers of the program and the goals and aims of the Federal Republic. However, it soon became clear that the original idea, a continual rotation of workers, was not cost efficient. The expense involved in bringing in and training new crops of workers each year proved formidable. In time, the disadvantages of rotation were perceived to outweigh the benefits. What clearly had begun as a temporary phenomenon gradually was transformed into one of longer duration and wider scope. With the economic recession of the late 1960s and the oil crisis of 1973, West Germany's labor shortage ceased, and unemployment reared its ugly head for the first time since World War II. The one- and two-year contracts, having been extended into a decade, now also extended demographically into the social field. Included were spouses sent for from the village, along with children and other kin, expanding into a full-fledged chain migration of a sort as unexpected as it was unprecedented in modern German experience. Approximately 1.5 million Turks currently reside in western Germany, making them the largest non-German population in Germany.

Thus began a new chapter in West German history, one that has highlighted a confrontation between, on the one hand, the ideology and legal structure of national and cultural homogeneity, and, on the other hand, a reality that defies and contradicts every thread of this idealized notion. An adequate analysis of the complexities and subtleties of this migration challenges the limits of an essay such as this. Bearing that in mind, however, the remaining portion of this essay attempts to explain some of these complexities by addressing multiple dimensions of this migration, in its historical, economic, and cultural contexts. To summarize, the dilemma of the Turkish workers has been that they found little acceptance in German society and yet little reason to return to Turkey. Despite the lack of integration, the Turkish immigrant community in Germany has in many ways become more rooted in the new land. Complicating the picture still further, as we shall see, are the deep divisions within the Turkish community, which Germans usually fail to see. The result is that the Turks are extremely vulnerable to the economic and political changes set off by the unfolding unification of Germany.

Problems of Guests and Definitions

Much of the social science literature on international labor migration has understood the movement of workers into Western European societies in the 1960s primarily as an economic phenomenon, where manpower was brought to the industrial core. For some, the migration initiated a new phase of industrial capitalism. No longer would the developed countries seek new markets for capital investments in the "less developed world"; rather, the industrial core would bring cheap labor to the source. This was thought by some to be the "new imperialism." Regardless of the interpretation of the migration, it was seen as the movement of workers, driven by the push of peripheral Third World poverty and underdevelopment and pulled by the booming economies of the industrial core. But the economic boom fueling the industrial core faded and left in its wake the demographic, legal, and social products and problems of the imported guest workers.

One of these problems stems, in a sense, from the impediment of a definition: the Turks and other migrant workers are popularly known as "guest workers" and officially known as foreigners, never as immigrants. The question remains of how "guest workers" are to be transformed into immigrants. The Federal Republic of Germany officially defined itself as a "nonimmigration land," politicians and citizens proclaiming the assertion "*Wir sind kein Einwanderungsland*" (we are not an immigration country) as a way of justifying the lack of civil rights for foreigners. It follows, then, that the migrant workers could neither be considered nor treated as immigrants. The epithet *Gastarbeiter*, guest worker, then, reinforced not only the migrant's nonpermanent and nonimmigrant status but also his or her identity as a worker. For it was the migrants' potential labor power that defined their presence in the Federal Republic and their absence from Turkey, just as it was this labor power that justified and rationalized their presence for the Germans. For guest workers, sociocultural and economic boundaries were explicitly and implicitly delimited between themselves and their hosts. Guests may, but need not be integrated, and guest workers may be easily dismissed, becoming the *Konjunkturpuffer*, the temporary, expendable economic buffer necessary for the production of West Germany's famous *Wirtschaftswunder*, the economic miracle.

Migration and the Failure of Development

Migration has not worked as its initial sponsors hoped because migrants usually do not return to Turkey, and, indeed, their emigration from their homeland has done little to encourage favorable economic change. The well-known economic "boom" of postwar Western Europe must be compared to Turkey's slow development, lack of technological know-how, absence of foreign investment, and high rate of population growth. (The population growth resulted from both a high birth rate and a dramatic decrease in infant mortality.) These factors provide a more comprehensive understanding of the complexities of emigration. Also, in an attempt to finance modernization, Turkey had borrowed heavily from the industrialized Western economies, incurring a phenomenally large foreign debt. Thus, any discussion of the political economy of this particular instance of labor migration must take into account the larger system as well as macroeconomic issues such as labor demand, balance of payments, and foreign debts.

Economist Suzanne Paine's study in the early 1970s, just prior to the 1973 recruitment stop (*Anwerbestoppe*), for example, correlated the remitted earnings of Turkish workers abroad with Turkey's foreign debt: $740 million was sent to Turkey, compared with the $678 million paid out by Turkey for imports such as mineral fuels, iron and steel and products, machinery, and motor vehicles. In addition, Paine's examination of Turkey's remittance economy manages to poke irreparable holes in some of the more naive theories that argue in favor of labor exporting. For example, an oft-cited 'plus' is that workers acquire skills abroad that they can then bring back when they repatriate. The problem, she points out, is that, first, only about 10 percent of Turkish workers receive training when abroad. Generally those who are unskilled when they emigrate return unskilled. Second, those who do manage to acquire some training abroad often find their training inappropriate for the very different Turkish labor market.[1]

Furthermore, Paine shows a correlation between inflation (of land and consumer items) and repatriated earnings. Those observers in favor of labor migration have often justified it by pointing out the advantage to the underdeveloped sending country of gaining access to much needed foreign exchange in remitted hard currency and its consequent potential role for increased production. Unfortunately, however, the investment patterns necessary for this situation have never been realized. Return migrants exhibit very little interest in making productive investments. Instead, savings acquired abroad and sent back to Turkey as remittances are most often spent on prestige goods and expensive property and housing. One common exception is investment in an independent business enterprise, such as the purchase of a taxi. This is consonant with the frequently expressed goal of "being my own boss."

In the early 1970s, the Turkish government, cognizant of the problem, established a bank, DESIYAB (Devlet Sanayî Isçi Yatîrîm Bankasî or State Industrial Worker Investment Bank), designed to promote programs to aid worker-owned and -managed cooperatives. These were to be financed by migrants, who would invest a portion of their salaries while working in Germany, and would be provided with employment upon their return. Out of nearly three hundred such joint endeavors, most were notorious disasters, and no more than two dozen even operated in the black.[2] The reasons for such astounding failure were many. Most of the failures stem from poor planning and management; for example, after serving as low-prestige, exploited assembly-line workers for twenty years in Germany, the cooperative worker-owners hoped to attain higher-status management positions for which they were untrained. An additional problem of management planning is revealed in the cynical anecdotes told about the factory cooperatives: many were allegedly located in inappropriate regions of Turkey for the specific sort of industry—a cement factory might have been built in an area lacking sand, or a sugar factory in a region lacking sugar beets. Also, the not unjustified lack of confidence in the Turkish economy inhibited many potential worker-investors, and thus the programs lacked sufficient capital to stimulate development of the sort originally envisioned by the designers of the program.[3] The ideology informing the government sponsorship of these cooperatives was socialistic in orientation and the model for the cooperatives was the Yugoslav one of worker self-management. (The cooperative program was instituted during Bülent Ecevit's tenure in office as premier when his Republican People's party had strong social democratic leanings. Though the cooperatives most likely would have failed anyway, the fact that Turkey's economy was experiencing a severe crisis in 1977–80, when most of the projects were attempted, did not help. During that period of social and political turmoil (which culminated in a military takeover) Turkey's economy actually contracted. The remittances, which with extensive multilateral international borrowing (from the IMF, World Bank, and other organizations) had kept Turkey afloat during the first four years of the oil crisis, no longer sustained the strained economy.[4]

Although the severe economic problems that Turkey experienced in the 1970s and early 1980s have eased, there is no sign of the expansive conditions that would induce Turks now living in Germany to return to the country that they or their parents left. At the same time, the Turkish community changed into one to which they were increasingly less likely to return.

The Fragmented Family: Social and Legal Considerations

A brief curtailment of recruitment in the late 1960s due to an economic recession was followed by a short period of granting work visas to Turkish women, not men. A major turning point in the history of this migration, the policy of granting visas only to women both led the way to family reunion, and perpetuated the family fragmentation already begun, albeit in a different form. The women who migrated were either single women from families poor enough to be willing to accept the ignominy implied by such an action or those who already were independent or marginal due to their own idiosyncratic histories, or, most often, were wives of men who had been denied worker visas and hoped to be brought to the Federal Republic as spouses of their worker-wives. These latter women often left children in Turkey to be cared for by relatives. When their husbands managed to join them in a year or two, the children frequently were left with grandparents in the village. No uncommonly did siblings find themselves split between the Federal Republic and Turkey, occasionally being shuffled back and forth, depending on variables such as timing of parents' work shifts, availability of child care, or acceptability of a school situation.

Meanwhile, many of the single male workers had returned to their villages in the summers and found their newly achieved earning power to be a desirable *başlik*, or bride price. They married, many brought their brides with them to Germany, and these women then found work. In 1973, over 40 percent of the Turkish women in West Berlin were employed. Kudat's findings of a year later show that "over three-quarters of the married Turks had their spouses, but only one-third of their children with them abroad."[5] The year that labor recruitment ceased, 1973, saw close to eighty thousand Turks in West Berlin. Five years later the Turkish population of the city had grown to one hundred thousand owing in large part to family reunion as well as illegal immigration. A selective reading of statistics, however, can prove misleading: the rise in sheer numbers does *not* indicate widespread family reunion tending toward greater stability. Rather, from 1976 to 1977 "about one-half of those returning to Turkey as well as entering Germany were youth under 18 years of age."[6]

The legal factors influencing family composition are many, and these in turn influence migration economics. In 1976, two-thirds of all Turkish men had their wives with them—more than the inverse of the figures from one decade before; and 27 percent of all Turks in Germany were women. More wives, and more children, meant that Turkish workers in Germany now spent much more of their wages on their families. As a direct result, the workers' remittances to Turkey dropped at this time and Turkey lost a great deal of badly needed hard currency. In addition, the high Turkish birth rate drove the population up 50 percent. "The net result is that despite the 1973 recruitment stop, in the fifteen year period between 1967 and 1982 the Turkish population in Germany grew from 172,400 to over one and a half million."[7]

The maximum legal age for children brought from Turkey has been eighteen. However, for over a decade, conservative party platforms have been lobbying to change the law and lower the age to six, a policy supported by the current Christian Democratic government. They justify this by claiming that after the age of six a foreign child is less "integratable." Clearly, a policy of this sort would only aggravate already serious problems of family fragmentation.

Until November 1981, the grown children of migrants were permitted to bring spouses from Turkey. New laws complicated the situation, mandating that the spouse in Turkey wait a minimum of one year after the time of marriage before being allowed to apply for a visa. The marriage's very foundation, then, is based upon a mandatory separation at its inception. Thus, the policy of family separation and fragmentation reproduces itself unto a second generation, and a third, as the young bride (*gelin*) often finds herself pregnant and husbandless throughout the minimum one-year waiting period.

Unemployment, Xenophobia, and the Greens

In the 1970s, the growth in the number of Germans unemployed was paralleled by an increase in popular resentment and xenophobia against the foreign migrants. The population of Turks, often said to be around two million, was constantly posed against the same number of Germans unemployed. Despite the fallaciousness of this reasoning—most of the unemployed Germans would not have considered taking the jobs occupied by Turks—for the popular press and the center-to-right political wing the Turkish problem came to be seen as one where "foreigners are taking our jobs."

Various solutions were proposed, discussed, and implemented. In addition to severe legal restrictions on family reunion, residence requirements, and the like, in 1983 a program of "go-home premiums" came into being. Under the terms of this program, monetary incentives were offered to Turks who agreed to cancel their work and residence permits and to return to Turkey. The expression used by Turks for the program translates as "killing passports" since one's passport became essentially invalid, or "dead," as far as any future possibility to return to work or live in Germany was concerned.

The program was a controversial one, and misleading as well. Advertisements for this program claimed that a family might qualify for up to 10,500 DM. However, once various sorts of deductions were made (for child allowance received, early pensions, and so on), the end sum of the premium was often considerably less. Even without the deductions, however, there was little in terms of productive investment that a returnee could do with this amount of money in Turkey, since the sum was insufficient to start any sort of business, buy a taxi, or the like. The issue of the "go-home premiums" was a very controversial one, and a certain amount of political activity was mobilized around it. The political Left became especially engaged in the issue, with Turkish and German grass-roots organizations and parties trying to educate foreigners about the disadvantages of the program. The premium program was short-lived, but unemployment has continued to grow, as has violence and resentment against the resident foreign community.

West Germany's Green Party involved itself in the movement to rescind the go-home premiums. The Greens, along with some branches of the Social Democrats and like-minded sympathizers, have consistently played the role of an opposition to the ruling Christian Democrats on many issues regarding foreigner policy. Many of these Germans would identify themselves as part of the loosely defined "alternative" community. (This is a sort of countercultural assemblage of people, life-styles, and institutions often directly opposing a right-wing establishment.) In some sense, these Germans of the alternative persuasion fancy themselves as the mediators between Turkish and German communities. The many alternative storefront community centers in Turkish neighborhoods bear witness to this commitment. Most of these are organized and managed by young Germans committed to "*Ausländerarbeit*" literally, "foreigner work" (in some ways roughly analogous to Northern whites in the 1960s active in the American civil rights movement), although Turks often are on the staff of such centers. The types of centers vary, from tenant rights groups committed to halting real estate speculation, to neighborhood development projects, to centers for Turkish girls and women offering free social work, psychological and legal services, literacy and language classes in Turkish and German, homework assistance for school-age girls, crafts, and sewing and cooking courses. In extreme cases, these centers may offer shelter and assistance to runaway girls and women.[8] There are also dozens of Turkish and German-Turkish storefront day-care centers, the *Kinderläden*.

The position of the German Left tends to be pro-integration and morally against any policy that would send the migrants back to Turkey. They feel that Germany has a responsibility toward the migrants, who were, after all, brought in order to help the Germany economy. This position has led to a great deal of discussion on "integration." The quotation marks suggest that what these Germans intend by "integration" is not necessarily what North Americans might suspect. The way in which the term is commonly used in this context implies what in North American would be called assimilation. A notion of multiculturalism or pluralism as it is understood in the United States is not generally part of this discourse. In other words, these advocates of integration would have the Turks dress, behave, and speak like Germans. Integration is not envisioned as a society where Turkishness looses its stigma; rather, it would be one where the marks of Turkishness fade away. Despite this idealistic vision, the recent history of relations between Germans and Turkish immigrants has been characterized by conflict rather than any sort of integration.

Labor Relations, Ethnic Relations

One arena where to be Turkish is indeed marked is that of labor relations. This is an area that has been characterized by tensions and an absence of solidarity. Foreigners have their own separate branches of trade unions, and the problems and issues for German workers are often quite different from those of their foreigner colleagues. For example, in the famous action at the Ford plant in Cologne in 1973, twelve thousand Turks staged a wildcat strike in support of five hundred coworkers, mostly Turkish, who had been fired. The workers, members of the large IG Metall (Metal Workers Union, one of the seventeen unions of the *Deutsche Gewerkschaftsbund* [DGB], German Trade Union Federation) found themselves isolated from their union. The local union official unsuccessfully attempted to persuade the strikers to return to work, and eventually "declared the Turkish work stoppage to be illegal and political in nature."[9] The strike was broken "by employers and police with the active co-operation of German union leaders and works councilors, causing a great deal of bitterness and anti-union feeling among foreigners." The union's cooperation with management, police, and, indeed, the Turkish embassy led to a violent confrontation between German trade unionists and "the striking foreign workers that left some eighty injured."[10]

The Ford Cologne strike served as a catalyst for many other strikes by foreign workers. During the period of the Ford Cologne strike, there were "over 80 strikes in West German factories involving around 122,000 workers in wildcat strikes in which Turks and other foreigners played a major role."[11] In 1973 West Germany saw about two hundred spontaneous strikes in which guest worker participation was central.

Not unexpectedly, then, did the *Anwerbestoppe*, the cessation of worker recruitment, come in late 1973. Some have called the militance of foreign workers an "underlying cause" of the stoppage.[12] (This was clearly not the only reason for it; as mentioned above, the international oil crisis and economic recession coincided with the wave of *Ausländerstreiks*, the foreigner strikes.) The DGB labor federation has supported the cessation of foreign labor recruitment:

> The DGB has consistently and categorically refused to accept the concept of permanent immigration. . . . The DGB has called for measures to encourage foreigners to return to their countries of origin. It continues to reject voting rights for foreigners in local elections, and opposes the European Trades Union Congress' demand for full social and labour market equality of foreign workers and their dependents.[13]

In fact, according to the DGB official who represented unions on the board of the Labor Office, Edmund Duda,

> In order to protect German employees, all legal possibilities must be utilized to send home foreign workers who are no longer needed. If they do not go voluntarily, regulations

which permit their expulsion will just have to be applied
more stringently.[14]

In the period since 1973, when unemployment was on the rise, workers'
struggles revolved around plant closures and redundancies. According
to labor law, work councils and unions were included in decisions about
firings and compensation.

> Many German employers have followed the strategy of using
> dismissals of foreign workers to cushion German workers from
> the effects of declining employment. On the whole, unions and
> work councils seem to have gone along with this policy.
> Indeed it could hardly have been carried out without their
> cooperation.[15]

This is not to imply, however, that there have not been situations
where united fronts of German and foreign workers produced mutually
beneficial results. As Castles points out, "there is growing awareness
that plant closures can only be effectively combated by a united labor
force."[16] In the early 1980s German and foreign workers together fought
against redundancies at three Frankfurt factories (VDM metal works,
Adler office machines, and Rockwell-Golde engineering works). Their
efforts proved successful in the latter two instances.[17]

Diversity in the Migrant Community

The divisions between segments of the German population find
parallel divisions within the foreign community. Although this essay focuses on the Turkish community, which makes up 50 percent of the
foreign workers, it should be remembered that many other national
groups are represented as well. First, reproducing the Germans' perception of them, the many nationalities place themselves within a hier-
archically ordered schema. European *Gastarbeiter*, from Christian—
that is, non-Islamic—areas clearly rank at the top. Italians, Greeks, and
Yugoslavs comprise this group. Spaniards and Portuguese, though less
numerous, also would be ranked here. Italians would probably be at the
top of the pecking order. The more distant and different from German
society—in terms of social, cultural, and physical proxemics—the
further down a group finds itself. That the Turks occupy the lowest rung
is indicated linguistically. The word "Turk" has come to be synonymous
with "*Ausländer*" as a sort of lowest common social denominator in
many contexts.[18]

Among the various migrant groups, internal differentiation is also
apparent. For example, urban Turks from western Turkey often feel little if any kinship with their poorer rural compatriots. Worse yet, from
their perspective, are the Kurds from eastern Anatolia, whom they re-

gard as little better than wild, primitive barbarians. The self-designated "westernized" urban Turks sense no end of shame and resentment toward their "backward, embarrassing" compatriots, who, they say, give *all* Turks, even the well-integrated, modern ones, a bad name. They also blame them for the considerable *Ausländerfeindlichkeit*—prejudice, ill will, stereotyping, and xenophobia—that most Turkish *Gastarbeiter* claim to experience.

Alternatively, the experience abroad proves liberating for many Kurds who, for the first time, find themselves free to express themselves as Kurds, and to use the Kurdish language. (It is illegal even to write in Kurdish in Turkey.) Kurdish political and cultural organizations and parties have proliferated in Western Europe at a rapid pace. This is in sharp contrast to the situation of Kurds in eastern Turkey, much of which is still governed by martial law. In Turkey, the Kurds are known as "Mountain Turks" and are subjected to severe repressive assimilationist policies. These include deportation to non-Kurdish regions and widespread imprisonment and torture for any suspicion of sentiments or expression of Kurdish self-determination.

Even in the foreign, German context, Kurds from Turkey sometimes complain that Turks resent them for speaking Kurdish and dismiss their claims of a separate identity. In Turkey, monolingual Kurdish children routinely experience severe corporal punishment when they enter first grade with no knowledge of Turkish. Ironically, in the diaspora situation Kurdish children also suffer because they can speak only Kurdish. In bilingual schools they are included under the Turkish rubric when they are assigned to foreigner classes. Yet when the teachers see that they are unable to communicate in either Turkish or German, they are sometimes presumed to be retarded and placed in special classes or schools for this "problem."

An additional dimension that often cross-cuts the urban-rural or Turkish-Kurdish one is based on religious affiliation, namely, the cleavage distinguishing the Turks and Kurds who are Sunni Muslim from those who are Alevi. Though large segments of the Turkish population, particularly urban middle and upper classes, the military, and the bureaucratic/civil servant class, consider themselves secular, much of the population remains devoutly Sunni Muslim. This is not insignificant in light of the sixty years of official governmental antireligious policy, education, indoctrination, and propaganda programs promoting westernization from above. But the Alevis complicate the picture. They are followers of a heterodox Shi'ite Muslim belief system. Population estimates for the Alevis range from five to ten million, a significant percentage of Turkey's population of fifty million. To religious Sunni Muslims the Alevis are worse than infidels. The Alevis are considered heretics, to whom all sorts of apocryphal, immoral traits are assigned. Having become accustomed to the role of underdog for centuries, the Alevis have, as a result, developed a practice of dissimulation. They have often found their way to the forefront of antiestablishment, leftist social movements. They identify with a tradition revering martyrdom and mysticism; indeed, many of their heroes were poet-bards, martyred by the Ottoman authorities. They have suffered executions and massacres in recent, Republican times, as well as earlier under the Ottomans. And Alevis are found within both Kurdish and Turkish communities. Some social scientists and some migrants as well believe that they represent a disproportionately high number of the Turkish *Gastarbeiter*.

Alevi identity assumes a complex myriad of expressions, depending on the perceived salient "other," which in turn implies a specific mode of affiliation. For many Alevis and Sunnis, whether Turks or Kurds, life in diaspora offers the first close encounter with each other. In some cases, centuries-old prejudices and traditionally informed behavior continue; at other times, it is overcome, giving way to their common "Turkishness" or *Gastarbeiter* identity. Some Alevis subsume their Aleviness in favor of a Kurdish nationalist or "ethnic" identity. Others, such as the Turkish-speaking Turkomen from western Anatolia, feel no kinship with Kurds and claim to be the original, purest of Turks, tracing descent to central Asian Turkic nomads. Still others strive for a national, political solution, envisioning an "Alevistan," similar to the Kurdistan advocated by Kurdish separatists.

With such activity within the Turkish migrant community it should not be surprising that different components within it exhibit vastly different responses to their lives in Germany and to the possibility of repatriation. For example, to date, very few Kurds and Alevis seem to have repatriated; the large minority of the repatriates are returning to central and western Anatolia, and to cities and towns.[19]

A growing response of second-generation young adults who, if not born, have been raised in Germany, has been to decide to remain even if their parents repatriate. More and more they are finding their way into German professions and workplaces—as Turks. Turkey for this group is a place with which they strongly identify on an affective level, but their practical associations are minimal. For many, Turkey is a place they have visited only a few times during school vacations. Moreover, it is well known that returnees often face serious problems readjusting. The legal and financial difficulties can be considerable, but the social reintegration often proves to be formidable. Frequently disillusion and disappointment lead to depression, as the returnees find themselves labeled "German-like" by their compatriots and as such are not socially accepted.

Germanness and Foreignness

When German-German unification monopolized West Germany's interests, priorities, and budgets, a question many asked was "What will happen to the Turks?" Will they be displaced by East German workers? Many experts believed that redefinition of German-German relations would lead to changes in government policy toward foreigners, ultimately resulting in fewer benefits and more restrictive political rights. For a time in 1989, growing pan-German nationalism—particularly acute in the wake of unification euphoria—seemed to be moving hand in hand with the growth of the extreme right neofascist party, the Republikaner, whose platform was unambiguously antiforeigner. More recently, a strong wave of German patriotism, which has still often been anti-immigrant, has been associated with the ruling Christian Democratic party.

With the unification of the two Germanys, the political rights that workers in the Democratic Republic enjoyed are lost, and subsumed to the terms and conditions of the Federal Republic. An interesting byproduct of the German-German merger is the transformation of the very meaning of *Ausländer*, "foreigner." It is an instance of the convergence and divergence of the categories of ethnic, foreigner, and native, in the case of East Germans. For forty years they had been citizens of a separate sovereign nation; they had been foreigners, or foreign natives at best. Now, in a matter of months, they are the native foreigners, yet of an extremely different order than the Turks, who, if not quite native, are at least the local foreigners. The newly arrived and reunited East Germans have publicly demonstrated time and again open resentment and xenophobia against the resident foreigners, who, they feel, are reaping the benefits they themselves deserve as Germans.

The group that somewhat mediates this opposition is yet a different category—those people or descendants of German stock who, due to fortuitous historical and political circumstances, live in what in 1937 were the eastern portions of the German Reich. Until the onslaught of East Germans beginning in September 1989, this population of so-called ethnic Germans constituted the largest new immigrant group of the past several years. Most of these ethnic Germans have come from present-day Poland, and allegedly most are monolingual Poles. In addition, it was supposedly relatively easy to claim ethnic legitimacy by purchasing a German genealogy on the Polish black market. The historical and moral dilemmas implied by this are considerable. Not least of the problems is that of implicit if not explicit racism, namely, that rather tenuous "German" Poles were immediately eligible for citizenship, full social services and assistance, and legal integration into West German society. By the same token, Turks born and educated in West Germany, speaking fluent German, are not eligible for this

privileged treatment, not being members of the correct ethnic—dare
one say racial—stock. But, after September 1989, this group of ethnic
Germans has been superseded by "real," no longer spurious, Germans
from the GDR. The relations between the long- established Turkish
community and the new arrivals assume different dimensions,
unfortunately often tension-ridden, as they compete for access to the
same jobs, resources, housing, and services.

Some Concluding Thoughts

At the beginning of this essay I discussed the origins of this
historical instance of migration. I mentioned the relationship between
the erection of the Berlin Wall, the onset of the Cold War, and West
Germany's sudden need for cheap labor. We have seen that the
opening of the wall has brought with it unforeseen consequences, for
Germans and Turks alike, and it has signaled a new chapter in the
postwar history of Germany, and ultimately for Turkey. Though the
conclusion to this story of migration has yet to be written, many
observers fear that the ominous signs for the future are already clear.
The legal and social structures that define the lives of the migrants can
be expected to change, and these changes most likely will privilege the
new Eastern Germans over groups such as the Turks. With the
tumbling of walls and regimes throughout Eastern Europe, the
definitions, boundaries and modes of political and economic inclusion
and exclusion have already begun to change at a rapid pace. With 1992
and the integration of Europe, the ramifications for migrants from
Turkey, an associate member of the European Community, look bleak
indeed.

Turkey for years has nurtured hopes about EC membership; after
the tumultuous events of autumn 1989, it would appear that Hungary,
Poland, and Czechoslovakia have jumped the queue.

Clearly, the relations between the migrants and the dominant
national culture—those who exercise authority over the prevailing
definitions of political and cultural discourse—are shifting. Thus,
aspects of Turkish identity and status in Germany are undergoing a
redefinition of a sort, in light of these changes. As the former East
Germans are politically incorporated into a unified Germany, we can
expect new sets of relations to emerge.

Notes

1. Suzanne Paine, *Exporting Workers: The Turkish Case* (Cambridge, 1974), 158.

2. One of the outstanding expectations is a wallpaper factory on the outskirts of (European, Thracian) Istanbul, which is also one of the original worker cooperatives. The worker-owners of this factory saw the need for instituting managerial training programs; they have expanded to the point where they can employ nonreturnees, as well as repatriates.

3. John Swanson Paine, "The Consequences of Emmigration for Economic Development," in *Papers in Anthropology*, ed. Robert Rhoades (Norman, Okla., 1979), 39-56; F. Bovenkirk, *The Sociology of Return Migration* (The Hague, 1974).

4. Currently, "free zones" are being developed in southwestern Turkey; "free" from tariffs and taxation, the government hopes that these areas will provide economic inducement to lure major foreign investment. Turkey has been considered a high-risk area for foreign investors, primarily due to its unstable political situation. New economic policies based on free-market economies, Friedmanesque ideologies, and a floating Turkish lira have been instituted in the last several years. However, a continual thorn in Turkey's fiscal side has been repeated public censorship by the European Parliament, the European Community (formerly the EEC), and other international organization, on the issue of human rights violations. This has hampered investors, who may believe that the iron-fisted, militarily enforced nominal democracy in Turkey is actually a repressive pressure cooker, and the possibility remains for a reversion to the situation of the late 1970s, when the country was brought to a near standstill, due to constant strikes and civil violence, often aimed against foreign business and military targets.

5. Czarina Wilpert and Ali Gitmez, "A Micro-Society or an Ethnic Community--Social Organization and Ethnicity amongst Turkish Migrants in Berlin," *Immigrant Associations in Europe*, ed. John Rex and Czarina Wilpert (forthcoming), 7.

6. Wilpert and Gitmez, 7.

7. Ibid., 6.

8. Such centers for girls and women can be quite controversial in the Turkish community as they generally do not permit men on the premises except on special occasions. In 1984 a Turkish man burst into one such center in Kreuzberg, asked for a certain person, and upon being told that there was no one there by the name, proceeded to shoot the young women working there, killing one and severely injuring a second. The attendance at such center radically dropped after the incident, as parents and husbands did not permit their daughters and wives to go any longer. The Turkish "progressive" community along with some German feminist groups held a sympathy demonstration not long after the tragedy. Despite the demonstration, such unfortunate inci-dents reinforce for many Germans the stereotype of the violence and oppression lurking in the Turkish patriarchal society.

9. Mark Miller, *Foreign Workers in Western Europe: An Emerging Political Force* (New York, 1981), 107.

10. Miller, 107-08.

11. Ibid., 109.

12. Stephen Castles, *Here for Good: Western Europe's New Ethnic Minorities* (London, 1984), 155.

13. Ibid., 155.

14. Ibid., 152.

15. Ibid., 155.
16. Ibid., 155-56.
17. Ibid., 156.
18. This paragraph and what follows are based on ethnographic research summarized in Ruth Mandel, "We called for manpower, but people came instead—The Foreign Problem and Turkish Guestworkers in West Germany" (Ph.D. diss., Anthropology, University of Chicago, 1988).
19. Many parts of eastern Anatolia, or Kurdistan, are in a state of virtual civil war, and have been under martial law. Obviously this extreme situation plays a role in decisions about repatriation.

AN INTERNATIONAL
PERSPECTIVE

12

Insiders and Outsiders: The Political Economy of International Migration during the Nineteenth and Twentieth Centuries

James Foreman-Peck

Migration within national boundaries may largely be understood in an unchanging political and institutional framework. True, rural-urban migration can create pressures for political change in major cities, as the French and many other revolutions bear witness. But imposing restrictions on the movements of citizens is generally difficult, at least in democratic regimes. International migration is quite different. Interest groups within a country can relatively easily use the domestic political process to frame formal or informal agreements over the international movement of workers to serve their own ends. They can do so because "outsiders" are not seen to deserve the same rights as "insiders." For this reason informal agreements to limit the options of would-be immigrant workers can sometimes be implemented at the level of the shop floor or the union, where the differences between insiders and outsiders are often felt most acutely.

An altruistic body politic would initiate some restrictions upon the international movement of workers for health and safety reasons and perhaps to improve or compensate for inadequacies in the flow of information about job opportunities. A real-world economy and polity may impose upon migrant workers institutions that reflect the interests of the dominant group of insiders.

How effective these political responses to migration are in influencing the volume and character of labor movements is not a question that will be addressed here. Some maintain that the U.S. Quota Acts of 1921 and 1924 were not significant reasons for the decline in immigration to the United States in the twenties.[1] Instead, the reduction came because of the virtually complete diffusion of information among potential migrants about opportunities in the New World. On the other hand, there is reason to believe that the U.S. Immigration Act of 1952 diverted Caribbean migrants to the United Kingdom and that the nineteenth-century exclusion of Chinese from the regions of recent European settlement by law and taxation was decisive in determining the population of those areas.[2] Although the importance of explanations of institutional change largely derives from the belief that such transformations can radically alter the options for human action, the subject of this chapter does not depend upon an acceptance of that view. Here the concern is only to consider whether political economy can explain why and how migration has induced political and institutional changes that in turn alter future migration.

The fundamental principle of political economics is that the establishment, maintenance, and demise of institutions can be understood as the outcome of the interactions of self-interested individuals and groups trying to do the best they can for themselves as they themselves judge.[3] In explaining any set of institutional changes, it is usually apparent that a variety of other influences must be invoked, including inertia, chance and "domino" effects, and perhaps culture and class solidarity. Consequently, such theories can hope to predict and explain only broad tendencies, on the basis of the selection of the appropriate set of initial institutional and behavioral conditions. The greatest value of these theories is in the ordering of historical experiences to reveal new insights and interpretations of what otherwise might be a mass of neglected facts, neglected because their significance has not been revealed by being placed in a wider, more systematic context. The study of political and institutional responses to international migration in the nineteenth and twentieth centuries is one of these neglected areas.

At the risk of some repetition, the following section outlines the major productive changes in the world economy of the nineteenth and twentieth centuries that influenced the migration of labor. The second section then sets out the theory of how economic parameters will cause different reactions to migration, and the third section examines how far theorizing is supported by and illuminates historical experience.

Migration in the World Economy of the Nineteenth and Twentieth Centuries

The world economy of the nineteenth century differed in certain fundamental respects from that of the twentieth century and created different conditions for international migration. Very marked reductions in transport and communications costs, burgeoning populations, and expanding industrial production in the Western world created the economic links that firmly bound national economies together, often for the first time. These changes caused a quantum jump in world economic development. Vast new areas were opened up to far more intensive farming and raw material extraction for the world market. In turn, high-productivity agriculture and mining allowed urbanization and a stronger demand for services and for industrial goods. Structural transformations required radical shifts in labor supplies, which were drawn in some cases from enormous distances. Immigrant workers were pushed or pulled by their beliefs that job opportunities were better in regions of recent European settlement, in the United States, Argentina, Canada, Australia, New Zealand, or South Africa, in the plantations of Malaya or Guiana, even in the sweatshops of East London, than in the countries of their birth. Migration of the free succeeded the forced migration of slaves, although indentured and convict migration continued throughout the century.

Other things being equal, workers preferred to move a shorter distance, within their own countries, to enhance their incomes. Apart from anything else, their budget constraints and the difficulty of borrowing on the expectation of higher future incomes limited their fare money and therefore the distance that they could migrate. The indenture contract, whereby a worker agreed to work for an employer abroad for a fixed period in exchange for the employer paying the passage money, was a device for avoiding this problem. Domestic industrialization reduced the pace of emigration (although the biography of Carnegie senior, discussed below, suggests this is not invariably true), as did decelerating population growth.[4] Scandinavian and German migration therefore declined toward the end of the nineteenth century as these countries industrialized. Emigration from Italy, Austria-Hungary, Spain, and Russia, by contrast, accelerated at the same time, mainly because of increasing population pressure and too slow a pace of industrialization. During the 1840s, agricultural disaster pushed families out of Ireland and Germany, where industry provided little alternative employment.

Throughout the nineteenth century the United States absorbed the largest number of migrants. The proportion of foreign-born in the total population remained around 14 percent between 1865 and 1920.[5] Other countries attained higher proportions—76 percent in New Zealand in

1864, 30 percent in Argentina in 1914—but because these economies were so much smaller than the United States initially, their total immigrant volumes were much lower.[6] The migrant population in the United States was highly concentrated. Nearly half the population of Manhattan in 1910 consisted of foreign-born whites, and 40 percent of the population of New York as a whole came into that category. Of the other cities with populations of half a million or more (Boston, Baltimore, Chicago, Cleveland, Philadelphia, Pittsburgh, St. Louis), only in Baltimore and St. Louis was less than one-quarter of the population born abroad. Migrants were more likely to be illiterate than the native white population and were more likely to serve a prison sentence.[7]

Similar characteristics could be noted of those Russian Jewish migrants to the United Kingdom who were driven out by the 1882 Russian May Laws. This was by far the largest foreign immigrant group in the United Kingdom. More than half the nearly one hundred thousand resident by 1911 lived in the London borough of Stepney, and most of them worked in tailoring, shoemaking, or cabinetmaking. They were more likely to be convicted of a criminal offense but less likely to obtain Poor Relief than natives.[8]

The nineteenth-century international labor market was segmented between European and Asian workers. Half a million indentured workers, 80 percent from India, migrated to the British West Indies between 1834 and 1918. Perhaps three-quarters of a million went elsewhere, but very few moved outside tropical areas.[9] Although the Chinese were temporarily imported to build California's railroads, to shovel Peru's guano, and to restart South Africa's gold mines after the Boer War, these were exceptions.[10] More typical Chinese migrant occupations were tin mining in Malaya or working on plantations in the Dutch East Indies.

A less abstract appreciation of the opportunities open to migrants in the nineteenth-century world economy can be obtained from individual biographies. The drawback of this approach is that the readily available biographies emphasize the successes rather than the average experience or the failures in worldly terms. The background to migration is the nineteenth-century transport revolution exemplified by Jules Verne's *Around the World in Eighty Days*. In some respects, transport truth had run ahead of fiction, for Verne's book was inspired by an advertisement by the travel agent Thomas Cook along the same lines. By the turn of the century this excursion was being offered for £450 first class. Not only transport facilities but the prevailing political order was favorable to at least individual migration throughout the nineteenth-century world, as the career of Heinrich Schliemann demonstrates. Born in Mecklenburg in Germany in 1822, Schliemann was a nineteen-year-old cabin boy when he was shipwrecked off the coast of Holland.[11] After his rescue he eventually found work as a clerk and bookkeeper. His extraordinary facility for learning languages promoted him to a post at St. Petersburg at twenty-four. While he was visiting California in search of his missing brother, the state entered the Union and Schliemann acquired American citizenship. Schliemann returned to Moscow where he made his fortune in indigo, cotton, and tea. He learned more languages and traveled round the world by way of Egypt, India, China, Japan, and America. A careful reading of classical authors led him to fulfill a childhood dream by discovering the site of Troy in 1870 and the "treasure of Priam" in 1876.

The other two immigrants to be considered here both left their home countries at the same age through their parents' attempts to improve their job prospects. Each immigrant pursued very different careers, but their paths crossed nonetheless. The spread of the power loom ruined Andrew Carnegie's master weaver father and so in 1848, when Carnegie was thirteen, the family left Dunfermline in Scotland for the United States.[12] Once settled in Allegheny, Pennsylvania, Carnegie began work as bobbin boy, twelve hours a day. His father never made a success of the move, but Andrew's enormous energy took him to superintendent of the Pittsburgh division of the Pennsylvania Railroad at twenty-three. From there he quickly moved into manufacturing, proving successful because of an attention to controlling costs that his competitors neglected. By the time U.S. Steel was formed in 1901, Carnegie's personal fortune amounted to $300 million. During his lifetime he gave away an even greater figure. Fifteen years after Carnegie emigrated from Dunfermline, Samuel Gompers left his native London. Like the Carnegies, the Gompers moved to alleviate economic distress. Gompers senior, a Jewish cigar maker, could not earn enough for his growing family. His union's emigration fund, the nineteenth-century alternative to unemployment benefits, therefore subsidized the passage to the United States.[13] In 1886 Samuel Gompers became first president of the American Federation of Labor. It was in this capacity that his career touched Carnegie's, for the AFL backed the famous and bloody Homestead Strike against Carnegie's steel company.

The major shift in the pattern of international migration and world economic development between the world wars came less because of economic changes than because of the altered political and institutional environment. Even allowing for the ending of extensive development in the regions of recent European settlement, it was much more the redrawing of national boundaries in Europe and restrictions such as the U.S. Quota Acts that disrupted the nineteenth-century pattern. Then the world depression of the 1930s hit the temperate zone primary product exporters, already suffering from falling prices, particularly hard. Nations such as the United Kingdom which had been net suppliers of workers to the world, became countries of net immigration as migrants returned. In France, the depression reversed the direction of internal labor migration as well, with a movement from the towns and industry back to the family farms.[14]

Rapid economic growth after the Second World War created an entirely new configuration of internal labor migration. Latin America and the Caribbean, formerly a host region for migrant workers, now became a source. International migration within Europe intensified. Some migration was a consequence of the Cold War and the Iron Curtain in Europe. As late as 1961 the construction of the Berlin Wall separated industry in the West from the workers in the East. Labor shortage in West Berlin was remedied by Turkish immigrant workers. For northwestern Europe as a whole, labor was drawn first from southern and eastern Europe, and then reserves in less developed countries were tapped. Before 1950, the majority of Italian emigrants left Europe, but as the postwar boom got underway they stayed in the continent, many of them going to Switzerland.[15] As Italian economic growth accelerated into line with population growth in the 1960s, migration from Italy began to decline. Greek migration showed a similar pattern but with a lag of almost a decade. Greek workers went mainly to America or Australia until 1960. Thereafter, they typically migrated to West Germany. Before the end of the decade emigration was on the decline as economic development at home progressed.

Imperial and postimperial links after 1945 now provided reverse flows to those of the nineteenth century. West Indians migrated to Britain and Algerians to France. Within the European group lacking colonial connections, some, notably Switzerland, Germany, and Austria, regulated labor inflows in accordance with economic conditions and were loath to encourage immigrant family settlement.[16] When in 1973-74 the next major downturn in economic activity occurred, this guest-worker policy allowed the host countries to repatriate labor and to avoid unemployed immigrants drawing on state benefits. At least for Irish emigration, these welfare state benefits, together with high taxation, had become an increasingly important influence upon the gains to be had from migration.[17]

The Institutional Economics of Migration

In a growing world economy the relative scarcities of land, labor, and capital in different parts of the globe will be changing all the time. Population expansion and capital accumulation vary from country to country. When coupled with transport costs, information flows, and political upheavals, these determine the growth, sources, and destinations of international migration in the first instance.

Propensities to migrate are then modified by political and institutional responses.

The state, which is the principal instrument of this modification, is concerned with migration policy because of the traditional obligation to provide "defense" or "security" (often on the pragmatic grounds that these services in fact keep the rulers in power). On these grounds, the entry of foreigners, as potential enemy agents, must be regulated if the security threat is believed to originate outside the state. A state exercised by the prospect of insurrection rather than invasion can afford to be more lax about immigration, although emigration, as a potential means of escape for police suspects, will prove difficult. An elementary prediction then is that immigration restrictions will be imposed in wartime and, since inertia is a major force in political life, they may continue in force during the peace.

Even if in practice defense and law and order have frequently been the excuse for domestic oppression, an altruistic state, maximizing the well-being of society, would still be obliged to provide these services in some form, and in doing so would be concerned with the regulation of immigration. Equally, an altruistic state would regulate migration for reasons of public health, safety, and information, where the market may not take into account the direct impacts on others of individual migration decisions. Disease can spread rapidly on board immigrant ships and can be transmitted to the host country's port of entry, unless preventive measures are taken. Criminals may flee the first state of their felonies and begin a second criminal career in a country of immigration. Companies that gain from immigrant fares may create false expectations of the returns from immigration, or information flows as to job opportunities over long distances may become attenuated, so that some state clarification may be needed.

More realistic than the altruistic state as an instrument of immigration policy is one that is controlled by the wealthiest or most powerful groups within it. Policy is then determined by the sources and distribution of national income. More specifically, the underlying questions for understanding the political response to migration are first, who gains and who loses from the migration? Second, which groups are in a position to do anything about it? Third, what are the costs of implementing political change relative to other reactions?

The simplest cases to analyze theoretically are those of slavery, serfdom, or other legal or political forms where the owners of land in both the source and the destination country exercise coercive powers over the rest of the population. An exogenous stimulus, such as population growth in one area or the enhanced profitability of cultivation in another because of improved transport facilities or industrialization, changes the balance in one labor market and brings pressure on adjacent markets. A landowner-managed state that has become further integrated into the world economy will experience appreciation of land prices, an appreciation that will increase as the labor available to work the land increases. The state will therefore encourage immigration by the most effective means that are politically expedient, including slavery, the transportation of convicts, or subsidized passages for immigrants.   Wages will rise less as immigration increases, and the greater will be the gains to the landowners in the host country. In the source country, the state will have diametrically opposed interests and policies, if subject to similar exogenous stimuli. Typically, security needs, to maintain the prime emigration age labor force for military service, will pull in the same direction of restricting emigration. However, potential source countries run by landowners or capitalists are not necessarily subject to identical exogenous changes as potential destinations.   These source states might then regard emigration as a safety valve that prevents pressure for domestic political change; those who object most strongly to the prevailing distribution of income and authority can leave instead of agitating for new institutional arrangements. On the other hand, they may wish to prevent the emergence of centers of political opposition abroad that cannot be controlled.[18]

Between labor-managed states subject to similar stimuli, migration policies are equally opposed in the simplest instances. Emigration raises wages and is therefore to be encouraged by migration subsidies to unemployed workers and to potential colonists.   Destination countries must exclude migrants because they drive down wages and reduce the chances that domestic workers will find jobs (unless migrants bring their own capital with them). Thus, landowner- or capitalist-managed destinations together with democratic or worker-managed sources are the political combinations most conducive to an institutional environment favorable to migration.   Conversely, democratic or worker-managed destinations and landowner or capitalist sources are a combination least likely to encourage international labor flows. When land and capital holdings are concentrated, landowner and capitalist-managed states are authoritarian. The limiting case is the Communist state, which owns all land and capital within its boundaries. A difference here may be that the state no longer maximizes immigration since no individual benefits from the process. However, the USSR and East Germany negotiated state-to-state agreements to import labor from Bulgaria, North Korea, and Vietnam as if they were attempting to optimize.

These conclusions about the institutional response to migration opportunities are modified when human capital is taken into account. Labor is not homogeneous but has acquired a variety of skills; a person trained for one job will not necessarily be able or willing to undertake another. In consequence, immigrant workers with different skills may be complementary to host country labor.[19] Such workers could boost the productivity of destination country labor rather than reducing it at the margin by expanding the labor supply. For the host nation, the desirability of this type of immigrant worker is enhanced when investment in education and training is typically undertaken by the state. The donor state spends the money, but host nationals gain the benefits, a phenomenon labeled the "brain drain" after 1945.[20]

Welfare state benefits and taxation are a more general manifestation of the same principle. The benefits are, in a number of instances, a form of investment in human capital, and therefore migration is encouraged from states with high tax-financed benefits to those with low, once the migrants have taken advantage of the investment. Another aspect of welfare state benefits is likely to prompt a different type of migration into the higher-benefit, higher-tax state; those who are eligible for benefits and do not anticipate paying the taxes.[21] Reflections such as these underlie "guest worker" programs, intended to allow entry to workers without their families, families who would make demands upon the tax-financed education, health, and perhaps housing services of the host country.

In the long term, the average investment in human capital might determine the willingness of workers to migrate for a given wage. The wage must yield a reasonable return on the investment. Labor unprepared to work for rewards lower than those prevailing in the potential immigrant area does not threaten the level of wages there. Net movement of labor takes place only when the economy expands and thereby helps to sustain growth. These considerations suggest that labor-managed host economies would permit certain types of immigration but would discriminate against migrants from low-wage areas and/or against those with skills already in abundant supply. With economic development the importance of human capital grows, and therefore discriminatory restrictions can be expected to increase.

States may adopt policies toward immigrant workers either unilaterally or by agreement with source countries. An extreme case is where both countries are subject to the same state control. Thus a democratic recipient may wish to restrict immigration in some way but may be prevented from doing so by a (democratic) imperial power that has an interest in keeping open areas for settlement. More politically explosive is the case where the host wishes to restrict the rights of immigrants whom a powerful imperial donor claims to protect. Normally the relative strengths of donor and recipient are crucial to the policies ultimately agreed upon. A small country of emigration cannot hope to have much influence over a large immigration state that can pursue immigration policies in splendid isolation. Bilateral agreements will be most common among states of equal strengths and shared interests. Agreements intended to equalize employment conditions of migrant workers between states remove the threat that low-wage migrants pose to indigenous labor while securing gains from extending the labor market. A weak state can act only negatively, forbidding nationals to emigrate.

Throughout the above analysis the problems of formulating and coordinating policy in the interests of the dominant group(s) within the state have been ignored. This omission is now remedied. Policy in most states, and the institutions that embody that policy, emerge as a result of conflict and bargaining among a number of groups. Other groups interested in influencing policy may be insufficiently concerned to undertake the costs of organizing and instead prefer to take a "free ride" or merely to accept adverse outcomes. In a democratic regime, whether enough people feel they are sufficiently intensely affected by migration to make their opinions felt must depend upon the distribution of migrants, among other things. If immigrants are spread uniformly over a country and over jobs, then under most circumstances their effects on labor and housing markets are too small to rise above the threshold of political perception. However, the need to go where the jobs and support facilities are known to be available, and the key role of earlier immigrants in providing this knowledge, mean that almost invariably migration is highly concentrated spatially and by occupation. Employment and housing conditions of native workers in the receiving trades and areas are likely to suffer severe adverse effects. To that extent their elected representatives will be made to feel that immigration is the burning issue.

In a state where the franchise is limited or not taken seriously, this type of political reaction will normally be ineffective, but similar bargaining problems may arise. Just as not all or only a minority of workers will feel themselves adversely affected, so not all capitalists will be able to gain from importing foreign labor. Some industries have the option in an open world economy of moving to other countries, if they feel domestic policies are not maximizing their net returns. Other industries cannot afford to be so footloose and therefore must invest more in lobbying on behalf of immigration. Landowners can only take what rents they can get when pursuing policies to advance their interests, in contrast to more mobile capital. They will therefore be inclined to fight harder for free immigration than will capitalists. The outcome of the above conflicts of interests depends upon particular conditions in each nation. A state where land is widely distributed in small holdings with little demand for labor outside the family would press for different immigration policies from one in which land was concentrated in the hands of a few.

When a great deal of immigration has taken place in a democratic nation, migrants themselves may come to be a significant force in politics, although they will not necessarily be more favorably inclined toward immigrants in general than the native labor force. To the extent that the labor market is segmented and less recent arrivals compete directly with more recent migrants, immigrant workers may oppose further migration, especially during trade depressions, more strongly than native workers, secure and insulated in their "primary" labor markets. A countervailing tendency may arise from foreign-born workers' being likely to favor future migrants from the same home country over either native or other immigrant labor. Preferred policies will therefore be so discriminatory that when migrants originate from a considerable number of different countries, an agreed-upon national policy is impossible.

In these circumstances, "democratic" immigration policies are likely to be pursued more sectionally, at the level of the trade union. The effectiveness and scope of these policies therefore depends upon factors that influence the formation and growth of trade unions. Industries with large plants and impersonal relationships between workers and management may be expected to show relatively high degrees of labor organization, as a means of defense against the arbitrary exercise of authority. A second basis for the prediction is that the costs of organizing a given number of workers are lower when they are concentrated in a few large plants. A low labor turnover, traditionally found in sectors with little female and casual employment, is equally necessary, for workers without firm-specific capital have little incentive to stay and bargain rather than to vote with their feet. Monopolized or "trustified" industry creates a surplus that labor might aim to capture by organizing. Finally, legal immunities and recognition of trade unions obviously encourage union growth. Immigration will be lower in sectors with these characteristics and under these conditions. Through control over the workplace a strong union can determine whether and which immigrants will be allowed employment in the primary, unionized sectors. Unions can ensure that immigrants are no threat to union members by permitting migrants to work only in the low-wage, high-turnover, nonunionized secondary labor markets. Without any central government legislation, immigration can be transformed from a substitute into a complement for domestic labor. An alternative, less selfish, strategy is to absorb the immigrants into the union, thereby ensuring that wages and conditions are not undercut.

Returning to government controls over migration, these may take a number of forms ranging from taxation to the enforcement of indenture contracts to outright prohibition. Taxes or subsidies on immigrants or emigrants can distinguish between more and less favored groups. They can be designed as either revenue or protective taxes. Once bureaucracies concerned with migration grow large, taxation may come to be mainly implicit, that is, forcing migrants to spend time and resources negotiating for visas. Subsidies are most easily and effectively payable on fares, since the money cannot be diverted to other purposes and constitutes a once-and-for-all commitment to selected persons. The indenture contract is even cheaper but must prove difficult to enforce where there is much free land or a large urban employment sector. Measures to support and assimilate newly arrived immigrants will reduce return migration and may be a particularly effective policy instrument. Special taxation, persecution, or harassment of those who the state wishes to emigrate, or of those who wish to emigrate but whom the state wishes to retain, may be effective but contravene a widely held belief that citizens, if not foreigners, should be treated equally. In all but totalitarian states these policies will be unsustainable in the long term for that reason. The model described above has adopted a simple view of motivation. Introducing ideology to the analysis, as a constraint or as a means of defining goals, could radically affect the conclusions. Nineteenth-century liberalism, social Darwinism, or nationalism might be responsible for policies other than those predicted by the simple political-economy model, if they were powerful influences.

The Political Response to Migration

The political response to migration was markedly different in the nineteenth century from that in the twentieth because of the pattern of economic development. Nineteenth century Europe, as a continent of net emigration, possessed no legislation on immigration of specific classes of foreigners, with the exception of Jews in Russia and Jesuits in Germany. On the other hand, immigrants had no general right to enter or to remain in a country of continental Europe, and the state claimed a general power of expulsion.

Geographical factors dictated a greater concern with national security on the continent than in the United Kingdom, a concern that was reinforced in some states by the repressive nature of their regimes. Germany required all residents, citizen and foreigner, to carry proof of identity but not a passport or identification papers. Russians needed a passport for emigration, and applicants were investigated by the secret police. If permission for emigration was granted, it was valid for only three weeks, and the cost amounted to an emigration tax. Not surprisingly, only about 10 percent of Russian emigrants were estimated to have the required passports at the turn of the century.[22]

Security considerations in the United Kingdom reached a peak of importance at the time of the French Revolution and the Napoleonic wars. In 1793, ship captains were obliged to report to customs officers the number and details of foreigners on board. Similar legislation was enacted in the United States in 1798. Much like U.K. legislation of the 1960s and the 1970s, the British statute of the end of the eighteenth century required foreigners to have a royal license before being allowed to settle in the country. The law conferred great discretion upon the Crown over the attachment of conditions to licenses, over the exemption of foreigners from licenses, and over the removal of foreigners. After the Napoleonic wars, immigration restrictions were gradually relaxed, as the security threat receded, but concern about the financial implications of freed slaves did promote legislation in 1832 that was in some ways a harbinger of the twentieth century and, in other ways, a marked contrast. Ship captains were required to declare whether any natives of Africa were on board and to supply a bond of one hundred pounds to reimburse any parish that had subsequently to support such a person.[23]

The abolition of slavery expanded the demand for Asian indentured labor and imposed conflicting pressures on the minimalist British state of the midcentury. The indenture contract was one of the more effective ways of encouraging and regulating international flows of migrant workers in the nineteenth century. Because the abolition of slavery in British colonies in 1834 gave the first great impetus to such migration, the contractual form has been identified with slavery, instead of as a means of overcoming labor market imperfections that made both parties to the bargain better off than they otherwise would have been. Between 1834 and 1837, the sugar planters of Mauritius imported about seven thousand laborers from Calcutta, typically on five-year contracts that guaranteed the worker five rupees a month together with food and clothing. The only control imposed by the colonial government of British India was that emigrants had to appear before a magistrate and to satisfy him as to their freedom of choice and knowledge of the conditions they were accepting.[24]

The British Parliament discussed this form of labor contract and suspended indentured emigration in 1837. A report of 1840 noted there were some bad masters in Mauritius and some apathetic or brutal ship captains, but that did not constitute a condemnation of the system itself. J. P. Grant's recommendations in this report formed the basis of subsequent policy. He proposed that a Protector of Emigrants should be located at each permitted port, that the laws of the colony of immigration should be examined before indenture be permitted, and that a return passage for the worker should be guaranteed. Indentured-labor migration to Jamaica, British Guiana, and Trinidad was authorized under these conditions in 1844. Eleven years later, when St. Lucia and Grenada applied for permission, the government of India objected to their labor laws, which were duly changed respectively in 1858 and 1856.

Indentured labor contracts were not confined to pairs of countries within the British Empire. Contracts between the Indian government and French, Danish, and Dutch colonies were agreed to between 1860 and 1872. The Indian government noted that emigrants were made better off as a result of the system, but because migrants were such a small proportion of the population as a whole, and therefore the well-being of the total population was unlikely to be affected, they saw no justification for spending money to encourage the system. Between 1842 and 1870 Mauritius took the bulk of the indentured workers, about three hundred and fifty thousand; British Guiana, Trinidad, and the French colonies hosted respectively approximately eighty thousand, forty thousand, and thirty thousand.

Colonial governments were typically those in which planter interests were powerful. Apart from the constraints imposed by the imperial power and the advantages that accrued from membership of an empire, their policies therefore most closely resembled those of Brazil and Argentina. At a time when communications were slow and information flow poor, abuses of indentured workers were not easy to prevent. Returning Indian immigrants from Natal in 1871 reported that, when their terms of indenture expired, they were expected to sign new indenture contracts. Otherwise they were treated with the same brutality as African workers, being whipped for alleged neglect of work. The Indian government did use its powers to prevent such abuses where possible. Countries outside the empire were less amenable to persuasion, and therefore the only policy option was to exclude them from the list of permitted destinations for indentured labor. Thus, by 1910 emigration to the French colonies had been suspended for twenty years as a consequence of complaints about the treatment of workers. By then the only non-British Empire country to which indentured Indian labor went in any numbers was Surinam or Dutch Guiana, where despite some serious riots, Indian government official opinion was impressed by the effectiveness of labor legislation.

As a destination for their migration and the controller of a port of embarcation, the British Empire also regulated Chinese migration. In 1853, Parliament relaxed the minimum physical conditions under which Asians could be shipped, but two years later the Chinese Passengers Act attempted to prevent abuses in the transport of emigrants from ports in the China Sea. The governor of Hong Kong was supposed to establish and enforce minimum conditions of shipment but was generally reckoned to have been rather ineffective in this regard.

American policy toward immigration was equally minimalist, but that was largely a matter of the ease with which immigrants could become voters and of the slavery issue. An anti-immigrant "Native American" movement became a force to be reckoned with from the 1830s, somewhat counteracted by the Democratic party's recruitment of foreign-born voters. The wave of immigration of the latter 1840s and 1850s encouraged a burst of nativist (and anti–Roman Catholic) sentiment that by 1855 suggested a nativist might win the presidency. As matters turned out, Northern nativists, often antislavery, were unable to ally themselves with nativists in the South. With the abolition of the slave trade, the Southern states could not encourage legal "immigration" of the type favored by their landowners. They were anxious to restrict free immigration so as not to disturb the federal balance between the states. After the 1856 presidential election, nativist support transferred from the Whig to the Republican party, which, however, made no formal concessions to them lest vital immigrant votes be lost.[25]

As a consequence of this balance of political pressures, at midcentury the first immigration legislation was concerned only with public health. New York led the way in 1847 at a time when ship fever (typhus) was rampant. Under New York law and a federal act of 1853, diseased or infirm immigrants were excluded. Not long after, the struggle between economic groups within the country at last came to be reflected in migration legislation. Congress passed a contract labor law in 1864 authorizing contracts made abroad to import foreign labor and permitting the establishment of the American Emigrant Company to act as an agent for American businessmen. The law was repealed four years later. Chinese workers were excluded in 1882, and acts requiring literacy tests were passed by Congress, only to be vetoed by President Cleveland and, later, by Taft. Through the influence of the Knights of Labor, contract labor—workers whose fares were paid out of subsequent wages—was excluded by acts of 1885 and 1889.[26]

The greater influence of capitalists and landowners, together with the needs of post–Boer War reconstruction, explain the Cape of Good Hope's exemption of contract labor from the provisions of that colony's Immigration Law of 1902. Otherwise, toward the end of the century, pressure for tighter immigration controls mounted in most countries. On three occasions during the 1890s, the British Trades Union Congress passed motions objecting to immigration. Recession had always been a reason for labor to press for restrictions, as rioting New Zealanders did in 1879. The Chinese were the first group to be targeted for exclusion, though at first, except in the United States, they were discriminated against only indirectly. New Zealand imposed a ten-pound poll tax on non-European immigrants, a figure that was increased to one hundred pounds in 1899. Natal introduced a European literacy test in 1897 to exclude Asians. Australia lacked the ability rather than the desire to limit certain types of immigration until the formation of the Australian Commonwealth in 1901. As long as each Australian colony adopted a different immigration policy, the policy of any individual colony could be circumvented by migrants entering through a different colony. As interim measures the colonies had to content themselves with special taxes. One of the first laws passed by the new Australian Commonwealth in 1901 restricted immigration. Like Australia and New Zealand, British Columbia adopted a discriminatory poll tax as a means of keeping out Chinese, one year after the American exclusion act. U.S. and other Canadian general immigration taxes were much lower, two dollars a head, than the five-hundred-dollar tax on each Chinese immigrant imposed by British Columbia in 1903.[27]

Nineteenth-century Latin America more closely approximates a set of host countries governed by landowning classes than the other regions of recent European settlement. Immigration rules, therefore, can be expected to differ from those elsewhere. Both Brazil and Argentina subsidized mass immigration to provide the elastic supply of labor that held wages down and rents up. Brazil, however, was distinguished by the central role played by slavery in the economy. Between 1800 and 1852, when the British navy ended slave imports, about 1.3 million slaves were transported to Brazil, amounting to more than one-fifth of the total increase in the country's population.[28] In contrast to the United States, slave breeding proved unprofitable and therefore, from the 1850s, immigration began to take off. Between 1885 and 1913, eleven million pounds was spent on immigration transport subsidies by the São Paulo and central governments. Presumably in Brazil an abundance of free land made indenture contracts unenforceable in the country of demand. It should be noted, though, that Brazil was not on the list of approved countries of immigration for India. The planters who paid for most of these subsidies through coffee taxes were happy to do so for two reasons: transport subsidies did not drive up labor costs and once the migrants were in Brazil, wages would be permanently lower even though the transport subsidy was paid only once per immigrant. During the period of rapid expansion of the São Paulo coffee sector, the subsidy policy was so successful that real wages of immigrants failed to rise between 1880 and 1914. A second indication of the success of the policy from the viewpoint of the planters was that immigrant living conditions were held so low that the Italian government tried to ban subsidized immigration to Brazil temporarily in 1902.[29]

Argentine expansion began in earnest rather later than Brazil's. Only in the 1880s did European weapons technology become efficient enough to defeat the Indians and drive them off their land.[30]

Ownership of that land then became very unequally distributed. Over 60 percent of pampas farmers were sharecroppers or cash tenants, whereas on the Canadian prairies, settled by migrants at much the same time, most farmers owned their own land.[31] The interest of large landowners in encouraging immigration was apparent to everybody, but the most effective way of doing so was not. A policy of providing free passages to Argentina for immigrants in the 1880s allegedly brought "a number of useless people, unfitted for any productive task whatever."[32] Such people could be filtered out only if migrants were required to make some financial commitment to the passage. Ultimately, Argentina had relatively little difficulty in getting labor; it received more European immigrants than any other Latin American country by 1914.

Subsidized migration to Australia at first sight seems to contradict the theoretical analysis. Fifty percent of arrivals in the 1870s were assisted and 10 percent in the 1890s.[33] As a democratic country Australia would be expected to restrict rather than to encourage immigration. Ad hoc supplementary conditions can be employed to save the theory, however; pressure to remove subsidies always mounted in recession, and Australia was a great distance from Europe by comparison with other host countries. When it is recognized that Australia was highly urbanized in the nineteenth century and that the subsidies were paid so that transport costs discriminated in favor of those trained in rural skills, the logic of Australian policy becomes clearer.[34] Rurally trained immigrants were a noncompeting group for the majority of Australians, providing complementary labor rather than substitute services.

During the nineteenth century the only regulations covering both host and source country of migration were provided by the existence of an empire. Not until the twentieth century do bilateral treaties emerge. Where the British Empire was concerned, Gladstone's conception of the relationship of Britain to her colonies had in the main been successfully implemented.[35] Immigration, as with other policy, was generally transacted by colonists as they wished, without coercion by the imperial power. The empire chose not to favor immigration from Britain over other European countries (although the majority of migrants did come from the United Kingdom). Only when the Australian states attempted to extend their anti-Chinese legislation to cover Indians, did the British government deny the bills the royal assent on the grounds that they discriminated against a country within the empire.[36]

Non–British Empire countries equally were not expected to discriminate against empire immigrants. If they did, then the Boer War suggests British migrants were likely to prove a Trojan horse. The discovery of gold at Witwatersrand in 1886 together with the cyanide extraction process caused an influx of foreign workers and capital, mostly British, into the Transvaal and Johannesburg. Transvaalers saw the immigrants as a threat to their newly regained independent, traditional way of life, while the migrants were upset by being denied the right to vote, by being exploited by the state-enforced dynamite monopoly, and by exorbitant railway rates fixed on political grounds. British demands, concentrating on the fair treatment of the "*uitlander*" migrants and especially on the admission to the franchise, culminated in the Boer War.[37]

Less radical solutions to migrants' rights were adopted by other source and host countries of more equal size and power. France and Italy negotiated the first bilateral labor treaty, which was signed in April 1904. France granted benefits and safeguards to the many Italian workers in France and also attempted to ensure that Italian competition would not be made more effective by low wages and poor working conditions. Italy agreed to complete the organization of its labor inspection service and to reduce the hours of work of women in industry.[38]

Reconstruction after the First World War and, in particular, France's need for labor multiplied similar treaties covering both industrial and agricultural, permanent and temporary workers. In 1919, France signed treaties with Poland and Italy. The following year an agreement was reached with Czechoslovakia, and later with Austria, Belgium, Romania, and Yugoslavia. The breakup of the Austro-Hungarian Empire required Austria to sign similar treaties with Czechoslovakia and Hungary in the 1920s, as well as one with Poland. Meeting Germany's demand for labor was facilitated by treaties with emigrant countries Poland, Yugoslavia, Lithuania, and Czechoslovakia.

Outside Europe, Portuguese Mozambique reached agreements on migrant workers with South Africa and British Southern Rhodesia. Imperial regulations governed migration from India to Ceylon and to the Straits Settlements and Malaya. In the New World, treaties were more problematic. The United States signed no bilateral agreements, and attempts to set up treaties between Italy and Brazil in 1921 and Poland and São Paulo in 1927 were unsuccessful. Source and host country were to pay for migration from the United Kingdom to the empire under the Empire Settlement Act of 1922, but the impact of the act upon migration was much less than its supporters had hoped.

Perhaps the most fundamental change in migration rules in the twentieth century was the American Quota Law of 1921. Immigration in any year was limited to 3 percent of the number of each nationality in the United States at the time of the 1910 Census. This did not produce the desired racial mix, which was fewer Southern Europeans and relatively more northern Europeans, and therefore the 1924 act reduced the quota to 2 percent of any nationality at the time of the 1890 Census. Particular industrial needs were accommodated by exempting Mexicans (for California agriculture) and Canadians (for logging). The Japanese joined the Chinese in the excluded category. This act had the effect of halving the 1921 quota. Further revisions were made in 1929. Granted that the United States was a democratic society, the introduction of the quota laws in the 1920s is predictable enough. The problem is to explain why they were not passed earlier. The severe rise in unemployment of 1921 naturally precipitated the legislation, but why did not the recession of 1907 produce the effect earlier?

As with pre–Civil War agitation the answer should probably be sought in the franchise and the importance of immigrant votes. Undoubtedly the political sentiment was there, as the Immigration Commission, which sat between 1907 and 1910, bears witness. Direct elections to the Senate from 1916 changed the rural-urban political balance, thus enhancing the political chances of immigration restrictions. Conceivably the opportunity for extensive development reduced pressure to restrict immigration but the closing of the frontier dates from 1890. Another hypothesis is that immigrant labor in general was of a different type, perhaps unskilled, from native, perhaps skilled, labor. Thus, immigration might have enhanced the productivity and wages of domestic workers. An alternative explanation is to recognize that other means of achieving host labor's ends were available apart from immigration restrictions. Discrimination against immigrants or in favor of selected groups of immigrants could be a preferred strategy, depending upon who controlled the relevant union or branches. That the skills and training of Irish immigrants to England in the 1840s fitted them for better jobs than they found is consistent with this interpretation.[39] On the United States railroads in 1910, immigrants accounted for one-half of all laborers but only one-tenth of the engineers and one-fourteenth of the ticket and station agents.[40] Admittedly, the immigrants may have been less well trained or less reliable than native-born workers. At Carnegie's Homestead works, control by the AFL-affiliated Amalgamated Association of Iron and Steel Workers ensured that the Welsh managed the rolling mills and the Irish, the Bessemer blast furnaces.[41] When vacancies appeared, the union would send abroad for immigrants of the "correct" nationality, rather than recruit locally. American union attitudes to immigrant labor were divided, most probably because so many trade unionists were foreign-born.

Unions controlled by domestic workers were almost invariably concerned that immigrants would undermine their bargaining position. That was one motive for unionizing them if possible. Thus, British union representatives at the beginning of the twentieth century complained of the Russian Jewish shoemakers and tailors' undercutting wages after Jewish union sections had dissolved.[42] British textile unions in the 1960s and 1970s successfully unionized Asian textile workers and thereby prevented any downward pressure on wages or removal of restrictive practices (ultimately to the detriment of the textile workers, who lost their jobs as a result of declining international competitiveness).[43] That unionization of immigrant workers was undertaken for the benefit solely of host-country labor has been a charge levied against the German unions of the 1960s, who have been accused of demonstrating little concern for the welfare of immigrant workers, once the threat they posed from outside the unions had been removed.[44]

The generally stagnant economic environment of the years between the world wars and heightened international tensions promoted restrictions on migration in most countries. Britain's 1905 Alien Immigration Act had turned out to be fairly innocuous. It was the First World War that tightened up the legislation as an emergency measure which was then embodied in the act of 1919. The following year a system of work permits was introduced. Commonwealth citizens remained free of controls, but the entry of Jewish refugees in the 1930s was restricted to avoid domestic political reactions comparable with those that had given rise to the 1905 act.[45]

After 1945, the great boom promoted new waves of migration. Frightened by the near invasion by the Japanese, Australia embarked upon a policy of encouraging immigration of selected groups in the hope that a larger population would make the country more secure.[46] Labor shortages in the face of strong demand played a part in the United Kingdom's reaffirming the right of Commonwealth citizens to enter. Until the American Immigration and Nationality Act of 1952 markedly reduced the number of Jamaican and other immigrants coming to the United States, new Commonwealth immigration to the United Kingdom remained small, however. Population growth in the Indian subcontinent contributed to Asian immigration in the United Kingdom exceeding West Indian from the beginning of the 1960s. The political reaction came quickly in 1962 when the first controls were introduced. In contrast to Germany and other European countries, employment vouchers were not used as a means of manpower planning but merely to limit the numbers of entrants. British immigration restrictions were further tightened in 1965, 1968, 1971, and 1981.

Increasing costs of human capital, together with a recognition of the complementary nature of shortage skills with those of the majority of the host-country labor force, encouraged the United States, Australia, Canada, and the United Kingdom from the mid 1960s to reduce discrimination by country of origin and to promote the immigration of certain skilled workers regardless of where they came from. Low-wage, less developed countries with poor working conditions suffered from this brain drain. The high-wage United States experienced an increase in professionally and technically trained immigrants, and thus saved on its costs of educational investment. At intermediate stages in the international wage hierarchy, the United Kingdom and Canada both lost, from emigration to the United States, and gained, from immigration from the less developed countries, with an indeterminate net effect.[47]

Bilateral agreements again began to flourish. West Germany reached agreement with Spain in 1960 for the equal treatment of workers, as did France and Algeria in 1962. As already noted, the break in the trend came in 1973–74. Democratic countries rid themselves of immigrant guest workers so that native labor would not suffer unemployment. The 11.5 million foreign workers in Western Europe by then had in any case reached the limit of the absorptive capacities of the host countries. Two years before the oil crisis, Switzerland had attempted to "stabilize" her migrant labor force, a policy that other Western European countries began adopting in 1972. Holland and West Germany banned the entry of non-EEC workers at the end of 1973 to protect native labor from the unemployment that then was emerging. In July 1974, France suspended immigration.[48]

American experience in the 1970s as a whole was rather different, with almost one-fifth of the increase in population being accounted for by those born abroad. When illegal immigration is added in, the proportion could rise above one-quarter.

Capital does not depend upon cheap immigrant labor, and to the extent that they were immediately absorbed into unions, immigrants in any case were not cheap. More effective for many large firms was to take work to the workers; capital migrated to potential labor-source countries instead of labor migrating to the capital-abundant host countries. Since the major world markets were also in host countries, and these states pursued increasingly restrictive trade policies, also to protect jobs, this strategy could be followed only to a limited extent. In a liberal world economy, a portion of West Germany's car industry that used a high proportion of immigrant workers would have been transferred to places such as Brazil, where the same American multinationals could have access to cheap and well-disciplined labor that had already contributed to Brazilian motor output exceeding that of the United Kingdom. The actual world economy of the 1970s and 1980s would not permit such major structural shifts. Instead, developed economies opted for more mechanization, including the introduction of robots, which in the absence of migration might have been introduced earlier.

Conclusion

Nineteenth-century intercontinental migration was mainly a response to the opportunities created by the imbalance between Western technological development and that of the rest of the world. In temperate zones, low-density populations whose economies were based on hunting or gathering could be displaced and their lands expropriated for Western-style development by Western labor for a world market.

In tropical zones, technological change, in particular transport costs, and expanding Western demand, were felt directly or indirectly. Thai rice cultivation expanded as an indirect effect to supply food for plantations or mines in other parts of the world that were producing sugar, rubber, or tin for the West. Workers in these activities were long-distance migrants, usually Chinese or Indian. Restrictions, statutory or social, upon where in the world economy they could work were intended to prevent these migrants from depressing Western wages.

As the regions of recent European settlement filled up, pressure mounted to exclude those who would only work for higher wages as well. In countries where labor had a large say in government, the interest in restricting immigration had always been present if foreign workers arrived in significant numbers or concentrations. In the United States, this tendency was attenuated by the rapid expansion of the nineteenth-century economy and by the desire and ability of some immigrant groups to favor their former countrymen over host-country or other source-country workers in employment. In the British Empire, restrictions on the migration of workers in either direction were officially frowned upon. Indeed, indenture labor contracts were supported to encourage Indian migration to tropical plantations. Where landowners or capitalists had the predominant influence in policy formation, as in Brazil or Argentina, immigration was officially encouraged because of the enhancement of land and capital values.

Whichever group controlled the state, when security was believed threatened, migration was restricted. In the more liberal states, the principal restrictions have been placed upon immigrants, whereas in repressive countries the major controls have concerned emigrants. The contrast between Western and Eastern Europe during the Cold War in this respect is particularly striking.

Twentieth-century restrictions, based upon fear of the costs of having to pay to support immigrants, are a reversion to the limitations of an earlier age, such as that of the English Old Poor Law. The new element is provided by the extraordinary reduction in the costs of international mobility, which would have been inconceivable two centuries ago. Cheap long-distance fares mean that workers in low-wage, high-population-density countries can find it economic to work in high-wage economies at much less than would indigenous labor. The economic logic of free labor mobility is a downward convergence of workers' living standards in the rich countries to those of the poor, unless immigrant labor is not, or can be prevented from being, a substitute for host-country workers.

The pressure for restrictions and/or discrimination then is entirely predictable. A willingness to accept highly skilled immigrants, an international form of poaching, is a positive aspect of restrictive twentieth-century policies from the viewpoint of the individuals concerned, if not necessarily for those who financed the acquisition of the skills. Equally so is the unionization of immigrant workers to avoid any undercutting of host-country wages. The negative side is the guest-worker policy, which allows in migrants for low-paid, unpleasant jobs that indigenous workers are not willing to undertake while refusing any general right of abode or permission to bring in their families. International class solidarity has been noticeably lacking in this respect as in many others concerning the rules governing migration. The pursuit of much narrower interests seems a better basis from which to explain and predict migration policy and institutions.

Notes

1. J. D. Gould, "European Intercontinental Emigration, 1915-1914: Patterns and Causes," *Journal of European Economic History* 8 (1979): 593-679.

2. W. A. Lewis, *Growth and Fluctuations 1870-1913* (London, 1978), 192; V. Bevan, *The Development of British Immigration Law* (London and Sydney, 1986), 76.

3. The principal sources of political and institutional economics consciously drawn upon here are B. S. Frey, *Modern Political Economy* (London, 1978), and D. C. North, *Structure and Change in Economic History* (New York, 1984). R. N. Langlois, ed., *The New Institutional Economics* (Cambridge, 1986) covers a wider range of methodological issues.

4. J. G. Williamson, *Late Nineteenth Century American Development: A General Equilibrium History* (Cambridge, 1974) chap. 11; Brinley Thomas, *Migration and Economic Growth: A Study of Great Britain and the Atlantic Economy*, 2nd ed. (Cambridge, 1973); D. Baines, *Migration in a Mature Economy: Emigration and Internal Migration in England and Wales 1861-1900* (Cambridge, 1985), finds only partial support for the view that internal migration in England and Wales was related to Atlantic migration.

5. Calculated from *Statistical Abstract of the United States, 1921* (Washington, 1922).

6. G. R. Hawke, *The Making of New Zealand* (Cambridge, 1985), 15.

7. Calculated from *Statistical Abstract of the United States, 1921*.

8. Calculated from the United Kingdom, *Census of Population 1911* (London, 1912).

9. S. Nicholas and P. R. Shergold, "Transportation as Global Migration," *Convict Worker*, ed. S. N. Nicholas (Cambridge, 1988).

10. Lewis, 185; P. C. Campbell, *Chinese Coolie Emigration to Countries within the British Empire* (London, 1923).

11. H. G. Wunderlich, *The Secret of Crete* (Athens, 1983), 10-12.

12. J. R. T. Hughes, *The Vital Few: American Economic Progress and Its Protagonists* (Oxford, 1973), chap. 6; J. F. Wall, *Andrew Carnegie* (New York, 1970).

13. H. Pollins, *An Economic History of the Jews in England* (London, 1982), 123.

14. Gary Cross, *Immigrant Workers in Industrial France* (Phila-delphia, 1983).

15. H. Rieben, "Intra-European Migration of Labour and the Migration of High Level Manpower from Europe to North America," in *North American and Western European Economic Policies*, ed. C. P. Kindleberger and A. Shonfield (London, 1971); J. Salt and H. Cout, eds., *Migration in Post-War Europe: Geographical Essays* (Oxford, 1976); C. P. Kindleberger, *Europe's Postwar Growth: The Role of Labor Supply* (Cambridge, Mass., 1967).

16. J. R. Gordon, "The Role of International Migration in the Changing European Labour Market," paper presented at the Confederation of European Economic Associations Symposium on European Factor Mobility, University of Kent, 1986.

17. C. O'Grada, "Determinants of Irish Emigration: A Note," *International Migration Review*, 20:3 (1986): 650-56.

18. M. Walker, *Germany and the Emigration, 1816-1885* (Cambridge, Mass., 1964).

19. Cornish miners were more likely to practice their trade abroad than to seek alternative work in the United Kingdom. G. Burke, "The Cornish Diaspora of the Nineteenth Century," *International Labour Migration: Historical Perspectives*, ed. S. Marks and P. Richardson (London, 1984).

20. J. Bhagwati, ed., *The Brain Drain and Taxation* (Amsterdam, 1976).

21. K. Jones and A. D. Smith, *The Economic Impact of Commonwealth Immigrants* (Cambridge, 1970), 159-60.

22. *Royal Commission on Alien Immigration 1903*, 464.

23. Bevan, 61-63.

24. *Report of the Committee on Emigration from India to the Crown Colonies and the Protectorates*, Cd. 5192 (1910) 46.13. For unfavorable views of the indenture system, see the essays by H. Tinker and P. Emmer in S. Marks and P. Richardson, eds.

25. W. Darrell Overdyke, *The Know-Nothing Party in the South* (Baton Rouge, La., 1950); D. M. Potter, *The Impending Crisis* (New York, 1976), 241-60.

26. C. Erickson, "Why Did Contract Labor Not Work in the Nineteenth-Century United States," in S. Marks and P. Richardson, eds.

27. *Royal Commission on Alien Immigration 1903*, 828. On the anti-Chinese riots in New Zealand, see J. B. Condliffe, *New Zealand in the Making: A Survey of Economic and Social Development* (London, 154).

28. N. H. Leff, *Underdevelopment and Development in Brazil: Vol. 1, Economic Structure and Change 1822-1947* (London, 1982).

29. International Labour Organisation, *The International Labour Organisation: The First Decade* (London, 1931).

30. G. di Tella, "Rents, Quasi-Rents, Normal Profits and Growth: Argentina and the Areas of Recent Settlement," *Argentine, Australia and Canada: Studies in Comparative Development 1870-1965*, ed. D. C. M. Platt and G. di Tella (London, 1985).

31. C. E. Solberg, "Land Tenure and Land Settlement: Policy and Patterns in the Canadian Prairies and the Argentine Pampas, 1880-1930," and C. F. Diaz Alejandro, "Argentina, Australia and Brazil before 1929," in Platt and di Tella.

32. A. B. Martinez and M. Lewandowski, *The Argentine in the Twentieth Century* (London, 1911), 118-20.

33. A. C. Kelley, "International Migration and Economic Growth: Australia 1865-1935," *Journal of Economic History* 25 (1965): 333-354.

34. J. B. Condliffe, *The Development of Australia* (London, 1930), 32.

35. P. Knaplund, *Gladstone and Britain's Imperial Policy* (London, 1927), 224.

36. Bevan, 67.

37. D. Hobart Houghton, "Economic Development 1865-1965," 13-15, and L. Thompson, "Great Britain and the Afrikaner Republics," 322, both in *Oxford History of South Africa*, ed. M. Wilson and L. Thompson (Oxford, 1971).

38. International Labour Organisation; *International Encyclopedia of Comparative Law*, ed. O. Khan-Freund (Tübingen, 1970), vol. 15, chap. 1; G. S. Goodwin-Gill, *International Law of the Movement of Persons between States* (Oxford, 1978).

39. S. J. Nicholas and P. R. Shergold, "Human Capital and the Pre-Famine Irish Emigration to England," *Explorations in Economic History* 24 (1987): 158-77.

40. P. Taylor, *The Distant Magnet: European Migration to the United States* (London, 1971), 197-98.

41. Hughes, 245. In formulating tariff policy, urban labor and capital joined forces against populist agriculture. Higher prices of manufactured goods, raised by import tariffs, tilted income distribution toward the manufacturing sector and away from populist agriculture. See P. A. Gourevitch, "International Trade, Domestic Coalitions and Liberty: Comparative Responses to the Crisis 1873-1896," *Journal of Interdisciplinary History* 8, 2 (1977): 281-313. This cannot explain the alliance between labor and capital in the United States unless immigrant labor was a noncompeting group or immigration controls had been imposed. Higher rewards to urban labor as a result of tariffs on manufactures would otherwise have been dissipated among a greater number of migrant workers that the better wages would have drawn in.

42. *Royal Commission on Alien Immigration 1903*, Minutes of Evidence paragraphs, 14383-5, 14739-42, 14758, 15523.

43. J. Singleton, "Lancashire's Last Stand: Declining Employment in the British Cotton Textile Industry, 1950-1970," *Economic History Review* 39 (1987): 106.

44. A. Lemon and N. C. Pollock, *Studies in Overseas Settlement and Population* (London, 1980), 154.

45. Bevan, 73-74.

46. R. L. Smith, "Australian Immigration 1945-75," *Population, Immigration and the Australian Economy*, ed. P. J. Brain, R. L. Smith, and G. P. Schuyers (London, 1979).

47. Bhagwati, 6-7.

48. Gordon; C. Kennedy-Brenner, *Foreign Workers and Immigration Policy: The Case of France* (Paris, 1979).

Contributors

RUTH AKAMINE (M.A., Columbia University) completed her undergraduate degree at Yale University, where the research for her article in this volume was done with Professor David Montgomery. She is currently an editor in the school studies department of Macmillan/McGraw-Hill School Publishing Company.

SURENDRA BHANA (Ph.D., University of Kansas) was, until December 1987, Professor and Chairperson of the History Department of the University of Durban-Westville, South Africa. He is currently Associate Professor of History and African and African-American Studies at the University of Kansas. Among his publications are *The United States and the Development of the Puerto Rican Status Question, 1936-1968*, *A Documentary History of Indian South Africa*, edited with B. Pachai, the edited collection *Essays on Natal's Indentured Indians*, and *Setting Down Roots: Indian Migrants in South Africa, 1860-1911*, coauthored with J. B. Brain.

DAVID BRODY (Ph.D., Harvard University) is Professor of History at the University of California, Davis. He is the author of *Steelworkers in America: The Non-Union Era*, *Labor in Crisis*, *Workers in Industrial America: Essays on the Twentieth Century Struggle*, as well as numerous articles on labor and social history.

JAMES FOREMAN-PECK (Ph.D., London School of Economics) is Fellow of St. Anthony's College, Oxford, and was Professor of Economic History at the University of Hull. He has also been Visiting Associate Professor of Economics at the University of California, Davis. He is the author of *A History of the World Economy: International Economic Relations since 1850*, editor of *New Perspectives on the Late Victorian Economy*, and has published in such journals as *Economic History Review*, *Business History*, *Oxford Economic Papers*, *Economic Journal*, and the *Journal of Economic History*.

CAMILLE GUERIN-GONZALES (Ph.D., University of California, Riverside) is Assistant Professor of History at Oberlin College. She has published articles in *Historia Mexicana*, in *Regions of the Raza: Changing Interpretations of Mexican American Regional History and Culture*, edited by Antonio Rios-Bustamante, and in *Guide to the Study of United States History outside the U.S., 1945-1980*, edited by Lewis Hanke.

JOHN J. KULCZYCKI (Ph.D., Columbia University) is Associate Professor of History at the University of Illinois, Chicago. He is author of *School Strikes in Prussian Poland, 1901-1907: The Struggle over Bilingual Education*, as well as articles in the *Canadian Review of Studies in Nationalism, Przeglad Polonijny*, and the *International History Review*.

JOHN H. M. LASLETT (D.Phil., Oxford University) is Professor of History at the University of California, Los Angeles. He is the author of *Labor and the Left: A Study of Socialist and Radical Influences in the American Labor Movement, 1881-1924*, and *Nature's Noblemen: The Fortunes of the Independent Collier in Scotland and the American Midwest, 1865-1889*. He also edited, with Seymour Martin Lipset, *Failure of a Dream? Essays in the History of American Socialism*.

RUTH MANDEL (Ph.D., University of Chicago) was a Social Science Research Council Post-Doctoral Fellow in Anthropology at the Free University of Berlin and is currently on the faculty at University College, London. She has published articles in *New German Critique* and the *Journal of Modern Greek Studies* as well as in two collections, *Muslim Travelers: Pilgrimage, Migration, and the Religious Imagination*, edited by James Piscatori and Dale Eickelmean, and *Conflict, Ethnicity, and International Migration*, edited by Nancy Gonzales and Carolyn McCommon.

DONALD NONINI (Ph.D., Stanford University) is Assistant Professor of Anthropology at the University of North Carolina, Chapel Hill. He has published a book, *British Colonial Rule and The Resistance of the Malay Peasantry, 1900-1957*, as well as articles in *Ethnos, Man, Dialectical Anthropology*, and *Kairos*.

DONALD REID (Ph.D., Stanford University) has been a member of the Harvard Society of Fellows and is presently Professor of History at the University of North Carolina, Chapel Hill. His publications include *The Miners of Decazeville: A Genealogy of Deindustrialization* and *Paris Sewers and Sewermen* as well as articles in *Comparative Studies in Society and History, European History Quarterly, Sociologie du travail*,

Social History, Journal of Social History, Annales du Midi, and *Radical History Review.*

DOROTHEE SCHNEIDER (Ph.D., University of Munich) is an Assistant Professor in the Department of History and in the Institute for Labor Relations at the University of Illinois, Urbana-Champaign. She is one of the associate editors of *The Papers of Samuel Gompers* and is the author of articles in *Labor History* and in *German Workers in Industrial Chicago, 1850-1910: A Comparative Perspective,* edited by Hartmut Keil and John B. Jentz, and author of *Trade Unions and Community: The German Working Class in New York City, 1870-1900.*

CARL STRIKWERDA (Ph.D., University of Michigan) is Associate Professor of History at the University of Kansas. His articles have been published in the *Journal of Social History, Comparative Studies in Society and History, International Labor and Working Class History,* and *Urban History Yearbook,* and in *Chance und Illusion/Labor in Retreat: Studien zur Krise der westeuropäischen Gesellschaft in den dreissiger Jahren/Studies on the Social Crisis in Interwar Western Europe,* edited by Wolfgang Maderthaner and Helmut Gruber.

Index